Best Ways to Make Money Now

By the Editors of **MONEY** Magazine

Oxmoor House®

Best Ways to Make Money Now

*Illustrations
By
Glenn Dodds*

Library of Congress Catalog Number: 90-64380
Hardcover ISBN: 0-8487-1020-7
Softcover ISBN: 0-8487-1050-9

Manufactured in the United States of America
First Printing 1991

Published by arrangement with Oxmoor House, Inc.
Book Division of Southern Progress Corporation
P. O. Box 2463, Birmingham, AL 35201

Best Ways to Make Money Now
Senior Editor: Clark Scott
Editorial Assistant: L. Amanda Owens
Designer: Nancy Johnson
Fact Checker: Frances C. Marshman
Copyreader: Kay Vance

Vice President, Editorial Director: Candace N. Conard
Art Director: Bob Nance
Director of Manufacturing: Jerry Higdon
Associate Production Manager: Rick Litton
Production Assistant: Theresa Beste

To order *Money* magazine, write to: *Money*,
P. O. Box 54429, Boulder, CO 80322-4429

Editor's Note

Every year presents its own opportunities, and despite talk of recession, government fiscal woes, and unrest in the Middle East, 1991 is no exception. Here to help you spot this year's opportunities is *Best Ways to Make Money Now*.

The fifth in a series of annuals from the Editors of *Money* and Oxmoor House, this book pulls together in one comprehensive volume some of the most important and useful information to appear in the pages of *Money* magazine in the past 12 months. In addition to telling you how to make more money on your investments, your savings, and in your career, we suggest ways to get the most out of what you earn by being a shrewd money manager and a savvy consumer.

In this volume, we offer timely help with every aspect of your financial life: your job, taxes (federal, state, and local), insurance, credit, budget, IRA, and estate planning, to name a few. We also outline strategies for navigating today's turbulent investment markets—stocks, bonds, mutual funds, and more. The real estate market in 1991 also presents a challenge—to say the least—and we give the lowdown to would-be buyers and sellers, as well as to individuals who want to improve their existing homes.

Best Ways to Make Money Now is designed to serve readers at every stage of their lives. Young families, for example, will learn how to raise kids without going broke—including ways to finance that notorious family budget buster, a college education. Meanwhile, those of you contemplating retirement will find out how to reach that goal—perhaps sooner than you think.

Lastly, in the final section of this book you will find our comprehensive ranking of the top mutual funds. An essential reference for fund investors, this 28-page listing shows the performance over one, three, five, and ten years of 960 funds in 22 categories.

We begin, however, with stories of individuals who have changed their lives for the better by changing careers. If you are a candidate for such a switch, we hope these examples will instruct and inspire. But whatever your circumstances, we believe this book can help change your life for the better. By enabling you to take control of your finances, it will speed you to your goals and grant you peace of mind in the meantime.

Caroline Donnelly

Caroline Donnelly
Assistant Managing Editor, *Money*

Contents

Do What You Want with Your Life

A generation or so ago, when everyone liked Ike and loved Lucy, the family's lone TV and the American dream came in simple black and white. A house was central to the dream, but central air wasn't. A basic $8,000 Levittown box with a carport was heaven. Come summer, the family piled into its Ford wagon and tooled off to Lake Watchama-sakee for a few weeks. In September, the proudest wish of all came true: Johnny boarded a Greyhound for State U. after working that summer to pay his tuition.

By the 1980s, the dream had gone yupscale. Home had become a 6,000-square-foot contemporary on three acres or a gutted and rehabbed townhouse in a gentrified ghetto. The rented cabin on the lake gave way to a second home high on an ocean dune. And you hoped to get there in a $40,000 Land Rover with four-wheel drive, a power sunroof, and an AM-FM cassette tape deck. Finally, in this updated version of the dream, your Tiffany, evenly tanned from a summer at the beach, jets off to Harvard.

Clearly, the American dreamers of three decades ago reached and surpassed their goals. The past 20 years of progress came with hidden costs, however. To acquire more and better of everything, just about everybody gave up free time and amassed a mountain of debt. What's more, while many made such sacrifices, not all reaped the rewards. Nonetheless, as a recent *Money* poll suggests, Americans in the 1990s are still dreaming. And their dream seems to be shifting back to its more traditional, less materialistic moorings.

Among the aspirations most often cited by *Money* subscribers in the poll was finding rewarding work. While income is important, more and more people are looking for job happiness first. In this chapter, you will find out how to change careers and earn what you want doing what you love. Included are tips on going into business for yourself, as well as detailed information on the hottest careers for the 1990s.

Experts predict that those entering the job market now will switch careers three times or more during their lives. Whether you are just starting out or are looking for a change, the key to being marketable in the 1990s is education. More than half the jobs created over the next decade will require at least some education beyond high school, and roughly a third of the total will go to college graduates. In addition, the number of jobs in fields requiring the most higher education—lawyers, electrical engineers, medical researchers, for example—will increase at twice the nearly 15% rate for all occupations. Economists predict that, if anything, a recession will accelerate this trend. During the last recession, it was the low-skill and manufacturing jobs that took the severest hit. As this job pool shrinks, the undereducated will have to settle for lower wages.

Once you find the right career, your happiness also will depend on how well you integrate it with your life outside work. The increase in two-income households—74% of women ages 25 to 54 were in the workforce in 1989, up from 49% in 1969—has made it more difficult than ever to juggle family and job responsibilities. Parents and would-be parents have to grapple with the question: How can you have a rewarding career while raising a family? "Having It All" on page 25 offers some strategies for handling maternity leave and the delicate negotiations with your company that sometimes arise.

Finally, it's interesting to note that despite the changes taking place in the job marketplace, the overwhelming majority of subscribers who responded to the *Money* poll were optimistic about their chances of achieving the American dream. Hopefully, with a little foresight you, too, can do what you want with your life.

How to Switch to a Job You Like and Still Make Money

Americans are discovering that using their talents to the fullest is more rewarding than simply chasing cash.

A growing number of people are discovering that shaking up their staid careers can be spiritually and financially therapeutic. Most career changers set out initially in search of happiness, not money. But many learn that doing what they love can make them prosperous, too—and, ultimately, financially secure.

In the following pages, *Money* looks at five people who sought self-fulfillment and found fortune as well, and the lessons drawn from their experience. They include: a bored attorney who became a highly successful wine critic; a disillusioned professor who networked his way to a secure corporate position; a cost analyst who ignored experts and won by retailing toys; two L.A. lawyers who made millions from high-style pizza; and a self-absorbed reporter who emerged as a selfless crusader.

Changing your life isn't easy, of course. Many who try fail—almost 25% of new small businesses cease to exist for one reason or another within two years. And even people who make it usually suffer periods of want. But for those who succeed, the rewards can be boundless—as the following profiles illustrate.

From Workaday Lawyer to World-Renowned Critic

Before Robert M. Parker Jr. went to France in 1967, his interest in wine was limited to gulping a few glasses of cold duck with schoolmates. So his first taste of French wine—ordered because it was cheaper than Coca-Cola—pleasantly surprised him.

Back at law school in the States, he became obsessed with wine and educated himself by reading books by the experts. A few years later, trapped in a tedious legal job in Baltimore, Parker—along with his wife, Patricia—formed wine tasting groups and ran off each summer to tour European vineyards. "We'd buy expensive labels that the critics raved about and find them disappointing," he says. "Gradually, I realized that many of the critics were into free samples and expense-paid tasting trips. There was no Ralph Nader in the field. It dawned on me that I could become that objective voice for consumers."

He talked his mother into lending him $2,000 in 1978 so that he could mimeograph 7,000 copies of his *Wine Advocate* newsletter and mail it, free, to members of wine groups. "I expected a flood of subscription orders," Parker laughs. Instead, he got only a trickle—but, at $10 each, they were enough to keep the newsletter afloat.

From the first, Parker's readers applauded his iconoclasm. "Wine writers traditionally have paid homage to sacred cows like Lafite-Rothschild, even when a wine was mediocre," he says. "I operated on the presumption that wines should be judged only by what's in the bottle, not by the label or price." He became blunt to the point of insult—describing wines as having "foul barnyard odors" or smelling like cat urine. He also introduced a simple 50-to-100-point scoring system that, to his dismay, some merchants began exploiting in their ads. He bought 70% of the wine himself—the rest were unsolicited samples—and paid all costs of his annual three-month tasting trips. At the end of 1983, with the newsletter grossing $200,000 a year, Parker finally quit his $47,000 law job. Today, with the *Wine Advocate* grossing more than $1 million (28,000 subscribers at $35 a year in the U.S. or $55 abroad) and five books to his credit, Parker is considered the most influential writer in the field—a reputation that promises to give him financial security for life, not to mention a net income at least triple what he used to make.

Still, Parker cherishes the nonfinancial rewards the most. He works from his home north of Baltimore, surrounded by the serene beauty of Gunpowder Falls State Park. Four days a week, he dictates into a tape recorder; two more days are spent tasting samples from about 100 bottles a day.

Six Lessons from a Wine Lover:

Start your new career in your spare time if possible. It's relatively risk-free; Parker, for example, waited five years before chucking his day job.

Work at home, at least initially, to cut costs. Like Parker and many others, you may decide to stay home permanently: The number of home-based workers swelled 15% in three years to reach 26.8 million in 1990, according to the New York City research firm, Link Resources.

Design your home work space to minimize distractions. When his wife got sick of losing her kitchen to wine tastings, Parker added a three-room wing that includes his sunny office, the entrance to his wine cellar, a tasting room stocked with 2,000 bottles, and an office for a full-time assistant who transcribes his tapes.

Don't scrimp on technology. Paul Edwards, co-author of the comprehensive guide *Working from Home* (Jeremy P. Tarcher), says the basic equipment will cost around $5,000, including one or more separate phone lines ($100 to install, $15 each per month); answering machine ($100); computer and software ($1,500);

printer (Edwards recommends a $650 ink jet or a $1,000 laser printer rather than a $300 dot matrix); fax ($800); and copier ($800). Parker, for example, says his $1,100 Murata fax is invaluable for communicating with wine buyers in European time zones.

If you have small children, arrange for child care during your working hours. "I just laugh when I see magazine pictures of mothers bouncing babies on their laps as they sit at the computer," says Ann McGrotha, a mother of two preschoolers who operates her human-resources consulting firm—MW Associates of Wilmette, Illinois—from home. "It just doesn't work that way." At the Parker household, Patricia chose to quit teaching French in order to stay home with Maia.

Set up a daily routine for when to start and stop. Parker's still working on this one. You might use the closing refrains of the "Today" show to get you started in the morning, and the arrival home of your spouse as the signal to quit at night.

From Mulling Kierkegaard to Touting Kilowatts

Ever since grade school, Fred Abbate wanted to become a teacher. While working on a philosophy Ph.D. at Columbia, he taught for three years at a small college and then became a professor on the Rutgers faculty in New Jersey after graduation. But five years later, he was growing restive. "The community of scholars I envisioned didn't really exist, and I felt isolated," he says. "At 36, with three sons to educate, finding greater financial stability was important. But even thinking about change was traumatic. Teaching was intrinsic to my identity. Who would I be if I changed that?"

So Abbate, who lives with his wife, Rosemary, in Moorestown, New Jersey, consulted career counselors. After making a list of what he wanted from a job, as they suggested, he started networking to find such a post—talking to friends, business associates, and others to whom he was referred. Finally, after more

than a year, a contact told him that Atlantic Electric—a New Jersey utility—was seeking a public affairs director. Within a month, Abbate landed the $22,000 job.

His first day was scary. "I took off my coat, sat at my desk, and was overwhelmed with a feeling of not knowing what to do next," he says. Fortunately, the phone rang, and soon he found himself swept up in learning his duties. "The primary difference was that in my former life, problems were something I analyzed—while in this one, they were something I solved," he says. And solved successfully. In the past 13 years, a string of promotions have led him to general manager of corporate communications at more than $90,000 a year—perhaps double what he might have made at Rutgers. True, he misses summer vacations. "But I don't miss much else," he says, including teaching. Why? "Because I teach a course in corporate communications at Drexel University on the side."

Seven Lessons from a P.R. Man:

Choose a new career where you can use what you know. Most people envision career changes in radical terms, like going from being a businessman to a brain surgeon. In fact, most successful changes allow people to simply transfer skills they have learned in one environment to another.

See a career counselor if you want help. Private counselors charge as much as $100 an hour. But some universities and community colleges, especially, offer similar services at little or no cost.

Research thoroughly any occupations that interest you. The table on page 16 can help you get started. Then move to the library for other sources, such as the U.S. Labor Department's *Occupational Outlook Handbook*.

Prepare an informative résumé. "I see so many résumés cross my desk that simply list past jobs," says Abbate. "I want to know what you've learned from that job. Focus on how what you know can help the employer, especially if you're aiming for a job that—on the surface—seems unrelated to what you've done."

After doing your homework, start networking. Place ads in trade publications, use your college alumni directory, consult headhunters. Talk to people at companies that attract you. Meet in their offices rather than at lunch, because you learn more about the company that way.

Keep in touch later. Follow up your visit with a thank-you note and then another note a couple of weeks later, perhaps enclosing a clipping about something you discussed. Continuing contact lets you become a known person so that later, when an opening pops up, your contact will call.

Don't give up. The average job hunt takes six months; dramatic changes like Abbate's usually take longer.

From Corporate Cost-Buster to Toy Dealer

In 1983, with the construction business slumping, the large Stamford, Connecticut firm that had employed Jim Askew for nine years started to freeze salaries and slash vacations. "None of that bothered me much," says Askew, an industrial engineer and cost expert. "I'd been brought up to be a team player—believing that if you worked hard and gave a little when times were bad, the company would always take care of you."

But when veterans in their fifties and sixties started getting laid off, Askew began having doubts. He decided to look around for other opportunities, preferably near the shore, where he and his wife, Kathy, had always wanted to live. Connecticut's waterfront was out of reach on Jim's $45,000-a-year salary. So, for the next year and a half, he mailed résumés to companies near the more reasonably priced New Jersey Shore. No luck. Then it dawned on him that he and Kathy could open their own business. But what? A liquor store seemed too dangerous. A bar or restaurant might leave little time for their kids.

One Sunday in August 1985, about 10 months later, Kathy spotted an ad in the *New York Times* for a children's toy and furniture store in Little Silver, New Jersey. "I figured that, even in a recession, people still buy baby furniture and toys," says Askew. But when they met the owner on Labor Day weekend, Kathy says, "there wasn't a customer in the shop." Afterward, their accountant and attorney reviewed the store's financial figures and advised them against buying it.

Most people would have quit then. But Jim and Kathy figured the owner had hurt himself by trying to compete with high-volume discount chains like Toys R Us. Jim's own financial analysis showed they could make it. Backed with $189,000 from the sale of their Stamford home, which had tripled in value in eight years, the Askews acquired Little Silver Mike's.

It wasn't until halfway through the first year, says Askew, that he finally relaxed because it was clear they had a winner. Sales of their high-end furniture (cribs from $300 to $1,000) and old-fashioned wooden or educational toys have grown from $200,000 the first year to $750,000 in 1989. Jim expected $850,000 in 1990, enough to provide more than double his old income.

Five Lessons from a Retailer:

Build a cash reserve. Ideally, it should equal about six months' living expenses. Failing that, a reserve of any size will help; the Askews, for example, started with only $10,000.

Reduce your debt, especially if your income will be uncertain at first. You may have to liquidate assets—as the Askews did with their home. Get several appraisals first. "Most people are good at comparison shopping when they buy but don't put the same effort into being smart sellers," says New York City financial planner Adriane Berg, who interviewed scores of career changers for a book titled *Changing Lanes, Cashing Out and Becoming Job-Free* that will be published by Dutton.

If you plan to open a business, get advice from others in the same trade. Potential competitors won't help you, so seek out businessmen without conflicts of interest. One source: Small Business Administration's Service Corps of Retired Executives (SCORE), reachable through 800-368-5855 or your nearest SBA office.

Count on working harder than you ever did as a wage slave. Happily, you can also count on enjoying it more.

Plow as much revenue as possible back into the operation, at least initially. "A lot of businesses fail because once money starts rolling in, owners don't have the discipline to use it to keep expanding," says Askew. "During our first year, for example, I took only $8,000 in salary."

From L.A. Law to Chi-Chi California-Style Pizza

Rick Rosenfield was grabbing lunch at the California Pizza Kitchen in Beverly Hills when a woman customer eyed the long line of diners waiting for a seat and said, "God, why didn't we think of this?" "I did," shot back Rosenfield, smiling.

The ex-lawyer has reason to be pleased with himself. In the six years since he and partner Larry Flax opened their first CPK restaurant with a fast-food menu specializing in salads, pastas, and pizza topped with barbecued chicken, duck sausage, and the like, their dozen stores have made them millionaires.

The two men became friends in the 1970s, working as federal prosecutors and then forming their own private Los Angeles law firm. By 1984, however, their work was no longer satisfying. Both were fascinated by the restaurant business, and they envisioned a chain of moderately priced restaurants serving gourmet pizza baked in wood-burning ovens. They leased a 1,800-square-foot space not far from their Beverly Hills homes and took unsecured personal loans of $100,000 each for the estimated $200,000 construction costs. The only

problem was, the contractor's estimate didn't include the $300,000 needed for ovens and fixtures. So one evening, with advice from their attorney, Flax and Rosenfield had to get on the phone to a number of well-heeled friends and raise the cash.

On opening night, "we were full at 5 p.m. and had people waiting in line," Rosenfield says. "I remember standing in the office above the restaurant hugging my 15-year-old son as both of us cried with happiness, because I'd really rolled the dice on this one. I'd gone into debt and had no savings to fall back on."

Today, with stores scattered from Atlanta to Hawaii, Flax and Rosenfield still hold 62% of the stock in the $22 million (sales) privately held company and are worth $19.4 million each. They may get even richer in a few years by going public. For now, though, their fondest dream is going international.

A Key Lesson from the Pizza Kings:

Be smart about how you raise cash up front. The best way is probably through a private placement, since you won't have to register the deal with the SEC. One simple type, used initially by Flax and Rosenfield, is the limited partnership in which you—as general partner—usually receive a management fee (often 5% of gross revenues) from the outset but none of the profits until the limited partners, or investors, recoup their stakes. Thereafter, you and the investors split the profits according to a pre-agreed schedule. By all means, get a good securities law attorney to set it up.

From Self-Absorbed Scribe to Selfless Crusader

In his former life, Jon Greer used to write about businessmen like Flax and Rosenfield. A financial journalist at the *San Francisco Chronicle*, Greer had drifted into the field because it was familiar: His father was a business reporter for the *Washington Post* and ABC radio. But Greer never felt committed. So when friends asked him in late 1987 to serve on the board of a shelter for homeless families near his Haight-Ashbury apartment, he agreed without giving it much thought. Once aboard, though, he saw that the shelter really needed him. Founded by the Hamilton United Methodist Church two years earlier, it had little cash, a slim staff, and an ever-growing parade of homeless at the door.

Greer took two weeks of vacation to straighten out the finances and almost immediately realized he'd need more time. He asked the *Chronicle* for a leave from his $40,000-a-year job. The paper said no. So Greer granted himself a leave—he quit. He began his new work by fund raising with a vengeance. He called executives at companies he'd once written about. Pals at the newspaper steered him to other corporations. And a friendly disk jockey aired a public service announcement that brought a $12,500 donation to buy beds.

Now, after three years of hard work by Greer and his staff, the shelter's budget has risen tenfold to $500,000; it operates around-the-clock rather than 12 hours a day; and it serves more than 700 homeless families a year, double the number in 1987. Greer's lot has improved, too—from the $6,000 in salary he drew when he started to $30,000 today.

True, that's $10,000 less than he used to make—but he's not complaining. "I finally realized that whatever I do for a living must directly affect people for the better," he says. Besides, he feels his earning potential may now be greater. "In journalism, I was probably earning close to my maximum. Now, I'm running a half-million-dollar agency and, as my experience grows, there's the potential to earn more to raise some kids of my own."

Three Lessons from a Fund Raiser:

Don't burn your bridges. Not only because you want a safety net in case your new life doesn't work out, but also because—as in Greer's case—the contacts from your old profession might prove extremely useful in your new one.

Accept trade-offs. Any career change involves sacrifices. To help focus on these, make a list of what you expect to gain and lose. You can avoid a lot of mistakes by knowing the trade-offs beforehand.

Don't be afraid to follow your gut. Since you're usually seeking happiness first and foremost, your instincts will be your best guide. As Harvard professor Abraham Zaleznik says, "The question the fast trackers asked in the 1980s was, 'Where can I make money the quickest?' I hope the next group's question will be, 'Where will I discover my true talent, contribute to society, and have the most fun?' If you answer that question, the money always follows."

A Checklist for Job-Changers

● Focus first on finding a career that will make you happy, not one that will make you rich.

● Concentrate on jobs that make maximal use of your skills, knowledge, and talent.

● Get advice from people who know the field you're interested in well.

● As you start a business, keep costs down—maybe by operating from home in your spare time.

● Establish a routine for starting and stopping work.

● Before expanding or investing, cut your debt and set aside an emergency cash reserve.

● Raise funds in ways that won't tie your hands later.

● Plan to work harder than you ever have before.

● Maintain a bailout plan in case your new effort fails.

● When in doubt, trust your own best instincts and intuitions.

21 Possibilities for Those Seeking a New Job

The ideal job would be prestigious, high-paying, and easy to get into—but real jobs aren't ideal.

Veteran carpenters, for example, earn more than nurses do, though the latter have higher

	Occupation	Approximate Time/Cost to Train	Prerequisite for Training	Rookies/ 10-Year Veterans	Prestige Score
FASTEST-GROWING JOBS	Secondary-school teacher	Two years/ $16,000	B.A. or B.S.	$19,600/ $29,600	63
	Registered nurse	Two years/ $9,040	High school diploma	$25,900/ $34,000	62
	Certified public accountant	Two years/ $16,000	B.A. or B.S.	$24,000/ $53,000	57
	Computer programmer	Six months/ $6,000	High school diploma	$25,000/ $46,000	51
	Retail salesclerk	None	None	$7,500/ $21,000	29
	Janitor	None	None	$16,500/ $29,000	16
MOST COMMON JOBS	Secretary	None	High school diploma	$16,326/ $28,051	46
	Farmer	None	None	$20,000/ $25,000	41
	Carpenter	Four-year apprenticeship	None	$18,000/ $45,000	40
	Truck driver	Six weeks/ $2,000	No recent driving offense	$23,000/ $35,000	32
	Assembly-line worker	None	None	$25,000/ $41,500	27
OTHER JOBS	Family physician	Seven years/ $60,000	B.A. or B.S.	$79,000/ $99,700	82
	Attorney	Three years/ $43,000	B.A. or B.S.	$40,791/ $105,796	76
	Dentist	Four years/ $58,000	B.A. or B.S.	$60,490/ $80,100	74
	Clergyman	Three years/ up to $43,000	B.A. or B.S. and a "calling"	$7,944/ $55,782	69
	Chemical engineer	Two years/ $16,000	B.S. in subject area	$32,150/ $51,500	67
	Restaurateur	None	None	$30,000/ $57,000	62
	Economist	Two years/ $16,000	B.A. or B.S.	$37,000/ $60,000	57
	Social worker	Two years/ $16,000	B.A. or B.S.	$23,000/ $32,000	52
	Stockbroker	80 hours/ $300	B.A. or B.S., works at NASD firm	$27,930/ $71,309	51
	Real estate agent	30 hours/ $200	None	$3,000/ $28,000	44

"Fastest-growing jobs" are expected to grow the most by 2000; "most common" have the most workers now; "other" are jobs of interest to readers. Average pay supplied by government, trade, and professional groups. **Compiled by D. Jacqueline Smith** status. And retail stockbrokers make good pay, but their prestige is middling. (The prestige scale, by the National Opinion Research Center, ranges from a low of 1 to a high of 100.)

Comments

To educate the offspring of the baby boomers, schools will need around 19% more secondary-school teachers by 2000. Salaries, though still low, are up 70% since 1980.

Some 10% of the 947,000 budgeted positions at hospitals and other health facilities were vacant in 1989, which helps explain why salaries were up 10% during the year.

Demand for accountants and auditors is expected to grow 22% by the year 2000, partly because both business operations and the tax laws are becoming increasingly intricate.

Because this skill is easily transported among companies, each year some 15% to 20% of programmers change jobs—a rate twice that of most professions.

Some salespeople prefer to be paid partly on commission, which can boost their annual salaries to two or three times the union rates shown at left.

The demand for janitors and cleaners is expected to grow 19% by 2000, but most of the new slots will be nonunion and, thus, will pay about 60% less than the union salaries cited here.

Top-paid secretaries must be capable of taking on mid-management functions, like preparing budget spreadsheets, ordering office equipment, and supervising other workers.

The number of farmers, now 2.2 million and shrinking, has dropped 12% since 1975 as smaller farms got swallowed by larger ones. (Income figures are for a mid-size dairy farm.)

With nationwide housing starts forecast to be down 1.5% in 1990 and up only 4% in 1991, try for work where starts are growing fastest: Arkansas, Louisiana, Oklahoma, and Texas.

This job has all the solitude that country crooners sing of but little of the freedom, partly because you have to go into hock to buy the 18-wheel rig (cost: $100,000 to $150,000).

In the auto industry, which keeps the most reliable figures, the number of assembly-line workers was down 27% from 1978 to 1988, while salaries rose 84% from 1978 to today.

Family physicians are increasingly in demand, since an ever greater share of graduates choose high-tech specialties to help pay off their average $42,374 school debt.

Beware of overcrowding. America already has one attorney for every 355 people—twice the rate in 1970—and law school entrants increased for the third straight year in 1989.

Cavities are down 36% since 1980, reducing that mainstay of a dentist's business, but demand for periodontal care, dentures, and implants will increase as baby boomers age.

Women are making inroads in this once all-male profession; they constituted 27% of all theological students in 1988, compared with only 10% in 1972. Still, few get pulpits.

Partly because of the demand for environmental and pollution control, chemical engineers—the top-paid engineering graduates—are getting bonuses of up to $10,000 when they take a job.

Restaurants and bars are the most popular type of start-up business today, and their failure rate is only half the 1.6% per year that prevailed in the first half of the 1980s.

Thanks to the growing complexity of domestic and international business, this increasingly prevalent corporate position has become a shortcut to the top.

Many new jobs are in company-sponsored employee assistance programs, which exist in 50% of Fortune 500 companies today, up from 5% a decade ago.

There are 17% fewer brokers working than before the 1987 stock market crash, and the survivors are being forced to produce more business—sometimes for lower commissions.

Because real estate agents work mostly on commission, this field is easy to enter but hard to survive in; a 1986 survey showed that one of five agents leaves his job within a year.

Fast-Track Careers for the '90s

The hottest jobs in the next decade will fatten your bank balance and enrich your life.

There was a time when following a career path was like climbing a ladder. Rung by rung, you ascended in a succession of orderly steps, each one with added responsibility, pay, status, and, you hoped, satisfaction.

No more. Today, when you reach for that next rung, it's likely to have been shifted off-shore, job-eliminated in a cost-cutting crisis, or transformed beyond all recognition by technology. Experts forecast that workers starting out now will switch careers—that's careers, not jobs—an average of more than three times during their lives.

Fortunately, these job-market changes are not all bad. As old professions are swept away, new ones roll in with unique opportunities. The trick to succeeding in this environment is to catch a wave early enough to ride it: to become a desktop publisher, for example, rather than an out-of-work typesetter.

To help newcomers to the work force as well as established professionals who are window shopping, here are the hottest careers of the 1990s. "Hottest" doesn't just mean fastest growing, although the 15 profiled here—and the 10 runners-up listed in the table on page 20—are all expanding rapidly. It also means careers that are relatively lucrative (most reach or approach six figures in salary), challenging, and—why not?—prestigious.

Be aware, however: This list is not the final word. While it tries to forecast the decade's major employment trends, the future always holds surprises, and some of the most exciting careers of the 1990s are still waiting to be invented.

Chef

Average salary: $35,000
Executive chef: Up to $200,000
Training: Associate's degree from two-year culinary arts program or three-year paid apprenticeship

These days, there aren't too many cooks in the kitchen. The steady climb in the number of women in the work force over the past two decades has meant a sharp reduction in home-cooked meals and an increasing reliance on restaurant fare. In fact, 45% of all adult Americans now eat at least one meal out on any given day, according to the National Restaurant Association. But the number of folks paid to turn out delectable dishes hasn't kept pace. In 1990, the American Culinary Federation predicted that there would be 250,000 openings for "trained culinarians" that year, though only around 140,000 new chefs would enter the field.

Novice cooks with lofty aspirations should head for big restaurant towns such as New York City or Los Angeles, where fat dining tabs tend to equate with higher salaries. In a business in which prestige really counts, insiders also advise taking a job in the best restaurant that will hire you, no matter how lowly the position.

To make it to the top, chefs also need stamina (they're often on the job 12 to 16 hours a day, six or seven days a week) and almost as much managerial ability as skill in whipping up soufflés. A talented chef with business acumen is the kind that will prosper in the 1990s.

Health-Care Cost Manager

Average salary: $75,000
Top executive: $200,000 and up
Training: Master's degree in business or public health, plus experience in hospital or HMO administration

With medical expenditures by private industry up 30% over the past three years, putting the brake on runaway health-care costs is a big priority for corporate America. Indeed, companies have devised a whole new position in the corporate hierarchy to handle the task: the health-care cost manager. Experts estimate that about 10% of Fortune 500 companies currently employ someone in this position. By 1995, 70% may have such a manager.

To slash a firm's medical outlays, the first move of a health-care cost executive is usually to contract with hospitals or physicians to provide treatment at discounts and to devise ways for employees to pick up a greater share of their expenses. As a result, the position requires people who can negotiate effectively with health-care providers and insurers as well as trade unions, which are likely to balk at paying more for coverage.

The best executives, however, quickly find more creative ways to keep the lid on expenses. Among their recent innovations: company-owned pharmacies (which fill most prescriptions at low cost) and corporate wellness programs (which offer seminars to teach workers how to prevent or cope with health risks).

Computer Graphics Artist

Salary after five years: $30,000 to $60,000
Top freelancer: $75,000 to $150,000
Training: B.A. in art or design preferred, plus computer courses

The latest generation of commercial artists is abandoning brushes and paint to work in a new medium: the personal computer. With the introduction of software specifically geared to their needs, the number of artists producing their work electronically quintupled between 1988 and 1990 to hit over 51,000.

Electronic artists use the computer for a variety of jobs, from setting type to creating graphs, charts, and color illustrations, most often for magazines, newspapers, and other print media. Many are employed by publishers and ad agencies, where the pay ranges from an entry-level $18,000 to $100,000 for department heads. Most artists, however, prefer the freedom and higher income that freelancing brings. After start-up costs of about $10,000 for a computer and printer, they can charge clients from $20 to $75 an hour. A successful freelancer working 40 hours a week can expect to make more than $100,000 a year.

Computer graphics artists can draw directly on the computer screen using an electronic pointer (known as a mouse) and keyboard, then print out the image instantaneously with text in place. This eliminates time-consuming steps such as sending the text to a typesetter and drawing a layout (essentially a blueprint that indicates how the type and illustration should be positioned on a page). No matter how sophisticated the tools, however, they can't stand alone. One thing the computer won't do is give you artistic talent.

Environmental Engineer

Average salary: $40,000 to $55,000
Top performer: $100,000 and up
Training: B.S. in civil, chemical, mechanical, or environmental engineering; M.S. in environmental engineering

Earth Day 1990 was not just a one-shot deal. Growing public concern over problems ranging from the oil-fouled beaches of Alaska to the polluted air of Eastern Europe is pushing up demand for environmental engineers. But fewer than 2% to 3% of all engineers—less than 50,000—now have the training and experience required for this specialty. There are 10 openings for every one environmental engineering graduate.

Environmental engineers usually specialize in what's known as either clean or dirty work.

The profession's clean arm typically does preventive work, investigating the potential causes of environmental damage and developing strategies to ward off pollution and other problems. For example, a so-called clean engineer might help to determine where to build a waterfront development so as not to destroy the area's ecosystem. Engineers who engage in dirty work are the heroes who come to the rescue when environmental emergencies arise—for example, donning protective gear to investigate firsthand why poisonous gas is seeping from underground pipes.

Whichever they choose, environmental engineers are expected to clean up financially over the next 10 years as demand for their skills

Careers with Real Potential

While these didn't make our top 15 fast-track jobs, they are surging because of emerging social trends. Financial planners will earn the most of this bunch, teachers and horticultural professionals the least. Registered nurses can expect the greatest number of job openings.

Career	Training	Avg. Salary/ Top Performer	Comments
Biotechnologist	M.A. or Ph.D. in natural sciences	$45,000/ $100,000	As biotechnology moves from the laboratory to the marketplace, demand is shooting up for scientists who research and develop cutting-edge products ranging from new drugs to biodegradable disposable diapers.
Commercial pilot	B.A. or B.S. plus commercial pilot's license	$85,000/ $170,000	Growth in air traffic plus the fact that 42% of today's airline pilots will retire in the 1990s should create a need for 62,000 new pilots. Defense cuts also are forcing the military to train fewer new ones.
Environmental lawyer	Law degree with courses in environmental law	$65,000/ $100,000-plus	Experts forecast that the number of environmental lawyers will triple by the end of the decade as governments pass more environmental laws and private corporations scramble to comply with them.
Financial planner	C.F.P. or Ch.F.C. preferred	$75,000/ $200,000	Though tax reform and stock market woes hurt this profession, prospects will pick up again this decade as the baby boomers reach their peak earning years and start to plan seriously for retirement.
Fitness professional	B.S. or M.S. in phys. ed., health, or nursing	$35,000/ $75,000-plus	The exercise boom has led to a growing corps of professionals who manage health and fitness programs. The outlook is particularly strong for those who set up in-house programs for private corporations.
Geriatrician	M.D. and geriatric fellowship	$75,000/ $100,000-plus	With the number of people over 65 expected to increase three times as fast as the population as a whole, and fewer than one doctor in 200 specializing in treating older folks, this field should expand rapidly.
Horticultural professional	B.S. in horticulture, landscaping, or turf	$30,000/ $65,000-plus	Opportunities are greatest in this multi-job industry, which includes landscapers, plant growers, and retailers, for those involved in landscape maintenance—for example, the upkeep of golf courses.
Information security specialist	B.S. in accounting or information systems	$50,000/ $75,000-plus	With computer crime costing U.S. companies $555 million in 1989, these experts are needed to devise and implement strategies to prevent theft of confidential data.
Registered nurse	A.A. or B.S. in nursing, plus licensing exam	$30,000/ $70,000-plus	The government expects that more than 600,000 new jobs will be created by the year 2000—nearly a 40% expansion—with the demand greatest in the fields of critical-care and home health-care nursing.
Teacher	B.A. or B.S. plus state certification; M.A. preferred	$31,000/ $56,000-plus	Rising enrollments will add to demand for 1.2 million new teachers this decade. Yet only 8% of college freshmen are interested in the career, compared with 22% of these students 25 years ago.

peaks. Meanwhile, dirty work, which some consider the most urgent environmental need, is likely to pay more than clean. Those specializing in hazardous waste—the real dirty work of the profession—are already commanding 25% more in salary than other engineers.

Physical Therapist

Average salary for hospital therapist: $30,000 to $42,000
Private practitioner: $100,000 to $120,000
Training: B.S. or M.S. in physical therapy; must pass state licensing exam

Physical therapy is the ultimate hands-on profession—but the hands are short these days. By the year 2000, the need for therapists will increase 57% to 107,000, estimates the Department of Labor, which dubs the occupation one of the 10 fastest growing of the decade.

Fitness buffs and the elderly are two expanding groups helping to fuel demand for therapists. Thirty- and forty-something weekend athletes are beating a path to the clinic door complaining of bursitis, tendonitis, sprains, and strains. The elderly are also increasingly seeking treatment to speed recovery from such ailments as strokes and broken hips.

The vigorous demand for therapists' services has helped spur a 30% jump in their salaries over the past few years. Another plus: Therapists can tailor their jobs to fit their needs by electing to work for themselves. Therapists who set up shop and continue to work 40-hour weeks can usually double their salaries within three to four years.

International Lawyer

Average salary for a fifth-year associate: $75,000 to $150,000
Partner: $200,000 and up
Training: Law degree, with course work in international law; fluency in foreign languages helpful

Twenty years ago, the term "international lawyer" was reserved for legal scholars and diplomats who negotiated treaties between countries. Today, it's applied to lawyers who help companies and individuals put together business and investment deals that transcend national borders, as well as litigators who represent clients when such deals unravel.

Demand for these attorneys is growing in proportion to changes in the global marketplace—most notably, the pending economic unification of Western Europe and the collapse of Communism in the Eastern bloc. Ten years ago, only the major companies did international business, so only they needed help. Today, small businesses, even mom-and-pop shops, are doing foreign transactions. Eventually, every major law firm in the country may have to offer international law experience to keep up.

Working for a foreign client involves reconciling disparities between legal codes as well as sorting through cultural differences, which puts an interesting spin on routine legal work, practitioners say. Another major perk is lots of travel, sometimes to exotic countries.

Industrial Designer

Average salary: $55,000
Top performer: $90,000 and up
Training: Undergraduate degree in industrial design or architecture

The recent commercial success of such innovatively designed products as the Ford Taurus and Black & Decker's Spacemaker line of home appliances has helped convince corporate America that good design pads the bottom line. A recent Gallup poll showed that 60% of senior management credit industrial design for the success of any given product. Lately, these managers have been backing their newfound conviction with both jobs and money. Over the past decade, openings for industrial designers have leaped 40%, while their salaries have doubled.

Industrial designers develop all manner of things, from stethoscopes to sleek new cars, from filing cabinets to fishing poles. The kinds of questions these designers wrestle with: Is the seat too high? Where should the buttons go? Is the steering wheel in the right place?

Over the past decade, companies making consumer products—auto, toy, appliance, and computer firms, in particular—have supplied much of the job growth in this profession. But in the 1990s, firms that sell raw materials are expected to hire many designers in an effort to find new customers. It's a lot more effective to show potential customers a finished product than it is to simply rattle off a list of great uses for, say, a particular chemical.

Software Developer

Average salary: $50,000 to $60,000
Top performer: $100,000
Training: B.S. in applied math, engineering, and computer science

Here's a career where a computer hacker can make real bucks—legally. Software design and engineering is the top growth area in the high-tech field. In 1989, employment at the top 100 personal-computer software companies shot up 23.5%. And the Congressional Office of Technology Assessment predicts that more than 100,000 new jobs will be created for software professionals by the end of the decade.

Software developers devise a plan for a certain computerized system—say, regulating the various monitors and instruments in an intensive-care unit—and then create the instructions that tell the computer how to accomplish that task. As more industries and institutions incorporate high technology into their daily operations, the designs and instructions become more complex.

Salaries have been rising to reflect the greater skills now required to design software: Between 1987 and 1990, they rose 19%. Salaries also are being inflated by the insufficient numbers of students entering the field. In 1989, only 10,688 graduates majored in computer science, barely up from 10,422 five years before, probably because students perceive the field is difficult without realizing how lucrative it can be.

Management Consultant

Salary after five years: $100,000 to $120,000
Top performer: $250,000 and up
Training: M.B.A. preferred, plus two years' experience in corporate research, marketing, or management

In 1989, management consulting was the top career choice of business school graduates in this country. Yet, there are still plenty of jobs to go around. Between 1985 and 1990, the consulting industry more than doubled to a $13.5 billion business employing about 80,000 people. Experts project the field will continue to grow by 20% a year throughout the 1990s, as corporate America searches for new strategies to contend with rapidly changing technology and a tough marketplace at home and abroad.

Corporations usually call in a consulting firm when they're trying to cope with major changes in their business, such as a dramatic loss of market share, or when they're contemplating a costly first, such as entering a new field. Depending on the project, the consultant might spend weeks or months talking to management, viewing operations, and collecting data to come up with a strategy to achieve the corporation's goal. After presenting the plan, it's then on to another company and another problem.

Heavy industry used to be the biggest employer of management consultants. Currently, the financial, computer, and health-care industries dominate, with high-tech information systems being the area with the greatest growth potential.

Would-be management consultants should note that this is a young person's field as well as a young profession. Only one in 10 consultants is a 10-year veteran, and almost three-quarters of consulting firms are less than 20 years old—although the big names in the business, like McKinsey and Towers Perrin, have been around since the 1930s. Major drawbacks include long hours (a 60-hour workweek is common) and a frenetic pace that some insiders claim is exciting in the early going but can quickly lead to career burnout.

Infertility Doctor

Researcher's median salary: $50,000
Private practitioner: $150,000 to $250,000
Training: M.D. plus a four-year residency in obstet-rics-gynecology and a two- to three-year fellowship in reproductive endocrinology

One out of every six married couples of childbearing age in the U.S. (excluding those who have been surgically sterilized) cannot conceive. This stunning statistic, attributable largely to the decision of millions of couples to postpone pregnancy beyond their most fertile years, has created a pressing need for repro-ductive endocrinologists, or infertility doctors.

While some of these specialists work strictly in the lab, researching the causes of infertility and helping to develop treatments, most opt to treat patients directly. Tools of the trade range from standard treatments, such as hormonal therapy and artificial insemination, to more advanced procedures, like in-vitro fertilization and embryo transfers.

The training that is necessary to become a reproductive endocrinologist—more than a decade of intensive work and study following college—is among the most arduous de-manded by any profession. But once the long prelude is finally over, the perks of the pro-fession are considerable. Among them: more regular hours than their medical colleagues (no patients going into labor in the middle of the night). Infertility practitioners can make as much as 50% more than obstetricians and gynecologists.

Mechanical Engineer

Average salary: $40,000 to $50,000
Top performer: $80,000 and up
Training: Undergraduate or master's degree in mechanical engineering

Gearing a career to the latest trend can get engineers in trouble—witness recent slumps in computer and defense industries that are hurt-ing the job outlook for electrical and aerospace engineers. But as the general practitioners of

the profession, mechanical engineers have the flexibility to move into all sorts of fields as the need arises. Given the general shortage of en-gineers, the need will definitely rise. By 1996, given current enrollment trends in engi-neering programs, the shortfall is expected to hit 18,000, according to the National Science Foundation.

One of the primary functions of the nation's 225,000 mechanical engineers is to design power-producing machines, such as jet engines and gas turbines, as well as power-using ma-chines, such as air-conditioning and drilling equipment. The skills involved can be applied to many industries. Where is the need most urgent now? The auto industry is seeking en-gineers who can develop anti-lock brake sys-tems, and big oil companies are looking for mechanical engineers to maintain and upgrade pumps and motors in their refineries.

Human-Resources Manager

Middle manager's salary: $40,000 to $70,000
Top executive: $100,000 to $165,000
Training: Liberal arts degree; M.B.A. increasingly common

As the baby-bust generation comes of age, the U.S. is facing its first labor shortage in 20 years. Changing demographics are transform-ing America's human resources into scarce re-sources. For every 10 jobs, there are eight applicants. Four are women, and three are immigrants.

Accordingly, one of the biggest challenges facing corporations in the next decade will be to recruit, train, and retrain an increasingly diversified staff—the heart of a human-re-sources professional's job. These managers also are on the front line of other key work-place issues, such as compensation, flexible-benefits programs, and child-care policies.

Salaries offer tangible proof of the increas-ing respect accorded human-resources ex-perts. In the past decade, total compensation (salaries and bonuses) for top human-re-sources executives at large companies jumped 75%, from $115,000 to just under $200,000.

Special Events Marketer

Average salary: $35,000 to $50,000
Top performer: $150,000 and up
Training: Experience in sales, marketing, or advertising; M.B.A. helpful

The corporate search for cost-effective ways to reach niche markets and stand apart from the competition has made special events one of the fastest-growing areas in marketing. In just five years, as the number of corporations pinning their names on special events has risen from 1,600 to 3,800, the industry has grown from $850 million to $2.1 billion. That means big demand for the specialists who plan, promote, and produce corporate-sponsored sporting events, festivals, and cultural activities.

As a rule, special events marketers work for an independent events agency, for a corporation with an in-house events department, or for an advertising agency. Getting ahead requires working your way up from pre-event preparations to directing events. Tasks along the way can include promoting the event with the media, negotiating contracts with technicians and stars, and on-site management. There is a downside: A flurry of last-minute preparations for each event often means 18-hour days for a week or two at a stretch.

Operations Research Analyst

Average salary: $45,000 to $55,000
Top performer: $150,000 and up
Training: B.S. in math, computer science, or engineering; M.S. in operations research or management science

Operations research analyst is more than just a fancy name for an old-fashioned efficiency expert. The computer is now the engine that makes this profession go and grow. The computer allows an analyst to process enormous amounts of information about a company's daily activities, then filter the data through mathematical models that help determine the most effective way to allocate human and financial resources, design work space, and distribute products or services. For example, the analyst might use the computer to answer questions such as: How many cashiers does a fast-food restaurant need to ensure that no more than three people are waiting on line at any given hour? Or how much should a hotel overbook to guarantee that most of its rooms are occupied most of the time?

Operations research specialists have always found jobs in the defense, manufacturing, and transportation industries. Much of the future job growth should come from telecommunications and service firms. All told, the Department of Labor projects a 55% rise in the field from 55,000 to 85,000 by the year 2000.

Bankruptcy Lawyer

Average salary for a fifth-year associate: $75,000 to $150,000
Partner: $200,000 and up
Training: Law degree; additional courses in finance strongly suggested

The merger-and-acquisition madness that characterized the 1980s has spawned a big business in bankruptcy in the 1990s, as companies stagger under the weight of debt that financed megabuck deals. The number of filings has nearly doubled since 1984, and bankruptcies are expected to grow another 30% to around 890,000 in 1992, according to the Administrative Office of the U.S. Courts. The number of cases involving assets of $1 billion or more is mushrooming, too. Eleven of the 25 largest industrial bankruptcies ever have been filed since January 1989. As a result, commercial bankruptcy law is one of the country's fastest-growing legal specialties.

Bankruptcy lawyers need to be as well versed in reading a balance sheet as they are with the legal intricacies of the bankruptcy code. They must help firms on the brink of insolvency stay out of bankruptcy court by negotiating contracts to restructure debt or sell assets. Once bankruptcy has been declared, these lawyers represent debtors or creditors in court. Both tasks frequently require lawyers to put in 50- to 70-hour workweeks.

Having It All

The question of the 1990s: How can you have a rewarding career while raising a family?

Finding a way for parents to raise their kids while holding down a job seems sure to emerge as one of the major workplace issues of the 1990s. More and more couples with newborns are grappling with the vexing questions of balancing work and family: How long should the new mother stay home with her baby? Should she return to work full time? Part time? At all? For families who need two paychecks to maintain their standard of living, the decisions are even tougher.

Chances are that when it comes to working out solutions with your employer, you will be in uncharted territory. While companies are increasingly willing to accommodate the needs of working mothers, many corporate benefits policies provide little guidance. And federal law doesn't help much either. The Pregnancy Discrimination Act of 1978, the only relevant federal statute, requires employers to treat pregnancy in the same way they treat short-term illness or disability. Typically, that means a woman may be certified as medically disabled for a week or two before her delivery date and for six to eight weeks afterward. But if your company offers even the disabled only five paid sick days a year that may be all you get when your baby is born. Your state's laws may give additional protection.

Beyond maternity leave is parental leave, also called family leave, a much broader benefit that allows time off for either parent to tend to a newborn or an adopted child; it can also permit a parent to stay home to care for a sick child or other relative. Parental leave, which

can last from a few weeks to a year or more, is virtually always unpaid, but it comes with a guarantee that the employee will be reinstated in the same or an equivalent job with no loss of pension benefits or seniority.

Parental leave can be especially onerous for small companies, which cannot afford to hold jobs open for long periods and where the loss of even one person can mean added work for everyone else.

Yet, it is getting harder for companies to duck the issue. The reason: 51% of women with infants under age two are now in the work force, up from 32% in 1977.

Some women are reluctant to take parental leave or even discuss it with their supervisors, for fear of being shifted to the infamous "mommy track," where raises are skimpy and promotions few. But there are women—and men—who are willing to make such a trade-off between work and family.

A growing number of large companies are experimenting with parental-leave benefits as well as flexible work schedules to ease some of the strain on working parents. Some of the more notable examples:

● In 1989, AT&T negotiated a contract with its two unions that provides a generous family-benefits package, including as much as one year of unpaid leave to care for infants or ill dependents.

● IBM now offers employees up to three years' unpaid leave—with full benefits—to raise children or for another "serious reason." Workers are assured their old job or a similar one when they return.

● Aetna Life & Casualty, whose nationwide work force of 45,000 is 69% female, instituted a family-leave policy in 1988 that permits men and women to take as much as six months off. One result: a 50% decrease in the number of women who decided not to return to work at the company after having a child.

● Campbell Soup Company has been a pioneer in family benefits; its on-site day-care center opened in 1983 and now handles 125 children. Campbell also offers leaves of as long as six months and allows job sharing, flexible hours, and part-time work. The company, which instituted the policies in response to employee requests, has found that making workers happy can pay off. "Not only does it reduce turnover, but it also reduces training costs because you don't have to train new employees as often," says a Campbell spokesman.

Most people will not find their companies that generous. Once you decide what you want, in fact, you should be prepared for some hard bargaining. So, along with your child-birth classes, you might consider a course in negotiating skills.

Margaret Meiers, now an employee relations adviser at Mobil, studied corporate policies on parental leave when she was a senior research associate at Catalyst, an advisory group on work and family issues. She proposes the following nine guidelines to help you devise your most effective strategy:

Learn your legal rights. Yes, you may have some—but finding out what they are can be tough. Not only do the rules vary from state to state, but they are in flux. If you are uncertain about local regulations, ask your state department of labor, or 9 to 5: National Association of Working Women (800-245-9865). For a chart explaining state family and medical leave laws, send $4.95 to the Women's Legal Defense Fund, 2000 P Street NW, Washington, D.C. 20036.

Investigate your company's policies. Start with the firm's human-resources booklets. Also, make a point of finding out what kinds of arrangements other employees have made and the benefits other companies in your industry provide. (Some human-resources departments will give you the information over the phone.) If your company is lagging its competitors, you might point this out to the human-resources manager, especially if the company is having trouble filling jobs.

If there is no policy at all, offer to help formulate one. The managing partner of a leading Atlanta law firm did that in 1984 when there were no precedents for dealing with her pregnancy. She asked for what she thought was reasonable—three months' paid leave. She got it, although the firm now offers lawyers only 10 weeks.

Decide what kind of leave you can afford. If your family needs two paychecks, you may not be able to take any parental leave, which is almost always unpaid. And unless you make a lot of money or don't need company-paid benefits, you may not be able to plan a long stint of part-time work either. To see where you stand, do some simple arithmetic. Determine how much you will have to spend on child care, commuting, and other job-related expenses, such as clothing. Then determine what your take-home pay would be. You may discover that you are barely breaking even. If you earn a salary in the high 20s, say, the numbers often don't make sense. You might find that you would be better off looking for another job or not working at all. Certainly, you would want to reconsider parental leave.

Significantly, a recent study by the National Council of Jewish Women involving 2,600 new mothers found that the mean income of the husbands of women who took parental leave was a solid $48,000.

Decide what you want—then decide what you would settle for. Suppose you would like six months away. Would you take four months off and two months of part-time work? If your spouse's job provides family health coverage, you might want to offer to forgo insurance in return for some extra time.

In some cases, it will simply not be possible for you to work out a plan that gives you everything you want no matter how flexible your company is willing to be.

Suggest ways of solving the problems your leave may create. Determine which of your tasks can be rerouted and what projects can be postponed. Perhaps your temporary absence could provide a training opportunity for a junior employee. You might also agree to handle a specific project during your time away.

Get it in writing. The most common mistake employees make is not to have arrangements put in writing. Make certain to discuss all the terms of your leave—including benefits, seniority, vacation accrual—with your supervisor, then send a confirming note and ask him or her to sign it. If you're concerned about seeming pushy, make the point to the person you are negotiating with that an oral agreement may not be honored if he or she moves to another post or leaves the company.

Keep in touch. Co-workers will often be hesitant to call you—what if they wake the baby?—so either call in, or give them specific times to reach you. It's in your best interest to stay abreast of what's going on in the office. It reminds co-workers that you are still part of the team, and it shows your boss that you have a serious interest in resuming a productive role with the company.

Plan your return. After your child is born, the scheme you worked out so carefully may seem all wrong. Maybe you will find that nothing matters to you as much as being home with your child—or, quite the opposite, that you are terribly eager to return to full-time work ahead of schedule.

If you do decide to change your plans, you may be in for another negotiation. Set up a meeting with your supervisor. Coming back to work sooner than expected will usually pose no problem. Getting permission to extend your leave or come back to shorter hours may be tougher. A better approach is to suggest trying a revised schedule for a month, and then meeting to assess it. Structuring in some evaluation time is essential to any kind of agreement.

Throughout, it's important that you treat the negotiations as a business issue and not as a personal problem. Remember that in many instances your employer is under no obligation to offer you parental leave or part-time work, so you may be beginning your discussions at a big disadvantage. On the other hand, if you are a valued employee or if your company is having trouble attracting and keeping talented personnel, you may have a lot of leverage.

And don't be put off by the fact that you are the first one in your company to raise the issue of parental leave. Explore all of the possibilities. The National Council of Jewish Women study found that only 15% of the expectant mothers were offered parental leave. But there was an encouraging finding: An enterprising 8% of the workers took the initiative and arranged their own. Company policy is one thing, but actual practice is another. A valued employee can often negotiate what he or she needs.

Survive the Financial Jungle

At some point, almost everyone gets frustrated managing his or her finances. Maybe your checking account won't balance. Or maybe you are overwhelmed by unpaid bills, with no savings to draw on. Maybe you simply can't deal with trying to figure out the amount and kinds of insurance you need. No matter how unwieldy your finances seem, the easy-to-follow tactics in this chapter can help you master them.

Don't think that you have to become a financial genius. Your prime goal should be financial health, not building huge assets. Even if your personal wealth is slight now, with proper planning you can get yourself into better shape easily and stay that way through retirement.

To create a financial plan, you have to begin by setting basic goals, such as owning your own home, starting a college savings plan, or building a nest egg for retirement.

If you're like most people, one of your goals will be to protect the assets you already have. You will need insurance for your car and your home or apartment, as well as health and disability coverage. But while no one should skimp on insurance, just about everybody pays more in insurance premiums than they need to. And all too often, the insurance you have doesn't give you the kind of coverage you need. "How to Protect Everything You Own" on page 40 can keep you from losing your home, your business—even your income—in a disaster.

Of course, you may also have goals that not everyone else shares, such as a vacation home in the hills. These desires should be part of your personal financial plan—just as long as you are able to identify the ones that are truly important to you. Chances are that you won't have the wherewithal to achieve all of your goals. Setting priorities forces you to be realistic. For example, you will probably regret directing all your saving toward buying a new Jaguar if it comes at the expense of Junior's college savings account. The financial fitness worksheets in this chapter will get you going in the right direction, helping you develop a budget.

A side benefit from examining your finances is that you will probably be able to spot some frivolous expenses that are busting you. For instance, if you paid your hairdresser or barber more than your grocer last year, consider a new hairdo and more home cooking. You don't have to turn into Jack Benny; just be less of an Imelda Marcos.

Most important, try to establish consistent savings patterns. During the 1980s, savers had it easy. To earn yields of 9% or more, all they had to do was put their spare cash in a money-market fund—almost any would do—or a bank certificate of deposit. You can kiss those days goodbye. There are still ways you can earn attractive returns on your savings, but you will have to work harder at it.

A Financial Fitness Checkup

This comprehensive diagnostic report will help you find the weaknesses in your financial plan.

The importance of knowing your financial strengths and weaknesses cannot be overemphasized. As a first step to taking control of your economic well-being, you should assess your goals. Once you understand what you want, use the worksheets on the following pages to figure your net worth and cash flow. They will tell you what you have and where it's going now. But don't stop there. Use the Monthly Budget Planner beginning on page 34 to monitor your income and outgo throughout the year. You'll be amazed at the improvement in your financial health.

Starting with the goals worksheet, list your objectives in order of their importance; then assess the resources that you have to work with. The personal balance worksheet will help you calculate your current net worth—the amount by which your assets exceed your liabilities. Most of the information required to complete this worksheet is easy to get. For financial assets, look at the statements you receive from your bank, brokerage, or mutual fund company and, if necessary, check the newspaper to update price quotations.

Your assets can be divided into two categories—liquid and illiquid. Cash, bank accounts, money funds, and investments such as stocks, bonds, and mutual-fund shares that can be converted to cash quickly are considered liquid. Between 15% and 50% of your assets should be liquid, and there should be enough ready cash in bank accounts and money-market funds to cover three to six months' worth of your living expenses. The most frequent problem that you find on a net worth statement is that too much money is tied up in assets that won't bail you out if you hit a rough spot.

Illiquid investments are harder to evaluate. Consult for-sale ads in your newspaper to find out the value of your home and any other properties that you own. Be sure to use conservative estimates for your car and your Persian rug because you might not be able to get their full worth if you had to sell them quickly. Your company benefits counselor should be able to tell you how much you now have in your 401(k) and other company benefit plans. And the tables in each of your life insurance policies and annuity contracts will indicate their current cash values.

Ideally, your outstanding loans—including mortgages—should be less than half your total assets. If the percentage is a lot higher, clearly you are carrying too much debt. When you are overburdened, any efforts you make to save are likely to be overwhelmed by the interest on all of your debts. In addition, appreciating property, such as your home and investments, should constitute more than half your total assets. If they don't, you are spending too much on personal possessions, such as furniture, that will decline in value as time passes.

To find out where you can raise money to improve your balance sheet, complete the cash-flow statement. This worksheet shows how much you earn in a year and where the money goes. The fastest way to find the numbers is to consult your last year's tax return. Expenses involving fixed periodic payments are also easy to reconstruct from your checkbook records. These costs include your mortgage payments or rent, charges for utilities, car loans, and insurance premiums.

The harder items to gauge are those that involve variable expenses, which are usually responsible for cash-flow problems. The best way to find out how much you spent last year on clothing, dining expenses, and the like is to go through your checkbook and credit-card statements for the last three months of the year and multiply by four. You should also add up your cash withdrawals for those months, multiply by four, and allocate the money as best you can among the expenses that you usually pay for in cash. One warning: Most people underestimate the amount that they actually spend by 10% to 20%.

Add up your living expenses and subtract the total from your after-tax income. The difference is the amount you have left over for savings and investments. Most financial planners say that the figure should be at least 7% to 10% of your after-tax income. If you aren't setting aside enough, cut back your credit-card spending and pay off your balances as quickly as possible. With credit-card interest rates

running as high as 22% a year, few other investments will offer as good a return.

The most difficult part of your financial fitness checkup is now over. Use the budget planner to stay on top of your finances.

Finding the Right Adviser

Even if you've always managed your own money—and done just fine—the need for professional help often arises when your life takes a major turn. To help you, more and more financial planners are offering what they call segmented or issue-oriented services. That is, they will help you solve a single problem.

While nearly all planners will try to help you with any problem, it's smart to hold out for a specialist. For example, if you need advice on paying for college, go to a planner who knows the intricacies of financial aid for higher education. Similarly, if your problem concerns long-term health care for an aging parent, be sure you're dealing with someone who has mastered state Medicaid regulations.

Finding such specialists can be difficult, since planners are neither licensed nor regulated. For recommendations, you can call the fee-only planners' trade group, the National Association of Personal Financial Advisors (800-366-2732), or the two biggest organizations of fee-and-commission planners, the International Association for Financial Planning (404-395-1605) and the Institute of Certified Financial Planners (303-751-7600).

Interview at least three candidates. Be sure to get several references and then telephone at least two to determine exactly how their problems were resolved.

Solutions to specific problems often require the planner to gather and assess as much information as in a full-scale workup. So you can usually expect to pay from $500 to around $1,500. Be careful, however. Don't let yourself be talked into putting more money into full-scale financial planning unless you're convinced that you need it.

Ranking Your Goals

Adequately assessing your goals, needs, and wants is the key to successful financial management. So before you begin to assess your finan- cial situation, you must first assess what is and is not important to your financial and emotional well being.

Objective	Of No Importance	Of Some Importance	Very Important	Essential	Short Term	Medium Term	Long Term
Reduce debt							
Build an emergency reserve							
Increase insurance coverage							
Buy a house							
Make home improvements							
Buy a vacation house							
Buy a car							
Make some other big purchase							
Have children							
Finance children's education							
Live more luxuriously							
Take an expensive vacation							
Take an unpaid leave from work							
Start a business							
Take early retirement							
Live well after retirement							
Other							

Your Personal Balance Sheet

Assessing your current net worth is the first step toward creating a long-term financial plan. This worksheet will show you how.

1. Cash and near-cash assets (bank accounts, CDs, T-bills, and money-market funds and accounts) _____

2. Stocks, bonds, and mutual funds _____

3. Total liquid assets (line 1 plus line 2) _____

4. Retirement savings (IRAs, Keoghs, 401(k) plans, and other company plans) _____

5. Real estate (value of your home, second home, and limited partnerships) _____

6. Cash value of life insurance and annuities _____

7. Collectibles (precious metals, art, and antiques) _____

8. Personal property (car, furniture, clothes, and jewelry) _____

9. Total assets (sum of lines 3 through 8) _____

10. Unpaid bills (taxes, mortgage, or rent, and charge-account balances) _____

11. Loans (mortgages, home improvement, car, education, and margin accounts) _____

12. Total liabilities (line 10 plus line 11) _____

13. Current net worth (line 9 minus line 12) _____

Your Cash-Flow Statement

Tracking your cash flow will show you how much you have to invest and indicate some expenses that you could trim.

1. Annual income (salaries; interest and dividends; child support or alimony; pensions; annuities; Social Security; rents; royalties; and fees) _____

2. Annual taxes (income and property taxes, Social Security contributions) _____

3. After-tax income (line 1 minus line 2) _____

4. Rent or mortgage payments and utilities _____

5. Food and clothing _____

6. Furniture and appliances _____

7. Recreation and entertainment _____

8. Car payments, repairs, and gasoline _____

9. Medical, legal, and financial expenses _____

10. Insurance premiums _____

11. Other _____

12. Total annual expenses (sum of lines 4 through 11) _____

13. Funds available for savings and investments (line 3 minus line 12) _____

Monthly Budget Planner

Keeping up with your money is necessary for day-to-day management of your financial affairs. This sample worksheet takes into account all of the expenses you incur in a month and will help you stay on top of your bills as well as your monthly income.

Month _____   **Total Monthly Income $ _____**

		Amount	Amount Paid	Due Date	Date Paid
EXPENSES (fixed)	**Mortgage/Rent**				
	Car payments				
	Loans				
	Insurance				
	Other				
EXPENSES (fixed variable)	**Electricity**				
	Gas/Fuel				
	Telephone				
	Gas/Auto				
	Water/Garbage				
	Food				
	Entertainment				
	Child Care				
	Other				

		Amount	Amount Paid	Due Date	Date Paid
OCCASIONAL EXPENSES	Household				
	Home Improvement				
	Clothes				
	Medical				
	Travel				
	Charitable				
	Political				
	Gifts				
	Miscellaneous				
INSTALLMENTS	Credit Cards				
	Other				
SAVINGS AND INVESTMENTS	Savings account				
	Money-market account				
	Stocks				
	Bonds				
	Mutual Funds				
	Other				

_____ − _____ = _____

Total Income   **Total Expenses**   **Net Income**

Are You Saving Enough?

You may be surprised by the amount you are really putting away. If it's not enough, there are smart ways to save more.

Americans have come to realize, as their parents and grandparents did before them, that the only sure way to meet future financial needs—from college education for the kids to a comfortable retirement for themselves—is to sock away money regularly. That's one reason the national savings rate, after bottoming out at 2.9% of after-tax income in 1987, rose to 4.6% for all of 1989 and recently was running at 5.1%.

Putting more aside is only the first step. Equally important is earning the highest safe yield. For instance, $20,000 in a 5.2% passbook savings account will grow to $55,100 in 20 years. Over that period, if you can raise your yield to 8.5%, your money will swell to $102,200. Achieving that 8.5%, however, is increasingly difficult—let alone 9%. So savers will have to work harder and smarter.

The following strategies should help. Keep both the size of your savings and your goals in mind. For instance, before putting money anywhere else, build up an amount equal to at least three months' expenses in a money-market fund for emergencies. Then, if your children's education is your top priority, consider buying zero-coupon Treasury securities for them. If retirement is your major goal, though, and you are still under 40, think about putting at least 50% of your savings into utility or other conservative stocks. And be sure to use dollar-cost averaging—regular purchases of the same dollar amount of stock—so that your money will buy more shares when prices are down and help insulate you against market swings. Here are nine savings strategies, starting with the simplest:

Earn higher interest on your bank balances. Switch the money you prefer to keep in federally-insured bank deposits to accounts that pay the highest possible interest. Keep only the minimum required balance in your no-interest checking account or 5% NOW account. Move any additional money—as well as any cash you have in a passbook savings account—to your bank's money-market deposit account, which will pay more.

Shop for high-rate CDs out of town. Although the astronomical rates once paid by the S&Ls of Texas and other economically troubled states are only a memory, some above-average yields are still available at financially-sound institutions. People often get nearly a full percentage point above hometown rates by sending money to a high-yielding bank out of state. (For other choices, see the Scorecard section of *Money* which every month lists the top yields in the country and ranks the safety of the issuing institutions.) Stock brokerages also offer above-average rates on CDs, though the S&L bailout has crimped the supply.

Open a money-market fund account and use it to pay bills over $250. Money funds do not carry any government insurance, but you still run almost no risk of principal loss. And with a money-market fund, you can earn higher interest—for example, 8% versus 5% on a typical

NOW account—while waiting for your checks to clear.

Because most money funds require that your checks top $250 or $500, use the fund for mortgage payments or other large bills; depend on your bank checking account to pay smaller bills. Or search out a money fund with no check-writing minimum.

Switch excess cash from your money fund to a short-term bond fund. Once you have accumulated an emergency reserve of at least three months' expenses in a money fund, move surplus cash to a short-term bond fund which invests in bonds with maturities of five years or less and offers a higher yield.

The highest safe returns are available from

Painless Tactics for Serious Savers

Hard-nosed savers aim to put away 10% of their pretax income each year. If you can't manage to set aside at least $1,000, though, consider the following tactics:

Pay in cash. That will teach you a lot about the difference between what you want and what you really need. Moreover, by paying cash you avoid finance charges. For example, trimming your credit-card balances by $500 this year can save you almost $100 in interest if your card issuer charges the average 18.6%.

Make bigger down payments. When financing your next major purchase—whether a new car or a new kitchen—put up as much money as you can. Not financing $500 at 12% over three years can keep $98 jingling in your pocket; not financing $5,000 saves you $979.

If you own a home, use a home-equity loan to consolidate high-rate debts. By replacing consumer debts at, say, 18% with a home-equity loan at 12%, you'll cut your interest costs by a third. In addition, the interest on a home-equity loan can be fully deducted on your income tax return. Consolidate $10,000 in car payments and credit-card cash advances with a home-equity loan, for example, and, counting the tax break, a taxpayer in the 28% bracket will save $936.

Eliminate one big expense a year. Skip your winter vacation, trade in your turbocharged sports car for an econobox, or ditch your health-club membership and use the "Y." No matter what the pain, the gain can be very impressive. Surveys show, for example, that typical *Money* readers could save about $2,350 per person by forgoing a trip abroad.

Don't pay for financial services you can get for free. Using only no-fee checking accounts, mutual funds, and credit cards can save you $100 a year or more. For instance, checking accounts can cost $60 a year; annual fees for credit cards typically range from $15 to $50.

Save your next raise. To squeeze out money for your 401(k), earmark your next raise for it. If you earn $40,000, for instance, a 5% raise will give you $2,000 for your account.

Take advantage of your company savings plan. If you aren't contributing to it now, you may be throwing money away. Reason: Most 401(k)s and other plans offer tax breaks; moreover, part of your contributions are often matched by your employer. Let's say you're in the 28% tax bracket, you sock away $2,000 a year, and your company kicks in a third of that amount. You'll gain $667 from your employer, and your tax savings for the year will amount to $746.

Use your flexible spending account. Don't pass up the opportunity to pay medical and dependent-care expenses with pretax dollars through these accounts. According to a survey by the Bureau of Labor Statistics, a family of four is almost certain to spend $1,000 a year on doctors, dentists, and prescription medicines. Your savings if you pay for them from an FSA can be at least $280.

Figure Your Real Savings Rate

The worksheet is designed to summarize all the new investments and savings you made in 1990, including reinvested earnings on existing assets. It excludes, however, changes in the market value of your holdings after you bought them. Money that moved from one location to another last year—such as the proceeds of stock sales put in your savings account—does not represent new savings. Such financial transfers should show up twice; as a debit on one line and a credit on another. If your savings rate is only around the national average of 5.1%, you should try to put aside more, though perhaps not much more if you are in your twenties or thirties and just starting out. If you are in your high earnings years of ages 40 to 60, however, and are trying to provide for a comfortable retirement, you should be saving considerably more than average—at least 15% and maybe a lot more.

NEW SAVINGS & INVESTMENTS

1. Cash balances. The 1990 change in the total balances of your savings and checking accounts and money-market funds.

2. Mutual funds. All the money you invested in new shares, plus capital-gain and dividend distributions you reinvested.

3. Other new investments. All the money you put into individual stocks and bonds, CDs, gold, real estate ventures, limited partnerships, and investment-grade collectibles.

4. Residential equity. The amount of principal you paid off on all mortgages, plus the down payment if you bought a home.

5. Profit sharing and other company savings plans. Your contributions and fully vested employer contributions in 1990.

6. Personal retirement plans. Contributions to Keoghs, IRAs, annuities, and other independent plans, plus their 1990 earnings.

7. Life insurance. The total increase in cash value of all policies, plus dividends credited to you in 1990.

8. Debts repaid. The amount of principal paid off on car loans and other nonmortgage balances, plus the reduction, if any, in total credit-card and charge account balances in 1990.

9. Other. A tax refund, for example, or an investment in a closely held small business.

10. Total savings. Add lines 1 through 9.

SALES OF ASSETS & ADDITIONS TO DEBT

11. Investments sold or matured and withdrawals from retirement plans.

12. New debts. The total of all your additional consumer debt, margin loans, home-equity loans, mortgage refinancing, and life insurance loans, plus any increase in your credit-card and charge account balances since December 31, 1989.

13. Total asset sales and new debt. Add lines 11 and 12.

14. Net savings. Subtract line 13 from line 10.

YOUR SAVINGS RATE

15. Your total income from all sources, including nontaxable benefits, interest, and dividends but not loans.

16. Your employer's contributions to pensions and profit sharing. The part of line 5 that represents employer contributions.

17. Life insurance adjustment. The total increases in cash value, plus dividends on line 7, minus premiums paid.

18. Your total income taxes. Include the federal, state, and local taxes you paid or will owe for 1990.

19. Total available income. Add lines 15 through 17 and subtract line 18.

20. Savings rate. Divide line 14 by line 19 and multiply by 100.

funds that hold the securities of top-rated corporations. Recently, one of the best-yielding funds sponsored by a leading management company was Vanguard Fixed Income-Short Term (800-662-7447).

Bond funds, in contrast to money funds, do not assure the value of your principal. But because short-term bond funds do not hold securities with maturities beyond five years, the losses you risk are less than a year's interest. Even if interest rates shot up by two percentage points, a typical short-term fund would lose less than 4%.

Savers who are willing to ride out greater price fluctuations may want to consider Scudder Short-Term Bond Fund (800-225-2470). The fund holds foreign bonds—whose value moves in the opposite direction of the dollar—as well as mortgage-backed securities and U.S. corporate issues.

Tax-exempt bond funds may provide an even higher after-tax return for investors in the 28% bracket or higher (married couples with taxable income of more than $32,450; singles with more than $19,450).

Beat bank CD rates with two- to three-year Treasury notes. For a $5,000 minimum investment, you recently could earn 8% on two-year notes and 8.2% on three-year issues—up to one-third of a percentage point more than on bank CDs of the same maturities. Better yet, interest on Treasury notes is exempt from state and local taxes, which effectively adds half a point or more in yield for many investors in high-tax states such as California and New York.

To avoid the usual $50 broker's commission, which would in effect cut a point off your first year's yield on a $5,000 purchase, buy Treasuries directly from a Federal Reserve branch.

Capture rising dividend yields with sound utility stocks. To meet long-term goals such as retirement, you may want to put up to 25% of your portfolio into electric and gas utilities that have boosted dividends at least 5% a year over the past decade. Such stocks offer both the prospect of growing yields and long-term capital gains. A utility with a 7% yield and 5%

annual price appreciation would offer a long-term total return of 12% a year.

Buy zero-coupon bonds for long-range goals. With yields comparable to those of regular Treasury bonds, zeros pay no cash interest but sell at substantially less than the face value amount that you receive when they mature and are redeemed by the Treasury. Such issues therefore are especially suitable for tax-deferred Individual Retirement Accounts and Keogh accounts, since otherwise you would owe annual taxes on interest that you do not receive in cash. If you have sufficient money from other sources to pay those taxes, you can also use zeros to save for college costs. Since the prices of long-term zeros are highly volatile, buy bonds that mature close to the time that you will need the money.

As an alternative, consider zero-coupon Refcorp issues, which are issued to finance the federal S&L bailout and recently yielded about three-tenths of a percentage point more than Treasury zeros.

Include blue-chip growth stocks in your retirement portfolio. If you have 20 years or more until retirement, such stocks or stock mutual funds are the best way to increase your capital. Over the past 64 years, stocks have returned 10.3% a year on average, including reinvested dividends, about twice as much as the return on corporate and government bonds and triple that of money-market funds.

Consider investing extra money for retirement in carefully selected deferred annuities. If you already have put as much as possible into both your tax-deferred 401(k) and IRA—the combined maximum allowed this year is $9,979—and you want an additional tax-advantaged investment, take a look at annuities. They work best for investors in the 28% and 33% tax brackets who are willing to lock their money away for 10 years or more.

The most attractive choices are variable annuities, which permit you to invest in stock and bond mutual funds without paying tax on capital gains or reinvested dividends and interest until the money is withdrawn.

How to Protect Everything You Own

Don't be caught with the wrong insurance—or worst of all—unprepared for disaster.

Vivid and terrifying images linger long after disasters like Hurricane Hugo or the California earthquake: roofless homes, burning buildings, grim tallies of injured and dead. Yet if you're like most people, you think such images could never include you. Or—if they ever did—that there is nothing you can do to prepare for it. Wrong on both counts. No matter where you live, complacency and fatalism can prove lethal to your finances.

Here's how you can protect yourself against disaster:

To safeguard your home: Check your insurance policy, then be prepared to prove your losses and fight for your claim.

Homeowners insurance will give top protection only when you have comprehensive coverage and are willing to stand up for your rights if your insurer balks.

The best policies all share two key features. First, they provide open perils coverage, meaning that you are insured against damage from any risk except those that are specifically excluded—such as earthquake, flood, war, and nuclear accident. (Less comprehensive policies protect you only against fire, wind, and a limited set of other calamities.) An open perils policy is usually referred to as Homeowners 3, and either that name or its abbreviation, HO-3, should appear on the first page of your policy. To obtain comparable coverage for your possessions, you must add an endorsement, often called HO-15. Second, the best policies contain a replacement cost clause that

obligates the insurer to pay the full cost of repairing or replacing your home—not just its depreciated value—up to the dollar limit of your policy. To get that protection, you must insure your home for at least 80% of the estimated cost of rebuilding it. (Your insurance agent can help determine the figure.) You need a separate endorsement to extend replacement-cost protection to your possessions. And check your policy limits on jewelry, fur, silverware, and collectibles losses; you may need to add special endorsements known as riders for expensive items.

Once you have your policy, review it with your insurance agent and ask for written answers to important questions. As further documentation, write out a room-by-room inventory of your possessions and attach photographs or a videotape. Save all receipts for sizable purchases. Keep this documentation away from your home—at your office, for example, or in a safe-deposit box.

If you do fall victim to a disaster, gather repair estimates before the insurer makes an offer. Otherwise, you might accept a lowball settlement that seems fair to your untrained eye. Don't accept offers that aren't at least close to your experts' figures. A claims process is a negotiation. If you have several detailed estimates to back your claim, you have a very strong case. And don't accept an offer of help from a public claims adjuster unless you feel you simply cannot do the job yourself. These freelance adjusters typically charge 10% of any payments you receive.

If you and your insurance company can't agree, write a letter to your state insurance commissioner. As a next resort, pay a lawyer $500 or so to resubmit your claim. But sue only if you don't mind waiting a year to collect your money and paying 25% or more of it to the lawyer. A cheaper, swifter route might be binding arbitration; the insurer should agree to split the fee, typically 2% to 3% of the disputed amount. And even after you settle, keep track of any unanticipated costs. Hidden damage is often found later, and if your contractor can document such problems, the insurer should pay.

To save a business: The big risk is not property damage but the eventual loss of revenues, employees, and customers.

Entrepreneurs who cope with small disasters daily often neglect to protect their businesses against truly big ones. Sometimes they buy insurance only against property damage—loss of buildings, equipment, and inventory. But such losses can be dwarfed by the cost of shutting down a business temporarily, moving to new quarters, paying key employees' salaries, and hiring other firms to fulfill your contracts so that you don't lose customers. You can get this kind of coverage by buying business interruption insurance.

Don't rely solely on insurance. Work out a disaster contingency plan that identifies potential emergency lenders, subcontractors to take over your work, and real estate brokers who can find you temporary space. Keep copies of essential records, such as work orders and financial statements, somewhere besides your office in case the originals are destroyed.

Should a disaster occur, make a detailed list of damage before you clean up, and document it with photos or videotapes. Besides supporting your claim, these could help you land a Small Business Administration disaster loan. The agency charges annual interest of only 4% if you can't borrow elsewhere, 8% if you can. You usually have to start repaying the loan after five months, although the SBA will sometimes grant extensions in special circumstances. The maximum term for an SBA loan is 30 years.

To insure your income: When buying coverage for your possessions, don't forget that you need to protect your earning power as well.

To avoid having to rely primarily on charity and public aid after a disabling injury, take a close look now at your own disaster plan. Ideally, you should have an emergency cash fund equal to at least three months' expenses. You might also open a personal or home-equity line of credit now for emergency borrowing. And your disability-income insurance should promise 60% to 70% of your before-tax salary, starting 90 days after injury and continuing until you resume work or reach 65. Such coverage is expensive when you buy it yourself— up to $1,300 annually for a 45-year-old non-smoking executive. Fortunately, most large companies—and about 25% of smaller ones— offer some employer-paid coverage. Also, if you're self-employed in California, you can buy into the inexpensive state disability fund. (New Jersey and Rhode Island have funds, too, but you must be incorporated to participate in them.)

In the event of a disaster, by all means supplement your income with public and private relief. The Red Cross provides food, clothing, and up to $1,000 for home repairs. The Small Business Administration can lend you as much as $100,000 to fix your house and $20,000 to replace possessions, whether or not you run a business. The Federal Emergency Management Agency offers grants of as much as $10,400 to people who suffer serious financial hardship, up to 26 weeks of unemployment benefits to self-employed disaster victims who can't work, and up to 18 months of housing assistance for those who are left homeless.

To cover floods and quakes: Insurance can be expensive, but it's worth buying if you're on shaky ground.

Most homeowners rely on luck to protect them from floods or earthquakes because standard homeowners policies exclude those perils. Special insurance is available, but it can be expensive, since people typically buy it only if they live in a high-risk area. So, even though trusting to fate may be your best defense, first make sure your risk is low.

Although private companies sell most flood policies, you cannot buy this government-guaranteed insurance unless your community is among the 18,000 that participate in the National Flood Insurance Program. Luckily, that includes almost every place with a serious risk of floods. In fact, you may already be insured if your home is in a region that the NFIP has designated a special flood hazard area—meaning that hydrologists calculate there is at least a 1 in 100 chance per year of a major flood. If those odds sound low, consider that they climb to greater than 1 in 4 over the life of a typical 30-year mortgage. Result: Federally regulated lenders—which include most banks and S&Ls—aren't supposed to give you a mortgage unless you're protected.

If you're not covered and want to be, find out from your insurance agent or the NFIP (800-638-6620) whether your community has joined the federal program. If it has, your agent should have a flood insurance rate map—or you can buy one from the agency for $5—that shows whether you live in a special hazard area, a moderate hazard area (flood risk: less than 1 in 100 but at least 1 in 500 per year), or a minimal hazard area (risk: less than 1 in 500 per year). Even on moderate- or minimal-risk ground, you may need protection:

Over 30% of insured flood damage occurs in such areas. The government-set premium usually ranges from $200 to $300 a year for a $150,000 house, regardless of where it's located. One exception: Insuring a house that doesn't meet NFIP safety rules in a special hazard area could cost up to $2,000 annually.

Judging your risks from an earthquake is more difficult. The U.S. Geological Survey offers maps that show major fault zones; you can see one at your planning agency or write to the Office of Public Inquiries, U.S. Geological Survey, Reston, VA 22092 for a free national map. Unfortunately, geophysicists are still unable to predict earthquakes with precision.

Most Californians, of course, would be well advised to carry quake insurance if they can afford it. The cost to protect a $250,000 frame house in San Francisco is $330 a year or more, depending on its age; in less quake-prone areas elsewhere in the state, the cost for a house of comparable style and price runs as low as $250. By contrast, in Memphis, which straddles a major fault line but hasn't had a big quake in 179 years, you would pay only about $100 for the same coverage. Prices bottom out at $50 or so in low-risk places like Tampa and Milwaukee.

When to Just Say No to Car-Rental Insurance

Add-ons are often too expensive and unnecessary.

You confidently stride up to the counter to rent a car. "I don't need the collision-damage waiver, since I'm covered by my credit card," you explain. The agent smiles and asks, "But what about liability? Or theft of personal property? And does your card cover you if the car is stolen?" Demoralized, you decide that $10 a day is a small price for peace of mind.

Confused about which extra insurance you need when renting a car? Join the crowd.

Many consumers still aren't sure whether they need collision-damage waivers. And recently, questions have been raised about other types of costly coverage peddled at the rental counter. Car-rental companies say the add-ons provide needed protection. "These packages are designed as a temporary safety net for people who may not have their own personal insurance," says Jan M. Armstrong, executive director of the American Car Rental Association. But at a recent meeting in Washington, a task force of the National Association of Insurance Commissioners criticized add-on insurance as too expensive and often unnecessary.

Here is *Money*'s guide to the most common add-ons to help you determine whether you need them:

Collision-damage waiver (CDW). Most rental agencies hold you responsible for any damage caused by an accident—no matter who is at fault—up to the car's market value. Among the industry's big four, Hertz and Budget hold clients responsible for theft and vandalism; Avis and National do not. All but Hertz also tack on "loss of use" costs, to recoup the rental fees the agencies could have earned if the car had been in service.

To eliminate your liability, you can buy what the rental companies call a collision-damage waiver or loss-damage waiver, usually for $7 to $12 a day. That's expensive, and the waiver itself is often riddled with exclusions. For example, many rental firms void the waiver if you were driving on what they deem a poorly maintained road.

What you should do. If you are renting in Illinois or New York, relax: Those states limit your liability to $200 and $100, respectively. (Many other states are considering similar limits.) Otherwise, check your own auto insurance. Most comprehensive policies cover a rented car's full value in case of theft, vandalism, or an accident; in addition, many pay for loss of use. And if you pay for your rental with certain charge cards, including most gold cards, you get full coverage for accidents, vandalism, theft, and loss of use when you decline the CDW. Two nonpremium cards that cover you: the American Express green card (800-528-4800, $55 annual fee) and the Chase Visa or MasterCard (800-441-7681, $20 annual fee). Also, consult your employer: Some firms have deals that cover their employees even when they are not traveling on company business.

If you find that you're not protected in some way, however, don't take any chances. If you're not covered by insurance or a credit card, then you should purchase the CDW.

Personal effects coverage (PEC). For $1 to $3 daily, you're covered for any personal property stolen from the car.

What you should do. Start by not leaving valuables in the car. Also, check your homeowners or tenants policy—almost all of them will cover your personal property even when it's outside your home.

Supplemental liability insurance (SLI). For about $5 a day, you're covered for all claims made against you by others involved in an accident.

What you should do. Some coverage is included automatically when you rent, but it's usually the minimum required by state law: as little as $10,000 a person up to a total of $20,000 an accident—not nearly enough. If you own a car, however, you presumably already have ample liability insurance. If you don't own a car, buy the extra coverage.

Personal accident insurance (PAI). This is just a fancy name for extra health and life insurance; it costs $1 to $3 a day.

What you should do. If you already have health and life insurance, pass up this extra. If you don't, the car-rental counter is not the place to buy more. Instead, talk to an independent insurance agent about getting coverage for every day of the year.

Track Down Winning Investments

Ever since the 1987 stock-market crash, economists have been warning that a recession was near. In 1990, it was definitely nearer, if not upon us. Consequently, the question that's probably uppermost on investors' minds is: How can I protect myself in bad times and the uneven times that follow? This chapter provides some answers.

Whether you experience hardship or pass through it all with nothing worse than a dim awareness of distant economic rumblings will depend on where you live and work and, above all, your financial preparedness. Don't try to outpsyche world crises or the U.S. economy, moving your money with each day's headlines. Rather, take measures that will safeguard your finances, regardless of events beyond your control.

Besides the obvious precautionary measures—protecting your job, building your savings and controlling your debt—stand by your stocks and bonds. Forget apocalypse now. While a staggering economy virtually guarantees further market gyrations, this isn't the moment to liquidate your assets and pour everything into CDs and money-market funds.

Market timing is notoriously difficult even in placid times; in volatile ones, timing is a prescription for mediocre returns and jangled nerves. A far better tactic is to arrange investments so that every new crisis doesn't provoke a headache.

The basic strategy: diversification. Keep the money you will need within five years where it is perfectly safe, such as Treasury bills, CDs, or money-market funds. Split longer-term dough fifty-fifty between equities and fixed-income securities. Push the balance more toward stocks if you're young, enjoy secure employment, or have a venturesome nature; beef up the fixed-income weighting if you're getting within five years of your goal or if you're just constitutionally risk-shy.

As for any fresh dollars you may have on hand for long-term investments, now is a good time to start cautiously looking for bargains. True, the Dow could always go lower but, since there's no way an investor can expect to catch the market bottom, you should start buying as soon as stocks look cheap. Be selective and don't rush in all at once. Instead, invest in stages: Commit equal dollar amounts every quarter, say—but no more often than once a week or for every 50-point drop in the Dow.

The social and economic changes taking place in this country and around the world will offer some fantastic investment opportunities in the 1990s. This chapter outlines the hottest investment trends of the decade, with special attention to the emerging European markets and the six regions in the U.S. where money can be made. You also find out how to forecast a stock's potential, protect your gains, and the ins and outs of municipal bonds and mutual funds, among other things.

If ever the temptation to hide out in money markets or CDs threatens to get the best of you in the months ahead, remember this: Recessions and bear markets all end eventually, and rebounds usually begin when the news seems bleakest.

The Hottest Investments of the Decade

Greed is out. Decency, the environment, and Eastern Europe are in. Here's how fund buyers can get in now on the emerging investment trends of the 1990s.

Long-term economic and social changes produce opportunities for big profits—if you are shrewd enough to get in early. Consider the lucky folks who played their hunch that Japan would become an increasingly dominant world economic power by investing in the Japan Fund back in 1980. By 1990, the fund had shot up 663.9%—the third-best fund performance of the 1980s.

But how do you find the next Japan Fund before it takes off? For every newspaper headline today, there's a new mutual fund tomorrow, or so it seems. Among hip new offerings are the Domini Social Index Trust, which has promised to be the first "socially responsible" index fund; Scudder New Europe Fund, which will try to capitalize on the changes taking place in Europe; and Shearson Lehman Hutton's 1990s Fund, a grab bag of stocks reflecting such trendy themes as the aging U.S. population and the rebuilding of the nation's rapidly deteriorating infrastructure.

To sort through the growing number of fund choices and find the trends that stand the best chance of delivering heady returns to investors in the 1990s, *Money* interviewed economists, portfolio strategists, and investment advisers. In addition to identifying six broad themes that are likely to shape society during the decade, the pros recommended more than a dozen mutual funds that seem most likely to prosper from the trends over the next five to 10 years.

Why funds? Simply put: They offer you the least risky way to invest in emerging social and economic trends. With funds, you get low-cost diversification as well as professional managers, who are generally better able than individual stockholders to recognize when a trend is petering out and that, therefore, the time has come to bail out. To reduce your risk further, you can use dollar-cost averaging to invest in these funds. With this technique, you put in the same amount of money each month, ensuring that you buy more shares when prices are low than when they are high.

Most of the funds recommended by the experts are diversified-growth funds that let you bet on a few trends with one investment. If you are convinced that a particular industry will take off and are willing to take bigger risks, you might consider a sector fund. These funds, which invest in a single industry, offer the possibility of big gains—or big losses. Before investing in them, you should already have a well-diversified portfolio of about $10,000. An aggressive investor can place up to 30% of that money in one or more sector funds.

The investment trends and funds most likely to deliver on them in the 1990s are:

The greening of America: Cleaning up on the environmental cleanup. Oil spills, acid rain, the greenhouse effect, and the depleted ozone layer—all are fueling a born-again environmental movement that should gather righteous steam as the nation moves toward the next millennium. Analysts project that annual spending on products and services to clean up the environment will double by the mid-1990s from about $100 billion in 1989.

Among the biggest beneficiaries: the $25 billion environmental-services industry, made up of firms involved in solid-waste management, pollution control, and toxic-waste disposal. "Many of these companies are going to grow about 20% annually over the next few years," says Lawrence Greenberg, manager of the $78 million Fidelity Select Environmental Services (3% load; 800-544-6666), one of at least four funds that invest primarily in environmental stocks.

Some experts feel these sector funds are especially risky now because the environmental industry has few established companies, and

they trade at high prices. Thus, you might opt instead for a diversified-growth fund with a solid performance record as well as an ecological bent. One of the best choices: the Janus Fund (no load; 800-525-3713). Janus recently had about 9% of its assets in solid-waste companies such as Wheelabrator and Chambers Development. "We're running out of landfill space," notes fund manager Jim Craig. "So companies that own landfills or help dispose of waste could double in value in three or four years."

You can also get environmental exposure through so-called socially conscious growth funds, which invest according to ethical guidelines. The fund with the most direct environmental commitment is eight-year-old New Alternatives (5.6% load; 516-466-0808), which invests in energy conservation and environmental service-related companies.

The Information Age comes into its own: Ringing up returns in cellular. In a world increasingly linked by fax, modem, phone, and computer, the telecommunications industry seems headed for another decade of torrid growth. Consider the fledgling cellular-telephone business. Although cellular networks covered only about 1.8% of the country in 1990, analysts predict that roughly 15% of the U.S. will be so equipped by the year 2000. As a result, the industry, which had sales of $4 billion in 1989, should grow at a 27% annual clip over the next four to five years.

Although the prospect of a phone in every car (see "Fax, Phone, and Fun in the New, Improved Auto Office" on page 151) already has carried many cellular stocks to lofty prices, analysts think they can go much higher—perhaps up another 30% annually over the next five years. Portable-phone junkies can reduce the risks inherent in such high fliers by getting their cellular fix through growth funds. One such fund is Founders Special (no load; 800-525-2440), which recently had part of its $46.6 million portfolio in telecommunications companies, chiefly those with fast-growing cellular businesses.

More conservative investors can get in on the telecommunications revolution through funds that hold the shares of less glamorous but steadily growing businesses such as the regional Bell networks. In an economic downturn, analysts say, these firms should prove more recession resistant than cellular firms.

Going global: Cashing in on the trade boom.
If the 1980s were Japan's decade, the 1990s may well be Europe's, as the 12-nation European Community moves toward a single market by 1992 and tantalizing new markets open up among its Eastern bloc comrades. Indeed,

economists predict that international trade, which grew at an annual rate of 5.6% throughout the 1980s, will power ahead at a double-digit pace for the next few years.

The opportunities in overseas markets, coupled with the shrinking U.S. share of the world equity market—today the value of all stocks traded in the U.S. amounts to less than a third of the global equity market, versus more than 50% in 1980—make a compelling case for American investors to keep 20% of their assets in foreign stocks.

How Much Risk Can You Tolerate?

More and more brokers are urging clients to take quickie psychological quizzes to determine "your investment personality." No matter what your broker says, these tests usually are mostly for his benefit. Any insights into your psyche can help him fine-tune his sales spiel and earn more commissions. Sometimes, though, a test can benefit you as well.

Guided by Baruch Fischhoff, a professor of psychology and decision-making at Carnegie-Mellon, *Money* designed this quiz to help you determine your own comfort zone:

1) A friend hints that Super Growth Cat Chow is about to acquire Mega-Mice Inc. The tip sounds irresistible, but your pal has been wrong before (more than a few times, now that you think about it). If you buy Super Growth and your shares slump, would you feel:
   a) Like a jerk?
   b) Somewhat sheepish; you can live with the loss, but you probably won't tell your spouse?
   c) That nothing ventured is nothing gained?

2) You are all set to invest $5,000 in an equipment-leasing limited partnership, and your money will be locked away for at least 10 years. Once the deal is done, will you think:
   a) "Isn't there some way that I can back out?"
   b) "Everything is going to be all right . . . I think."
   c) "Great!"

3) You own 50 shares of Locust Valley Lockjaw, a blue-chip stock with a vertical track record. The Dow was off 2% yesterday and another 3% today—but Locust has fallen even more. What do you say to yourself in the middle of the night?
   a) "Two more points, and I'm outta here."
   b) "Think my broker will mind if I wake him up?"
   c) "Should I play tennis tomorrow—or golf?"

4) A few months ago, you bought $10,000 worth of 30-year Treasury bonds, expecting interest rates to drop and give you a big profit. But several well-known economists have just predicted that rates are about to rise. Are you:
   a) On the verge of bailing out?
   b) So distracted by the forecast that you can't concentrate on your job?
   c) Holding tight?

It doesn't matter if you are a buy-and-hold investor or a trader. If you didn't answer "c" on all the questions, you should carefully weigh the emotional toll before investing. It's possible that you can't stomach the anxiety of losing money, even temporary paper losses. You may want to chain yourself to the mast and buy mutual funds or hire a professional to manage your money. Be honest about how you might feel if something unexpected happens in the market. It will.

One strategy for global investing: Think small—small emerging growth companies, that is. In the 1990s, expect a much higher rate of growth and greater price appreciation from these foreign firms than from big, established businesses. Many of the larger stocks are now so widely followed that it's difficult to find hidden values.

One mutual fund that focuses exclusively on small foreign stocks is $147 million T. Rowe Price International Discovery (no load; 800-638-5660), which recently counted companies such as Bangkok Investments, a financial services company, and Singapore Marine, a shipbuilder, among its biggest holdings. But you can also get a hefty helping of emerging foreign enterprises with Vanguard World International Growth (no load; 800-662-7447), which invests in small as well as medium-size companies. Its recent holdings included Otra, a Dutch building supplier, and Joshin-Denki, a Japanese consumer electronics chain.

Investors willing to take above-average risks might consider regional funds, which have recently outperformed their more diversified brethren. The best region, many advisers believe, is Western Europe, where the economy is expected to grow by 3% annually over the next five years, compared with 2.2% for the U.S. One fund specializing in this area is the $84.3 million Financial Strategic European (no load; 800-525-8085).

If you are reluctant to load up on foreign stocks, or if you can afford to invest in only one mutual fund, you might want to choose a well-managed domestic fund with substantial overseas holdings. For example, Fidelity Magellan (3% load; 800-544-6666), whose 28.4% compound annual return over the past decade made it the top-performing equity fund of the 1980s, recently held a 15% stake abroad. And Acorn (no load; 800-922-6769) recently kept 22% of its small-stock fund's portfolio in overseas equities.

The baby boomers hit fortysomething: Making money on midlife crises. Tired of hearing about yuppies? Well, take heart: Those annoying urban professionals aren't so young anymore. The leading edge of the baby-boom generation has already entered its early forties. And by the year 2000, the number of people ages 45 to 54 will have jumped a whopping 46%, the biggest increase in any age category. This age wave undoubtedly will have a profound impact on all aspects of the American economy, particularly because the baby boomers will be entering their peak earning years. Expect boomers' saving and spending habits to boost the profits of the industries that cater to their needs and whims—from specialty retailers to entertainment companies to financial services firms.

Several top-performing mutual funds lately have been moving hefty portions of their portfolios to an aging baby-boomer beat. For example, the Merrill Lynch Fund for Tomorrow B (no load; 800-637-3863) has virtually all of its portfolio in stocks that reflect baby boomers' tastes, including Coca-Cola, American Express, and Sara Lee.

Baby boomers who postponed childbearing until their thirties and forties will join other new parents to create a 1990s baby boomlet. The under-18 population, which shrank slightly during the 1980s, is expected to grow by 2 million. The new parents—along with the growing number of boomer grandparents—should greatly boost demand for toys and children's clothes.

Rebuilding America: Investing in the country's infrastructure. The most chilling reminder yet of the urgent need to rebuild the nation's long-neglected infrastructure came during the 1989 earthquake in California when a section of the Nimitz Freeway in Oakland collapsed, killing 42 people. Many experts say the tragedy might have been averted had the antiquated highway been reinforced.

Repairs and renovations of the country's highways, bridges, tunnels, and other structures will require a boost in capital spending by state and local governments from $95 billion in 1990 to $156 billion in 1995, according to the Government Finance Officers Association, a professional organization. Those dollars should benefit a variety of businesses—chief among them contractors, steel companies, and equipment makers. The returns on these capital-goods stocks could outpace consumer shares by 75% over the next three to four years.

Although the timing is not yet right for heavy wagers on companies involved in rebuilding the infrastructure—these cyclical concerns could get hammered in a recession—you might consider a small investment in $38 million Mackenzie American (5.75% load; 800-456-5611), recently the only mutual fund fully committed to the infrastructure theme. And the fund's tendency to increase its cash investments in uncertain times could cushion any short-term stock losses.

Alternatively, you might make a modest investment in a diversified fund that owns stocks in infrastructure niches. For example, the $78.5 million Counsellors Capital Appreciation Fund (no load; 800-888-6878), recently invested 2% of its portfolio in companies that build electrical plants.

The graying of America: Profiting from the health and longevity of senior citizens. Over the next 10 years, the number of people in this country who are 65 or older will climb by nearly 11%, while the 75-and-over set will jump by 26%. Medical advances are making this age wave possible; in turn, the larger elderly population will boost demand for health-care products and services. As a result, analysts predict the $650 billion health-care industry will grow 10% to 15% annually over the next five years.

In anticipation of this bonanza for medical products and services companies, several growth-fund managers have loaded up on health-care stocks. For example, Columbia Growth (no load; 800-547-1707) recently had 11% of its portfolio in companies with a medical mission.

Moderately aggressive investors might do well to put some money in a sector fund that invests solely in health-care companies. A good choice is $130 million Vanguard Specialized Health Care (no load; 800-662-7447), which carries a below-average risk rating as measured by Mutual Fund Values. "Health-care spending now makes up about 11% of the U.S. economy," points out manager Edward Owens. "With the aging population, it could reach 15% by the end of the century." At which point, investors can start betting on the trends that will sizzle by 2010.

Getting in on the European Boom

Communism's collapse could make the Old World the site of the most enticing—and treacherous—stock market plays in the 1990s.

Mutual funds are ideal for Americans who lack the expertise or resolve to become fluent in transatlantic stock picking. But the direct route is gaining popularity among seasoned shareholders eager to broaden their U.S. portfolios and profit horizons with European stocks. If you're one of them, begin by weighing the advice of the Eurostrategists introduced here. They know the investor's atlas of the Old World is being altered by powerful—and unpredictable—tectonic forces. Colliding with each other are movements for democracy in Eastern Europe, unification in Germany, and the integration of the European Community's 12 western economies by 1992. The challenge for Americans is to overcome a collective detachment from European markets and discover sensible ways to profit from the changes now transforming them.

The most vexing issue is not the trend but the timing. For example, it could take as long as a decade to close the gap between low-wage Eastern Europe's vast potential and its current economic mess. To attract foreign investment, these countries must make their funny-money currencies convertible in the West via devaluation, which carries twin curses of rampant inflation and shortages of goods. To make products competitive on world markets, the East must break up state monopolies, close obsolete plants, and suffer the consequences of rising unemployment and factory unrest.

The hope is that free national elections in most Eastern European nations will create governments with the legitimacy to ask their people to endure more economic pain. The danger is that the new leadership will buckle under the strain. "I don't want my money in Europe when the Eastern Europeans suddenly realize that democracy doesn't quickly lead to prosperity," says Jim Rogers, a wealthy Wall Street dropout and Columbia University finance professor. "European markets could be at the mercy of massive uprisings in—and immigration from—the East that the Soviets will be powerless to contain."

"German and Austrian stocks have soared on expectations of a huge flow of new orders from Eastern Europe, which has no money to buy anything. What's actually going to happen is a huge flow of funds to Eastern Europe. This will soak up excess capital that previously went into European stock markets, which I submit will be affected in an adverse way."

A much more upbeat, though still realistic, case is made by David Roche, Morgan Stanley's European strategist in London. Money managers exploring Europe often cite Roche's far-sighted research (first published in April 1989) on the interplay of perestroika and 1992's single market, which he sees as the flip sides of a new Greater Europe coin worth owning for long-term gains.

For Eastern European reform to succeed, however, massive injections of Western capital will be necessary, Roche says. "The next two

years represent a 'black hole' in Eastern Europe which we should plug if capitalism is not to fail with communism. But after that (1993), Eastern European states will start to create wealth."

Roche feels that the long-term potential of Eastern Europe and its developing market of 428 million people will have a positive effect on the growth and cyclicality of Europe's economies and that this makes Europe's bonds and equities fundamentally attractive. Consequently, investors should look for economic setbacks in the East and the ensuing buying opportunities. "There will be horror stories that make markets go bump in the night," he predicts. "But then, you either believe communism is dead and won't be restored or you don't. My advice: Keep the faith."

Your Stake in Perestroika

To that end, Roche recently singled out the top perestroika plays in his European model portfolio of 89 stocks. Those he recommends are viewed as chief beneficiaries of the marches toward capitalism in the East and a single market in the West. With the exception of Danieli, an Italian machinery maker, all are quoted (in local currencies) in the *Wall Street Journal's* overseas markets listings. Several conveniently trade as American Depositary Receipts (ADRs) on U.S. exchanges or over the counter. Price quotes and direct purchases of stocks sold only on European exchanges can be handled by major full-service brokerages in the U.S. and discounter Fidelity Brokerage Services. Commissions are comparable to those on U.S. stocks.

Information technology. Leaders in telecommunications, office equipment, and electrical engineering should see fatter order books and profits as the East's vacuum-tube economies enter the electronic age. Roche recalls visiting a government ministry in Eastern Europe that had 3,500 employees but only one photocopier and no fax machine. "These economies are dominated by industrial output of things people don't want to own themselves," he explains. "But people want services, which run on technology and knowledge." He recommends two pioneers of East-West trade. France's CGE Group is Europe's titan of telecom, with $23 billion in annual sales. Germany's $36 billion Siemens excels in office equipment, factory automation, and medical technology. "Over a third of Soviet hospitals don't even have running water," notes Roche.

Capital equipment and transportation. The mid-century state of communist industry was neatly captured by TV images of East Berliners puttering across the border in their clunky, smoke-belching Trabants. Factories hatching such ugly ducklings are just as outdated. Roche figures it takes twice as much steel to produce a car in the East as it does in Western plants with efficient casting equipment. His favorite supplier of such machinery, with 30% of its orders from Russia, is Italy's Danieli. Also look for the auto, truck, and rail divisions of Italy's Fiat to build on the $41 billion holding company's existing joint ventures in the East.

Banking and insurance. Roche says large German institutions stand to profit most from the

The Disappointing Earnings of Ethical Mutual Funds

Disciples of socially responsible investing have long contended that you don't have to settle for second-rate returns if you put your money in a so-called ethical mutual fund to keep your conscience clear. But that view has recently been challenged by an analysis of the 10 funds with the longest track records. "Someone who invested in the average-performing portfolio of a fund category would have earned 10% a year more than the ethical investor," says the study's author, Sam Mueller, associate professor of sociology at the University of Akron. What's more, the study also determined that the shares of ethical funds were more volatile than those of the competition.

Mueller reviewed the performance of the funds for the five years through 1988 (except for Parnassus Fund, which had a four-year record). To make his sample as wide as possible, Mueller included five funds that might not meet many investors' definition of socially responsible investing—namely, avoiding the securities of companies that invest in South Africa, pollute the environment, or engage in unfair labor practices. Two money-market funds that Mueller reviewed—Working Assets and Calvert Social Investment-Money Market—differ from other money funds only slightly; for example, their managers don't buy Treasury issues, since they help finance defense spending. Three others are Pioneer stock funds that eschew only tobacco, gambling, and alcohol companies.

Still, even if these funds are excluded, the study's overall findings stand up: Over a five-year period, socially conscious funds annually lag their competition by an average of one percentage point. True, two of the funds did beat their category averages: New Alternatives (516-466-0808), which invests in alternative energy and environmental companies, was up 82% over the five years; and Dreyfus Third Century (800-645-6561), a growth fund, returned 74%. But on a risk-adjusted basis, only Dreyfus Third Century outperformed its growth-stock category average. Its manager can buy defense stocks, though the fund hasn't held any for a year. Parnassus, Calvert Managed Growth, and Pax World all underperformed their categories by more than a point.

Supporters of ethical funds note that they are fairly new and that their managers' performance should improve over time. "Socially responsible investing is just coming into its own," says Amy Domini, who recently launched an index fund of 400 ethical stocks, the Domini Social Index Trust. Besides, for some investors seeking to make the world a better place, giving up 10% of their return may seem a small price to pay.

East's acute need for financial services, in part because of their dual roles as lenders to—and major shareholders in—local companies expanding in post-communist Europe. Such alliances provide big head starts for Deutsche Bank, the country's richest in assets, and the third-ranked Commerzbank. Similarly, he's keen on German insurers because perestroika should lead to greater privatization of property. "If individuals own their homes, shops, or factories," he reasons, "the first thing they do is to insure them." Small investors, however, may be put off by the formidable share price of his Frankfurt-listed pick, Munich Reinsurance (which was selling for 2,125 marks, or $1,266, in June 1990).

Not to worry, says Marc Alexandre, head of Paris' Atlantic Finance, one of Europe's top independent research firms. He thinks Italy's biggest insurer, Generali (which sold for 39,995 lire, or $33, during the same period), is equally well positioned to expand in the East. "Until World War II, Generali was Central Europe's main insurer and still has strong name recognition there," he explains. "Yet, none of this potential is reflected in the stock price, as is the case with its competitors in Germany."

Alexandre says other perestroika sleepers abound on the lethargic Milan exchange. In 1990, the average stock sold at 3.4 times cash flow versus 6.3 for European and 7.6 for U.S. issues. One reason is that Italian savers were hooked on tax-exempt government bonds, then yielding 11.5%. "The Milan-listed capital-goods firms we follow are already doing more business in the East." He recommends Comau, a world leader in industrial robotics; and Sasib's savings shares, which recently sold at a 27% discount to the common of this specialist in food-packaging equipment.

The Urge to Splurge

Nigel Ledeboer, chief portfolio manager at G.T. Management in London, saw total assets of his firm's 10 open-end Eurofunds surge threefold to $2 billion in the 7 months between November 1989 and June 1990.

Ledeboer's closed-end fund, G.T. Greater Europe, can and will invest aggressively in small, unseasoned, privately held companies—even Eastern European (when that's possible, he adds). Initially, however, he's placing some long-term bets on anticipated stronger consumer spending on the Continent spurred by German unification and hordes of tourists en route to or from the East.

"French firms selling high-margin luxury goods will be among the biggest winners," says Ledeboer. He likes three brand names on the Paris exchange: Clarins, a maker of skin-care products; Remy Martin, a cognac vintner; and Yves Saint Laurent, the designer's fashion and perfume company. He's also impressed with the growth of Accor, a hotel chain, and Canal +, a French pay-TV service expanding in West Germany, Belgium, and Spain. "Competition is finally coming to Spanish TV," says Ledeboer. Accordingly, he recommends a TV broadcaster listed in Madrid: Antena 3.

Hidden Values

From Alliance Capital's London office, Glenn Wellman oversees a stable of four stock funds enlarged by a $252 million offering of Alliance New Europe. The closed-end portfolio is a direct competitor of G.T. Greater Europe. "Europe will be this decade's great long-term-growth story," predicts Wellman, who sees economic gains (adjusting for inflation) of 4% to 5% a year in the 1990s, double the region's average in the 1980s.

He believes that unrecognized bargains currently abound in Europe's fragmented auto components sector. Reason: Most investors mistakenly view the group as unglamorous captive suppliers to their national auto industries. "The stocks are already cheap relative to their steady earnings gains of 10% to 15% a year," he explains. Yet, growth should accelerate as more Western and Japanese car companies rush to open plants and dealerships in Eastern Europe.

Consider Volkswagen, Europe's premier automaker and Wellman's hands-down favorite to grab the pole position in post-communist markets. In 1990, the company agreed to invest $2.9 billion in a joint venture to assemble subcompact VW Polos in East Germany. "While Volkswagen made headlines," he says, "dozens of its suppliers quietly cut their own production deals in East Germany. Others are coming East on the coattails of Volkswagen's competitors." Standouts in his view are Germany's Continental and FAG Kugelfischer; France's Valeo; and Italy's Magneti Marelli.

High on Hydro

Many analysts worry that the Revolution of 1989 will hopelessly delay the long-awaited economic consolidation of Western Europe. Not Guy Rigden, Eurostrategist at UBS Phillips & Drew, the Union Bank of Switzerland's London-based investment bank. Trade barriers will continue to fall, he says, as Europeans recognize how deregulation's bitter pill is stimulating the region's sweet gains in investment, employment, and consumer spending.

"One of the surest ways to play this boom is via utilities," says Rigden. "New demand and regulatory reforms should greatly reward the most efficient producers." High on his list of stocks to buy are three electric companies whose capacity is concentrated in low-cost hydropower: Spain's Iberduero; Germany's Viag; and Austria's Verbund.

Finally, investors should proceed carefully, but a strategic, long-term commitment to the European market makes sense. That way the performance of your portfolio won't depend entirely on the health of the U.S. economy.

Why Smart Investors Are Going Regional

Some places are hot while others are not. Here are six regions in the U.S. where savvy investors will make money in the 1990s.

In the past nine years, a pattern of powerful regional business cycles has taken shape, offering opportunities for investors who can spot the hot regions and pick the key players. National business cycles haven't been repealed entirely. Softness in enough parts of the economy can still produce a countrywide recession, but that is less likely than in the past. Now we have a more diversified economy, where exports and other international factors play a bigger role.

To choose the best regions for investors in the 1990s, *Money* looked first at projections of growth in jobs and population by the economic consulting firm DRI/McGraw-Hill. Areas where jobs are expanding attract migration. And that in turn fuels retail spending, adding more jobs and ensuring strong growth. Employment in the six standout regions that *Money* identified is expected to expand in the 1990s by 15% to 22%, compared with a projected 13.8% national average. Population in the six areas will grow 9.5% to 23%—against 7.2% nationally.

In addition, better climate and lower living costs in states in the southern half of the country will draw more jobs and people, according to DRI and U.S. census projections. And many economists believe that the federal bailout of failed savings and loans will boost the economies of Texas, New Mexico, and other states where S&L problems have been acute. By one estimate, over 30 or more years, Texas could receive $4,775 more in federal funds per resident than its citizens pay out in federal taxes, thanks to the bailout. Upshot: The move to the Sunbelt of the 1970s and early 1980s—interrupted by the oil bust in the mid-1980s—is resuming. That explains why most of the hot regions are in the Sunbelt.

Regions were ranked on the basis of investment opportunities. For example, the Southwest outside Texas—an area that is expected to be tops in both jobs and population increase—stands only third on the list because of a paucity of large, publicly traded companies positioned to cash in on that growth. Prime investments, according to *Money*'s advisers, are either in businesses dependent on a regional economy's fortunes (retailers, banks, utilities) or rooted in a region by its raw materials or transport system (a barge line hauling commodities from Texas on inland waterways, for example).

How much money should you invest regionally? Portfolio analysts note that the risk varies from region to region and cycle to cycle, but they generally recommend that you commit no more than 10% to 15% of your portfolio to such investments.

Here is a closer look at the regions that were selected. Note that where individual states—Florida, Hawaii, and Texas—have distinct economies, they have been treated as regions unto themselves:

Texas

Bouncing back from a decade when its growth business was bankruptcy law, Texas is expected to outpace the national economy handily through 2000. Job growth is projected at 1.6% a year, compared with 1.3% nationally. The Texas economy now lives and dies less on the swing in oil prices: Energy accounts for 15% of the state's economy, compared with 27% in 1981. Over the next 10 years, Texas should see steady and predictable growth. Cheap office space and low living costs already have led 49 companies—including Exxon and J.C. Penney—to move to the Dallas area in the past three years. Office construction has begun in that area for a number of relocating companies, including GTE Corporation and MCI Communications. Forecasters also believe that housing construction will pick up in the near future. All of this building should benefit Justin Industries, a maker of building materials, with estimated 1990 annual revenues of $300 million.

Petrochemicals are also perking along, with companies planning to expand production by 15% for two major products, ethylene and propylene, in the Houston area. A major beneficiary could be Kirby Corporation, which is the country's largest operator of inland tank barges.

In the energy sector, many analysts believe that rising demand for environmentally clean natural gas, nudged by government regulation and an end to the oversupply of the past decade, will push up prices 25% by the early 1990s. Consequently, they are recommending gas exploration companies such as Enron and Arkla.

Fund of the Southwest (4.75% load; 800-262-6631) invests mainly in firms doing business in Texas and five other states—Arizona, Arkansas, Louisiana, New Mexico, and Oklahoma—and outperformed the S&P 500 in 1988 and 1989.

Pacific Northwest

Even before its piney vistas and superior cherry pie were getting prime-time praise on ABC-TV's "Twin Peaks," the Northwest was attracting settlers. Jobs and the simple, clean-air life will keep them coming. Observers look for a rapid inflow of new residents, plus strong income and employment gains. Washington and Oregon are projected to add new jobs at about a 2%-a-year pace—double the national rate—in the early 1990s and 1.5% later on.

The region is coming off unsustainable boom levels: nearly 100,000 new residents and about 5% job growth in 1988 and 1989. But new businesses have built in something this region never had before: stabilizing economic diversity. To its traditional mix of airplane manufacturing and lumbering, the Northwest has added a burgeoning technology sector. And soaring trade with the Far East—from importing clothes to exporting high-tech components—is fueling growth.

Foreign passenger-plane orders keep swelling the backlog at Boeing, which still generates 15% to 20% of Washington State's economic activity.

In the timber and paper business, torn over the endangered spotted owl, pending restrictions on cutting timber on federal land could benefit Weyerhaeuser. The company owns 2.9 million acres of timberland in the Northwest—double the acreage owned by its closest competitor.

The Composite Northwest 50 Index Fund (4.5% load; 800-543-8072) closely reflects the northwestern economy. The fund holds 50 stocks at a time within industry sectors weighted by their contributions to personal income in the region.

Southwest outside Texas

By the year 2000, the lonesome mountains and deserts of this region will be alive with the sound of development. Nevada is forecast by DRI/McGraw-Hill to be No. 1 in both population and job growth, while Arizona, Colorado, New Mexico, and Utah are among the top 10 states for both categories after growth picks up by 1992—though parts of the region are still

Beat the Pros with this High-Yield Strategy

It may sound too good to be true, but there really is a sure, easy, and safe way to beat the stock market: Buy the 10 highest-yielding stocks in the Dow Jones industrial average. Once a year, in January, say, replace any stocks that no longer rank among the top 10. Don't make more frequent adjustments, because the commissions would eat too deeply into your returns.

Calculations by John Slatter, an analyst with the Cleveland brokerage Prescott, Ball & Turben, and Harvey Knowles, a Merrill Lynch broker in Cincinnati, support the high-yield theory. Since 1968, a portfolio of the Dow's 10 top yielders provided a total return of 1,557%, compared with only 426% for the average's 30 stocks as a group. There were, moreover, only four years in which the 10 high yielders underperformed the Dow, usually by small margins, while they outperformed it by five percentage points or more in 11 years. Better yet, you can currently adopt Slatter's strategy with less than $6,000—enough for 10 shares of each stock and your broker's commission.

Why does the system work? Slatter and other analysts give two reasons:

First, dividends contribute far more to returns than most investors realize. Over the long term, the market returns about 10% a year, and half of that comes from dividends.

Second, a high yield frequently signals that a stock is depressed. Usually the tide eventually turns, and investors who buy a stock when it's down can earn a substantial yield while they wait for the price to rise.

Some pros use systems like Slatter's, but most follow other approaches. One reason: Mutual-fund managers, for example, often must strive for strong short-term results, and Slatter's system requires time.

Investors can try to improve their returns by homing in on the high-yielding Dow stocks that analysts favor most. Slatter, however, warns against being influenced by analysts' expectations, noting that the whole point of the system is to save you from your own fallible judgment. The stocks you decide to leave out inevitably end up being the best performers.

coping with economies stunned by real estate problems. Casinos account for 45% of the Nevada economy, but much recent growth has come from small manufacturing companies in such fields as medical instruments and aerospace parts. Many are refugees from high-tax California, and unfortunately most are not publicly traded.

Among stocks you can buy, some analysts favor Southwest Airlines, with revenues of $1.1 billion and a heavy schedule of short-hop flights throughout the region. Industry analysts say Southwest is a low-cost airline with a high level of customer satisfaction. For income-oriented investors, there is U.S. West, which provides phone service for all of the region (except Nevada), plus the Pacific Northwest. Rising business telephone use should keep the company growing. Analysts believe U.S. West's dividend, recently yielding 5.3%, could increase by 5% a year over the next five years.

Hawaii

The Japanese appetite for Hawaiian land has kept a real estate run-up going at a time when markets elsewhere are melting. Honolulu housing prices rose 25% in 1989 alone. With Hawaii's population expected to expand nearly 20% by 2000, the state will add new jobs at a 1.7% annual rate—30% faster than the national average. The real estate boom should continue because there is strong foreign demand for residential and commercial space and very little supply.

How does an investor enter this pricey scene? Not through REITs or companies solely in local real estate; they tend to be too heavily in debt. Instead, analysts suggest two companies with large Hawaiian real estate holdings that stand to benefit from Asian demand as well as other operations. A big favorite is Alexander & Baldwin, with revenues of $770 million. The company grows sugar cane and operates the largest shipping line hauling freight between the islands and the U.S. West Coast. And Castle & Cooke, with revenues of $3 billion, owns 98% of the island of Lanai,

where it opened a new luxury resort in 1990. The company also includes the pineapple producer Dole Food, which it plans to spin off soon. The two parts could become worth more than the current stock price.

Florida

With sand and sun and Mickey Mouse to attract tourists and new residents, Florida is forecast to be the decade's second-fastest-growing state in population after Nevada. Retirees will be prominent among the arrivals, but jobs are also expected to increase at a robust 2.1% annual rate.

One way to invest in this vigorous growth is through Advanced Telecommunications, which has 10% of the Florida market for long-distance services. Advanced, which concentrates on small businesses, figures to have annual earnings growth of 20% over the next five years.

And then there's the Orlando play. In addition to the Mickey and Goofy gang, a movie studio in Orlando opened in 1990 by Universal is drawing big crowds, including a flood of foreign visitors drawn by a weaker dollar as well as the Hollywood-comes-East ambience. A company positioned to profit from the fun-biz boom is Major Realty, a developer that owns 274 acres adjacent to Universal. Hotel chains are inquiring about the site, the company says. Some analysts believe that its real estate alone may be worth $30 a share, which is more than two times its recent stock price.

Another strong tourism entry is Miami-based Carnival Cruise Lines, the nation's largest such line. Look for Carnival, with estimated 1990 revenues of $1.4 billion, to more than double its earnings in the next five years. Analysts expect the company's shipbuilding program to raise passenger capacity 50% by 1995.

Southeast outside Florida

This slice of the Old South—the Carolinas, Georgia, and Virginia—will enjoy a 13% population spurt in the 1990s. That's not up to

Florida's dizzying 20%, but it's almost twice the U.S. rate. The region is expected to add jobs at a healthy 1.4% a year. The mild climate and below-average living costs will keep attracting companies and households from the Northeast and Midwest.

Southeastern regional banks, the best of which never took on many of the bad loans that crippled their cousins in the Southwest and Northeast, are a strong buy now. The stocks remain cheap—selling at price/earnings ratios about half those of the overall stock market—after being knocked down in anticipation of stringent federal audits that are now partially complete. A leading North Carolina bank, NCNB, based in Charlotte, has assets of $68 billion and operates throughout the Southeast. The company also has a large Texas subsidiary that figures to profit in the years ahead.

Automation has allowed the textile industry to build new plants in the southeastern states. With a dominant position in the market for polyester fibers, Unifi can increase prices readily. Unifi acquired one of its major competitors in 1986, and the company is now financially strong enough to expand again through more takeovers.

Southeastern growth could also provide business for Ryan's Family Steak Houses. The company, which is based in Greer, South Carolina, has 49 of its 119 cafeteria-style restaurants aimed at middle-income families in the Southeast.

The Appeal of Tax-Exempt Munis

You don't have to sacrifice safety to earn above-average yields on these investments.

Municipal bonds should be a serious consideration for any tax-burdened portfolio. Their appeal is easy to understand: in mid-1990, for example, luscious tax-free yields of 6.8% on nationwide long-term muni-bond funds were equivalent to taxable yields of 10% for investors in the 33% federal bracket (or 9.4% for those in the 28% zone). And because the payouts from single-state funds are exempt from state and sometimes local as well as federal taxes (if you live in the state in which the bonds were issued), such choices can deliver even more appealing after-tax yields. By contrast, long-term Treasuries during the same period paid only about 8.6%, and high-grade corporates about 8.8%. In 1990, munis became the new high-yield investment of choice, replacing widely disparaged junk bonds.

But watch out. The road to those kinds of rates is strewn with an uncommon number of hazards. First, there are the income robbers: the funds' occasionally punishing sales and management fees. Then, there's the spectre of an interest-rate spike that could deflate some bond prices. Most troubling of all, though, are two comparatively new threats: the dubious quality of the bonds bought by many funds seeking to boost yields and the heightened risk that bond-rating agencies will lower the grades on many munis as growing financial strains finally cripple state and local governments.

Thus, if you're already in a municipal bond fund—especially a single-state entry—consult your fund's most recent semiannual report and submit the portfolio to a new round of scrutiny. Determine whether you should seek a new fund or, perhaps, diversify into alternative muni funds as you add to your investments. Similarly, if you're considering joining the tax-exempt fun, take off your party hat and get out your magnifying glass.

Fortunately, there are still plenty of worthy tax-exempt fund selections to choose from. What is more, the muni market has some powerful factors working in its favor. Chief among them: demographics. As they enter their peak earning years, baby boomers are likely to buy more munis to shelter their growing taxable incomes. Yet, the number of new issues is dwindling, partly because the Tax Reform Act of 1986 severely limited the types of municipal bonds that qualify for tax-exempt status. Greater demand—spurred even more by today's rising state and local tax burdens—should provide a floor under muni prices, making them as a group the most stable fixed-income investment of the early 1990s.

In scoping out municipal-bond funds, be sure to evaluate the following factors:

Yield. This should be your first consideration. Although muni funds often outpay their taxable counterparts, that's not always the case. Before you plunk down any money, always determine the muni fund's taxable equivalent yield—that is, the rate that a taxable bond fund would have to pay to match the muni fund's yield. You can calculate the taxable equivalent yield for an ordinary muni fund by dividing the fund's yield by 0.72 (if you are in the 28% bracket) or by 0.67 (if you pay at the 33% rate). To evaluate a single-state fund's payout, divide the muni fund's yield by the following somewhat obscure divisor: 1 minus your combined federal and state bracket expressed as a decimal. For example, a California investor with a combined federal and state bracket of 42% would divide the 6.7% yield recently available from a typical California single-state fund by .58 to get a taxable equivalent yield of 11.6%.

If your calculations reveal that muni funds offer an edge over the taxable competition,

make sure that the fund you're considering—or are already in—won't blow the advantage. To do that, consider . . .

Credit quality. Yawning budget deficits—the byproduct of heavy borrowing to repair infrastructure without cutting back on municipal services—are threatening the ability of many state and local governments to repay their debts. Some observers expect a dramatic increase in the number of problems and defaults among tax-exempts in the next several years. Moreover, many localities, unable or unwilling to enact tax increases to shore up their finances, are turning increasingly to revenue bonds to meet their capital requirements. These bonds, backed by future income from specific projects, usually are riskier than general obligation bonds, which rely on tax revenues to pay investors. The net result: a far larger pool of risky munis.

Therefore, now more than ever, emphasize safety in your muni holdings. Stick with funds that invest 90% or more of their portfolio in bonds rated A or better—including 40% to 50% or more in AA and AAA issues. To get this data, scrutinize the fund's semiannual report or phone its service hotline.

Steer entirely clear of high-yield muni funds, which sometimes invest from 30% to 60% of their portfolios in unrated bonds or those rated BBB or below. Their slight yield advantage is not worth their extra risk. Particularly worrisome is the prospect that demand for marginal tax-exempt issues could evaporate if muni investors suddenly get religion. Result: The more adventurous funds could post losses to rival the 15% to 20% plunges that many high-yield corporate funds took in the wake of the recent corporate junk-bond debacle.

Investors in single-state funds, now available to residents of 31 states, must bear another quality factor in mind. True, the yields are sweeter. But you're sunk if your state or regional economy turns sour. So limit your single-state holdings to 60% of your muni portfolio. Make that 30% if the single-state fund's after-tax yield advantage over national funds is less than half a point—the extra return simply isn't worth the risk—or if you live in a state with financial troubles.

Maturity. When economists are predicting a near-term increase in interest rates, conservative investors should keep as much as 75% of their muni holdings in intermediate- and short-term funds. (Short-term funds have an average maturity of about one to three years; intermediates, five to 12.) But the sharply lower risk of principal losses should more than compensate for the reduction in income.

For example, if rates were to rise by a full point, the shares of short-term funds would fall by only 1% to 2%, and those of intermediate-term funds by 5% to 7%. By contrast, long-term muni portfolios could sustain capital losses of at least 8% to 10%.

Fees. The fees and sales charges described in a fund's prospectus can sometimes do more than a portfolio manager's skill to determine shareholders' returns. Avoid funds that assess front-end sales charges, which range as high as 8%, or exit fees of up to 6%. For example, if you had invested $10,000 in the Mutual of Omaha Tax-Free Income Fund (initial sales charge: 8%) at the beginning of 1987, your account would have grown to $11,204 through March 31 of 1990. By contrast, in the no-load Fidelity Municipal Bond Fund, your shares would be worth $12,279—even though both funds had almost identical expense ratios (0.63% and 0.50% of assets per year, respectively) and total returns (21.8% and 22.8%) over the period.

Also, choose a fund with annual expenses below the muni-fund average—recently 0.83% of assets. For example, Thomson McKinnon Tax-Exempt's 1.7% annual expense ratio ate up a quarter of the 7.1% yield that the fund earned on its portfolio in 1989, leaving only 5.4% for shareholders. By contrast, the Vanguard Municipal Bond Long-Term Portfolio, with a similar 7.3% yield but a much lower expense ratio of 0.27%, paid 7%.

How to Assemble Your Own Bond Portfolio

The credit problems looming over the municipal-bond market pose special risks to holders of individual bonds. Most notable: A single default can sink the performance of a small portfolio. So can a rating downgrade if you try to sell a tarnished individual issue before it matures. (Ratings are based on an evaluation of a company's financial strength by Standard & Poor's, Moody's Investors Service, or Fitch's Investors Service.)

Even so, buying bonds directly offers advantages that may be worth considering. Unlike funds, for example, individual bonds pay fixed yields and ensure the return of your principal upon maturity. And trading costs are low—about 2% when you buy and sell $5,000 worth of bonds.

If assembling your own portfolio appeals to you—and consider doing so only if you can afford to buy at least five different issues at a minimum cost of $5,000 apiece—just be sure to follow these risk-reducing guidelines:

Plan to hold your bonds until they mature. That way, you won't suffer a loss if a credit downgrade reduces their trading value.

Invest at least half of your portfolio in bonds rated AAA or AA by Standard & Poor's. Top-rated issues are less likely to default. Pre-refunded tax-exempts, which are backed by escrow accounts of U.S. Treasuries, are the safest munis of all.

Avoid municipal bonds that pay unusually high yields. Be wary of issues that yield more than half a percentage point over the average yield on AAA bonds of similar maturity. Such lofty payouts may signal financial weakness that could lead to a default.

Diversify. Invest at least half of your portfolio in bonds with maturities of 10 years or less to guard against rising rates. And buy bonds from a variety of issuers in different states.

If you intend to sit tight with your muni holdings for several years, you might sidestep the high-fee fund dilemma by buying shares in a municipal-bond unit trust instead. Offered by brokerages and sponsors such as Nuveen and Van Kampen Merritt, the trusts maintain unmanaged portfolios of munis that are held to maturity. (Funds, by contrast, constantly buy and sell bonds to maximize returns.) The sales charge is 4% to 5% of your investment. But over seven years or longer, the trusts' low annual fees of about 0.15% make them less expensive than funds. Another plus: Trusts—unlike funds—have a fixed maturity date upon which you can expect a full refund of your principal.

But the trusts' inability to make strategic shifts in their holdings can sometimes spell trouble for investors. During the next several years, for instance, many high-coupon bonds bought by trusts formed in the early 1980s will be called—that is, redeemed at face value—by municipalities eager to retire such expensive debt. Result: sharply lower yields for shareholders. Being locked into a trust's long-term portfolio—their average maturity is about 20 years—also may cause you to miss out on higher yields if interest rates rise after you invest.

Lately, another way to buy a readymade muni portfolio has been gaining popularity: new closed-end municipal-bond funds. The funds' offering prices include commissions of up to 7%, however, and their share prices typically drop in value during the months after the funds first come to market.

Once on the secondary market, the prices of closed-end funds fluctuate according to investor demand and changes in the value of the funds' portfolios.

Make Sure Your Money-Market Funds Are Safe

Not all funds are alike. It's important to ask the right questions before depositing your hard-earned cash.

Are money-market funds really as safe as their sponsors claim? Small investors seem to think so. They poured $27.3 billion into the funds in the first three months of 1990—nearly twice as much as in the previous quarter. But while no money fund that meets today's rigorous standards has ever suffered a loss, there have been a few close calls resulting from defaults on securities held by funds. Some critics contend that a few fund managers are taking unwise risks to boost yields and attract deposits. Money funds are still relatively safe investments, but investors should realize that the degree of risk varies among funds. To help you pick the most secure haven for your cash, consider the following answers to the most frequently asked questions about money-market funds:

What advantages do money-market funds have over bank money-market deposit accounts? First and foremost, money-market mutual funds pay more. These funds, which invest in corporate and government short-term debt obligations, generally offer yields that are 1.5 to two percentage points above those of money-market deposit accounts (MMDAs). Also, money funds provide more free services. You can generally write any number of checks at no charge, although many funds have a $100 to $500 minimum for them. By contrast, MMDAs usually limit you to six transactions a month by mail—only three of which can be checks. Money funds, however, unlike MMDAs, are not federally insured for up to $100,000.

Could you lose money in a money fund? It's possible, although no one ever has in a fund that meets today's definition of a money fund. To keep share prices at $1, the Securities and Exchange Commission requires money funds to limit their average maturities to 120 days. Many fund managers, however, reach for high yields by investing in issues with longer maturities than the money-fund average of 45 days. In theory, this could cause losses. More

Classic Broker Sales Pitches for Load Funds

Brokers have bad-mouthed no-commission mutual funds ever since First Investment Counsel Corporation (now Scudder Income) began competing with broker-sold funds in 1928. But with industry-wide commissions off 54% compared with their peak three years ago, investors need to be especially wary of the tired—and often inaccurate—putdowns that salesmen sometimes aim at no-loads. Some broker classics:

No-load funds have higher annual fees, which cost you more over the long run than up-front sales loads. Brokers are fond of saying ominously that "all that money for no-load advertising has to come from somewhere." True, it does. It comes out of the management fee that shareholders tithe over to fund sponsors each year. But the fact is, total annual expenses at no-loads, including management fees, shareholder servicing charges, and the like, come to roughly the same as at load funds, usually between 0.75% and 1.5% of assets per year.

You are better off with a load fund because you get the benefit of my advice in making your selection. Having a broker look over your shoulder can be an advantage—but only if he or she is more able than you to pick a winning fund. Some brokers may indeed be investment sages. But evidence suggests that many others are not. Between 1985 and 1990, for example, 75% of the money invested in broker-sold funds went into bond funds, which rose 61%

even as stock funds were soaring 117%. No-load investors, meanwhile, steered only 48% of their money into bonds.

The fund I'm recommending is better than the competition, even after the load. It is true that some load funds have performed so strongly over the years that shareholders did come out ahead. The problem: You can't project past performance into the future. All you know for sure is that a load fund starts the race with a handicap.

In one particularly creative variation on this pitch, a broker with Edward D. Jones & Company presented Gay Courter, a Crystal River, Florida novelist, with a sheaf of computer printouts showing that the net asset value of several top no-loads had not risen as much over the past 10 years as that of the fund he was pushing, the 5.75% load Investment Company of America. The broker warned Courter that without capital gain and income distributions, the no-loads would have provided almost no growth.

True, but irrelevant. The real measure of a fund's performance is its total return—the combination of appreciation in net asset value plus the value of reinvested income and capital-gains payouts. On that basis, the load fund and the no-loads were equally good performers. Courter, meanwhile, decided to put her money into two solid no-loads, Vanguard Wellington and Twentieth Century Heritage, and kept the commission for herself.

than a decade ago, First Multifund for Daily Income extended its average maturity to almost two years. (With such a portfolio, First Multifund would qualify as a short-term bond fund today.) When interest rates shot up more than two percentage points in late 1978, investors lost 6¢ a share.

Some money funds are currently jeopardizing their $1 share prices in a much more serious way—by investing in risky, high-yielding paper. During 1989, seven large issuers—including Integrated Resources, a financial services firm, and Mortgage & Realty Trust, a real estate investment trust—defaulted on almost $1 billion of commercial paper. So far, fund companies have paid the tab; Value Line, for instance, bought $23 million of bad paper from its money fund and T. Rowe Price $42 million. If the fund companies had not paid the costs, losses of 1¢ to 3¢ a share could have been passed on to shareholders.

How can you be sure that your fund isn't loaded up with all sorts of dangerous junk debt? The SEC requires that money funds invest only in issues with the two highest credit ratings or unrated securities that the fund's directors judge to be of comparable quality. Top ratings, though, do not guarantee safety, because an issuer's finances can deteriorate after the rating is awarded. Both Integrated Resources and Mortgage & Realty Trust were rated investment-grade just a month before they defaulted.

To play it safe, stick with funds offered by the largest management companies and look for funds that have no more than 1% of their assets in the securities of any single issuer. As a simple rule of thumb, you should invest in money funds with more than $1 billion in assets; only about one in eight funds qualifies. Such funds are likely to be highly diversified, and their sponsors could probably absorb any losses resulting from defaults.

Will you actually get the yield your fund advertises? No. A fund's advertised yield is calculated by annualizing its payout for the past seven days, and that figure can be far different from what you will get over the coming year.

Your return will depend on how interest rates vary and how well your fund's managers adjust to them. Rather than looking at seven-day yields, you should compare funds' returns for the past 12 months. The best way to assess a fund's managers is by their performance record.

Should you invest in the fund with the highest seven-day yield? An above-average yield can mean that the manager is temporarily waiving management fees—or that he is risking poor returns later. For example, the fund may be stretching its average maturity beyond 60 to 70 days, which could cause its yield to lag if interest rates suddenly rise. Worse yet, the fund could be investing in securities that don't deserve their high grades. Ask your fund's representative about its portfolio; the safest funds have maturities of less than 60 days and hold only government issues or those rated tops (A1 or P1) by agencies such as Standard & Poor's and Moody's.

In addition to yield, you should also look at a fund's services and other features, which are listed in its prospectus. Fidelity Spartan, for instance, keeps its management fee low partly by charging $2 for each check you write. Also, be sure that you can afford the fund's minimum investment, which can range anywhere from $100 to $20,000.

Should you avoid funds that are temporarily waiving their management fees? Not at all—enjoy the free ride while you can. Just realize that funds do this to attract new customers by boosting yields. They can start charging fees at any time, unless their prospectuses state otherwise.

When does it make sense to invest in a tax-free money fund? Such a fund is worth considering if you're in the 28% or 33% federal tax bracket, because your yield is likely to be higher than the return from a taxable fund after taxes are taken into account. For example, if your bracket is 33% and you invested in a fund yielding 5.79%, your taxable-equivalent yield would be 8.6%—a better deal than the typical taxable fund yielding just under 8%.

Cost-Conscious Fund Investing

With mutual fund expenses on the rise, it's more important than ever to keep a close eye on your fund costs.

Sure, you glanced at the fees listed in the prospectus when you first invested in your mutual fund. But what was so bad about sacrificing a few tenths of a percentage point of your return to annual expense charges when your fund was earning 16% a year or more?

Not so fast. That was the roaring 1980s. Welcome to the no-nonsense 1990s, when many analysts foresee much more modest annual gains, perhaps 8% to 11% on average for stock funds and 6% to 9% for bond funds. In such times, your fund's cost structure can be a crucial factor in your investment results. Moreover, those little annual fees that seemed so inconsequential just a few years ago have been rising like a hot-air balloon in the Mojave Desert. In fact, in many if not most cases, the proliferating charges (such as the insidious 12b-1 fee that typically docks shareholders up to 1.25% of assets per year to pay for advertising or commissions to sales agents) have sprung up precisely where the old 8.5% front-end loads many funds used to charge have diminished or disappeared.

In short, the fee grabbers are everywhere. In such an environment, it pays more than ever to be a cost-conscious investor.

First, some specifics about those rising tabs. According to Lipper Analytical Services, the average annual operating expenses of a large sample of stock and bond funds, expressed as a percentage of average net assets, had risen to 1.2% by 1990, up from 0.9% in 1980—a 33% jump. Among 1,020 funds with assets of $100 million or more, 91 sock you for more than

1.5% in operating expenses each year.

Some smaller funds, with assets of $50 million or less, tend to charge even more on average than do their larger cousins—frequently saddling investors with expenses of 2% or more. That's partly because smaller funds don't benefit from economies of scale and partly because many invest in costlier-to-research corners of the market (like over-the-counter stocks). Similarly, international and global stock funds can be 20% to 25% more expensive to operate than comparable domestic funds because they do business overseas.

Now for a look at how those not-so-innocent little charges can eat away at your returns. Consider identical $10,000 investments in two pure, no-load funds—that is, two that assess neither up-front nor back-end sales charges. Let's assume that one fund's annual operating expenses, which are always deducted straight from your account, are a full percentage point higher than the other's (say, 1.9% of assets a year versus 0.9%). Let's further assume that both funds achieve investment returns of 10% a year, compounded annually, for 10 years. At the end of that time, you'd have $25,937 in the fund with lower fees and only $23,674 in the higher-fee choice. The difference: $2,263. After a little under nine years, in fact, the cumulative toll of a 1% annual hit (as from a 12b-1) has a more debilitating effect on your account than does an 8.5% up-front load.

Fortunately, you can prevent annual fees and other charges from crippling your account. The obvious first step is to just say no-load, or at least low-load, and invest only in funds with sales charges of 3% or less. Independent research has consistently shown no difference in performance between load and no-load funds on average.

Another vital tactic, naturally enough, is to stick with funds that keep a tight lid on total annual operating expenses. You'll find expense information detailed within the first few pages of fund prospectuses. On average, total expenses for diversified stock funds run about 1.3%; for specialty or sector funds, roughly 1.7%; for taxable bond funds, about 1%; for tax-exempt bond funds, around 0.8%; and for money-market funds, about 0.65%.

In large part, the rise in fees reflects changes in the fund industry. To cash in on the vast appetite for mutual funds during the bull market, many companies raced to open hundreds of new portfolios. A lot of them were more-costly-to-run specialty funds, and all must now compete in a more crowded marketplace. That has led many fund distributors to step up advertising or offer attractive compensation plans to brokers. At least 60 fund families use 12b-1s as part of such arrangements.

Another reason for today's higher fund expenses is steeper operating costs. Industry spokespersons say some increases are justified. Not only do investors want more fund selections, but they expect expensive new services, such as 24-hour toll-free telephone price quotes, liberal check-writing and exchange privileges, and monthly statements that consolidate balances in several fund accounts.

Fair enough. But the bottom line for fund investors is, well, the bottom line, and high expenses can pull it down. While there is no doubt that superior management can overcome the drag of a high expense ratio in a given month, or even over a one- or two-year period, not many fund managers can offset this drag over long periods of time.

One other problem with rising annual fees applies to 12b-1s specifically. They simply haven't lived up to their promise. To be precise, when they were first sanctioned by the Securities and Exchange Commission in 1980, fund analysts saw them as a way to foster the growth of fund assets. As the funds grew (or so the theory went), shareholders would benefit because as assets swelled, overhead would be spread over a larger base and total operating expenses would come down. But it didn't work out that way. According to a 1990 study conducted for the SEC by Charles Trzcinka, a management professor at the University of Buffalo, 12b-1 fees have no significant impact on the growth of a fund's assets, and funds with high 12b-1s tend to have higher overall expenses and lower overall returns. Therefore, if you want to make money on mutual funds, you should focus on expenses first and then performance.

Forecasting a Stock's Potential

How P/E ratios can lead you to the best buys in the market.

No single piece of financial information can disclose all of a stock's mysteries. If you had to choose just one, though, the stock's price/earnings ratio—its price divided by the company's earnings per share—would tell you the most. In particular, a P/E signals professional investors' expectations about a company's future earnings growth. The higher the P/E ratio, the more investors think the firm will grow over the next five years or so.

Similarly, a relatively low P/E means that investors expect sluggish growth or at least a highly uncertain future.

Of course, the pros are sometimes wrong. The biggest profits come from finding a fast-growing company whose P/E is relatively low because other investors have not yet recognized its prospects. As earnings increase, the stock's price is likely to move up even faster. The reason: Once investors recognize the company's growth potential, they will value its shares at a higher price/earnings ratio.

In effect, P/Es level the playing field, enabling investors to compare dissimilar companies and spot bargains. A simple way to think about this is to imagine that you are in a supermarket trying to pick a detergent. Faced with several brands in boxes of different sizes, you have to read the stickers on the shelf, which list the price per ounce for each brand, to make a fair comparison. P/E ratios work the same way by giving you a price per dollar of earnings.

In an effort to make P/Es even more useful, analysts have come up with endless variations. The most frequently quoted P/E—the one in newspaper stock listings—is based on a stock's current price and the earnings reported by the company for the past four quarters. This *trailing P/E* has the advantage of reflecting actual results, not estimates. Its disadvantage is that the earnings are out of date.

A better indication of a stock's value is its *current P/E*, which steps into the near future. To arrive at this ratio, you add the stock's reported results for the past six months to analysts' estimates for the next two quarters. You can get earnings estimates from your broker or the *Value Line Investment Survey*.

The best P/E—especially for a fast-growing company—is often the *projected P/E*, a ratio that is based on analysts' forecasts of earnings for the coming year.

To understand how these three P/E ratios differ, consider MCI Communications, a long-distance telephone company. Based on trailing earnings, MCI had a P/E of 15.5 in March 1990, compared with 14 for the average stock in Standard & Poor's 500-stock index. But because of MCI's fast profit growth, its current

P/E was 13, and its projected P/E for 1990 was only 10.2. If you looked just at the trailing P/E, you might conclude that MCI is high priced. In fact, many analysts considered the stock to be undervalued, given its projected growth rate, which was more than twice that of the average stock in the S&P 500.

In gauging whether a stock is a bargain, you need a benchmark. You can compare a stock's

Six Different P/E Yardsticks

Price/earnings ratios tell you how investors are valuing a stock, based on its growth prospects. These are the P/Es that analysts rely on most often:

Trailing P/E. A stock's current price divided by the company's reported earnings per share for the most recent four quarters.

Current P/E. A stock's current price divided by the sum of earnings per share for the most recent two quarters plus analysts' estimates of earnings per share for the next two quarters.

Projected P/E. A stock's current price divided by analysts' forecasts of earnings per share for the next four quarters.

Analysts compare a stock's P/E with these benchmarks to see if the stock may be a bargain:

The market's P/E. The price/earnings ratio of the average stock in Standard & Poor's 500-stock index—or in the S&P index of 400 large industrial companies.

The industry's P/E. The average P/E of stocks in the same industry as the company that is being analyzed.

The stock's historical P/E. A stock's typical P/E in the past. For each year, the stock's average price is divided by its earnings for that year, and then those P/Es are averaged.

P/E with the market's P/E—as we did with MCI. Analysts sometimes use the S&P index of 400 industrial companies instead of the S&P 500 as a proxy for the market. (The S&P 400 is the 500 minus 100 transportation, financial, and utility companies.)

A stock's P/E divided by the P/E of the over-all market is called the stock's *relative P/E*. A quick way to scan for out-of-favor stocks that could be bargains is to look in a newspaper's financial pages for shares with trailing P/Es below the trailing P/E of the S&P 500. Most stock pickers would consider a relative P/E of 0.8 or less a sign that a stock may be cheap. Be sure to check brokerage research, though, before you buy a low-P/E stock. Sometimes shares are cheap because the company has serious problems.

Since stocks in some industries typically have above-average or below-average P/Es, you may get a more accurate gauge of how expensive a particular stock is by comparing its P/E with that of other stocks in the same industry (known as the *industry's P/E*), or with the company's own past P/E ratios (called the stock's *historical P/E*). Take Ford, for example. The stock's trailing P/E was recently 4.4, its current P/E 4.6, and its projected P/E 4.3. These low ratios, however, don't necessarily indicate that the stock is a great bargain. Because auto-makers are cyclical companies whose earnings fluctuate considerably with changes in the economy, investors usually value them at P/Es less than half that of the overall market.

Comparing Ford's P/E with that of the average auto stock—recently 4.8—or with Ford's own average P/E during the past five years—about 3.9—gives a better assessment. Using this criteria, Ford would seem to be a reasonable buy, according to some value-oriented stock pickers, but it is no bargain by historical standards.

Protect Your Gains with the Right Buy and Sell Orders

Getting caught by rising or falling stock prices when you trade could cost you money.

Let's say your broker recently persuaded you to buy 100 shares of Amgen, a volatile biotech company, for $46. Now you see on the stock ticker that Amgen is trading at $82.50. So you reach for the phone to tell your broker to lock in your profit by selling you out. Wait! Don't make that call yet.

You are about to place a market order. It's simple and frequently used, but it can cost you money. A market order instructs your broker to buy or sell shares at the prevailing price. Your order probably will be executed a minute or two after it leaves your broker's hands, but as much as 10 minutes can elapse from the time you begin your call until your trade takes place.

That may not pose a problem on slow trading days. But if stocks are rising or falling rapidly, the price when your shares are sold may be far different from what you expected it to be when you decided to sell. For example, when the Dow Jones industrial average falls some 30 points in half an hour, a volatile $40 stock could drop as much as $2 while you are talking to your broker. Fortunately, there are other ways to place orders that can protect you against sudden price changes and without costing you any more in broker commissions. By selecting the right type of order, a shrewd investor can reduce his risk and pick up a little extra profit.

One common alternative to a market order is a simple limit order. With it, you specify the maximum price at which you are willing to buy or the minimum at which you would sell. For example, if you favor General Motors because of its 7.3% yield but think the stock is not likely to move suddenly higher, you might place a buy order a dollar or two below the stock's market price (recently $41). A limit buy order at $39 or better means that your order

would be executed only if the stock's price fell to $39 or less. By contrast, if you were selling GM and placed a limit sell order at $43 or better, it would be filled only at $43 or above.

Limit orders at a given price are executed in the sequence that they are received by the specialist handling the issue on the floor of the New York or American stock exchange. (Orders on stocks such as Amgen that are bought and sold through the NASDAQ computer network—the most important part of the over-the-counter market—are executed in sequence by an automated system.) This means that if your stock trades only briefly at the limit, your order may not be among the ones that are filled.

There is, however, a simple way to jump

Stock Reinvestment Plans Pay Off in the Long Term

Shareholders who do not need investment income to live on often spend their dividend checks anyway, frittering away the money without even thinking about it. But there is a convenient way that you can use your dividends to make your stockholdings grow.

More than 1,000 corporations have dividend-reinvestment plans (DRIPs), which allow investors to plow dividends back into shares, generally without any brokerage fees. And in more than 100 such plans, the dividends buy stock at a 3% to 5% discount.

The effect of dividend reinvestment is striking. If you had bought 100 shares of AT&T for $1,950 five years ago and reinvested your dividends, which then provided a 6.2% yield, you would now have nearly 124 shares worth $5,624. Had you spent the income, you would have only your 100 shares worth $4,550.

Purchasing stock through a reinvestment plan can also improve your returns because it offers a painless way to dollar-cost average. This strategy consists of buying equal dollar amounts of a stock at regular intervals. When the stock's price is down, you get more shares and thereby lower your average cost.

Some DRIPs offer a feature that is especially

attractive to dollar-cost averagers. These plans let you invest cash in addition to your dividends. That means you can steadily accumulate stock without paying high commissions and without having to buy round lots of 100 shares at a time.

Reinvestment plans have a couple of minor drawbacks, though, that you should be aware of: First, you may have to pay a small fee—$5 to $10, for instance—when you buy or sell stock. (For a plan's specific terms, ask the company's shareholder relations department for a prospectus.) Second, you will have to pay tax on your dividends even if you reinvest them.

There are several sources that provide complete listings of companies with dividend-reinvestment plans. Among them: Evergreen Enterprises (P.O. Box 763, Laurel, MD 20725; 301-953-1861; $28.95 a copy) and Moneypaper (1010 Mamaroneck Avenue, Mamaroneck, NY 10543; 914-381-5400; $25 a copy).

Because DRIPs compound your dividends, they enhance your return most on stocks with above-average yields. You should also look for a company that has strong fundamentals. The company should show rising earnings and dividends, as well as a healthy balance sheet.

ahead of the line: Since most investors set limits at round-number prices, you can put yours an eighth of a point higher or lower. Rather than placing a buy order on AT&T at $35, for instance, make your limit $35⅛. That way, you'll be filled before all the $35 orders.

The risk that other orders may be filled before yours points up the main disadvantage of limit orders: You have no guarantee that you will actually buy or sell your shares. When you place a limit order, therefore, you have to specify the length of time that it will be effective. If you don't, your broker will assume that the order is a day order—one that will be executed only if the stock reaches the price limit during that day's trading. The alternative is an open order, also known as a good-till-canceled order, which will remain in force until it is filled or you explicitly cancel it.

To get a feel for an appropriate limit price, follow a stock closely for a month, noting how much it moves when the overall market has strong up or down days. A limit order too close to a stock's current price will not produce much more profit than a market order, while a limit too far away may never be filled. You should set a limit at a price where the stock has traded within the past 30 days and no more than 10% away from the current price.

Market and limit orders are usually the only types available on OTC stocks, but New York and American exchange issues allow for other orders; the most important of these is known as a stop-loss. It essentially sets a floor beneath a stock in which you have a paper profit—or a price ceiling on a stock that you have sold short. When a stock trades at or beyond your stop price, your shares will be sold as soon as possible at the market price. For example, if you had bought Deere at $61 and were holding it at $67 now, you could protect half of your profit by setting a stop at $64. If the stock declined by $3, your shares would automatically be sold, locking in $3 of profit.

With a good-till-canceled stop, adjust the stop price as your stock appreciates. In the case of Deere, for example, you should raise your stop from $64 to $67 if the stock hits $70. This strategy is called using trailing stops.

Setting a price on a stop presents the opposite problem of choosing a buy limit: Your objective is to pick a price far enough below the stock's current level that the stop is unlikely to be triggered by day-to-day fluctuations. Set the stop about 5% below the current level of a stock you own, so that you will be sold out only in a serious decline.

There is one type of order to avoid: the discretionary order, which allows a broker to buy or sell as he sees fit. These orders create potential conflicts of interest for the broker and can land you in an arbitration dispute.

How to Profit from the S&L Crisis

Little-known Refcorps offer attractive yields for conservative investors.

Any investment connected with the savings and loan debacle sounds about as worthwhile as a stock tip from your loudmouthed brother-in-law. But hear this one out. A byproduct of the S&L mess, government-backed bonds known as Refcorps are nearly as safe as Treasuries and pay at least one-quarter of a percentage point more yield. Recently, 30-year Refcorps offered 9.15%, compared with 8.85% for 30-year Treasuries.

Moreover, Refcorps could provide big capital gains if interest rates decline, as expected, in the next two years. If rates fall by one percentage point from current levels by mid-1992, for example, a 30-year Refcorp would deliver a total return of about 30%.

Because of Refcorps' attractive yields and capital-gains potential, bond experts regard the issues—sold by stockbrokers in minimum amounts of $1,000—as excellent choices for conservative long-term investors.

The Refcorp advantage stems from Congress' eagerness to keep the S&L bailout's cost ($60 billion and growing) from being counted as part of the federal deficit. When legislators first tackled the collapse of federally insured thrifts in 1987, they created the Financing Corporation and authorized it to issue $10.8 billion of 30-year bonds. Under the government's quirky bookkeeping rules, that money would not be part of the deficit.

Even though the Financing Corporation's bonds carry yields as high as 9.43%, analysts warn that they are not the best choice for safety-minded investors. True, the bonds' principal is backed by zero-coupon Treasuries. And the interest payments are met from the premiums that S&Ls pay to the government for deposit insurance. But the interest payments are not backed by the Treasury.

By 1989, it was clear that confronting the S&L disaster with the Financing Corporation's $10.8 billion was like trying to extinguish a forest fire with a garden hose. So Congress created another agency that could raise larger sums of money more cheaply, the Resolution Funding Corporation (Refcorp), and gave it the authority to issue $30 billion of bonds. Again, their principal is backed by Treasury zeros. The interest is paid out of the Federal Home Loan Bank system's earnings from loans to savings institutions and proceeds from the sale of failed thrifts' assets. But most important: If these funds aren't enough to meet interest payments on Refcorp bonds, the law directs the Treasury to make up the shortfall. Because of this requirement, for all practical purposes Refcorp issues are just as secure as Treasuries.

If Refcorps are so safe, why do they pay more than Treasuries? The reason is simple. Because Refcorps are new, they are not well understood by most investors. In addition, the bailout agency has issued only $18.5 billion of Refcorps, versus the $3.1 trillion of outstanding Treasuries. The difference in volume—and the fact that Refcorps are not a direct obligation of the Treasury—means that they will always yield a bit more. But analysts say that the yield advantage eventually will diminish as investors become more familiar with Refcorps.

In deciding which Refcorps to buy, you have two choices: bonds that pay interest every six months or zero-coupon bonds that make no periodic interest payments but are sold for much less than the face value you will receive when the bonds are redeemed at maturity. Cash-paying Refcorps have maturities of 30 or 40 years. Zeros come in a full range of maturities, from three months to 40 years. Just like Treasuries, Refcorps cannot be called in early and their interest is taxed on the federal level but is exempt from state and local levies. (With zero-coupon Refcorps, you must pay federal taxes on the interest that accrues each year, even though you don't actually receive the money until the bonds mature.)

To minimize transaction costs, analysts recommend that you buy at least $20,000 of Refcorps at a time. For a purchase of that size, the costs would amount to about $200—or 1% of face value—which is comparable to the relatively low cost of buying the same dollar amount of a blue-chip stock.

If you're a conservative investor trying to plan for a specific cost in the future, such as retirement, zeros that mature when you will need the money are the best choice. On the other hand, analysts say, investors who simply want to add safe, long-term bonds to their portfolios might look at the 30-year, cash-paying issue. Aggressive investors betting on a decline in rates might consider the 40-year bond or zeros with maturities of 20 years or more. While prices of long-term zeros are the most volatile, such bonds could provide total returns as high as 70% if rates turn down in six months or so and fall by one percentage point by 1992.

Follow the Money Trail to Big Performers

When reporters Bob Woodward and Carl Bernstein sought to unravel the mystery behind the 1972 Watergate break-in, a key source told them: "Follow the money." The strategy worked for them—and it could work for you.

At least, that's the message for investors from Laszlo Birinyi, former director of equity analysis at Salomon Brothers. He says that small investors who follow money-flow trends can capture profits on stock moves. All you have to do is zero in on the actual dollars being committed to buying or selling individual stocks. The most important indicator of future price performance is the eagerness of major investors to put money into a stock. And the most reliable way to gauge that eagerness is to count up the dollars they're willing to lay on the line.

Birinyi relies on his own sophisticated computer software system to add up the dollar value of all trades that take place at a higher price than the previous transaction and subtract all those made at a lower price. He says small investors can get the same information, however, from any one of the major brokerages that track money flow electronically. Most will supply money-flow data on a few stocks for no charge. Once you have the numbers, interpreting the results doesn't take much detective work. If you learn that investors are pouring money into a stock, despite a sagging price, then you know their interest is genuine, and the shares will rebound and continue to head up. But if they're unloading their stock, even on price rises, you probably should avoid it.

Birinyi first hit upon his money-flow system while he was working as a trader in the mid-1970s for Mitchell Hutchins. "I learned to look beyond a stock's closing price, which rarely tells the whole story," he says. In fact, according to Birinyi's research, about 20% of all advances and declines registered at the final bell conflict with the dollar amounts of those stocks bought and sold during the day.

Birinyi offers this hypothetical example: Consider a stock that trades four times in one day. At the opening bell, 100 shares trade up 25¢, followed by a transaction involving 50,000 shares down 25¢. Then, in the afternoon, a 200-share trade comes in up a quarter, and just before the close, 10,000 shares change hands down 25¢. Result: The stock price—which is determined by the amount investors are willing to pay for their trades, not the number of shares involved—is unchanged for the day. But money-flow watchers know that the big 10,000- and 50,000-share investors were willing to take small losses to get out—an important sign of impending weakness for the stock price.

In addition to tracking money flow, Birinyi also encourages small investors to take advantage of ways in which they have an edge over their institutional counterparts. In a trendless market, for example, the individual investor can use volatility in a way the big guys can't. One strategy is to study the trading range of a company you like over a three-month period. Then, using a discount broker to minimize transaction costs, put in a limit order—an instruction to buy or sell a stock at a specific price—to buy whenever the price nears its recent low. Finally, enter another limit order to sell your issue at its recent high—and let volatility pay off for you.

Moreover, Birinyi says, small investors can often spot opportunities for profit that institutions overlook, particularly in consumer companies that they deal with every day. His favorite example: Woolworth, whose stock rose 71% between 1983 and 1985, mostly on buying from individual investors who recognized that the discount chain had successfully upgraded its stores. The average institutional money manager is not likely to shop at Woolworth, Birinyi says. But individual investors did and realized the company's potential.

All too often, individuals fail to act on the opportunities they understand best—and as a result lose out. Birinyi notes, "If the small investors who bought Japanese cars in the early 1980s had also spent some of their money on the stock of Japanese car makers, they might be driving Rolls-Royces today."

The New Mania for Coins

Buy rare, buy near-perfect, and buy American. And make yourself an expert on price. Or you may pay mostly for hype.

Talk about exciting times. If the fall of Communism, the reunification of Germany, the imminent decline of apartheid in South Africa, and the junk-bond Walpurgisnacht aren't enough, try the brave new world of rare coins: In 1990, dealers, telemarketers, and stock brokers mounted what may be the biggest promotional blitz ever seen for the minted metal.

Many individuals soured on stocks and bonds are attracted to the turned-up flame of rare coins. Are those glittering profits authentic? Is rare-coin investing as low risk as some of its boosters are claiming? Or is coinmania merely destined to become the tulipmania of the 1990s?

Wall Street's sudden interest in coins is not hard to explain, given customer disenchantment with mainstream investments. Stockbrokers want new alternative investments they can sell to clients. Coins, which once might have seemed an eccentric choice, have been taking on investment legitimacy by looking more and more like stocks and bonds. Merrill Lynch and Kidder Peabody have launched multimillion-dollar limited partnerships to sell to investors.

There are now many grading services, but only three enjoy wide investor confidence: the Numismatic Guaranty Corporation of America (NGC), the Professional Coin Grading Service (PCGS), and the American Numismatic Association Certification Service (ANACS). The services assign a grade to a coin submitted to them by dealers. Prices of these coins range from around $250 to $250,000, with some

going for upwards of $1 million. The uncirculated, and rarest, coins are graded MS60 (MS stands for mint state) to a perfect MS70. Proof coins, struck by the U.S. mint for collectors but never meant for circulation, are graded PR60 to PR70. Coins that have been circulated—and show dents, scratches, and rubbing marks—are assigned one of 19 grades, from 1 (for poor) to 58 (for "about uncirculated"). Unless a coin is so rare that it exists only in poorer condition, MS65—free of any blemish detectable by the untrained eye—is usually the minimum grade for investment.

Independent grading has enabled investors to buy and sell coins sight unseen. And this in turn has allowed the investor to shop for price: If a buyer doesn't like what one dealer is charging for a specific coin with a specific grade from one of the three main services, he can call around until he finds an identical coin at a better price. Grading has trimmed dealer markups, but they still range widely—from 8% to a stiff 30%. It would take three years to overcome that 30% hit on a coin that appreciated 10% a year, not counting storage costs.

Another move to make coins trade more like conventional securities: the introduction of an electronic market called the American Numismatic Exchange. It offers an alternative to the cumbersome buying and selling mediums of auctions, coin shows, and telephone trading. This computer network allows 175 coin dealers to bid on PCGS- and NGC-certified coins. It also lets investors buy and sell more quickly and at less volatile prices.

While the moves toward securitization have helped investors, coins are not stocks, and the market in them is nothing like the stock market. Coins are limited-edition art objects, so valuation of any issue is inherently subjective. Coins are collectibles. They have only one fundamental, supply and demand, while stocks go up and down on such basics as earnings outlook and new products. And demand is sometimes hard to gauge—there may not be a bid on a coin every day—particularly when the market is being primed so vigorously.

What's more, trading remains completely unregulated by any major government agency. And coins are not a liquid asset, no matter what some dealers may tell you. While industry improvements have made it possible to sell some coins in a single day, an investor might wait weeks and, in some cases, months for the right price for a very rare and valuable coin.

Bottom line: Coins are not the sure bet that their shrillest boosters claim. Before you buy, be sure to follow these guidelines:

Learn about rare coins. Go to coin shows (listed in *Coin World*), talk to dealers and collectors, and read every book and journal you can get your hands on before buying a single coin. The successful investor needs knowledge to identify and follow the 200 to 400 kinds of U.S. coins that have genuine investment potential.

Source books include the annual *Coin World Guide to U.S. Coins, Prices & Value Trends* (Amos Press, $4.95); *A Guide Book of United States Coins* (Western Publishing, $7.95), known as the "red book"; and the *Investor's Guide to Coin Trading* by Scott A. Travers (John Wiley & Sons, $24.95). The American Numismatic Association and the Federal Trade Commission have jointly issued an excellent free guide, *Consumer Alert: Investing in Rare Coins* (ANA, 818 North Cascade Avenue, Colorado Springs, CO 80903).

Find a reputable, experienced dealer. Best bet: someone in business in the same area for at least 10 years who is a member of the Professional Numismatists Guild (P.O. Box 430,

Van Nuys, CA 91408) or the Industry Council for Tangible Assets (25 E Street NW, Washington, D.C. 20001). These groups have established stringent guidelines for ethical conduct and can give names of dealers. Ask for references from dealers' clients and from a bank.

Do your own price homework. Deciding what you are willing to pay requires knowledge of the price history of a coin. Look for undervalued material—what's selling well below market highs—especially in a rising market. You can find wholesale prices in one of these publications: *The Certified Coin Dealer Newsletter* (weekly; P.O. Box 11099, Torrance, CA 90510; one year, $99); *Coin World* (weekly; P.O. Box 150, Sidney, OH 45365; one year, $26); and *Numismatic News* (weekly; 700 East State Street, Iola, WI 54990; one year, $24.95). You should always bear in mind the need to factor in your dealer's markup, which can sometimes change an undervalued coin into a pricey one.

Avoid the esoteric. U.S. government mintages are the only reasonable coin investments for the beginner because they enjoy the broadest collector and investor market. Paper currency, foreign and ancient coins, and issues by such short-lived governments as the Confederate States do not have enough buyers and sellers to support an active market.

Store safely. Do not leave your coins with the dealer or even at home. You'll have to add rent—$25 a year—for a safe-deposit box to your coin costs, but it's worth it to avoid theft of one-of-a-kind coins.

And how about those partnerships? While the Merrill Lynch deals are accessibly priced, professionally managed, and diversified, you pay for all that with 15% sales fees and annual management fees, as well as markups. And at $50,000 apiece, the Kidder partnership is aimed at a fairly exalted market. Besides, coin partnerships are like gold stocks: You might feel more secure having the genuine article than a piece of paper.

Make Sure the House Fits

If you belong to one of the nation's 58 million home-owning households or aspire to join the club, you will be relieved to know that doomsayers' predictions of a collapse in the housing market are more attention-getting than accurate. Like many specious arguments, though, the house-bust thesis contains a kernel of truth. House prices will probably rise only about 5% a year on average in the early 1990s, roughly matching or only barely exceeding inflation, and in some years prices won't keep pace at all. That's a far cry from the late 1970s, when annual gains of 12% or more routinely left inflation in the dust. And it's certainly no replay of the rapid 20%-a-year or more price rises that spoiled owners in many housing markets, mostly on or near the coasts, in the second half of the 1980s. But a bust, with prices crashing 40% to 50% coast to coast? That's unlikely unless we see a 1930s-style depression, and no one is seriously predicting that. Making sure your biggest investment is your best is the goal of this chapter. To get a solid start, consider the following major housing trends of the 1990s:

As incomes rise nationally, house prices will appreciate more than in the 1980s but less than in the 1970s. In the past decade, the national median sales price for the typical single-family house, recently $94,000, actually fell after adjusting for inflation. In the go-go 1970s, by contrast, house prices outgunned the consumer price index by an average of almost 3% a year. Look for something in between during this decade, with home appreciation rates generally running nose to nose with, or barely edging out, inflation's expected 4.5% to 5% average annual pace.

The affordability squeeze is likely to ease. For the first time since the Depression, the percentage of U.S. households owning homes has fallen—from 65.6% to 63.9% between 1980 and 1988. Yet, ownership rates should stabilize this decade and might even inch up. The baby boomers are in their prime earning years, and they're more likely to be able to afford a home now.

Buyers will gain the upper hand over sellers in many regions and market segments. While prices should keep up with inflation, a glut of listings from owners anxious to trade up and a relative dearth of first-time buyers will force some sellers to accept demands for price cuts and the sharing of closing costs. For advice on how to benefit from this buyers' market, see "Searching for the Perfect Home" below.

Buyers can count on speedier service from lenders—and may enjoy single-digit mortgage rates for much of the decade. As the thirtysomething crowd meanders into middle age, economists expect them to start saving madly. The resulting flood of capital would make more money available for borrowers and, thus, help drive down mortgage interest rates. Experts expect fixed-rate mortgages to fall to 8% and maybe as low as 7% in the mid-1990s. Lenders are already competing hard for business, which means more options for homebuyers, as explained in "When Price and Financing Matter" beginning on page 81.

Environmental concerns will grow for both buyers and sellers. Look for buyers to be more attuned to indoor air quality, outdoor noise pollution, and underground water contamination. As explained in "The Signs of an Unhealthy House" on page 87, by the end of the 1990s, you may not be able to sell a house or get financing for one unless it's been subjected to rigorous environmental screening.

Searching for the Perfect Home

In today's buyers' market, you can afford to take your time and get picky, picky, picky.

With FOR SALE signs appearing on more lawns across the country, the balance of power has clearly shifted from home sellers to buyers. As a result, shelter seekers in the buyers' markets of the 1990s should be as finicky as Morris the cat. These days, you can hold out for the house that precisely suits your taste and needs. Of course, as long as fantasies outstrip incomes, no one can get absolutely everything he's ever dreamed of in one house. There just aren't enough $50,000 waterfront mansions 10 minutes from work to go around. So before beginning any house hunting, even in a sluggish market, you need to decide which features you absolutely must have and which you could compromise on. (Price is a separate consideration, as "When Price and Financing Matter" on page 81 explains.)

A thorough investigation of the housing market you're considering will help you focus your search. Not everyone has to conduct a house hunt with the precision of a Marine drill team. Still, you would do well to map out a strategy. Get some professional assistance from a knowledgeable real estate agent. This will save time, since brokers can subscribe to a publication or computer data base known as the multiple listing service; it will have descriptions of all the homes listed in the style and price range you desire.

But with brokers desperate to sell homes today, there's no reason to tolerate one who takes your quest any less seriously than you do. Your broker should, for example, be willing to traipse through as many houses as you want; it's reasonable to look at 10 to 20 listings in one community. Ideally, the broker should also clue you in to upcoming house auctions. Never forget, though, that when you're ready to make an offer, your broker's allegiance will be to the seller—the person who will be paying him or her the commission out of the sale proceeds.

Choosing the Area

Before scuffling through a single house, select a few neighborhoods or communities in which to concentrate your search. More than any other factor, the area itself will determine your quality of life and your house's investment potential. Maximize that potential by singling out places where housing values are likely to meet or exceed inflation's pace. To identify them, ask a local planning board or economic development office for the area's current employment growth rate. If it is 3% a year or more, a steady stream of buyers should keep house-price gains above average.

The areas you shop should also feature the qualities that buyers value most. You can scope out such traits just by driving around: entertainment outlets and access to public transportation and major highways, for example. Others require a little gumshoe work. For instance, to see whether the community has a low crime rate, stop by the police department and find out the level of burglaries and violent crimes in the past year compared with other nearby communities of the same size. A top-flight school system is also a strong selling

point and certainly a major factor if you have school-aged children or soon will. Surprisingly, most parents do not demand the schools with the highest elementary or high school achievement test scores in the area. Instead, they prefer ones whose students perform at average to above-average levels. Apparently, parents would rather have their child be a star at a good school than a mediocre pupil at a superior one.

You can get essential education data for public schools from the state board of education; for private-school information, ask the school's admissions director or headmaster. Get an independent assessment, too; for $49, SchoolMatch (800-992-5323; 5027 Pine Creek Drive, Westerville, OH 43081) will evaluate a specific public school system or private school against others in neighboring areas or anywhere in the U.S.

Don't judge schools purely by the numbers, though. Meet with principals and tour facilities. Be sure to ask whether the neighborhood school has the capacity to enroll your child. In some fast-growing areas, local schools are filled to capacity and new kids get bused elsewhere.

The planning board can fill you in on local issues like land use, business migration, and area environmental hazards—all of which help set house-price trends. By finding out where future business growth will be located, for instance, and then looking for a home in the vicinity, you can buy in at today's lower prices and sell tomorrow after prices have escalated. Just be certain that the locality has a master plan that prevents commercial and industrial development from overwhelming residential areas. Lax zoning regulations can turn a once tidy neighborhood into a cruddy one in a trice. Press for information about recent developments that could erode home values, such as major employers fleeing the area and taking enough jobs with them to hurt the local economy. New, unpopular businesses—a huge mall down the street that might cause traffic congestion, for example—can also dampen housing appreciation. So can environmental dangers such as hazardous-waste dumps or high radon levels.

Housing Markets around the Country

Until now, Sacramento was famous largely for its tomato juice and a lamentable pro basketball team. But as the table shows, California's capital could soon become the king of U.S. housing appreciation, with home prices rising a total of 60.1% through 1995 *after* adjusting for inflation. That's the prediction of the WEFA Group, a Bala Cynwyd, Pennsylvania economic forecasting firm.

In the early 1990s, the strongest housing markets will generally be mid-size cities with diversified economies. In addition to Sacramento—which is drawing migrants from San Francisco, 90 miles southwest, where prices are about 138% higher—WEFA predicts solid profits for owners in Pittsburgh and Portland, Oregon. But WEFA expects home prices to decline, after factoring in inflation, in New York City, St. Louis, and New Orleans. Times will be particularly tough in the Big Easy, where flat oil prices, stalled employment, and scant income growth may cut house prices by nearly 11% by 1996.

Metropolitan Area	1989 median sales price	Annual income required for buyers*
Anaheim, California	$246,267	$83,000
Atlanta	82,941	28,000
Baltimore	96,628	32,600
Bergen/Passaic Counties, N.J.	190,269	64,100
Boston	183,205	61,700
Buffalo	72,322	24,400
Charlotte, N.C.	89,625	30,200
Chicago	107,216	36,100
Cincinnati	77,258	26,000
Cleveland	75,659	25,500
Columbus, Ohio	78,673	26,500
Dallas/Fort Worth	93,108	31,400
Denver	85,604	28,800
Detroit	74,614	25,100
Fort Lauderdale	85,857	28,900
Hartford	167,124	56,300
Houston	68,504	23,100
Indianapolis	71,352	24,000
Kansas City	71,389	24,100
Long Island	163,905	55,200
Los Angeles	217,629	73,300
Memphis	78,160	26,300
Miami	86,387	29,100
Middlesex/Somerset Counties, N.J.	174,719	58,900
Milwaukee	79,489	26,800
Minneapolis/St. Paul	87,338	29,400
Monmouth/Ocean Counties, N.J.	162,929	54,900
Nashville	81,445	27,400
New Orleans	70,677	23,800
New York City	183,137	61,700
Newark	200,370	67,500
Norfolk/Newport News	97,710	32,900
Oklahoma City	54,073	18,200
Orlando	81,413	27,400
Philadelphia	107,700	36,300
Phoenix	79,046	26,600
Pittsburgh	66,681	22,500
Portland, Oregon	70,112	23,600
Riverside, California	124,130	41,800
Rochester, N.Y.	78,849	26,600
Sacramento	110,492	37,200
Salt Lake City	69,780	23,500
San Antonio	65,384	22,000
San Diego	174,638	58,900
San Francisco/Oakland	262,763	88,500
San Jose	214,136	72,200
Seattle	107,377	36,200
St. Louis	77,530	26,100
Tampa/St. Petersburg	72,838	24,500
Washington, D.C.	144,259	48,600
U.S. Median	**$94,019**	**$31,700**

Note: *Gross income needed to buy the median home assumes a 20% down payment, a 10%, 30-year fixed-rate mortgage, and that the buyer's mortgage equals 25% of gross income. Source: WEFA Group.

1989 inflation-adjusted appreciation rate	Projected inflation-adjusted appreciation rate	
	1990	1990-95
+ 14.1%	+ 1.9%	+ 24.0%
− 1.8	+ 0.5	+ 3.8
+ 4.5	+ 3.3	+ 15.7
− 2.1	+ 0.5	+ 6.8
− 3.7	+ 2.4	+ 28.8
+ 4.9	+ 2.8	+ 20.8
+ 5.4	+ 3.0	+ 1.2
+ 4.5	+ 5.0	+ 22.5
+ 5.9	+ 2.8	+ 8.0
+ 4.7	+ 3.2	+ 3.0
+ 3.9	+ 4.4	+ 13.9
+ 1.9	+ 1.0	+ 2.3
− 0.7	+ 4.5	+ 19.5
− 3.4	+ 2.9	+ 17.0
+ 0.9	+ 4.8	+ 20.5
− 5.2	+ 0.3	+ 19.4
+ 6.3	+ 2.9	+ 8.5
+ 3.6	+ 3.1	+ 19.7
− 3.8	− 2.0	+ 17.2
+ 3.6	+ 2.4	+ 9.0
+ 16.8	+ 3.0	+ 12.8
− 2.7	+ 1.3	+ 26.1
+ 0.2	+ 1.6	+ 18.9
+ 5.8	− 0.3	+ 14.3
+ 2.1	+ 0.5	+ 5.9
− 2.9	+ 0.2	+ 3.3
+ 2.5	+ 4.5	+ 18.7
0.0	+ 1.9	+ 3.9
− 8.2	+ 0.8	− 10.8
− 7.8	− 1.7	− 2.2
+ 3.6	+ 4.1	+ 13.4
− 5.0	− 2.2	+ 4.1
− 8.9	+ 3.1	+ 11.2
− 2.0	+ 3.4	+ 20.3
− 0.1	+ 0.7	+ 7.4
− 6.3	− 2.4	+ 2.8
+ 0.7	+ 7.8	+ 50.2
+ 3.9	+ 3.8	+ 33.2
+ 12.2	+ 3.6	+ 22.0
− 0.5	+ 1.2	+ 5.2
+ 11.8	+ 7.8	+ 60.1
− 1.7	+ 1.7	+ 12.0
− 4.1	3.9	+ 3.9
+ 14.0	+ 1.5	+ 7.0
+ 20.1	+ 2.1	+ 11.1
+ 10.1	+ 1.9	+ 16.7
+ 13.1	+ 1.8	+ 6.4
− 5.2	− 2.3	− 3.1
+ 7.0	+ 4.3	+ 22.8
+ 3.9	+ 2.1	+ 15.6
0.3%	**+ 4.5%**	**+ 5.2%**

Sunbelt shoppers especially should ask their agents about the prospective impact on local home values of the Resolution Trust Corporation (RTC)—the federal agency charged with selling off properties once owned by failed thrifts. In hard-hit areas like Austin, RTC-owned houses and condos make up a stunning 11% of brokers' inventory. Congress has told the RTC not to unload such properties for less than 90% to 95% of their appraised value. But real estate analysts worry that appraisals might have to be lowered to sell these houses. If that happens, people who bought earlier might see their homes drop in value. Beware of areas where the RTC might unload acres of raw land for below-market prices, too. Such sales could enable builders to erect new, inexpensive homes and undercut appreciation on existing residences.

Commuting time will also play a major role in dictating where you live. Let your tolerance for traffic—or lack of it—be your guide. To gauge commuting time accurately, don't rely on the broker's estimate. Make the commute yourself. And do it during peak rush hour—not in midday when traffic tends to be lighter.

Since property taxes in many places can easily run $200 a month on a $150,000 house, you should compare tax bills on homes that interest you with others in the area. Remember, you're not interested in what the current owner is paying but what you will owe once you move in. To find out how to calculate what your taxes would be, call local assessors. This is especially important to know these days when cash-strapped local governments are raising property taxes faster than you can say Howard Jarvis.

Choosing the Home

Once you've winnowed your choices down to a few neighborhoods, start house hunting. Keep in mind that for resale potential, detached single-family houses on lots of one-quarter to one-half acre are hands-down favorites for most buyers.

An attached house doesn't necessarily doom you to meager appreciation, though. Some markets are now so expensive that shoppers must bend their preferences to their budgets. As a result, builders have come up with a new type of housing: attached move-ups. These are basically large townhouses with grand and glitzy kitchens and baths that are still 15% to 20% less than detached homes of comparable size and quality.

Think about how much time, energy, and money you'll want to commit to home maintenance and repairs. If you don't keep your home in superior condition, it could be a tough sell when you're ready to move out. Houses built before the 1950s may have more character than freshly built ones, but they require greater care, too; houses more than seven years old often cost $1,500 or so a year to maintain, versus a few hundred dollars for younger ones.

If you want the joys of home ownership without much of the drudgery—and are willing to forgo some privacy and potential appreciation—consider a condo or a home in a cluster development, where the condominium or homeowners association maintains the exterior of your house and the common grounds for around $100 a month. Or concentrate on developments still under construction. Don't be taken in by a shiny veneer, however. To check the quality of the builder's materials and workmanship, interview people who bought homes from him within the past year. Also, call the local Better Business Bureau and see whether any complaints have been filed against the builder. You might want to find a builder whose homes come with an insured warranty at no additional fee to you. This policy will cover losses due to faulty electrical, plumbing, and heating and cooling systems within two years and major structural defects within 10 years.

As for style, you will appeal to the largest number of potential buyers when you eventually sell if you stick with houses that are more ordinary than daring. That means, for example, passing up a $500,000 house in a $200,000 neighborhood. A 2,000-square-foot, four-bedroom house with virtually no backyard might also be a tough sell someday since the typical buyers for such a home—families

with children—usually want a large lot. You should be especially chary of falling for custom-built homes with avant-garde architecture, because potential buyers who share your preferences may ultimately be harder to find.

Take care to choose a house whose architectural style adds to its value. Increased mobility has widened the range of acceptable styles—good ol' boys in Houston are now buying that old Texas standby, the English Tudor—but regional preferences can still run strong. In New England, for example, ranch-style houses are as popular as Ceausescu posters in Bucharest and, thus, could become a tough sell for you someday.

It's important, of course, to be certain that a home's layout fits the way you really live. Families with small children, for example, often prefer a kitchen that opens onto the family room, so Mom or Dad can keep an eye on the kids while preparing meals. Parents should also be mindful of traffic patterns within the house. No, not special lanes for little Mikey's Big Wheel, but the route you must take to get from room to room. Ideally, in a household with young kids, the family room should be well clear of the formal dining room where you will entertain adult friends. Parents of teenagers often prefer that the master bedroom be placed as far away from their kids as possible—preferably on the opposite side of the house—to save them from noise.

You may also need a room that's not found in every home. For instance, a household with a grandparent or a boomerang child—one who moves back in after college, a divorce, or job layoff—may prefer a house with an accessory apartment and a separate entrance. Dual-career couples may find a home office to be indispensable.

Finally, with so many places to choose from, don't be afraid to let comfort help you select a home. Deluxe features like French doors, large kitchens, and spacious bathrooms will make your house brighter and more livable and will probably add value. Feathering your nest in the 1990s will not only make your time at home more enjoyable, but it should make it easier to find an eventual buyer when you're ready to fly.

When Price and Financing Matter

Go ahead: Choose a house with your heart. But use your sharpest business skills to negotiate the terms of the deal.

Remember when escalating prices made your dream house seem out of reach? That was then, and this is now. Shrewd home buyers today can pull off spectacular deals on prices and affordable financing, especially in soft real estate markets. Make sure you capitalize on your advantage. Otherwise, if you pay too much for a home today, you might be forced to take a loss when you sell one day. When the housing market was hot, you could count on appreciation to bail you out if you overpaid. That's not true anymore.

As a buyer-borrower, you will have somewhat less leverage with mortgage lenders than with sellers. That's because many banks, savings and loans, mortgage companies, and credit unions have recently stiffened their underwriting policies in response to a U.S. mortgage delinquency rate that hit 6% in the mid-1980s versus 4.1% in the 1970s. As a result, these days, you won't find many lenders making 5%-down mortgages or no- or low-documentation loans. Nevertheless, lenders are competing furiously for business, so there's no need to settle for the first loan dangled before you. By sifting through the traditional menu of fixed- and adjustable-rate mortgages (ARMs), as well as a smorgasbord of newer options like the seven-year balloon and 10-year ARM, you can find a loan tailored to your needs. And if you'll be relocated by your employer, your company might even pick up some of your financing costs (as more than 40% of major corporations now do, according to the Employee Relocation Council).

To squeeze the greatest concessions out of sellers and lenders, you must first gauge the health of the local housing market. The lousier it is, the more pressure you can exert. A tip: Ask your real estate agent for the average length of time that unsold houses are lingering on the market. If it is 90 days or longer, you are in a buyers' market and can call the shots with sellers and, to a lesser extent, lenders. You should also be realistic about how much house you can afford. As a rule, your housing costs—including insurance and taxes—should not exceed 28% of your gross income. This means you can afford a house costing roughly three times your gross.

Dealing with the Seller

Once you're ready to zero in on specific houses, nose around to determine how anxious the owners are to sell. For example, ask your agent which owners have recently lowered their listing prices by at least 3%. That's often an indication an owner is ripe for a low-ball offer. Never forget, though, that your agent's first allegiance will be to the seller—the person paying him or her the commission. You also stand an excellent chance of negotiating price cuts with sellers who have lived in their houses more than seven years or so. Such owners may be sitting on large enough equity cushions to let them accept a lower price and still post a sizable profit. Furthermore, assuming you have the stomach for it, you could adopt vulture tactics—homing in on owners experiencing financial difficulties. Likely targets: people in mid-divorce, heirs who must raise cash to pay estate taxes, and sellers who, having already bought homes, are stuck making double-barrel mortgage payments each month.

You and the owner can haggle over three financial matters: the sales price, your closing costs—those niggling yet substantial home-buying expenses ranging from title searches to home inspections—and the possibility of seller financing. It's unreasonable to expect to ravage the seller on each, though. Instead, try to bargain on the house price as much as possible. Then, if you think the seller might bend further, press for the other concessions.

Start your negotiations these days by making an aggressive opening bid orally through your agent. This bid should factor in the strength of the local market and the owner's eagerness to sell. Never use the owner's listing price as the basis for your initial offer. Rather, you should peg your bid to the home's market value. To determine this figure, ask your agent for a competitive market analysis showing the prices that comparable houses have sold for within the past six months. Then, instruct the agent to draw up a purchase agreement with your offering price, and be sure the contract gives the seller a strict time limit of three to five days for responding. As a general rule, your offer should be no higher than the lowest price paid for a comparable house in your area during the past six months. If the local market is depressed and houses typically remain unsold for four months or more, you can try offering 10% below the past half-year's lowest sales price.

When you're ready to make a prudent bid,

The Choices in Home Mortgages

Lenders now offer so many types of mortgages that the selective home buyer can easily find one to match his wallet and taste. Here are the most common varieties, their recent interest rates, and brief guidelines for choosing a deal that is perfectly tailored to your needs.

	On a Loan of $100,000			
Mortgage Type	Recent Interest Rate	Initial Monthly Payment	Annual Income Needed To Qualify	Best For
30-Year Fixed Rate	10.16%	$889	$38,100	Buyers who demand stable payments; deals are most appealing when rates drop below 10%
Fixed-Rate Biweekly	10.32	451 (biweekly)	38,200	Paying off your loan faster without owing higher monthly payments
15-year Fixed Rate	9.86	1,066	45,700	Quickly building home equity—if you can afford the high monthly payment
Seven-Year Balloon	9.66	853	36,500	Buyers who expect to move or refinance within seven years, paying off the loan
One-Year Adjustable (Treasury Index)	8.18	746	32,000	Borrowers who need a low initial rate to qualify for a home or ones who think rates will soon fall
Adjustable (Tied to Cost-of-Funds Index)	8.28	753	32,300	Getting a low initial rate plus rates in later years that won't fluctuate as much as those on Treasury adjustables
30-Year Graduated Payment	10.55*	639	25,900	Borrowers who need a low initial rate to qualify for a home but can afford payment increases that kick in after the first year

*Actual loan rate; monthly payment and income needed to qualify are based on the first-year rate of 6%.
**Source: HSH Associates, Butler, N.J.

don't fall for that favorite harrumphing line of real estate brokers to buyers: "I wouldn't insult my client (the seller) with an offer that low." In fact, this is simply a ploy to get you to raise your offer. If a broker refuses to pass along your bid—and in a soft market anything within 20% of the market value should be seriously considered—get yourself another agent.

If you decide to buy a freshly built home, gird yourself for tough bargaining. Builders are often loath to cut sales prices because they know that when the word gets out, prospective buyers of other homes in their subdivisions will demand the same breaks. However, builders occasionally get desperate. For example, a builder may be ready to talk when there is a large inventory of new homes in his area— nine months or more. Your local home builders' association may be able to give you such data. Any foreclosed homes for sale in or near a builder's subdivision suggest another chance for dickering since a builder may have to accept less money just to compete.

Typically, a seller will make you a counteroffer in-between your bid and the original asking price. It's generally not worth haggling any further if the seller comes back with a figure within 3% or so of the price you want. But if you still consider the price too high, let the counter expire. Then make a new bid for an amount between your first offer and the seller's counter. (If you're uncomfortable with negotiating, hire a buyer's broker who will do it for you. Some charge hourly fees of $65 to $100; others keep a percentage of the sales price, usually 3% or 3.5%. Call the Real Estate Buyers Agents Council, a national trade group, at 800-359-4092 for names of buyer's brokers near you.)

If you and the seller reach an impasse on price, direct the agent to ask for other concessions that will indirectly lower the house's cost. You can stipulate, for example, that the seller will pick up some or even all of your closing charges, which can easily total 5% of the purchase price—$7,500 on a $150,000 home. Try to lay on the seller the points, or loan-processing fees, your lender will charge for your mortgage. One point is equal to 1% of the

mortgage amount; lenders typically charge buyers one to three points. Of course, if the seller pays your points, you can't deduct their cost on your tax return.

Another cost-shaving tactic that's worth considering is asking the seller to lower your mortgage rate for the first few years through what's known as a buy-down, which many lenders offer. This is an especially sound move if you're worried about affording the monthly mortgage payments on the house. Lenders vary their buy-down terms. But in a buy-down on a 10%, 30-year fixed-rate $100,000 mortgage, for example, the seller might pay your lender an up-front fee of about $5,100, lowering your interest rate to 7% in the loan's first year and cutting the monthly payment from $878 to $665. The rate would then climb one point each year until it locks in at 10% in the fourth year.

Mortgage-related costs aren't the only ones you can try to get the seller to pay. Others include a title search (cost: about $200), title insurance ($300 to $600), and appraiser fees ($175 to $300). You'll make any purchase offer contingent upon a home inspection report, naturally. If the inspector finds major structural defects or even many minor flaws and you still want the house, have your agent rewrite the contract so that the seller will deduct necessary fix-up costs from your purchase price. In a soft market, you can also demand that the seller pay for—or at least split—the $150 to $300 cost of the inspection itself.

Finding the Best Financing

Once you've hammered out the purchase contract for a house, turn your attention to lining up the most suitable financing package. This means not only scouting out the lowest mortgage rate, but also comparing what lenders require for closing costs such as their attorney's fees as well as appraisals and points. You may be charged between one and four points. But most lenders will let you pay fewer points in exchange for a higher interest rate. For example, instead of owing two points for a 10%, 30-year fixed-rate loan, you could pay only one point but your rate would be 10.5%. If you expect to stay in your house for more than five years, you'll probably owe less in overall financing charges by paying more points now and getting the lowest possible mortgage rate.

Don't forget to ask your employer about mortgage assistance. Colgate-Palmolive, for example, pays up to one point in mortgage origination fees for any employee who has been with the company for six months or more.

Your first mortgage decision will be whether to go for a fixed- or adjustable-rate loan. That choice will hinge on three factors: how much you can afford each month, how you feel about fluctuating payments, and where you think interest rates are headed. A 30-year fixed-rate mortgage lets you know in advance exactly what your monthly mortgage payment and interest rate will be for the life of the loan. Adjustable-rate mortgages or ARMs are more affordable initially. But their interest rates and monthly payments can rise or fall on specified anniversaries of the loan—usually once a year—depending on the trend of short-term interest rates. While ARM rates may appear low, when they are adjusted, lenders add two to three percentage points, called the margin, to an interest-rate index such as one pegged to Treasuries maturing in one year. Rates on most ARMs, however, cannot be raised by more than two percentage points a year or six points over the life of a mortgage. Still, even if short-term rates haven't budged, the rate on your ARM will go up in the second year.

These days, you are probably better off with a fixed-rate loan. Rates of 10% or so are low compared with those during most of the 1980s. And you'll get a real bargain with an ARM only if rates drop at least two percentage points over the next few years and then don't head back up. If you think rates will fall but want the option of locking in a rate long term, consider a convertible ARM. After the first year, but before the sixth, you can switch out of the ARM and into a fixed-rate loan, usually for a $250 fee. The new rate will be about one-half of a percentage point more than what lenders are charging at the time for 30-year fixed loans.

Don't be hasty about going with a lender merely because the institution is pushing speedy service or discounts on such goods as appliances and cars. You may pay dearly for the speed and convenience of one-stop shopping. The real estate agent often gets a fee of one-half of a percentage point of the mortgage amount for making the loan, which raises the cash you will need at closing—by, say, $500 on a $100,000 loan. And by signing up on the spot, you forgo the chance to shop around for a more competitive rate and terms.

The fastest way to compare local lenders is to scan a current listing of their mortgage rates and terms. Your daily newspaper may publish such a mortgage table. Many real estate brokerage offices also offer guides to mortgages in their areas. Otherwise, order a similar list from one of the companies that conduct weekly surveys. HSH Associates has mortgage data for more than 20 lenders in each of 30 U.S. metropolitan areas (800-873-2837; $18). *The Peeke Report* gives a similar roundup for buyers in Maryland, Virginia, and Washington, D.C. (301-840-5752; $20).

There are now a multitude of mortgages aside from the standard 30-year fixed and one-year Treasury ARM. To help demystify the marketplace, here is a quick rundown with the pros and cons of each:

The FHA 30-year fixed-rate loan. If you'd like to lock in a low fixed rate on a 30-year loan but can't raise the normal 10% to 20% down payment, look into the Federal Housing Administration's mortgage insurance plan offered by many lenders. It permits 3% down on the first $25,000 of a home's value, 5% for the rest. The catch: The maximum FHA loan amount is generally $67,500, but in high-cost housing markets such as Boston and Los Angeles it's $124,875.

The biweekly mortgage. Consider this loan if you want the dependability of a fixed-rate deal and want to pay off your loan fast. A biweekly is similar to a standard 30-year fixed-rate mortgage except instead of making, for example, an $850 payment each month, you make a $425 payment every two weeks. Since you end up with two extra payments a year, equity builds more quickly and you can pay off the loan in 21 instead of 30 years. (Many lenders will let you transform nearly any mortgage into a biweekly.) Institutions offering biweeklies—as about 25% do—may require you to keep your checking account with them so they can automatically withdraw your mortgage payments from the account. So if you don't have a predictable cash flow into your checking account, avoid this arrangement. Otherwise, you could be stuck paying bounced-check

How to Buy Homeowners Insurance

Before you can move into a house, your lender will require you to buy homeowners insurance. Don't shrug off this expense—typically $300 to $600 a year on a $100,000 house—as another forgettable closing cost. As the victims of Hurricane Hugo and the Bay Area earthquake learned, adequate coverage can mean the difference between ruin and recovery.

The best policies adequately protect your house, its contents, and you—the latter against lawsuits if someone is injured on your property or, for example, sues you when your lovable pooch wanders down the street and takes a chunk out of her calf. Buy the broadest coverage you can afford. Be aware, though, that policies usually cover a home for only 80% of its replacement value—what it would cost you to rebuild. Insurance against flood and earthquake damage is never part of the standard package. Home buyers in flood-prone areas should ask their agents for coverage from the National Flood Insurance Program, a federal plan that costs about $200 to $300 a year for a $150,000 house. To get quake coverage, you typically must buy what's known as an endorsement; some companies sell the insurance as a separate policy. The price depends on where you live; in California, you might pay $300 to $600 a year for a $200,000 house.

Most policies automatically insure your belongings like furniture and clothing for half the coverage you carry on your house. If 50% seems low—for example, if you are a home electronics fiend—pay for more protection. Contents coverage of 70% might raise your annual premiums by 10% to 15%. Certain valuables have their own coverage limits. For instance, theft losses on jewelry and furs are generally insured only up to $1,000; silverware, $2,500. For extra protection, you'll pay from 40¢ per $100 of additional silverware insurance to $4 per $100 for jewelry.

Almost all policies automatically provide $100,000 of personal-liability insurance for you and your household. It's cheap to raise that protection, and in today's litigious society it's probably wise. For another $5 to $15 a year, you can get $300,000 of coverage. You might need even more, though, if you are a tempting target such as a highly paid executive. If so, ask your agent about an umbrella policy—excess liability insurance that comes in $1 million increments above your homeowners and auto insurance protection. Cost: about $150 a year for $1 million in coverage. Homeowners policies also generally pay additional living expenses—up to 10% of your home's coverage—if you must evacuate during rebuilding.

Tell your agent you want a guaranteed-replacement-value clause that requires the insurer to pay the full cost to repair or rebuild your home. Otherwise, you'll get reimbursed only up to the policy's limit. Also, get replacement-cost coverage for your belongings so you won't be docked for their depreciation. Expect to pay 10% to 15% extra for each clause.

Most policies come with a $250 deductible—the amount you must pay per loss before the insurer provides benefits. By raising the deductible to $500, you can shave 5% to 10% off your premiums. Many insurers also offer discounts of 10% if your home has a fire or security alarm that rings at a nearby fire or police station.

fees of $10 to $20 to your lender. And you shouldn't bother with a biweekly mortgage if you don't have the discipline to make payments every other week.

The 15-year fixed-rate loan. If you hate owing anybody anything and want to build up home equity as quickly as possible, this may be the mortgage for you. By cutting the repayment term in half, a borrower with a $150,000 mortgage on a $185,000 house can save $41,000 in total interest payments at a rate of 10% compared with a 30-year fixed-rate loan at 10.25%. And after 10 years, he'd have reduced the loan's principal by $74,135 versus only $13,071 on a 30-year fixed or $36,450 on a biweekly. What's more, the interest rate on a 15-year mortgage is usually about a quarter of a percentage point lower than that on a 30-year fixed. So why doesn't everybody take advantage of this great deal? Steep monthly payments—roughly 20% higher than those on a 30-year mortgage.

Alternative adjustable-rate mortgages. While most ARM lenders offer one-year adjustables tied to Treasury securities, some banks prefer to use other indexes. One common type is the 11th District cost-of-funds index (COFI), which reflects the interest that West Coast banks generally pay depositors. COFI ARMs are roughly half as volatile as their Treasury counterparts. These deals are common among lenders in California; elsewhere, you may have to make a special request for them.

If you'd like an ARM but the prospect of a new interest rate each year rattles you, search for a lender that offers three- or five-year adjustable loans. These ARMs may give you more protection from higher interest rates— but they also prevent you from benefiting promptly if rates fall. If you don't expect rates will drop much, however, a three- or five-year ARM may provide a lower rate than a 30-year fixed without the roller-coaster moves of a one-year ARM. Should you need a loan for more than $187,450—known as a jumbo—consider a 10-year ARM. Its rate remains constant for 10 years and is usually slightly lower than that of a 30-year fixed-rate jumbo.

The seven-year balloon mortgage. If you will probably sell the house you are buying within seven years—the average length of home ownership today—this innovative loan can lower your payments a bit compared with a fixed-rate mortgage. Here's how the mortgage works: Even though the loan comes due in seven years, monthly payments are kept low because they are calculated as if you had a 30-year mortgage. The rate is set as much as a quarter to a half a percent below that of a conventional 30-year fixed-rate loan, reducing your monthly payments by, for example, $40 on a $100,000 loan. When the mortgage comes due in seven years, you can either pay it off, extend its term for 23 years at about a half a point higher than the going rate for 30-year loans, or refinance with another lender. Unlike most ARMs, these balloons have no rate caps, however. Thus, if interest rates soar in seven years, so will your monthly costs if you don't pay off the loan.

The 30-year graduated-payment mortgage. This loan is best if you can't afford to buy a home with a conventional fixed or adjustable loan. A graduated-payment mortgage artificially lowers monthly payments during the first five years by basing the payments on a rate that's far below the actual loan rate. Then the payments rise by about 7.5% annually as the borrower's income goes up (or so he or she hopes). After the fifth year, payments remain constant, pegged to the loan's true rate. On a $100,000 graduated-payment loan at 7.5%, for example, monthly payments would run $705 in the first year and would rise to $1,012 at the start of the sixth year, remaining at that level for the next 24 years. The catch: Since the low initial payments usually don't cover the interest on the loan, the principal balance grows rather than shrinks during the first seven years or so—a feature known in banking circles as negative amortization. So if you want to sell your house during that period and its price hasn't risen, your sale proceeds may not cover your mortgage balance and any broker's commission. You'd then have to tap into your savings to pay off the mortgage—not what you expect when you first buy a home.

The Signs of an Unhealthy House

To safeguard your health as well as your home's value, be sure to perform a rigorous checkup before you buy.

Environmental hazards can imperil your family's health—and wealth. Because of that, giving a house and its environs a thorough going-over for potential health hazards ranging from cancer-inducing radon gas to high moisture levels that may lead to respiratory problems is now a crucial step in buying any home. Already, mortgage lenders increasingly require that appraisers take such dangers into account in determining a house's market value. If a problem is severe enough—a house sits near a toxic-waste dump, for example—banks may simply refuse to finance the deal.

First, conduct a diagnostic review of any house you are seriously considering by hiring a home inspector, who should check at least the following:

Structural components. Check walls, floors, and the roof for water stains or cracks, and window casings, doors and frames, stairs, and the attic for structural damage.

Electrical system. Inspect the main electrical panel for aluminum circuit wiring that could cause fires; outlets to be sure they are properly attached and grounded; and the fuse box for proper amperage.

Plumbing. Fixtures such as toilets and sinks should be free of leaks and have adequate water pressure.

Heating and cooling. Check to be sure they work and deliver airflow to all rooms.

Foundation and basement. Cracks and water seepage could indicate structural damage.

To identify a nonstructural problem like contaminated soil, you may have to find a specialist such as an environmental engineer who'll charge $75 to $150 an hour to test for trouble. Don't reject a house simply because it may pose a health problem. Many hazards are not life threatening, and those that are can often be eliminated relatively inexpensively. Following are hazards found in homes today and the health risks they pose in descending order from most to least common:

Inadequate ventilation. A good ventilation system that gets rid of stale air indoors and brings in fresh air from outside is one of the most critical elements in making your home healthy. To rid the house of harmful pollutants, install a central exhaust fan in the attic or basement. The fan should be vented to the bath, laundry, and kitchen, where moisture buildup can cause mold. An exhaust-fan system, including ductwork for proper venting, costs $300 to $400 if it is put in as the house is built. Installing such a system in an existing house, however, can easily run $1,000. If that price seems too steep, put separate fans in each bathroom and, over the stove, an exhaust hood vented to the outside. Cost: $50 to $100 per installation.

Excess moisture. In today's well-insulated homes, moisture from cooking and bathing can easily accumulate and cause respiratory problems. High humidity can also damage a home's structure, causing rot in walls, roof rafters, and sheathing. You can avoid moisture buildup by keeping the relative humidity in your home between 30% and 50%. To do that, attach a humidistat, which costs just $30 or so, as a control for the exhaust fan in your ventilation system. This way, the fan automatically pulls moisture from the house when humidity rises above the desired level.

Combustion gases. If your home has gas-, oil-, or wood-burning appliances, including furnaces—as roughly 70% of homes do—be sure that combustion byproducts such as carbon monoxide, nitrogen dioxide, and moisture are being vented outside the home. Start by examining the furnace. If the area around the flue pipe that connects the furnace to the chimney is black, backdrafts may be allowing gases to seep into your house. This problem stems from an inadequate supply of air to the furnace area. Installing an air-intake vent to the furnace, at a cost of $100 or so, will usually correct it.

If you have a wood-burning stove, make sure the door to the combustion chamber fits snugly. You can also prevent gases from escaping into the house by installing air-intake ducts in wood-stove fireboxes and fireplaces. Cost: about $100.

Poor water quality. Whether your water is from a municipal supply or a private well, you should have it tested for radon, pH and calcium levels, iron, bacteria, microorganisms, organic substances such as pesticides, and inorganic chemicals such as lead or arsenic. A national mail-order testing service recommended by consumer groups is WaterTest Corporation of America (800-426-8378). To test for all these contaminants, expect to pay about $190 for a kit that tells you how to take samples and interpret the results. Lead and radon are probably the most hazardous problems you may encounter in your water. Lead can leach into the water from lead solder in copper pipes. To solve leaching from lead solder, which was banned as a plumbing material in 1986, install a reverse-osmosis water

treatment system that rids your water of lead and such other impurities as bacteria and calcium. A model such as the Everpure Ultimate 1 that fits discreetly under a sink sells for around $825 including installation.

If your water comes from a well, radon—the odorless gas identified by the Environmental Protection Agency as the second leading cause of lung cancer after smoking—can enter the water underground and then be released in the air inside the house. An activated-carbon system, which costs about $200, will eliminate this hazard.

Formaldehyde. The two greatest household sources of this toxic chemical are particleboard subflooring—prevalent in houses built since the mid-1960s—and urea-formaldehyde insulation. To check the subfloor, pull up the carpet or a floorboard in a closet and look for boards made of glued wood chips and flakes. You can spot the insulation by checking the attic perimeters or behind electric-outlet cover plates for a telltale light-brown foamy mass or powder. To reduce emission from particleboard, apply two coats of sealant such as Deft Clear Wood Finish, available in hardware stores for about $32 a gallon. There is no practical way to completely seal off vapors from urea-formaldehyde insulation. Removing it is prohibitively expensive, as the material lies between exterior and interior walls. Since the peak levels of vapor are released in the initial years, avoid any house that has had this insulation installed in the previous four years.

Lead paint. Lead paint was used in about two-thirds of houses built before 1940, about one-third built from 1940 to 1960, and even in a few built after 1960. Some state health or housing departments will test houses for lead paint at no charge. If it turns up, take action. Cover cracked or peeling paint with wallpaper or drywall. Doors and moldings should be removed and sent out to be chemically stripped. Any removal done on-site should be performed by trained professionals to reduce the amount of harmful lead dust. Ridding an entire house of lead paint can cost from $5,000 to $15,000. To get the names of qualified removal services, call your city or state health department.

Asbestos. This cancer- and lung-disease-causing substance is usually found in the insulation surrounding pipes or hot-water heaters and in textured ceilings in houses built from 1900 through the early 1970s, when publicity about its ill effects forced it off the market. If you spot a substance you suspect is asbestos—a chalky cardboard-like material—contact a lab about how to take a sample for testing. Expect to pay $40 to $50. If the asbestos is not crumbling, leave it alone. If it is crumbling or you plan alterations that will disturb it, remove or seal the hazard. To avoid getting ripped off by sleazy companies that charge as much as $10,000 to rid your house of this substance, call the local office of the EPA for the name of a trustworthy professional.

Pesticides. When misapplied, pesticides used to kill off termites and other insects can seep inside, leaving toxic residues that can linger for years. The most dangerous are chlordane, heptachlor, aldrin, and dieldrin—chemicals now banned as termite treatments but used as recently as 1988.

Before making an offer on a home, get a history of pesticide use from the sellers. To determine the risks of a particular substance, call the EPA's pesticide hotline at 800-858-PEST. If you discover that the house was treated within the past 10 years with chlordane or any other banned pesticide, you'd be wise to pass on the place entirely. You should also reject a home if it's been treated more than three times during the past 10 years with any termite pesticide.

Radon. Scientists believe that the risks from this radioactive gas, which is produced by the natural breakdown of radium in soil, are serious enough that you should test any house you're considering. The substance is thought to be found at levels high enough to cause cancer in about 10% of U.S. homes. For a rough estimate, buy a so-called charcoal-type test kit, such as Air Chek. To get a kit, call 800-247-2435.

The EPA has not determined an acceptable level of exposure, but you should consider taking action if the level exceeds two picocuries per liter of air, the equivalent of smoking about three cigarettes a day. If the test registers two to 20 picocuries, then before you buy the house, get a cost estimate of bringing the radon level below the two-picocurie level. Your best source for such estimates is radon-reduction specialists.

If the reading is higher than 20, don't buy until you get a more accurate reading from an alpha-track detector or electret-ion chamber, which measures radon levels over a three- to 12-month period. Lowering the radon concentration in a home may be as simple as spending $200 to caulk and seal cracks in the basement walls and around the ceiling of the top floor of the house. But an older house with concentrations of 100 picocuries or more may require adding a subslab ventilation system—a set of pipes inserted into the foundation and vented to the outdoors—at a cost of $1,500 or more. To avoid disreputable contractors, use only radon reduction specialists listed with your local EPA office.

Toxic waste. Soil or ground-water contamination from toxic-waste dumps or underground storage tanks should be among your foremost concerns in evaluating a homesite. If a house is within one mile of a dump or has fill dirt that came from an old landfill, the soil may be contaminated with toxic matter. Two major risk sources: radioactive refuse from dentists' offices and PCBs (polychlorinated biphenyls), which are cancer-causing agents found in discarded transformers and batteries. To find out whether a home or land is near a dump or has fill dirt from one, check at your local public health office. To test the soil, contact the agriculture department of a nearby university or hire an environmental engineer. Such professionals are listed in the Yellow Pages and typically charge $75 to $150 an hour. Abandoned underground heating-oil tanks also pose a danger. Your best clue: a pipe sticking out of the ground near the house or in the backyard. For advice on how to eliminate this toxic risk, call the EPA at 800-424-9346.

Should You Move or Remodel?

You can often get the house you want without moving. But renovate because you love the place, not because you figure to profit on the deal.

If you own a house, you've undoubtedly also daydreamed about living in the perfect one: with spacious sun-filled rooms, a regal bath, a country kitchen with lots of cabinets and counter space, and a private retreat for getting away from it all. During those musings, you probably assumed that this ideal house was out there somewhere—maybe even under construction right now—if only you could find and afford it. Actually, you may already be living in it, though it may not seem so. Many people feel they are misfits in their own homes. The life-style of the 1990s simply doesn't jibe with the life-style that most houses were built for. Fortunately, a renovation that redesigns the existing space within your house—or creates additional rooms where necessary—can custom-tailor your home precisely to the way you live.

Millions of Americans have discovered that improving often beats moving in today's ho-hum housing markets. With home prices nationally projected to rise at roughly 5% a year, it may take three or more years of appreciation to recoup the transaction costs of buying, selling, and moving. Result: To get the house you want, you're sometimes better off staying put and fixing up. Then, too, many owners of period-style homes get a charge out of restoring their residences. There also can be powerful emotional attachments to staying put, especially for families. The children are often settled in school, and the parents have a network they can rely on, from friends to relatives

to babysitters. It's hard to rip all that up just for a bigger house somewhere else. Remodeling can also solve problems encountered when you outgrow your house, such as the need for an extra bedroom for a new child.

If you, too, might want to undertake a big improvement project, it's essential to find ways to keep your costs down and your potential payback up. For starters, don't try to justify a splashy renovation by claiming it will make a great investment. In a 1989 National Association of Home Builders (NAHB) survey of 1,600 people who remodeled their homes, respondents estimated that on average they added 95¢ of value for every dollar they spent. Actually, unless you are starting with a house whose value is well below that of others in the area, you will probably be lucky to get back anything near that much when you sell. More often than not, as is the case with such jobs as building a 12-foot-by-16-foot sunroom addition, you may get back just 60% or so of your investment. Keep in mind, too, that remodeling costs vary by region. For example, a recent *Remodeling* magazine survey estimates it now costs roughly $36,500 to build a 400-square-foot family room addition in pricey Los Angeles, compared with only $25,000 in Columbia, South Carolina. (For average costs and paybacks of projects, see the table opposite.)

For some owners, merely spending a few thousand dollars on home-furnishing touches can customize a house for a lot less than an expensive structural overhaul. No longer must you feel constrained to decorate all at once in a single and often expensive motif, though. Rather, today's more adventurous owners now gradually fill their homes through a sophisticated mix: perhaps a $2,000 French country-style armoire here, a hand-painted $395 Italian faux marble table there.

Should you decide, however, that the way to make your house most livable is through a major renovation, you can help prevent the project from turning into a financial folly by adhering to two simple rules. The first is the 20% rule: Don't undertake any project that will raise the value of your home to more than 20% above the most expensive houses in the neighborhood. Spend more on the job, and you'll have real trouble getting your money back when you sell.

Rule No. 2 is to remodel when the housing market in your area is in a slump. During a frenzied market, competition between builders and remodelers for contractors and supplies bids up both materials and labor costs. In addition, remodelers feel more confident about charging higher prices when customers are lining up at their doors. Your remodeling costs can be 10% to 20% lower when the housing market is slow in your area.

One of the best ways to add space is by transforming your attic into a more functional room. This is a particularly useful technique in tight urban settings and neighborhoods where

The Value of Different Remodeling Projects

As this table of U.S. averages shows, you are unlikely to recoup 100% of your investment on these common renovation jobs, listed from the greatest payback potential of 88% to the lowest. A kitchen remodeling tends to hold the most value, since the room is usually a major draw for buyers. Doing a job yourself can save you as much as two-thirds of the cost of hiring a contractor, but you should factor in the value of your time to calculate your true savings.

Project	Cost If Done by a Contractor	Materials Only	Cost Recouped at Resale	Comments
Renovate the Kitchen	$20,641	$7,224	88%	Adds more value than most remodeling projects and can really help to sell a house; go for high-quality cabinetry; don't stint on storage and counter space
Add a Bathroom	10,151	2,538	85	The 85% payback presumes you are adding a second full bath to a house with just one; returns drop sharply when you add more than two baths
Convert the Master Bedroom into a Suite with Bath	21,074	4,847	79	Combining two bedrooms to form a private retreat has become a popular project; makes an older house competitive with newer homes at resale
Build a Family Room	31,223	7,494	78	Do this off the kitchen to create an open gathering area sought by new-home buyers; resale value drops if the addition's style clashes with the rest of the house
Put in a Family Room with Fireplace	35,169	8,402	76	A family-room hearth adds comfort and coziness to a new addition, and many buyers are big on fireplaces
Remodel a Bathroom	7,568	2,422	73	A useful project in houses 25 or more years old; hedonistic splurges like a marble tub and vanities can easily push costs to $30,000
Construct a Deck	5,109	2,146	67	An inexpensive way to add usable space to the house, though the payback is relatively low; returns are slightly higher for decks with scenic views

Source: *Remodeling* magazine. ©1989 Hanley-Wood Inc.; materials costs by Home Tech Remodeling and Renovation Cost Estimator

small lots preclude adding on. Though normally shunned as a dark, cramped, dusty area with inadequate headroom, an attic can actually be converted into an open, bright home office or an extra bedroom with bath when renovated by a skilled architect or contractor. Typical cost: about $15,000 to $25,000, roughly $1,200 to $2,400 more with skylights.

The basement is another area that lends itself to carving out room. For roughly $25,000 to $35,000, you could turn an unfinished 24-foot-by-40-foot basement into either a rec room plus bath or two extra bedrooms and a bath. But don't expect to recoup more than 50% or so of what you spend. It's hard to get enough light into most basements. As a result, home buyers don't value extra living space there very highly these days.

Since kitchens and bathrooms are prone to show their age, many homeowners launch their renovations in these areas. In addition to bringing your home into the 1990s, renovating these rooms can make it easier to unload your house at resale time. The demand for a modern, fully-equipped kitchen is so powerful among home shoppers that you can usually count on recouping a higher percentage of what you spend on a renovation there than with any other project—88% on average. You will get a more modest payback when remodeling an existing bathroom—about 73% on average—but adding a second full bath to a house that has only one can boost your payback to 85%.

Many couples with children now choose to add privacy and luxury by putting in master suites with bed, bath, and separate areas large enough for, say, a small gym or a study. The most cost-efficient way to achieve this effect is by combining two bedrooms. Expect to pay $15,000—roughly $45 a square foot. But toss in splurges such as enlarging the existing bath to include a whirlpool tub and walk-in shower, and the price tag can easily float above $20,000 to $25,000. Though adding a master suite can let you recoup 79% of your money, real estate brokers caution against this project if you won't have at least three bedrooms left after eliminating one. Reason: A two-bedroom house is a hard sell in most communities.

If you're already using your square footage to the max but your family still feels claustrophobic, look into a room addition. The cost will depend on the size of the addition and the materials you use, but figure on paying roughly $70 to $100 per square foot. To increase its payback potential, design the addition to compensate for any weaknesses in the house's present layout. If your home has a tiny kitchen segregated from the family room, for example, an addition that creates a family room opening onto the kitchen will add the most resale value.

As land costs rise and houses get shoehorned onto smaller lots in many densely populated areas, homeowners are also looking for novel ways to get the most out of the outdoor space they have, often by creating what some design mavens call an outdoor room. A patio or deck, for example, offers the chance of getting extra functional space at a low cost, particularly if you build it off the kitchen, family, or dining room where it can be used for alfresco entertaining. You might pay only $4,400 to $5,600 for a 16-foot-by-20-foot deck made of pressure-treated pine; 25% to 50% extra for more durable redwood or cedar. A deck doesn't usually add much to resale value, although you stand a better chance of getting a decent payback if the deck looks onto a mountain, lake, or ocean.

Another way to elevate the satisfaction you get from your outdoor space, if not your home's value, is to use trees and shrubs for decoration and privacy. For instance, by spending as little as $2,500 to plant dogwoods, Japanese maples, and shrubs like yews and azaleas, you can fashion an outdoor sanctuary. With leisure time at a premium, however, you'll probably want to scout out low-maintenance landscaping techniques. One way to make caring for your property easier is to use bark chips or pachysandra as ground cover. Then, too, while horticultural scientists haven't yet come up with no-mow lawns, an improved breed of grass known as fescues requires far less watering and fertilizing than more common varieties. So instead of spending time taking care of your property, you can relax and watch it take care of itself.

Paying for Remodeling Projects

Before your contractor hammers the first nail, be sure you've shopped shrewdly and pounded out the best deal on your renovation loan.

Picking the ideal loan to bankroll your home improvement project isn't nearly as much fun as shopping for the perfect whirlpool tub. But to prevent your hard-earned bucks from being drained away by astronomical interest rates or fat loan fees, you must draw the blueprint for your financing before the renovation work begins. For small fix-ups costing $3,000 or less, try to sidestep a loan altogether and pay for the project out of savings.

Even if the interest is tax deductible, it's far cheaper to avoid interest payments entirely and use cash. But assuming your plans are more ambitious than merely putting a fresh coat of paint in the family room, you will probably need a loan.

Fortunately, now is a terrific time to grab one. Want choices? You've got them: home-equity credit lines, standard home improvement loans, mortgage refinancing, and unsecured personal loans are only a few of your options. Looking for bargains? No sweat. Many banks, savings and loans, and even major brokerage firms are so eager to lend that they are slashing interest rates or waiving fees.

For large loans, such as $20,000 or more, you're usually better off with a so-called secured loan. Example: a home-equity line that taps the equity in your house, which you pledge as collateral. The relatively low interest rates—typically three to four percentage points below those on other renovation loans—and a long repayment period of up to 30 years

can keep your monthly payments manageable. If you bought your first house within the past few years, however, chances are you have little, if any, equity to borrow against. So your only choice may be an unsecured loan. Many lenders will make home improvement loans of as much as $20,000 even on houses with no equity cushion. And since unsecured loans don't require you to pledge your house as collateral, lengthy title searches and appraisals aren't needed. You can usually count on getting your money within a week, compared with four weeks for a secured loan. The downside: Unsecured loans' higher rates and shorter repayment periods dramatically boost monthly payments.

Even if you use your home as collateral, the actual size of the loan you get ultimately depends on your ability to make monthly payments. As a rule, lenders demand that monthly carrying costs for all your debt not exceed 37% of your gross monthly income. So if your monthly salary is $5,000 and you already shell out $1,500 a month for your car loan and mortgage, a bank isn't likely to let you take on more than another $350 a month in payments. Thus, even if you have $150,000 in home equity, you won't qualify for more than $34,000 on a 30-year loan at 12%: Since interest rates can vary wildly even among the same types of loans, they should be your first screen for comparing financing deals. You should be particularly wary of lenders dangling super-low teaser rates that can get marked up faster than merchandise on Rodeo Drive.

If you find you've fallen for such a come-on, you have an escape hatch. The 1988 Home Equity Loan Consumer Protection Act lets you back out of an equity-line agreement without losing your application fee up to three days after you apply.

Rates, of course, aren't your only concern. Be sure you also grill the lender about fees. For a secured loan, you will usually face much the same closing costs as you would when taking out a mortgage: a $150 to $200 application fee and $300 to $400 for a property appraisal and title search. You may also pay one to three points (each point equals one percent of the loan or line). These fees can easily hit $1,000 on a $20,000 home-equity loan. With an unsecured loan, up-front costs are usually limited to a credit-check charge of up to $50. While you should look for a loan with both low fees and a tantalizing rate, usually a loan has one or the other. If you're borrowing $20,000 or more for 15 years or longer, opt for the better rate. But if you're doing a small project and will pay off the loan quickly, your total costs will be lower if you go for the lowest fees.

Banks and S&Ls stock the widest choice of loan types and terms, but credit unions often have the best deals on home-equity lines. By offering a narrower range of loans than other lenders, credit unions lower their costs and pass the savings along to borrowers. If you don't belong to a credit union, you can snag top home-equity terms by shopping in the month or so before the April tax-filing deadline. Lenders often waive fees then to lure customers who've been 1040'd to death. Don't overlook unconventional sources: Many company 401(k) plans allow you to borrow with no fees and at a rate close to prime. Life insurers usually let you borrow up to 100% of the cash value of your life insurance policy. The rate: a soothing 8% or less. Here are details on popular financing options:

Home-equity line. The premise behind most equity lines is the same: The lender appraises your house and then lends you up to 80% of your equity—that is, the market value of the house minus the mortgage balance. You draw on the variable-rate line by writing checks against a special account the lender sets up or, in some cases, by using a credit card tied to your loan account.

The combination of low rates and the convenience of borrowing by simply writing a check makes these loans ideal for large projects where you will be paying a contractor over several months to a year. It also slashes your interest costs. With other loans you get your cash in a lump sum and immediately begin paying interest on the entire loan. But with an equity line, the interest clock doesn't start ticking until you write a check.

Some lenders offer balloon lines that allow you to pay only interest during the loan's term, then require full payment when the loan comes due, usually in 10 years. Avoid such deals. If the value of your house falls, you may not have enough equity to cover that big balloon payment. You are better off with a line that requires regular principal payments. Under one new arrangement, the lender freezes your line after a set number of years—usually five or 10—and then requires you to pay the balance on the loan over the next five to 10 years.

Home-equity loan. As with an equity line, you are borrowing against the value of your house that exceeds your mortgage balance. But instead of drawing down cash as you need it, the lender gives you a lump sum and you make regular monthly payments, usually over 10 to 30 years. Also, unlike lines, home-equity loans can have a fixed rate, usually set two to three percentage points above prime. Thus, choose one if you want the comfort of knowing exactly what your monthly payments will be.

Refinancing your mortgage. Another way to tap the built-up equity in your home for remodeling is to refinance—that is, take out a new mortgage based on today's higher value of your house and pay off your old mortgage. For example, if your house is worth $125,000 and your mortgage balance is just $60,000, taking out a new mortgage for 80% of your home's value would free up $40,000 for renovations after paying off your old mortgage. The hitch: You pay closing costs of $2,000 to $4,000 on the entire new loan versus $1,500 or less in fees if you take out a $40,000 equity line. Refinance only if you can grab a new mortgage rate at least two percentage points lower than your present one. Otherwise, it will take more than five years of savings from the lower rate to recoup the closing costs.

Home improvement loans. These loans, which come in secured and unsecured versions, work best for one-shot projects that cost less than $10,000. But the short repayment period of five to seven years makes monthly payments a stiff $233 on a $10,000 five-year loan at 14%. If that's too steep, check out Title I home improvement loans backed by the Federal Housing Administration. You can borrow up to $17,500 and take up to 15 years to pay it off. The longer term lowers monthly payments by roughly 40%. Title I loans can be used for improvements such as remodeling a bathroom, but not for luxuries like adding a pool.

Unsecured personal loan. If you need more than the $10,000 maximum for many home improvement loans but lack the collateral to qualify for an equity line, an unsecured personal loan may be your only option. Drawbacks: You will pay an interest rate six or more points above prime and get just three to five years to pay back the loan. Approvals are quick (usually three days or less). But unless your project is a small one costing $5,000 or less, skip it.

How Renovation Loans Compare

Below are typical terms that lenders offer for renovation loans. To get the top deal, home in on the interest rate, fees, and tax status of the loan. Lines, equity loans, and refinanced mortgages carry the highest fees, but their lower rates make them the best choices for large projects. You should also consider the loan's term or length. You pay more interest on longer loans, but you can lower your monthly payments by 40%.

Type	Recent Rate	Interest Deductibility	Term	Amount (Minimum/Maximum)	Fees
Home-Equity Line	12% (adjustable; maximum rate of 15% to 18%)	100% for proceeds going toward home improvements, provided total debt on primary residence and second home doesn't exceed $1.1 million	Five to 30 years	$5,000/80% of home equity	Zero to $600 plus up to two points
Home-Equity Loan	13% (fixed); 12% (adjustable; maximum rate of 15% to 18%)	Same as for home-equity line	Five to 30 years	$5,000/80% of home equity	$200 to $600 plus typically three points
Refinanced Mortgage	10.2% (fixed); 8.2% (adjustable; 14% maximum rate)	Same as above. Caution: Interest on proceeds used to pay old mortgage is fully deductible if that loan was made on or after October 13, 1987. Otherwise, write-off may be subject to limits.	30 years	$40,000/80% of home's market value	$600 to $850 plus up to three points
FHA Title I Loan	13% to 15% (fixed)	100% if secured by house	Five to 15 years	$1,500/$17,500	Zero to $1,000
Home Improvement Loan	12% to 14% (fixed)	100% if secured by house; if unsecured, zero beginning in 1991	Five to seven years	$1,000/$20,000	Zero to $50
Unsecured Personal Loan	15% to 18% (fixed)	Zero starting in 1991	Three to five years	$1,000/$25,000	Zero to $50

How to Manage Your Contractor

The remodeling process is rarely heavenly, but you can take steps to prevent it from turning into a living hell.

Some 8,200 owners complained to Better Business Bureaus about their home remodeling contractors in 1988; only nine of the 137 types of companies tracked by the BBB generated more gripes. Clearly, fixing up is hard to do. What can go wrong? What can't? In Pentagonian fashion, major home renovations costing $10,000 and up are legend for their cost overruns, missed deadlines, and shoddy workmanship. Add to that several months of dust, disorder, and din, and—well, you get the idea. The truth is that it's almost impossible to hire someone to create a master suite, remodel a kitchen, or convert a basement into a playroom without disruptions or screwups. But there are numerous ways of preventing or at least minimizing the financial and construction snafus that so often bedevil renovations. The three keys: choosing reliable professionals, hammering out detailed contracts with them, and holding them to the agreements.

First, though, decide precisely how and what you want to remodel or renovate. A critical pre-remodeling step is honestly appraising whether you have the temperament to put up with the aggravation of a renovation. If your remodeling job will consume more than 50% of your home's living space, you will probably need to camp elsewhere until the work is done.

Finding the Help You Need

Start any renovation by asking yourself whether you can handle alone small fix-up projects like installing light fixtures or floor tiles. Some excellent how-to books, such as the *Reader's Digest Complete Do-it-yourself Manual* ($22.95) and the *Home Repair and Improvement* series ($10.99 per book; published by Time-Life Books), may be all you'll need. No matter how handy you are, you will need professional help for big jobs. Relatively straightforward improvements—a new kitchen, for example, or a room addition that doesn't change the structure of your home—can most easily be handled by a contractor who does both design work and construction. Such contractors often call their companies design/build firms. The contractor will then subcontract carpenters, plumbers, and other workers, buy materials, organize work schedules, and follow the job's day-to-day progress.

If you plan something that will dramatically change the design of your home, such as replacing two bedrooms with a master suite or opening up a kitchen to include a family area, you will probably get the best results by hiring two types of experts: First, either an architect or an interior designer to plan and oversee the project and then a contractor to build it. Architects are best for jobs involving structural changes such as moving walls. Interior designers generally specialize in making existing rooms more livable. For instance, they can devise a more appropriate lighting system and order hard-to-find furniture, wallpaper, and other accessories. You'll pay an architect or designer a fee of roughly 10% to 15% of anticipated construction costs.

Your Yellow Pages probably lists dozens of contractors, architects, and interior designers, so selecting ones to improve your home can be a daunting task. Neighbors or acquaintances who have had work done similar to the renovation you plan can refer you to likely candidates. Beyond that, here's how to narrow your search:

Start by writing to professional organizations for names and phone numbers of architects or interior designers in your area. The local chapter of the American Institute of Architects can refer you to registered architects who have passed state licensing examinations. Similarly, the local chapter of the American Society of Interior Designers will provide information on its members who have graduated from a four- or five-year degree program.

Set up appointments with at least three architects or designers. Then, explain what you want, why you're remodeling, and how you expect the changes to mesh with your lifestyle. Most will meet with you for an hour or so at no charge to discuss your ideas. Before you hire an architect, be sure he or she has handled projects similar in scale to yours; many specialize instead in new construction.

Investigate contractors by asking local architects and designers for referrals. In addition, call your local builders association for names of contractors who are among the National Association of Home Builders' 130 certified graduate remodelers. These people have at least five years of experience owning or managing a remodeling company and take continuing-education courses. Interview at least three contractors and ask them for rough estimates of their fees for your project. Don't jump at the smallest fee. The guy with the low bid may take his profit out of the job by using shoddy materials or taking shortcuts.

When you've identified a promising contractor, find out the answers to the following three questions:

Is he solvent? The biggest disaster is watching your contractor go out of business in the middle of a job. In addition to the delay, expense, and inconvenience of finding someone to finish the project, you may face claims from subcontractors who have not been paid for their work on the job. For a clue to a contractor's financial stability, ask for names and phone numbers of his regular subcontractors and suppliers. Then call them to see whether he typically pays promptly. If he has been slow lately, that may be a signal of money trouble. Also, be wary of newcomers; an estimated 90% of new contractors go out of business within five years.

Is he reliable? Contractors rarely say no to a job. You'll get your best gauge of reliability by visiting at least one of the contractor's clients who recently lived through a remodeling project like yours. Any reputable contractor will gladly provide such references. Find out how well the contractor met his deadlines and estimated his fee. Since problems probably arose during the renovation—they nearly always do—ask whether the contractor handled them satisfactorily. Inquire, too, whether the work and materials matched the standards originally agreed upon by the owner and contractor. In addition, be sure the contractor will be using his regular team for your job, not the second-string pickups he might use when he's juggling a number of projects. If he tells you the staff he'll assign have worked with him for less than six months and most of the subcontractors have never worked for him, find another contractor.

Is he honest? The Better Business Bureau can tell you if any complaints have been filed against a contractor. You might also check his probity by getting in touch with local suppliers and architects.

Getting the Contract Right

A contract from an architect or interior designer, usually a one- to eight-page document, spells out fees and payment terms, as well as a general description of the work the pro will do. For example, the contract might say that your architect will offer three alternative detailed designs and will visit the job site at least once a week. Ask your lawyer to review the contract.

You need to bear down especially hard on a contractor's contract because of its minutia. Every aspect of the renovation should be included. Even a modest job might call for two to three pages of specifications, known in the trade as specs. For $5.95, the American Homeowners Foundation, a private group, will provide an eight-page model agreement that you can compare with yours (1724 South Quincy Street, Arlington, VA 22204). If anything is missing from your contract, such as deadlines, brand names, or descriptions of materials, write it in before signing.

Be certain that your agreement also lays out the following information:

The price calculation and your payment schedule. There are two types of contracts: fixed-price and time-and-materials. A fixed-price contract guarantees your costs. If anything comes up during the renovation that will change the project, you and the contractor must then sign an official change order noting—and agreeing to—any additional related expenditures. In a time-and-materials contract, you will get only a rough estimate of the job's cost. Your actual fee will depend on the hours of labor and expenses ultimately incurred. A fixed-price contract is safer, since you lock in costs early.

With either type, stipulate the payment schedule. On a fixed-price contract, never pay more than 30% of the anticipated cost when you sign the contract. The rest should break down roughly this way: 30% midway through the job, 30% when the major work is done, and 10% after all remaining details are complete. Make payments for a time-and-materials contract every two weeks or so to cover ongoing costs.

The precise materials. Will you get pre-built, modular cabinets or the more expensive custom-made cherry ones? Other key concerns: the thickness and exterior finish of new walls; ceiling textures; brand names and styles of windows, doors, plumbing fixtures, and appliances; and the number of electrical plugs, lights, and switches in a room. Material names and descriptions won't always be familiar, so ask for catalogue pictures or visit showrooms if necessary.

What Makes a Home Sell When Nobody's Buying

Get real about price, be fanatical about your home's appearance, find a clever broker, and try a little creativity.

Throughout the country, the arithmetic of the housing market, long the seller's staunch ally, has changed sides. Yet, even in beleaguered markets, some homeowners sell without delay or disappointment because they actively take steps to make their homes stand out. In buyers' markets, houses aren't sold—they're marketed. First, you must differentiate your "product" in buyers' minds, just as if you were Gillette bringing out a new razor. Some useful tactics, such as sprucing up your home, are time-tested. Others are new or demand special attention in today's soft marketplace: choosing and using a skillful real estate agent or broker; setting a realistic price; and perhaps even offering buyers special come-ons, like a year's prepaid property taxes. Most of all, you have to be willing to work at it. Use the following strategies:

Choose the sharpest merchant. Find out what it will really take to move your house by hiring a professional marketer—namely, a clever real estate agent. In a softening market, you may be tempted to try to preserve your profits by selling your home yourself and avoiding the agent's commission (typically 6% or 7%, but slightly lower in a few spots). That's unwise. A sharp pro will advertise your home expertly, show it skillfully, and mediate deftly with your buyer. Equally important: Only agents can list homes on your area's multiple listing service, the publication or computer data base informing other agents and prospective buyers about your house. In many areas, the service is the entry point for buyers in eight of every 10 sales.

For recommendations of agents, ask neighbors who recently sold homes like yours, and read real estate brokerage office plaques or ads denoting their most recent top sellers. Invite at least three agents to your house for their listing presentations, where they'll spell out their marketing plans and how much they think you can get for your home.

If you can't decide between two otherwise equally qualified agents from different brokerages, lean toward the firm that has more agents in your area. Most agencies encourage their salespeople to show the firm's own listings first so the brokerage won't need to split the commission with a competitor. That could help give your house greater exposure faster. Moreover, odds are that a larger agency will have a fatter advertising budget.

Once you've selected an agent, tell him or her you want to sign an "exclusive right to sell" listing contract. With this arrangement, the agent collects a commission if the home sells during your listing period, even if you actually find the buyer yourself. By promising not to sell the house out from under your agent, you encourage him or her to work as hard on your house as on other listings. Be sure your listing contract has an escape clause that kicks in after no more than 90 days. This way, your agent will know you expect quick action. If the house hasn't sold by then but you are still satisfied with the agent, you can always renew the agreement.

In a sluggish market, don't even suggest amending the contract to slice a few points off the broker's commission. Look at it from the broker's point of view. Who would you work harder for: an employer who paid you 6% or one who insisted that you take 3%? Similarly, in a cold market, resist the temptation to sign with a discount agency that charges only 3% or so. Homes listed with discounters tend to generate low interest among selling brokers, who understandably would rather split 6% than 3%. Moreover, many cut-rate agencies also require sellers to pay for their own advertising or even show their houses themselves.

In fact, rather than trying to cut commissions, you might consider offering a bonus to the selling agent if the home gets snapped up for, say, 97% of the asking price. It could be cash—for example, 1% of the selling price in addition to the normal commission—or merchandise, such as a pair of airline tickets to anywhere in the continental U.S. Real estate developers and builders offer such incentives regularly.

Price it to sell. Perhaps the most common and damaging mistake sellers make in weak markets today is clinging to yesterday's prices. When sales are spotty, what your new neighbors paid for their place last year—or even three months ago—may not be much more relevant to your home's market value than what the Dutch paid for Manhattan. By asking too much initially, you squander the critical first 30 to 45 days of the listing period. Your freshly spiffed-up house will look its best in those early weeks, and it will be shown more, as agents bring by their current stable of shoppers. Lose those buyers and you will have to wait for new prospects to trickle in.

Your agent will recommend an asking price based on recent sales of what he or she considers comparable homes. Pin down the agent. Ask for the addresses of those homes and their sales dates. Then drive by to ensure that the homes are comparable to yours.

Decide on a rock-bottom selling price, then set your initial asking price no more than 3% to 5% higher. If possible, come in just under the next lowest multiple of $10,000 (for example, at $149,000 rather than $150,000). Not only is there a psychological difference between the two prices, but since many agents screen homes for buyers by computer—searching for, say, all homes listed for less than $150,000—you are likely to wind up on many more buyers' itineraries.

Spruce up what you've got. The tougher the market, the closer to impeccable your house should be before you list it. In a buyer's market, there may be 10 homes competing for every buyer, so you have to make sure your house does just that: competes. While major remodeling and landscaping projects usually don't pay, minor repairs and cosmetic makeovers generally do—in a quicker sale, if not a higher price. From the outside, your home must look well cared for and welcoming, two components of the vital first impression brokers call curb appeal. New shrubs and flowers seem to be particularly persuasive.

Inside your home, concentrate on making rooms look sunny and immaculate. You may be able to give the home a more open feel by putting some furniture in storage. Overall, your goal should be to make it as easy as possible for potential buyers to imagine themselves living in your house. When buyers have an abundance of choices, as they do in soft markets, they tend to look for reasons to cross homes off their lists. So if your interiors include a lot of personal decorating flourishes, make them over in conservative schemes.

Create a package that stands out. Remember that promotions work best when they are pitched to the right customers. If you have what might be considered a smallish starter home, consider enticing cash-strapped buyers

with an offer to pick up part of their closing costs. To help a buyer qualify for a mortgage, you could float the idea of a mortgage buy-down, in which you pay a lender a flat sum to lower the interest rate on the buyer's mortgage for the first few years. On a 30-year $100,000 mortgage, it might cost you $2,636 to lower the rate from 10.5% to 8.5% for the first year and 9.5% for the second, reducing the buyer's monthly payment by $146 to $769.

Trade-up buyers, who can often count on sacks of cash from the sale of their previous home, tend to be less impressed by financing incentives. For these buyers, you might consider throwing in a $1,000 redecorating or landscaping allowance or a year's prepaid lawn maintenance service. Other incentives, such as an offer to pay first-year country club membership fees, sometimes will draw buyers to slow-selling upscale homes.

Even the most creative promotions will be useless if buyers don't know about them, so make sure that the word gets out to both agents and potential buyers. For example, you might encourage your agent to hold an open house for other real estate brokerages before officially putting the house on the market. Give the invited brokers a reason to visit. The enticement could be as simple as hors d'oeuvres and wine in the kitchen or as corny as a drawing for a frozen turkey.

To help get the word out to buyers, target your advertising. If you have a starter home, for example, leave leaflets at a nearby rental complex where young couples may be waiting to make the leap to ownership. If your intended buyer is more affluent, mail a description of your home to local corporations' human resources directors, who will know of executives transferring in.

Rethink your sales strategy. Monitor the progress of your sales campaign by getting updates from your broker after every showing. Find out what objections prospects are voicing and adapt your strategy accordingly. If buyers seem to prefer newer houses than yours, consider spending $300 or so on a homeowners warranty. Sold through most real estate agencies, such warranties often pay for repairing a house's air-conditioning, heating, or plumbing system during the first year of occupancy. Whenever you cut your price sharply or alter your selling strategy in any major way, have your agent re-list the home with the multiple listing service. The repackaging may induce brokers to give your house a second look.

If your home hasn't sold in three months, it may be time for a new broker. Warning signs: your house is not attracting much buyer traffic, the agent does not keep you regularly informed of prospects' reactions, or he or she is slow to return your calls. Give your broker a chance to explain the situation. But if you're unimpressed, search for another.

If nothing seems to work, you may be tempted to grab a home purchase plan. Some 80% of large firms offer such programs to transferees. The company typically agrees to buy your home for the average of two appraisals—one paid by you and one by your firm. The employer—or a relocation company it hires—then sells the house. Some real estate agencies and developers offer similar promotions. Warning: Resist them. You could end up paying a stiff price for their bailouts. For example, some builders try coaxing sellers into buying languishing units by offering to purchase their old homes at only 70% to 90% of the appraised value. The developer may further cover his risk by charging top dollar for your new home.

A last resort may be to put your house up for auction. This does not eliminate the need for sprucing up the place. Even in a tough market, if you spend the time and money on marketing up front, you almost always save time and money in the end.

Tax Tips for Sellers

Selling your house can provide the biggest tax break of your life: You may be able to defer the taxes on your profit for years or even avoid ever paying them. The trick is understanding how the IRS calculates house-sale gains. The basics:

You can snatch a once-in-a-lifetime exclusion from taxes on as much as $125,000 in capital gains if you're married and file separately, and if you are 55 or older and owned the house and lived in it as your principal residence for at least three of the past five years. If you and your spouse file jointly, only one of you must meet the tests to claim the exclusion.

A seller who doesn't qualify for the exclusion but is buying another principal residence usually gets a tax deferral of his gains. The two IRS hurdles: You must buy or build the new house within two years before or after the sale and your new house must cost at least as much as the so-called adjusted sales price of your old one.

The second stipulation is trickier than it seems. You may incorrectly assume that if you bought a house for, say, $80,000 and will now sell it for $125,000, you have a $45,000 capital gain and must therefore buy a home for $125,000 or more to defer the taxes on it. Actually, to calculate the gain accurately, you have to factor in such things as closing costs and home improvements. Fortunately, the extra pencil pushing can help slash your taxes. In the prior example, if you had spent $8,000 on improvements to the original house, you could knock down your capital gain at least to $37,000 ($45,000 minus $8,000).

Naturally enough, all sales require some IRS paperwork. If you will either claim the $125,000 exclusion, defer the taxes on your sale, or have a loss, file Form 2119. Taxable gains must be reported on Schedule D.

Should you die before paying taxes on your deferred gains, your house will become part of your estate. Then any federal estate or state death taxes due will depend on the overall value of your assets. If they total $600,000 or less, your estate won't owe federal taxes. But beware: Many states have lower cutoffs for setting taxes. New York, for instance, taxes estates above $108,000.

Escape from Tax Hell

What's your tax bracket? If you answered 15% or 28%, you were wrong. No American can afford such a quaintly simple view anymore. Your federal bracket is only the beginning. If you were a resident of New York City in 1990, you paid up to 7.375% of taxable income to the state and 3.4% to the city. On top of that, you paid a combined state/local sales tax of 8.25% and, if you were also a homeowner, a 9.4% property tax. You would also be reeling from new user fees, a higher cigarette tax, and an expansion of items covered by the sales tax—all imposed that year. With a household income of $61,372—the recent average for a *Money* reader—you could easily be facing a top federal, state, and local bracket of 41%. And you wouldn't even be in the jurisdiction with the heaviest taxes. New York ranks only No. 7, behind Utah, Idaho, Maryland, the District of Columbia, Oregon, and, the worst of all, Hawaii.

Though the specifics vary around the nation, the message does not: State and local taxes are on fire. Today, you can't do serious tax planning unless you take state and local taxes into account. For some, these are getting to be almost half the size of their federal income tax bill. This chapter aims to bring you up to speed. "The Taxes That Hit Closest to Home" on page 104 explains how state and local taxation has proliferated, how it is affecting people's tax lives, and, most important, the strategies you can use to fight its inexorable creep.

In a recent *Money* poll, some 41% of those surveyed said that since federal tax reform in 1986, their property taxes have risen faster than both their state and federal income taxes. (For ways to cut your property taxes, see "Challenging Your Tax Assessment" on page 107.) They felt, however, that those property taxes are being spent more wisely than state—and far better than federal—revenues.

This animus toward Washington resonated throughout the poll. By 37% to 25%, the respondents found the federal tax code less fair since reform; by 53% to 16% they called it more complicated. So it's not hard to see why most polled subscribers who employ a tax preparer found him or her to be a hero: 52% declared their pro's work very good, 36% good, 10% fair, and only 2% poor.

The good news is that the people who answer your questions at the IRS have increased the accuracy of their advice. Still, the agency's incredible workload makes for inevitable errors and you could be one of the some 36 million people receiving notice that they owe additional tax and penalties this year. For help responding to those frequently erroneous notices, see "How to Fight Back When the IRS Is Wrong" on page 118.

With Congress considering new ways to change the tax code, your federal tax planning this year will be more important than ever (See "Smart Ways to Beat the Feds" on page 110). Happily, that will also be your best defense against the explosion in state and local levies. Reason: Of the 43 states with income taxes, 35 base them on federal returns, usually asking you for a percentage of what you pay the IRS, or using your federal adjusted gross income or taxable income as the starting point for their own computation. So take this short course in tax planning and ease the burden on all three levels—federal, state, and local.

The Taxes that Hit Closest to Home

State and local increases make the feds look almost friendly. Here are seven ways you can fight back.

If you didn't feel the squeeze of rising state and local taxes in the past decade, you're probably feeling it now. According to the annual survey by the National Conference of State Legislatures, 30 states enacted tax hikes in the first six months of 1989 alone. On the local level, a recent survey by the National League of Cities found that 148 of 362 cities—41%—increased property tax rates in 1989. Another 69% took the less drastic option of increasing existing user fees, while 36% enacted new fees. These fees are chiefly for water and sewer service, garbage collection, and recreation programs—"free" services once supported by general tax revenue.

Such a pounding pace of increases adds up, especially when you consider the array of taxes you may be getting hit with. A hike in the income, general sales, or real property tax is hard to miss. User fees are less conspicuous but still costly, as are taxes on real estate transfers, gasoline, cigarettes, alcoholic beverages, hotel lodgings, motor vehicle registration, utilities, estates, inheritances, and even privately owned parking spaces and lottery winnings. Moreover, in many places, property taxes aren't restricted to real estate. They can also be applied to tangible personal property, such as cars, and to intangible personal property, such as stocks and bonds. Unfortunately, the forecast is for a continuing steady downpour of state and local taxes. Consider the signs:

● Problems that were not nearly so acute a decade ago, such as drug abuse and prison overcrowding, demand hugely increased spending. Meanwhile, the federal deficit has grown, provoking Congress to shift the funding of federally mandated programs, such as Medicaid and nursing-home reform, onto the states.

● Federal aid to states has declined on average 1.5% a year over the past decade. In inflation-adjusted dollars, that's a drop from $105.9 billion in 1980 to an estimated $91.1 billion in 1990.

● Cities, for their part, are reeling from the loss of both federal and state aid. At its peak in the mid-1980s, federal general revenue sharing provided $4 billion a year to cities and counties—a fifth of all the aid. That well ran dry in 1986. Hard-pressed state governments have also had to curtail the rate of growth of aid to cities.

● For 1990, thirty-five states projected fiscal year-end budget reserves below 5% of total spending. Unlike the federal government, cities and states (with the exception of Vermont) are legally barred from operating in the red. Many states will have to cut spending sharply or enact explicit tax increases, or both, simply to balance their budgets.

Worst of All: Property Taxes

If you are like readers polled by *Money*, the tax you find to be rising fastest is the one that literally hits home—the property tax. The reasons for property tax hikes are as varied as the rates and assessments applied in neighborhoods around the country. National figures do confirm a general upward movement, though: Following a brief period of decline that ended a decade ago, annual property tax rates have increased from $29 for every $1,000 of personal income in 1981 to $32 per $1,000 in 1987.

But the gentle rise in rates belies the explosive nature of some of the recent increases. Of course, in an appreciating housing market, bills can leave homeowners crying for relief even when rates go down. Take Fairfax

County, Virginia, just outside Washington, D.C. Eight years ago, an $82,000 house was assessed for 100% of its value and taxed at a rate of $1.47 for each $100 of valuation, yielding a total tax bill of $1,205. By 1989, tax rates had dropped to $1.19 per $100 of valuation. The house had appreciated to $181,000, however, for a property tax bill of $2,154, a 79% increase. In addition, localities in Virginia and many other states levy a tax on personal property.

Often the only route to property tax relief is to enact or increase another tax, a strategy that voters are loath to embrace. In Oregon, for example, voters have repeatedly rejected a statewide sales tax, some of the proceeds of which would be shared with local governments. Thus, strapped for revenue, localities lean more heavily on homeowners.

The Sleeper: State Taxes

While *Money*'s poll confirmed a growing awareness of burdensome property taxes, it exposed relative ignorance of the costly conspirings at state capitals. That bliss will soon end. Nine states enacted income tax hikes in 1989. Among the broadest hikes were those in Connecticut, Illinois, Massachusetts, Montana, and Vermont.

A state with low or no income taxes, on the other hand, is almost certain to deliver a heavy sales tax punch. Of the seven states that impose no personal income tax on earned or unearned income—Alaska, Florida, Nevada, South Dakota, Texas, Washington, and Wyoming—five derive most of their revenue from the sales tax. Such levies range from a high of 7¢ on the dollar in Washington to a low of 4¢ in South Dakota. In some Washington jurisdictions, the combined state and local sales tax rate goes as high as 8.1%.

The rate alone is only half the story: Your actual sales tax load depends on what is taxed. For instance, taxpayers in Indiana and Massachusetts both pay a 5% sales tax. But as a share of income, the burden can be nearly 50% higher in Indiana than in Massachusetts. Reason: Massachusetts exempts food, heating fuel, and many clothing purchases. Of these, Indiana exempts only food.

States have been steadily increasing their sales tax base. Last year, 25 states began taxing out-of-state mail-order sales; several states and the District of Columbia also tax various services such as videotape and equipment rentals, cable TV, public relations, landscaping, and building maintenance.

Although many cities are facing budgetary hardships as well, local sales tax increases are uncommon, primarily because they are difficult to enact: Nearly half of the cities surveyed are restricted by state law from increasing the sales tax. Thus, only 5% of those surveyed boosted the sales tax during the 1989 fiscal year; the preceding year, 8% did so.

Despite the upward pressures, no one is predicting the kind of tax revolt that occurred in the late 1970s and early 1980s. One reason for the relative calm is that, unlike today, a decade ago state coffers were overflowing.

How to Fight Back

There are a number of steps you can take to protect yourself from high state and local taxes, short of moving:

Take full advantage of federal deductions for state and local taxes. If you itemize on your federal return, you can write off state and local income taxes, real estate taxes, and personal property taxes that are based on the item's value. Don't overlook the less obvious deductions, however, such as taxes for a prior year that you pay during the current year as a result of an audit or filing an amended or late return; contributions to state disability funds in California, New Jersey, New York, and Rhode Island; employee contributions for state unemployment insurance in Alabama, Alaska, and New Jersey; and in 16 states, all or a portion of the license fees for your car. Your local tax authority can guide you as to what portion of the fee is federally deductible.

Learn where your state's tax law is more generous than the federal code. Expenses that may not be federally deductible are allowed by many states, such as political contributions, a portion of your rent, and medical expenses that fall below the federal deductibility threshold of 7.5% of your adjusted gross income. Some states also extend credits not available from the federal government, such as renters' credits in California and Hawaii and, in several states, credits for installing energy-saving equipment. To reduce taxes for two-earner couples, some states allow married people to file separately, even if they file a joint federal return. Ask an accountant or consult a state tax handbook, available in most libraries, for a listing of deductions, exemptions, and credits.

Also, learn where your state is more punitive than the feds. Many taxpayers wrongly assume that federal rules automatically apply to the states. Among the snares: 10 states and the District of Columbia will not grant an extension for filing your state income tax return simply because you have requested a federal extension. Also, if you make estimated tax payments, you must underpay your federal liability by $500 before you're hit with a penalty, but the cutoff can be much lower at the state level. And if you have a refund coming, there is no federal penalty for late filing, but several states, including California, can dock a late filer's refund.

Consider tax-free investments. Most municipal bonds issued in your state of residence pay interest that is exempt from federal, state, and local taxes—a break that can be especially valuable in high-tax states such as California, Massachusetts, and New York. For instance, a New York City couple in the 28% federal income tax bracket—which works out to a 35.69% combined federal, state, and local bracket—who buy munis yielding 7% (minimum investment: $5,000) would have to find a taxable investment paying 10.88% to make as much money after tax.

For an initial investment of about $1,000 to $2,500, you can get into municipal-bond funds that hold the obligations of your state only and, thus, provide the same federal, state, and local tax exemptions as individually held muni-bonds. You may have to settle for slightly lower yields from single-state funds than from national funds that hold securities from many states, but the added tax savings could make up the difference.

If you do invest in a national muni-bond fund, the portion of your payout that is attributable to your state's bonds is exempt from state and possibly local taxes. Check your year-end statement or call the fund to get the amount. For your savings, you might consider single-state money-market funds. U.S. Treasury securities also pay interest that is free of state and local tax, although it is subject to federal tax. You can invest in Treasuries individually or through government bond funds. The funds' yields are generally one-half to one percentage point lower than those on individual Treasuries. Be sure to ask if all or just part of the yield is state-tax-exempt in your state, since some government funds hold federal agency securities, whose interest is not always exempted.

Research an area's taxes before you move. Among the key considerations: only the District of Columbia and five states—Indiana, New Mexico, and Utah and, in certain cases, North Dakota and Vermont—exempt interest on out-of-state munis from income tax; 13 states tax Social Security benefits that are federally taxable.

Challenge an unfair property assessment. Successfully appealing such an assessment could save you hundreds of dollars a year in property taxes. (See "Challenging Your Tax Assessment" below.) You are on solid ground if the assessment is based on incorrect or overlooked information. The assessor may have overstated your home's square footage, for example, or neglected to give you a tax credit for being 65 or older, a veteran, or disabled. Perhaps your house suffered damage or your area experienced a general drop in housing prices. Begin by calling your local assessor's office. If the local office can't help, file a challenge with your community board of appeals—a simple, usually cost-free procedure. If the appeals board rejects your challenge, you can go to court or the state review board, but you will probably need to hire a lawyer.

Plan your estate. Half the states impose estate or inheritance taxes independent of federal estate taxes. Consult an attorney for ways to reduce or eliminate such taxes through charitable gifts, trusts, and other strategies. (For more information, see "Making Your Legacy Trouble-Free" on page 186.)

Challenging Your Tax Assessment

Are you paying more than your fair share of property taxes? Here's how to cut that bill by upwards of 20%.

You probably don't have to look beyond your own backyard for a homeowner who's steamed about his property tax bill. In fact, local property taxes, which are up nearly 50% over the past five years in some places, may well be the fastest-rising tax you pay.

More galling still, if your area's housing prices have turned soft, your tax bill may reflect your home's higher value of several years ago. Or your tax assessment, even if it's up to date, may simply be wrong. Experts estimate that 40% of the time overworked tax assessors set incorrect values on houses—most often in the tax collector's favor. The assessments are typically 5% to 20% too high and cost homeowners $150 to $1,000 in extra taxes each year. Assessing property is not an exact science. It's a process, open to interpretation and change.

As homeowners have found, however, you can make the process work to your benefit—if you know how to complain to city hall. Real estate consultants insist that if you have evidence to support your case, you can get a reduction. The most obvious time to consider a protest is right after you receive a new assessment. Many localities, in fact, allow homeowners to appeal only within 14 to 60 days after such notices are mailed out. Wholesale reassessments of all homes in an area, known as revaluations—"revals" to assessors—typically occur every two to eight years. Otherwise, you can expect a reassessment after you make a substantial renovation, such as adding a room or a swimming pool.

Revenue-hungry municipalities often use revals to hike assessments aggressively as a means of bringing in extra tax receipts. Some towns reassess homes at 10% or 20% over their market value. The city officials know that even if you appeal and win, they will have a nice interest-free, short-term loan in the meantime.

You needn't wait for a reassessment to appeal, however. Many older valuations rest on incorrect or outdated information that can be challenged at any time. When housing values soar, cities often race to reassess properties and sometimes let assessors base their estimates on quickie drive-by visits rather than on careful home inspections. As a result, for example, your home's square footage can be mismeasured.

If you think your assessment seems excessive—perhaps after comparing yours with your neighbors'—you can fight the battle yourself or you can hire a local property tax consultant. Since consultants typically charge steep contingency fees of about 50% of your first year's tax savings, as a rule you are better off on your own, armed perhaps with a book such as *Taxpayer's Survival Kit* (Tax Management Group, 4845 Ronson Court, San Diego, CA 92111; $54.95) or *How to Lower Your Property Taxes* (King Associates, 143 South Road, Chester, NJ 07930; $39).

Start by visiting your local assessor's office and asking for a copy of the worksheet, known as the property record card, that he used to estimate your home's value. Also, pin down the meaning of any abbreviations or codes on the card. Question him closely to learn exactly how the municipality calculates your assessed value working with the information on the card. Finally, ask for a list of all available exemptions, such as those for war veterans or homeowners aged 65 or older, so you can be sure you received any you deserve.

When you get back home, verify all the information on your property card. The data will include your house's age; square footage; number of rooms and fireplaces; the condition of your attic, roof, and garage; descriptions of

Learning Assessor-Speak

To challenge your property tax bill successfully, you must understand assessor-speak. Here are plain-English definitions of five important terms:

Equalization ratio. The relationship between house values set by assessors and current sales prices, expressed as a percentage. Sometimes known as the sales ratio.

Millage. The property tax rate expressed in thousandths of a dollar. If the tax levy is 50 mills, a homeowner will pay $50 for every $1,000 of assessed valuation.

Reassessment. The tax assessor's revision of a house's value for tax purposes, for example, after you undertake a substantial renovation.

Revaluation. An area-wide revision of all tax assessments, often done every two to eight years.

Statutory ratio. The percentage of market value at which houses are assessed for tax purposes.

the heating and air-conditioning systems; the size of your lot; and both the quality of your view and of the neighborhood. Make sure that the card also notes any features that detract from your property, such as being located next to a freeway or an industrial park.

Your next task—determining whether your assessment is fair—may be far more complicated. Some localities assess property for tax purposes at fair market value—that is, what you would get if you sold. In most communities, however, assessors estimate the home's market value and then apply a formula, known as the statutory or classification ratio, to arrive at the tax assessment.

If your community has just gone through a reval at full market value, you need only that number to figure out whether you are indeed being treated fairly. Otherwise, ask the assessor for the statutory ratio, as well as for the current equalization ratio, which lets you compare assessed values with actual selling prices of properties.

For example, say that you believe your house is worth $150,000. The town has it assessed for $32,500, the statutory ratio is 25%, and your equalization ratio is 65%. What does the town think your house is worth? First, divide the assessment ($32,500) by the statutory ratio (25%). Result: $130,000. Next, divide this figure by the equalization ratio (65%). The result: $200,000. That's 33% more than your own $150,000 estimate. (Because the computations can be complicated and vary dramatically, you may want to seek help from a clerk at the county board that oversees assessments.)

Of course, you can't simply march into city hall with your arithmetic and expect your house will be revalued to $150,000 from $200,000. Rather, you must prove it by collecting evidence of the current market values of three to five nearby houses like yours that have been sold recently, ideally no more than six months before your assessment. Your assessor or a local real estate agent can probably provide that information.

To make sure the houses you cite are similar, compare their property record cards, if your assessor will let you see them, or look up their sales records in the county courthouse.

Also, drive by each house to verify that the exteriors and locations approximate your home's, being careful to adjust the sales prices accordingly. Should your research show that the assessor's market value of your house is at least 10% out of line, you have an excellent chance of winning an appeal.

If your town's revaluation was done more than two years ago, your home's assessment may now be out of line. Check by asking the assessor for a copy of the latest assessment/sales ratio study, which shows how assessments stack up to sales prices. If the ratio is 65%, for example, it means that homes in your area are assessed at 65% of their selling prices on average. Therefore, if your assessment is, say, 75% more than the fair market value of your house, you're overassessed.

You generally appeal an assessment at an informal meeting with the assessor at which you can point out factual errors on your property card. Be sure to bring along any useful documentation. For instance, if your property card has the wrong square footage, present your survey proving the correct figure.

If the assessor rejects your challenge, you can fill out an appeal form, usually available from the assessor, requesting a review of his decision by the local board of appeals, which is typically made up of three to five local business people. When you go before the board, take along your sales comparisons and other relevant evidence, such as recent appraisals, photographs, or floor plans. Give board members photocopies of your documents before you summarize your appeal orally. Conclude your challenge by proposing an alternative assessment. Above all, don't antagonize the board by losing your temper.

In most cases, you'll receive the board's decision by mail within six weeks or so. If you lose but still believe you have a solid case, you can appeal to a higher level, often a state review board that follows a procedure much like the local one. Should you lose there, you can go on to a state tax court. Before you do, though, ask yourself whether an extraordinary amount of money is actually at stake. The cost of hiring a lawyer—typically $250 to $1,000—should not exceed the tax savings you think you can win.

Smart Ways to Beat the Feds

A little planning can save you a lot of money. Take advantage of these tax-cutting moves for the coming year.

It is never too soon for you and your tax professional to plot a tax-slashing strategy. Almost all serious tax savings are made in such a deliberate, unrushed way. Acting early on the following advice offers you the best hope for substantive relief from federal taxes over the next year or two:

Make gifts early. The income thrown off by an interest- or dividend-bearing gift will show up on someone else's tax return, not yours. The sooner you make the gift, the greater the shift of income. If the gift is to a child under 14, remember that unearned income of more than $1,000 will be taxed at your rate. Children 14 or older pay taxes at their rate, typically 15%, compared with their parents' 28% or 33%. The law allows you to make as many tax-free gifts as you wish but limits them to $10,000 a recipient ($20,000 if given together with your spouse).

Turn passive losses into more lucrative active ones. If you have invested in a business but aren't actively involved in running it, the tax law regards your investment as passive. Your income from it can then be offset only by losses on other passive investments. But if you spend more than 500 hours a year working at the business—except for rental properties, which are subject to a far less stringent requirement—the investment generally qualifies as active, giving you several tax joys. Chief among them: Losses may be used to offset income from any source, including salary. Tax

experts recommend that you block out your 500-plus hours in January. You might need to devote 12 or 13 weeks to helping run a retail business you own a piece of, so if you start early, you might find a couple of weeks in February and two more in April, and so on. The important thing is not to wait. If you suddenly wake up to this need in September, how will you be able to squeeze in the required hours before the year is over?

Pay off your personal debts. 1990 was the last year you could deduct any of the interest on consumer loans. (For 1989, the write-off was 20%; for 1990 it was 10%.) And you can reap a fairly fabulous bonus in the bargain: For instance, by paying off a credit-card balance that bears typical annual interest of 19%, you get the equivalent of a pretax 26% investment return if you are in the 28% bracket. If you can't afford to liquidate your personal debts, don't try to fool the IRS about the interest on them. The agency will be looking in particular this year for taxpayers who, say, disguise personal debt as business loans so that they can deduct all of the interest.

Fund IRAs and Keoghs early. You should invest at least a portion of your contribution to these retirement accounts at the start of the year rather than waiting until the last minute—April 15 of the following year. The difference in tax-deferred earnings becomes substantial in 10 or 15 years. For example, if you deposit $10,000 a year in a Keogh in

January and it earns 10% a year, your balance 15 years later would be $375,004. If you wait until the last minute each year, however, you would wind up with only $329,846, a difference of $45,158.

Start a paper trail to preserve your child-care credit. You must file Form 2441, identifying your care giver by name and Social Security number (or taxpayer ID number in the case of a day-care center). If you don't, you can't take the credit of up to $720 a child for care of kids 13 or under. The IRS wants the data so that its computer snoops can cross-check your care provider's tax return and make sure that you made both Social Security and unemployment insurance payments for him or her. Here, too, you must file the proper forms (942 for Social Security and 940 for unemployment insurance) or lose the child-care credit and get socked with penalties.

Explore optional benefits at work. Working parents with joint incomes of at least $20,000 can come out ahead by forgoing the tax credit and paying child-care expenses from a flexible-spending account at work. (If you use the account to the maximum for child care, you can't also claim the credit.) In the 28% bracket, a couple with one child would save $1,400 by paying for care from a flexible-spending account, but they would get only $480 by taking the child-care tax credit. You must give your employer the child-care provider's taxpayer identification number or Social Security number. The IRS allows you to put aside as much as $5,000 of your before-tax salary in such an account for child-care expenses. Depending on your company's plan, you may have to set up the account before the end of each calendar year. If you've missed the deadline for this year, make this a high-priority item for the coming year.

Take another look at series EE savings bonds. These simple investments are gaining new respect. Since EEs are free from state and local taxes, they have considerable allure for upper-bracket residents of tax-heavy states. Moreover, for bonds purchased after December 31, 1989, the interest on EE bonds is free of federal taxes if the proceeds are used for higher education expenses for you, your spouse, or your child. There are restrictions, however: Most notably, the benefit phases out for a married couple filing jointly with adjusted gross income of $60,000 to $90,000, or single parents with AGI of $40,000 to $55,000.

Start keeping tax-smart records. Being fastidious about documenting your deductible expenses can save you lots of tax dollars. If you use your car for business, for example, the IRS lets you either take a flat 26¢-a-mile deduction for 1990 or—if you keep careful records—write off your actual work-related expenses for gasoline, auto insurance, parking fees, tolls, and other car costs.

Married with Deductions

If you and your spouse both earn taxable income and normally file a joint tax return, you might want to do a little arithmetic to see if you'd pay less tax by filing separate returns. You may find that you can then claim deductions that you lose by filing jointly.

For example, if one of you had hefty, unreimbursed medical expenses, only the amount that exceeds 7.5% of your adjusted gross income (AGI) is deductible. Let's say your joint AGI totals $70,000. Your unreimbursed medical bills would then have to top $5,250 before you could deduct anything. But if you filed separately, the AGI of the spouse who incurred the costs might be low enough to enable him or her to take the deduction.

Make sure, however, that the pluses of filing separately outweigh the minuses. First, your tax rate may be slightly higher than if you file jointly. Second, you won't be able to take some credits, such as the one for child-care expenses that can save you as much as $1,400. And if you receive Social Security benefits, generally half of them will be taxable because you will not be able to apply the usual base amount exemption, which protects your benefits from taxes.

Shift that stock. If you have appreciated shares that are ready to be sold, consider making a gift of them to your child if he or she is 14 or older. Your child can then sell the stock, paying tax on the capital gain at his or her rate—typically 15%, as opposed to your 28% or 33%. On a gain of $10,000, your family will save $1,300.

Share that stock. One variation on the stock transfer is to register the shares jointly in your name and your child's. This way, you give him or her half the stock as well as half the tax on the dividends. When the stock is sold, the child pays tax on half the gain at 15%. For example, on $20,000 of securities yielding a 10% profit, the first $500 that goes to the child would be tax-free; on the other $500, he would owe $75 in taxes versus $280 if you had kept the shares in your name. This approach is useful to parents who want to retain some control. To avoid gift taxes, the value of the child's portion of the stock must be $10,000 or less—$20,000 if given jointly with your spouse.

To avoid a big capital-gains hit, give an investment to charity. Tax experts suggest this little-used technique to clients who have highly appreciated securities that are not throwing off much income but would result in a heavy capital-gains tax if sold. You contribute the securities, usually at least $25,000, to an irrevocable charitable remainder annuity trust and designate a relatively small percentage of their value, perhaps 4%, for the charity after a specified number of years. You decide how much income you want from the trust annually, working out the numbers from IRS tables with your tax lawyer or accountant, whose fees should be negligible. The trustee, named by you, then sells the securities and reinvests the proceeds. Since it is an irrevocable charitable trust, it pays no tax on the gains. You also get a small one-time tax break based on the present value of what will eventually be your contribution.

Fashion your own annuity. This tactic is simpler than it sounds and, in fact, is encouraged by many nonprofit organizations for donors willing to put up $5,000 or more. Here's how the transaction works: You make a contribution, for example, to your university, on condition that it set up a charitable gift annuity that will pay you an annual sum. The size depends on the amount of your gift and your age—the older you are when you make the gift, the larger your annuity payment. At age 60, you might get a return of 7%. The value of the annuity cannot exceed 90% of the contribution. Such annuities last for the life of the beneficiary. You can start receiving checks right away or defer them. Either way, in the year you make the gift, you get a one-time deduction based on the difference between the amount you have given and the value today of all the projected annuity payments. For example, at age 60, you would receive $3,500 a year for life from a $50,000 gift. The value of those payments at the time you make the gift is $26,500, producing a deduction of $23,500. The paperwork is minimal: a one-page agreement between you and the institution.

Consider tax-saving funds for the generous. Another charitable arrangement that can help you as well as your favorite charity is a pooled-income fund. Such funds operate much like mutual funds, but they are administered and invested by educational institutions and other charities. Your gift is pooled with others, and you and the other donors share the returns. When a donor dies, a pro rata portion of the fund goes to the charity. Your deduction depends on your age, the fund's rate of return, and IRS tables—an equation the charity can run off for you. Pooled funds are simple—no lawyers are required—but still give you all the tax advantages of the trusts, including income, deductions, and lower capital-gains and estate taxes.

Look into a life insurance trust. This can be an effective move to protect your wealth from estate taxes. A life insurance payout is often enough to propel the total value of a middle-income breadwinner's estate above $600,000, which triggers federal taxes. You can avoid the problem by placing your life insurance in an irrevocable trust for any beneficiary. As with all irrevocable trusts, you must give up all ownership rights to the policy; for instance, you can't borrow against it. To avoid any taint of ownership and to reduce taxable assets further, you can fund the insurance premiums with tax-free gifts to the trust, using a portion of the annual gift exclusion of $10,000 for singles and $20,000 for couples. The transfer of a life insurance policy to the trust must take place more than three years before your death.

Protect retirement funds. If you are planning to retire this year and move to a state with lower taxes, have your company send your pension checks directly to you. Some states— California and New Jersey in particular—will pursue you for income taxes if the authorities can claim that you earned your pension there. More states are looking into this potential revenue source, so check before you move.

Roll over that lump sum. Accountants often tell people that with the low federal income tax rates today, they should make lump-sum withdrawals from tax-deferred retirement accounts such as 401(k)s, pay the taxes, and reinvest what's left. Tax experts say, however, that you preserve more of your funds and ultimately earn more by rolling over your retirement money into an IRA, where it can continue to grow untaxed.

IRS Phone Advisers Are Getting Better—Finally

And now for some relatively comforting news. *Money*'s third annual survey of the folks at the IRS who answer your queries by phone showed they did passably well—a big improvement over past years. In *Money*'s 1988 survey, these employees, officially known as taxpayer service representatives, dispensed erroneous advice nearly half the time. In 1989, after the agency reformed its training program, the figure dropped slightly to 41%. In 1990, Uncle Sam's helpers answered only 28% of *Money*'s questions incorrectly.

What gives? IRS spokesman Henry Holmes credits the training program. The 11-week regimen now puts more emphasis on problem areas. But he modestly adds: "There is no doubt that our accuracy rate needs improvement. We're trying to find ways to ensure better-quality service." Efforts include keeping more seasonal temps full time and getting more temps to return annually. All IRS service representatives also now have what the agency calls "probe and response" booklets to guide them through follow-up questions on difficult tax issues.

Each year, *Money* placed calls to 100 IRS service reps across the country. Each respondent was asked one of 10 questions, and each question was posed to 10 different reps. The 1990 questions, typical of what reps are likely to encounter, were prepared with the help of C.P.A. Martin Nergaard of Hansen Jergenson & Company in Minneapolis.

Most service reps aced the questions if they could look up the answers in a 1040 instruction booklet or in a basic IRS publication. But they tended to give misleading advice if they had to dig. For example, nine of 10 gave incomplete replies when asked whether you could deduct a deceased person's medical expenses on his or her final income tax return. All of the reps correctly said yes, but only one said that it was necessary to include a statement waiving the right to deduct the expenses on the deceased's estate-tax return.

Service reps were generally genial, with a few ugly exceptions. When a Boston rep was asked to send a written confirmation of his advice, he gruffly replied: "You have to call Washington for that. If you don't think the answer is good enough, you can come in to the IRS in Boston and discuss it with someone on the first floor." He was wrong as well as rude: He should have said that you could get a written reply within 10 days if you sent your question in writing to a local IRS office.

Getting Your Taxes—and Your Accountant—Under Control

The 10 most critical questions to ask your tax pro.

Does this scene sound familiar? It's mid-March and you drop by your accountant's office, just as you do every year. You deposit a wad of papers on his or her desk—W-2s, 1099s, and assorted other records—and chat briefly, as much about the weather as about taxes. Twelve minutes later, you're back on the street. What you've just accomplished may have given you an enormous sense of relief, but it hasn't done a thing to help cut your taxes. In fact, you've just blown your biggest opportunity of the year to get your tax life under control.

Truth is, a tax pro isn't likely to perform aggressively on your behalf unless you take an active role in managing your partnership. That doesn't mean you must immerse yourself in the 648-page *U.S. Master Tax Guide* or look over your accountant's shoulder while he or she prepares your Form 1040. After all, you're probably paying a pro anywhere from $50 to $150 an hour to interpret the tax law and crunch numbers for you.

Your job is to keep your accountant abreast of everything you do that affects your tax bill. And since you can't possibly be aware of what all those items are, you'll need to know the right questions to ask. The following can serve as a checklist:

Am I taking all of the deductions and credits I'm due? This is the if-you-ask-only-one-question question. A good accountant will give you a master list of write-offs to review. Did you know, for example, that you can claim a $102

credit if you bought a new diesel-powered car in 1990? Make that $198 if you bought a diesel-powered light truck or van.

Of course, in most cases, you should also try to bunch miscellaneous itemized deductions, such as unreimbursed business expenses, since they are deductible only to the extent that they exceed 2% of your adjusted gross income (AGI). The same advice applies to unreimbursed medical expenses: You deduct only the portion above 7.5% of AGI. Loading up on such expenses every second year, for example, can put you over the top.

Are there any gray areas that could affect my return? Gray areas are where great C.P.A.s shine. Since taxpayers are constantly challenging the Internal Revenue Service's interpretation of the law, some recent court rulings could cut your taxes. For example, cases involving the home-office deduction have resulted in write-offs being allowed for musicians who practice at home and business consultants who work there. A classic example is the deductibility of work clothes. In general, the cost of uniforms and other work apparel, including their cleaning and repair, is deductible only if you need the clothing for work and it isn't suitable for wear during your off-hours. Still, musicians have been permitted to deduct the cost of formal wear, and plumbers have written off special shoes and gloves.

How will marriage—or divorce—affect my taxes? Unless you have already handed a huge, nonrefundable deposit to a caterer, give your accountant some say in choosing your wedding day. You might save enough on taxes to pay for your honeymoon. If you and your intended earn comparable incomes, the marriage penalty—the additional tax you pay as joint filers over what you would owe if you filed as singles—generally makes it worthwhile to postpone your nuptials until next year. Reason: Your marital status at year-end determines your filing status. But it pays to tie the knot posthaste if, for example, you sell stock for a significant gain and your fiancé(e) conveniently suffers an offsetting loss.

Divorce can present innumerable tax traps, so you and your lawyer should seek your accountant's help in negotiating a property settlement. Your pro can also value some of the assets that may be on the bargaining table in a divorce, such as a pension. Once you reach a settlement, don't deviate from it without consulting your tax expert.

Can I cut my tax bill by reporting my child's unearned income on my return? Parents can claim unearned income of a child under 14 on their returns starting with the 1989 tax year—if the child had no withholding or estimated tax payments and received more than $500 but less than $5,000 in interest and dividends. Any amount below $500 is tax-free because of the child's standard deduction; above $5,000, a separate return must be filed for the child. The tax will be about the same whichever course you take, but there are other factors to ponder. By counting your child's unearned income as your own, for example, you will increase your net investment income and be able to claim a larger deduction for investment interest if you buy stock on margin. On the other hand, you'll also raise your adjusted gross income, thus making it harder to write off miscellaneous itemized deductions and medical expenses.

Should I worry about the alternative minimum tax (AMT)? You should if you intend to acquire shares in your company by exercising incentive stock options, give appreciated property to charity, or take big deductions for depreciation, real estate taxes, or state and local taxes. These are some of the tax preferences that can trigger the AMT, which is intended to minimize the value of very large write-offs. If the AMT threatens you this year, meet with your accountant sometime between late summer and mid-October to compute your tax under both regular and AMT rules. You pay whichever tab is higher. Once you run the numbers, you may find you shouldn't make a big charitable contribution this year because the appreciation in the value of property you contribute is added back to your income under the AMT. Some states have their own version of the minimum tax. Escaping it may require additional planning by you and your accountant.

Am I doing everything I should to protect the tax-favored status of my retirement accounts? Misinterpreting the rules pertaining to retirement plans can cost you a bundle. Consider what happened to one man who wanted to withdraw $2,000 from his company-sponsored, tax-deferred savings plan. In the past, employees could take out their contributions without penalty. But this individual didn't realize that the plan's bylaws had changed to prohibit partial withdrawals. So when the man asked for $2,000, he received a check for $43,000—the sum of his contributions plus their earnings. The unhappy man had to write checks for $19,300 in taxes and a $4,300 early-withdrawal penalty.

It is also important to consult a tax pro before deciding whether to keep a lump-sum distribution from a company retirement plan or roll it over into an Individual Retirement Account. If you keep the cash, for example, you may be eligible to calculate the tax on it using favorable five- or 10-year forward averaging. If you decide to roll over a lump sum, you can put only its taxable portion into an IRA. If you roll over after-tax money by mistake, the IRS will slap a 6% excise tax on it—unless you catch the error and rectify it before the filing deadline.

There's even more to discuss with your tax pro if you're an entrepreneur or a moonlighter. For example, you must set up a Keogh plan by December 31 even if you don't intend to contribute to it until you file your tax return next year.

What should I consider before buying a second home? Your accountant can help you reap the greatest tax rewards—and negotiate the maddening tax complications—of a rental or vacation home. Ask him or her to figure out whether you should treat the property as a business or a second residence. To qualify a property as a rental, you can use it only 14 days a year or 10% of the time it's actually rented, whichever is greater. But the Tax Reform Act of 1986 restricted the deductibility of rental losses against other income and reduced

many other tax breaks associated with rental properties. As a result, you may be better off treating your hideaway as a second residence, because your mortgage interest and real estate taxes on the property will then be fully deductible.

What's the best way to borrow? With the deduction for consumer interest about to vanish in 1991 (you could deduct 10% in 1990), maintaining a credit-card balance is just plain dumb. Talk to your accountant about using an interest-deductible second mortgage or home-equity line of credit to pay off your consumer loans.

If you're suffering from a short-term cash-flow crunch, your accountant might suggest that you take money out of your IRA. You will not incur taxes or penalties as long as you redeposit the money within 60 days. You can, however, pull off this neat trick only once a year.

Am I having enough withheld from my salary or paying enough estimated tax? Withholdings from your pay plus estimated tax payments must equal the lesser of 90% of your tax liability this year or 100% of your bill last year. Otherwise you'll get socked with a penalty, now about 11% of the shortfall. You shouldn't necessarily adjust your withholding and estimated tax payments to match last year's tax liability, though. If you sold a business or stock for a large capital gain last year, you don't want to pay estimated taxes based on the assumption that your income is going to be just as high this year. Instead, ask your accountant to do a projection based on your expected income this year.

What should I consider before taking a capital gain or loss? Your tax pro can help you determine whether you can use a loss to offset all or part of a gain. Losses are deductible dollar for dollar from capital gains and generally up to $3,000 of ordinary income each year. Remaining net losses can be carried forward and used to offset capital gains or income in future years. If deferring a stock market killing until next year makes sense, you

Flexible Spending Accounts Offer a Terrific Deal

Tax-advantaged flexible spending accounts (FSAs) for health-care expenses, available to employees of about one in three large companies, are more attractive than ever. If your employer offers you one, you should probably grab it.

FSAs allow you to set aside pretax income from each paycheck for two kinds of expenses: generally up to $3,000 a year for medical bills and $5,000 for dependent-care costs. The money in your account is exempt from federal income and Social Security taxes, as well as most states' income taxes.

In the past, health-care FSAs had at least one drawback: You were not fully reimbursed for a bill until you had enough money in your account to cover it. This year, however, your employer will reimburse you as soon as you present a medical bill. So if your expenses are bunched early in the year—some expensive dental work, for example—your company, in effect, will give you an interest-free loan. You will, of course, repay it in the course of the year as money is deducted from your paychecks. Unfortunately, dependent-care expenses will still be reimbursed the old way—when your contributions cover the expenses.

can sell short against the box. To do so, instruct your broker to sell borrowed shares to lock in your gain. In the new year, you hand over your own shares to repay the loan. Another defensive strategy is to buy a put on the stock that doesn't expire until next January. The put gives you the right to sell a specific number of shares at a stipulated price within a designated period. You can exercise the put and protect your gain if the stock's price sinks. If the stock continues to soar, however, you should let the put expire. When you sell the stock in the new year, you'll realize your gain less the price of the put.

A Break for Home-Office Users

The Tax Court opens the door for deductions.

The home-office deduction is one of the most closely guarded goodies dispensed to taxpayers by the Internal Revenue Service. If you qualify for it, you can deduct part of your rent or your home's light and heat bills, and you can depreciate the portion of your house you use as an office. Since almost anyone can dream up a need for a tax-cutting home office, the IRS for years has allowed the deduction only for people who earn their income at home or meet clients there.

So you can imagine the consternation at the IRS in January 1990 when the U.S. Tax Court signaled that it will henceforth allow deductions for home offices that are essential to running a business, even if you do the actual work someplace else.

This change throws open the dispensation to many doctors, accountants, sales people, computer programmers, caterers, musicians, contractors, moonlighters, and others who work at home because they don't have offices elsewhere. Still shut out: the legions who bring home work from a regular job and do it in the family den.

Before you start ordering color-coordinated desktop publishing gear, bear in mind that the IRS has not given up. In March of that year, the agency took the highly unusual step of announcing its intention to fight the Tax Court's decision and cautioning taxpayers that it would continue to deny questionable home-office deductions.

At the heart of the fight is the definition of what constitutes the focal point of your business. To counter widespread home-office abuses—teachers, for instance, were claiming write-offs because they corrected papers at home—Congress in 1976 required that the office space in your home had to be used exclusively and on a regular basis for your trade or business. In addition, you had to run your business out of the office or see clients or patients there.

To clarify the rules, the Tax Court in 1980 established the focal point test. Essentially, this held that a taxpayer's principal place of business—the focal point of his activities—must be where he provides goods and services and generates revenues. If, however, you administered your business from a home office but actually performed your services and generated your income elsewhere, you were out of luck.

All that changed when the Tax Court ruled in the case of Dr. Nader E. Soliman of Gaithersburg, Maryland. In 1983, he was working as an anesthesiologist at three hospitals in the Washington, D.C. area. Since none of them provided him with the office he needed to schedule appointments, bill clients, and prepare lectures, he converted one of the three bedrooms in his McLean, Virginia apartment. Following the letter of the tax law, he used the room exclusively and regularly—around three hours a day—for business.

That wasn't good enough for the IRS, which said Dr. Soliman had failed the focal point test. Since he performed his services and earned his income in the hospitals, the agency argued, they were his principal place of business. The agency denied deductions of $1,259 for home-office expenses and depreciation and $3,758 for the business use of the car that the doctor drove from his apartment-office to the three hospitals.

In Tax Court, his lawyer argued that without an office the doctor would not have been able to sustain his practice. The court agreed, noting that the law was not enacted to compel a taxpayer to rent office space rather than work out of his home.

In effect, the court overruled its own focal point test. From now on, according to the decision, if you have an office at home that is essential to your business, spend substantial time there, and maintain no other office, you are entitled to home-office deductions even if you earn your income elsewhere.

Tax professionals are confident that the decision will be upheld. The consensus among other pros *Money* interviewed: If you qualify under the new ruling, take the write-off. In addition, if you think you qualified in earlier years, review your returns for the past three years—as far back as you can go in amending returns—and file Form 1040X for refunds.

How to Fight Back When the IRS Is Wrong

Four basic letters can help you prevail when the agency demands extra tax money from you that it doesn't deserve.

If recent history is a guide, some 36 million notices of additional tax and penalties due will appear in mailboxes around the country this year. More than 35% of those notorious notices can be attributed to one of four common failings by taxpayers: making math errors; filing tax returns late without the benefit of an official extension; declaring income, interest, or dividends that differ from the amount your employer, broker, or bank reported paying to you; failing to send in the right amount of quarterly estimated taxes.

In 1989, the IRS' letter-writing blitz took in an estimated $15.3 billion in taxes and penalties—an average of $425 for every notice mailed. Yet, behind that apparent triumph of tax law micro-enforcement lurks a sloppy little secret: A convincing case can be made that at least $7 billion of that money should never have been collected at all because around half of those imposing official notices were inaccurate. Consider the following:

● A 1988 study of IRS letters to taxpayers by the federal watchdog General Accounting Office turned up so much evidence of errors that at a congressional hearing on the matter Republican Representative Christopher Shays of Connecticut questioned how the IRS could even contemplate prosecuting anybody when

47% of all the written responses to taxpayers are incorrect.

● Interviews by *Money* with leading tax lawyers and accountants as well as IRS officials support the GAO findings. Charles Peoples, IRS assistant commissioner for returns processing, admits flatly: "We don't have good methods for detecting and correcting errors."

● A telephone poll of *Money* subscribers by the Gallup Organization in late February 1990 revealed that half of that generally higher-income group have received such notices—one in four in the past two years. A stunning 45% of those who contested their notices report that the IRS claims were totally incorrect, and an additional 24% said that they were at least partially wrong. What's more, of those who challenged the IRS on their own, 53% wound up paying nothing and another 17% succeeded in getting the bill reduced.

The IRS declined to comment directly on *Money*'s findings. Wilson Fadely, an agency spokesman, instead cited an internal study that showed a 9.1% error rate in notices sent out in February 1990.

But here's what really stings. Millions of taxpayers are paying up whether or not they should, even though 69% of *Money* subscribers polled, who put up a fight, report that their notices were at least partially inaccurate. Clearly, individuals are caving in to questionable demands for more money that would propel them to the phone in a second if the bill came from some bank or credit-card company. What they ought to be doing is fighting back against IRS inefficiency.

Why such abject submission? Reason No. 1 is simple, undifferentiated fear of fighting. The IRS is infamous for Star Chamber audits, summary confiscation of property, and all-seeing, imperious independence. So when a taxpayer spots that ominous envelope, !RS seal, and OFFICIAL BUSINESS stamp, panic strikes. It's not surprising, then, that two-thirds of the IRS' $15.3 billion take in 1989 was from first notices alone. A second reason for taxpayer timorousness is that the notices tend to be confusing, compounding the maddening complexity of tax law itself. And finally, tax professionals attest that all too many intimidated taxpayers fear that if they don't pay, they will suffer far worse. They begin to imagine that the IRS will come to audit them and perhaps end up questioning all sorts of deductions in the process.

Who ever stops to realize that the army of about 3,300 IRS tax examiners managing the annual flow of more than 120 million notices and follow-up letters are low paid (typical starting wage: $14,573 a year) and poorly trained? They are not at all like the sharp lawyers and C.P.A.s you meet when you're called down to the local IRS office for an audit. Furthermore, about a third of the total 115,360 IRS work force are only temps hired for the crush of the filing season, often trained for a week and thrown onto the barricades.

Who among taxpayers would guess that the agency's data network is really an antiquated system designed 28 years ago, a sagging patchwork of Sperry Univac, Honeywell, and Control Data equipment and outdated magnetic tape that gets shipped around the country not electronically but in planes and trucks?

And who would think that a federal agency would have to operate under such squalid working conditions? At the IRS Service Center in Andover, Massachusetts, for example, 3,400 employees labor in a dreary, largely windowless space the size of five football fields. Mail clerks, who begin the processing of returns, sit at paper-shuffling nightmares called Tingle tables. Each clerk confronts 18 bins, stacked three high, into which he or she is expected to sort 265 returns and related documents an hour. To combat this mind-numbing work, many clerks wear headsets tuned to their favorite rock stations. The roof leaks so strategically that during heavy rainfalls, employees have to position wastebaskets on top of their computers to prevent them from being drowned. Supplies are so limited that if you need a stapler, you may have to barter your calculator with another worker for it. The end result: According to a 1988 GAO study of four IRS processing centers, Andover had to undergo the highest rate of adjustments—that is,

Late Filing

Department of Treasury
Internal Revenue Service

If you have any questions, refer to the information

Date of this notice:
Social Security Number:
Document Locator Number:
Form: 1040

Tax Year Ended: 1988

Call: 512-462-8600 LOCAL AUSTIN
1-800-424-1040 OTHER TEXAS
or
Write: Chief, Taxpayer Assistance Section
Internal Revenue Service Center

Request for Payment

Our records show you owe $46,730.73 on your income tax. If you believe this amount is not correct, please see the back of this notice. Make your check or money order payable to the Internal Revenue Service. Please write your social security number on your payment and mail it with the bottom part of this notice. An envelope is enclosed for your convenience. Thank you for your cooperation.

If you write, be sure to attach the bottom part of this notice. Include your telephone number and the best time to call.

Allo

Tax

Aug. 11, 1989

Internal Revenue Service
Austin, Texas 73301

Gentlemen:

Enclosed is an affidavit responding to your notice and assessment for allegedly filing and paying our 1988 tax return late. A copy of that notice is enclosed.

It is in error. We filed our return on April 14, 1989, and it was apparently lost in the postal system. We are enclosing copies of the check we sent with our 1040 and the checks written in sequence before and after that check. As you will see, they were all dated April 13.

Please change your records and abate the additional tax, penalty and interest due, according to the notice.

AFFIDAVIT

We hereby state that our 1988 U.S. Individual Income Tax Return, Form 1040, was mailed to the Internal Revenue Service in Austin, Texas 73301, on Friday, April 14, 1989.

_____
Taxpayer

_____
Spouse

_____
Date signed

_____
Date signed

Certified to and sworn before me:

_____
Notary

The post office is the likeliest late-filing culprit. If you wisely sent your return by certified mail, receipt requested, just write to the IRS stating when you mailed your return and enclose a copy of your receipt. Otherwise, send the IRS a letter and a notarized affidavit—like the ones above—plus copies of the check you sent with the return and the ones just before and after it to further verify the date. Consult the story for more guidance.

work done over again—because of errors.

Andover is no isolated case. Conditions at other IRS processing centers are equally Dickensian. One inevitable byproduct: In 1988, according to an agency-wide IRS study, 2 million documents—tax returns, 1099s, and the like—could not be located when IRS employees went looking for them in the files. Such chaos translates into low morale and an annual agency-wide turnover rate of 20%.

The Game's Five General Rules

Knowing what you now do about what's behind that high rate of errors in IRS notices, you can see that the agency's problems quickly become your tortures. So you are ready to move on to the next phase of your fight-back training:

Rule 1: Never ignore an IRS notice. The agency may be wounded, but it can still bite. The computer that cranks out these letters is programmed to send you a series of five to nine, depending on the purported error. Each letter arrives some four to five weeks after the preceding one—unless you send a response that stops them—and each is more threatening in tone until you are finally facing a lien on your bank account, wages, or other assets.

For example, a typical math-correction notice starts calmly enough: *As a result of an error we have corrected on your return, you owe the IRS $1,990.20. If you believe this amount is not correct, you may want to check your figures against ours. If you believe we made a mistake, please write to us and include the bottom part of this notice.* About five weeks later the first follow-up letter arrives, its tone noticeably darker: *The federal tax shown below has not been paid. It is overdue. Please pay it today.* Four weeks after that, the third letter shows up, with OVERDUE TAX printed accusingly across the top. The fourth letter grows ominous: *You did not respond to our previous notices. As a result, your account has been assigned for enforcement action.*

The fifth letter plays hardball. In the upper left corner is the legend: PAST DUE FINAL NOTICE (NOTICE OF INTENTION TO

LEVY). READ CAREFULLY. The body of the letter goes on to say: *This is your final notice . . . If full payment is not received within 10 days from the date of this notice, additional interest and penalties will be charged. A notice of federal tax lien may be filed . . . Your property or rights to property may be seized . . .* If the taxpayer still fails to respond, the lien process begins, and 30 days later an IRS revenue officer calls on the taxpayer to collect. If he is unable to arrange payment, he then puts a lien on assets. Most likely target: your bank account.

Rule 2: Respond quickly. When you get a notice, first check your records to determine who is in error. If it's you, send off your check within 10 days, and the matter will likely be ended. If the IRS is wrong, you can call in response—a local IRS phone number and 800-424-1040, the agency's national switchboard for such matters, are listed on your notice. Most practitioners, however, feel you should never phone. Chances are you'll get a busy signal or someone who can't help you anyway. Besides, even if you get some help, you'll have no record of it.

Instead, you should write to the IRS and send your response by certified mail, with a return receipt requested, and have all documents photocopied for your records. That way, if the only answer you get to your rebuttal is yet another computer notice—which is common—you can reply again, this time enclosing copies of your previous correspondence and of your certified mail receipt.

When you do win, you may not receive any IRS acknowledgment that your case has been settled. The notices will simply cease. Experts say that if the IRS stops sending threatening notices for 90 days after your reply, rest easy: No news is good news.

Rule 3: Keep your response simple but sharp. "A sixth-grade letter," one accountant calls it, so that the ill-trained, underpaid, overworked tax examiner will have no problems with it. Sentences must be like the ones in the sample letters that accompany this story—short and clear, addressed solely to the issue of your notice. No outrages, overexplanations, or

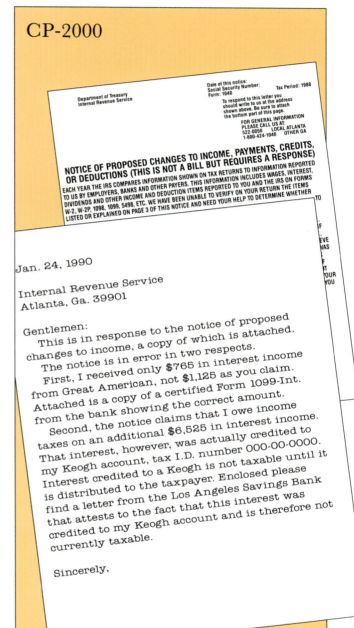

CP-2000

Department of Treasury
Internal Revenue Service

Date of this notice:
Social Security Number:
Form: 1040   Tax Period: 1988

To respond to this letter you should write to us at the address shown above. Be sure to attach the bottom part of this page.

FOR GENERAL INFORMATION
PLEASE CALL US AT:
522-0050   LOCAL ATLANTA
1-800-424-1040   OTHER GA

NOTICE OF PROPOSED CHANGES TO INCOME, PAYMENTS, CREDITS, OR DEDUCTIONS (THIS IS NOT A BILL BUT REQUIRES A RESPONSE)
EACH YEAR THE IRS COMPARES INFORMATION SHOWN ON TAX RETURNS TO INFORMATION REPORTED TO US BY EMPLOYERS, BANKS AND OTHER PAYERS. THIS INFORMATION INCLUDES WAGES, INTEREST, DIVIDENDS AND OTHER INCOME AND DEDUCTION ITEMS REPORTED TO YOU AND THE IRS ON FORMS W-2, W-2P, 1098, 1099, 5498, ETC. WE HAVE BEEN UNABLE TO VERIFY ON YOUR RETURN THE ITEMS LISTED OR EXPLAINED ON PAGE 3 OF THIS NOTICE AND NEED YOUR HELP TO DETERMINE WHETHER

Jan. 24, 1990

Internal Revenue Service
Atlanta, Ga. 39901

Gentlemen:
    This is in response to the notice of proposed changes to income, a copy of which is attached.
    The notice is in error in two respects.
    First, I received only $765 in interest income from Great American, not $1,125 as you claim. Attached is a copy of a certified Form 1099-Int. from the bank showing the correct amount.
    Second, the notice claims that I owe income taxes on an additional $6,525 in interest income. That interest, however, was actually credited to my Keogh account, tax I.D. number 000-00-0000. Interest credited to a Keogh is not taxable until it is distributed to the taxpayer. Enclosed please find a letter from the Los Angeles Savings Bank that attests to the fact that this interest was credited to my Keogh account and is therefore not currently taxable.

    Sincerely,

This is the IRS' name for a program that matches income reported on your tax return with the totals sent in by a third party such as your employer, bank, or broker. If the IRS finds what seems to be a discrepancy, out goes a CP-2000 notice. Triple-check your records if you receive one: It's particularly error-prone. If you spot a reporting flub, ask the third party for a letter of correction and a new statement. But don't wait for a reply. Send a letter like the one above to the IRS with a copy of your correction request.

Estimated Tax

DEPARTMENT OF TREASURY
INTERNAL REVENUE SERVICE
ATLANTA, GA 39901

Date of this notice:
Taxpayer Identifying Number
Form: 1040   Tax Period: DEC. 31, 1988

For assistance you may
call us at:
522-0050 LOCAL ATLANTA
1-800-424-1040OTHER GA
Or you may write to us at
the address shown at the
left. If you write, be
sure to attach the bottom
part of this notice.

CORRECTION NOTICE – REFUND DUE TAXPAYER

WE HAVE CORRECTED AN ERROR ON YOUR RETURN FOR THE ABOVE TAX YEAR. THE CORRECTION IS EXPLAINED BELOW. YOU MAY WANT TO CHECK YOUR FIGURES AGAINST OURS. IF YOU BELIEVE WE MADE A MISTAKE, PLEASE WRITE TO US AND INCLUDE THE BOTTOM PART OF THIS NOTICE. YOU ARE ENTITLED TO THE REFUND SHOWN BELOW UNLESS YOU OWE OTHER TAXES.

March 1, 1990

Internal Revenue Service
Atlanta, Ga. 39901

Gentlemen:

This letter is in response to your notice dated Feb. 15, 1990, a copy of which is attached. The notice reflects a discrepancy and balance due of $12,000 in my estimated tax payments as reported on my 1988 income tax return plus a penalty of $668.40. Your assessment is wrong.

I am enclosing copies of canceled checks (front and back) to document estimated payments in the amount of $24,000.

The payments were made in the following amounts on the following dates: April 14, 1988: $6,000.00; June 12, 1988: $6,000.00; Sept. 13, 1988: $6,000.00; Jan. 10, 1989: $6,000.00.

Please note that two of the checks amounting to $12,000 were from my wife, Mary Taxpayer, who files a joint tax return with me. Her Social Security Number is 000-00-0000, which is different from mine.

Our tax the previous year, 1987, was $23,552. Since the amount paid in 1988 of $24,000 exceeds the tax paid in the previous year, 1987, there is no underpayment of estimated tax for 1988.

Please adjust your records in accordance with our documentation and cancel the notice of additional tax, penalty and interest due.

Sincerely,

If you receive this notice, the headline may offer some momentary relief: CORRECTION NOTICE—REFUND DUE TAXPAYER. But as you wade through the molasses-like prose, you will discover that the IRS is accusing you of not keeping up with your promised estimated tax payments. When you sort out the problem, with the help of the accompanying article, send the IRS a letter based on the model above and enclose copies of your canceled checks as proof of payment.

justifications. Just the facts: You're wrong. I'm right. Here's the evidence.

Rule 4: Follow up forcefully. However quick, accurate, and complete your reply to the first notice may be, in most cases that will not be the end of the matter. Often, a first response crosses in the mail with a second notice. (In fact, although that first notice says you have 30 days to reply, you may not receive it until a few days before the deadline.) If that happens to you, send the IRS a copy of everything you mailed the first time, citing the document locator number on the notice, usually in the upper right-hand corner, with a covering letter explaining that on such and such date you answered the first notice, evidence of which is enclosed.

If you receive a third notice from the IRS, it is clear that your reasoned responses are not being appropriately acknowledged. At that point, it is time for you to phone the problem resolution officer (PRO) at your local district office or service center. The PRO can go to a computer terminal, pull out your case, and, if he or she thinks it's warranted, stop any further action, including a property lien that is about to be carried out.

By most accounts, this is one part of the system that does work. Tax professionals report substantial success by phoning these officers, who handled 407,000 cases last year, taking an average of three weeks a case. PROs are not supposed to handle your problem unless you have received at least three letters or encountered rudeness or inefficiency on the part of IRS personnel over your case. Some will give you unofficial guidance earlier than that, however, such as finding the right person to whom you should write next.

Rule 5: Get outside help if you need it. In most cases, the dispute revolves around facts that you can supply yourself, with the help of one of our sample letters. But if the issue turns on a technical point or an application of the law, call in a professional tax adviser. Not only will you get the argument properly and clearly presented to the IRS, but you will also gain the added respect you may need from the examiner reading your response. Remember that the examiner typically has only a high school education and fewer than three years on the job. He or she will tend to assume that a C.P.A.'s reading of a complex tax matter is more authoritative than the opinion of an amateur like yourself.

Aside from the general rules, there are important points to know about each of the IRS' four common notices. These specifics will help you deal intelligently with the agency, as well as give you useful insight into the IRS' all-too-fallible ways:

Math-Error Notice

This letter lands in your mailbox when the IRS thinks it has caught you in a simple arithmetic mistake or taking too many deductions for dependents or perhaps using the wrong tax table. Last year's math-error notices assessed penalties such as one-half of 1% of additional tax due for each month it is owed plus interest.

While there are no official figures on errors made or abatements—IRS-speak for the elimination of penalties—granted on these notices, tax professionals report that this is a major area of IRS goofs and cite two particularly weak links in the processing system. First, soon after your return arrives at a local service center, a data-entry transcriber—typically a $7-an-hour GS3 with one week of training—punches the essential information into a computer: your name, Social Security number, filing status, number of dependents, total wages, taxable interest, taxable income. That transcriber clerk, who might well be expected to process at least 460.4 returns an hour—7.7 a minute—has only to strike a single wrong digit when entering, say, a deduction to make a math-error notice likely.

This erroneous information passes electronically with all the other data from your return to the National Computing Center in Martinsburg, West Virginia, where every single tax return in America is processed. In the millisecond that the computer there takes to review

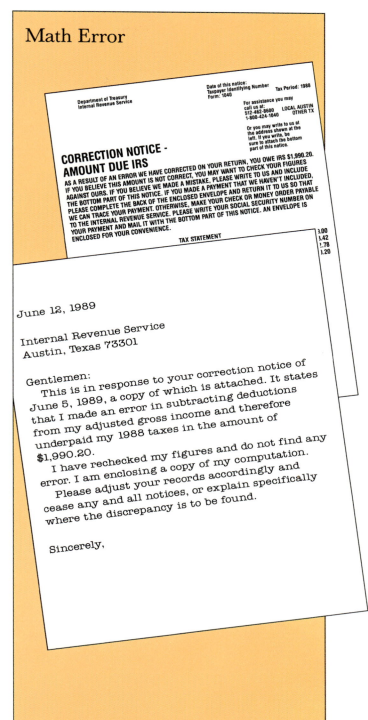

Math Error

A simple mistake in arithmetic by you can trigger the math-error notice. Or IRS staffers can create the error by miscopying data from your return. If the IRS is in the wrong, once you send off your version of the above letter, chances are you will never hear of the matter again. See the "Math-error notice" section of the accompanying story for more details.

your return, it picks up the supposed mistake and confirms that a mistake notice should be sent to you. That information goes back to your local service center. Next, to double-check, one of the GS4 tax examiners compares the data in the notice with your actual return. But pressed to perform quickly, he all too often misses the mistake. Out goes the notice to you.

If the IRS created the error, turn to the sample letter on page 123, fill in your particulars, and append any computation you have that will support your version. If the notice neglects to tell you exactly where the mistake supposedly lies, which is sometimes the case, your first letter should demand specifics and include a statement that you have rechecked all of your computations and do not find any errors. When the IRS gets back to you with details, then proceed with your version of the model letter.

Late-Filing Notice

If you miss the tax-filing deadline this year—your return must be postmarked by midnight on April 15—and fail to file a Form 4868 for an extension to August 15, you will be liable for a penalty of as much as 5% of the tax owed for each month you are late, up to a maximum of 25%. The 1.5 million late-filing notices sent out in 1989 generated revenue of $1.14 billion. Each notice says REQUEST FOR PAYMENT across the top and lists the tax already paid, plus the amount of the penalty and interest.

Tardy taxpayers are supposed to be rooted out by another $7-an-hour GS3 clerk in the Receipt and Control section at the local service center. This employee, handling a peak load of as many as 283 documents an hour, stamps the date on your return if it is postmarked after the deadline, attaching your envelope.

The stamp alerts the data-entry transcriber (again a GS3) down the line, who then pulls your return and codes the lateness information along with your other essential data into the computer. Then it all goes to computer central at Martinsburg. If "delinquent" is

coded on your return, the master computer calculates your penalty and orders your local center to mail you a late-filing notice. One way the IRS sometimes errs in this process: Your return arrives on time but languishes in the land of the Tingle tables. When a clerk finally picks it up, instead of checking its postmark, he stamps it with that day's date—your late-filing notice is as good as in the mail.

You might head off this headache entirely by including a letter with your return showing what the tax code calls "reasonable cause" for your lateness (or see sample letter, page 120). Tax examiners in the collection department have the authority to accept your excuse on the spot. They simply consult their adjustment manual and run down a list of more than three pages of acceptable excuses. Some are allowed without documentation, such as the death or serious illness of the taxpayer, a family member, or the tax preparer, or destruction by fire of a taxpayer's residence and tax records. Others leave the decision up to the examiner—for example, that you were unavoidably out of the country at filing time, or you were unable to obtain certain records to complete your return on time. One familiar reason for lateness: The post office fouled up.

CP-2000 Notice

This is the Big Brother notice, the one that results when the computer can't exactly match the entries on your return with data supplied by your employer, broker, bank—any business or other source that pays you money. It is, as IRS Commissioner Fred Goldberg asserts, no less than a massive audit of 40% of all taxpayers. The 3.5 million CP-2000 (the CP stands for Compliance Program) notices sent out in 1989 carried penalties ranging up to 25% of the tax due plus interest.

The master computer in Martinsburg does the matching and catching, again ordering your service center to mail out the notices. But before that happens, one of those low-paid tax examiners checks the Martinsburg findings against your return, looking for errors. Have you listed the income elsewhere on the return?

Or called income "interest" when it was in fact dividends? Or listed the amount correctly as dividends but entered the name of the paying company incorrectly? If you simply drop the "Inc." from a company's name, for example, and the 1099 form carries it, the computer can't make a match. Banks are frequent 1099 offenders, inflating with a faulty computer keystroke the amount of interest you actually received from them, or assigning income from a child's trust to the parent's Social Security number. Also, IRS data-entry transcribers often trigger an erroneous CP-2000 notice when transferring basic data from a return to the computer. This happens when they switch Social Security numbers of two taxpayers as they riffle through hundreds of documents an hour.

When the source of a CP-2000 error is a third party—your employer, bank, or broker—write immediately to the offender requesting a revised, corrected form. Don't even wait for a reply. Instead, send your explanation to the IRS immediately—use the sample letter on page 121 as your guide—along with a copy of the request for a correction you have just sent to the third party.

Estimated-Tax Notice

If you pay estimated taxes and your quarterly payments don't add up to either 100% of the tax you paid the previous year or 90% of the present year's bill, you face an interest penalty based on the tax you still owe. The Martinsburg computer tracks you, updating your file quarterly by checking the amounts you pay each quarter, as well as your filing dates. This is how the IRS can hit you at the end of the year for nonpayment in one quarter, even if you catch up and pay the full tax due by the end of the year.

Once again, the computer at Martinsburg receives the basic data on your return from your service center, tracks your payments, and determines whether to order the issuance of a notice for discrepancy in estimated tax. The 1.7 million such notices that went out in 1989 brought in $668 million.

IRS officials and tax professionals agree that there is one widespread reason for errors in this notice: pervasive mishandling of credits from one year applied to the next.

If you get such a notice, pull out your files and be guided by the sample letter on page 122. If at first or even second try you don't succeed, you—or better still, your tax pro—may have to take your first letter and strip it of polite language. Start your next letter like this:

"You have assessed an additional underpayment of estimated tax penalty.

"YOUR ASSESSMENT IS WRONG!"

Then go on to demand a resolution of the matter within three weeks of the date of your letter. If that doesn't work, call the problem resolution officer. One way or another, you will win.

Surprising Write-Offs

As you reach for every possible tax deduction, here are some less-than-obvious medical expenses that might not have occurred to you but are legitimate, if you qualify:

• A reclining chair, if a doctor prescribes it to relieve your cardiac condition.

• A wig, if a doctor says you need it for your mental health.

• Clarinet lessons, if an orthodontist says playing it will straighten your teeth.

• A facelift, if recommended by a doctor.

These expenses may seem deductible, but they aren't:

• Dance lessons, even if recommended by a doctor as physical or mental therapy.

• A hotel room for sex therapy, whether or not your physician recommends it.

• A vet's treatment of your sick pet.

• Getting yourself tattooed or your ears pierced.

Get Ready for an Expensive Child

Parents want everything this great country has to offer for their kids. But getting it won't be easy. The government says that if you have a baby this year, you will spend $265,249 on the basic necessities in raising the child to the age of 22—plus $100,000 to $300,000 to put him through a four-year college. Add piano lessons, summer camp, and at least some private schooling, which many parents consider nearly mandatory, and you're staring at $750,000. If you are like most parents, you are already wondering how you can afford your kids. For some answers, see "How Much Will Your Children Cost?" on page 128.

The biggest financial strain on families in the 1990s will be the cost of their children's higher education. It's not necessary to dwell on the importance of college: Those who graduate earn an average of 50% more than those who only finish high school. Over the next 20 years, the gap will surely widen.

Americans can be the keenest of consumers—dickering with car dealers, driving dozens of miles to discount outlets to save a few bucks on a Calvin Klein skirt. Yet, until recently, even sharp shoppers were timid and trusting when it came to choosing a college. Now that's beginning to change: Parents and students are more sophisticated and determined to get answers to questions rather than simply be in awe of the neatly manicured lawns or the record of the football team. For help, see "Picking the Right College" on page 134.

To be a good college consumer, all you need is the diligence and skeptical instincts you would bring to, say, the hunt for a house. This chapter will help you learn the right way to organize your college quest, suggest the best investment strategies, and give you a grasp of the baffling financial aid system.

Here are some things to keep in mind during your search: The cost of getting an education will keep climbing. While moderating from the punishing pace of the 1980s, tuition and room-and-board increases are still expected to outrun general inflation by about two percentage points a year.

That is a frightening thought to families with small children looking ahead to six-figure bills for a bachelor's degree. But you have several ways to cope with the high cost of learning. By beginning a savings plan when your children are young, you can build up a substantial college fund. And the financial aid system can provide surprising amounts of help to families who qualify, particularly at expensive schools.

But don't base your choice on price alone. You should be trying to find a setting where your child will thrive, and that means looking at several factors. School size is one obvious issue. Kids who need more personal attention may fare better at a smaller school. Academic atmosphere is also important.

There's no doubt that a thorough college search requires a serious investment of time and energy. It's not something you do with one book, sitting down at one time. But think about the kind of money you're investing—and remember that your child will carry his college experience with him for the rest of his life. Doesn't it make sense to take a long, hard look before sending your kid off to school?

Also covered in this chapter is another important, if less obvious, problem concerning children and money. Americans give their children $9 billion a year, yet few parents make an organized effort to teach their progeny essential money skills. "The Best Way to Teach Your Kids about Money" on page 131 offers some suggestions.

How Much Will Your Children Cost?

The answer can be upsetting—and you need to make the right financial moves now to meet the truly staggering expenses you will face.

Let's start with the basics. The U.S. Department of Agriculture says the average family earning $50,000 or more will spend $265,249 to feed, clothe, and shelter a child to age 22. Add to that the cost of an education—college, and in many cases, private preschool, elementary, and high schools—as well as the other amenities of growing up middle class, and the expense of raising a child can easily be hundreds of thousands of dollars more.

Parents already know intuitively that children are expensive, of course. Economists say that part of the reason couples are having smaller families—an average of only two kids in 1989, versus 3.7 at the height of the baby boom in 1957—is that they fear the expense of a large brood. But few have actually calculated the impact on their budget. Indeed, it is to help them comprehend the enormity of the expense that the full effects of inflation are included in all numbers cited here.

Fortunately, there are steps couples can take to prepare themselves. Having children makes you realize you're not immortal—that it's time to buy life insurance, save for college, and figure out some way to support yourself in retirement.

Curiously, the cost of child rearing is high, not because the basic expenses have changed, but because the price of extras like a college education—once considered a luxury but now almost a necessity—have gone through the roof. Food, clothes, and shelter for a single child consumed about 30% of average family spending in the 1960s and roughly the same proportion in the 1980s, according to Princeton sociologist Thomas Espenshade. But a year's tuition, room, and board at a private college, which claimed 28% of median family earnings in the 1960s, absorbs 35% today, while the bite of a year at Harvard has shot from 42% to 57%. The one piece of good news: Expenses at state universities have remained stable at about 14% of median family earnings, but that's only because state taxpayers have been generous enough to pick up the difference. In addition to college ($300,134 for four years at an Ivy League institution), there are all the other advantages that middle-class families like to provide—music lessons ($5,145 for six years of piano), hobbies ($1,500 for a personal computer), summer camp ($27,606 for eight summers), and so on. When you include them, you reach totals that leave parents gasping.

Moreover, a series of social, demographic, and economic trends threaten to make child rearing even less affordable in years to come:

More preschoolers will need child care or nursery school. Nearly a quarter of all families with children are headed by a single parent today, compared with only 10% in the mid-1960s. And the proportion of households with two wage earners has jumped from 44% to 57% in that time. With experts forecasting that both trends will continue, an increasing number of parents will pay $2,000 to $10,000 a year for group day care or $9,000 to $20,000 for full-time, in-home child care.

More parents will send their kids to private elementary and secondary schools. As families fled America's failing public education

system during the 1980s, enrollment at private institutions rose 17 times faster than at public schools. With top private academies charging $5,000 to $10,000 a year, the cost can easily equal that of four years at an expensive college.

The cost of private higher education will continue to outpace inflation. It won't go up twice as fast as the consumer price index, as it did in the 1980s, but its rate of increase should hover one to two percentage points above inflation's. The trend may not abate until the baby boomers' kids swarm onto campus starting in 1995—thus allowing colleges to spread their fixed costs over larger student bodies.

Slower housing appreciation will give families less equity to tap. Many couples count on second mortgages or home-equity loans to bail them out if they need money for college. The assumption is that home values will increase considerably; however, the price of most single-family homes will rise at rates only one-half to one percentage point above inflation in the 1990s—not the three points over inflation of the 1970s and 1980s.

Marketers will be blitzing your kids with tempting ways to spend money. With lures like the Simpsons and Ninja Turtles, a recent *Forbes* magazine reports, retailers sold some $60 billion in goods aimed at youngsters ages four to 12 last year—up 25% from 1988—and may sell $75 billion this year.

For many of today's parents, college costs and retirement costs will collide. The growing number of couples who wait until their thirties or forties to have a baby will not finish putting that child through school until within 10 years of their own retirements. If they run short of cash, they may have to borrow from a tax-deferred retirement account, remortgage their home, or take on other loans just when they should be paying down debt and maximizing their savings.

But wait! Don't let these dismal facts persuade you to put your kids up for adoption.

Even couples who are just starting families, and who, thus, face the biggest expenses, have several factors working for them.

The most important is income. The average college graduate's income rose at a rate about two percentage points above inflation during the past two decades, according to estimates based on Census Bureau figures, and that small-sounding edge can have dramatic effects.

Additionally, many of today's baby-boomer parents could receive a sad but helpful windfall when their own parents pass away. Americans 55 and older hold assets of $6.5 trillion—the largest pool of inheritable wealth ever amassed in a single country. The only question is how much of those riches will actually be passed on? Since people are living longer these days, medical expenses—including nursing-home care—could swallow some of that pot. Furthermore, Congress is debating whether to reduce the $600,000 that people can pass to their heirs without incurring any federal estate tax.

To be safe, we recommend you leave inheritance and the possibility of your income topping inflation out of your financial plan. There are other factors, however, that you can control. Some dos and don'ts:

Boost your savings, and do it today. Starting soon makes a big difference. To raise the $300,134 required to give a 1990 baby an Ivy League education, for instance, you would need to put $8,165 a year into an investment earning 9% annually if you began now. But if you waited until the child entered first grade, your annual bite would rise to $15,400.

Put your savings where they will earn the most over the long haul. There are few good savings vehicles for college these days. Among the available options, though, the Series EE U.S. savings bond offers significant advantages for families with adjusted gross income of less than $60,000. Their earnings on these variable-rate bonds that now pay 7% are completely tax-free if the money is used to finance college (though the federal tax break phases out as the couple's AGI approaches a $90,000

cutoff). Traditional savings instruments such as EEs, zero-coupon bonds, and CDs should make up only half of your portfolio, however, if your child is at least 10 years away from entering school. The rest should go into more aggressive investments, such as growth stocks or no-load growth mutual funds. They usually pay more and, while they are riskier, the fact that you will hold them for years makes you less vulnerable to short-term fluctuations.

If you think you might qualify for college financial aid, don't put savings in your child's name. Parents traditionally park college money under their young one's name, since that way the first $500 in investment income is tax-free; the second $500 is taxed at the child's tax rate; and only the portion over $1,000, if the child is under 14, gets taxed at the parents' usually higher level. And after age 14, all earnings past $500 are taxed at the child's rate. If a child has substantial wealth, however, his financial aid package suffers, since he must contribute 35% of his assets a year toward his education, while his parents need pay only 5.6%.

If both parents work, consider whether one of you should stay home and raise children. Child care is not the only expense you incur when both of you have full-time jobs. There are also costs for commuting, business clothing, meals at work, and so forth. When you add those up, it may be better all around for one parent to take care of the kids and go back to work later. This is especially so if you learn to live on one salary and then save the entire second salary when the child raiser returns to work.

Set realistic goals. Chances are you will find that you simply cannot afford everything you want for your kids—private secondary schools, for example, plus an expensive college. If you can't, remain open to compromise. You could send your offspring to one of the many excellent state-supported colleges, or you could find alternative ways of financing, such as those outlined in "Figuring Out Financial Aid" on page 140 or "Going for a Loan" on page 143.

The Best Way to Teach Your Kids about Money

We give our children $9 billion a year—mostly for the wrong reasons and with little guidance.

No doubt most parents would agree that learning to manage money is part of becoming responsible. Yet, few make any organized effort to teach their kids from an early age how to earn, spend, save, borrow, and invest. Even a conscientious parent could use some help. For example, experts in both child psychology and financial planning suggest that allowance should not be used to punish or reward. A family should not operate the same way as a marketplace.

What authoritative evidence there is suggests that many kids aren't taught essential money skills. A recent survey by the Joint Council on Economic Education, for example, found "appalling ignorance" of monetary concepts among high school students, two-thirds of whom couldn't even define "profit." No wonder young people mismanage their money. "They enter college expecting to maintain the same level of life-style they had in their parents' homes," says Charlene Sullivan, associate professor of management at Purdue University. "They see credit as a permanent source of funds, and they get into trouble."

Schools are partly at fault. Few have either the resources or expertise to teach money management. Still, most responsibility falls on the parents—since wisdom about money, like basic honesty or good manners, begins at home. Whether you realize it or not, how much you save, borrow, give to charity, and so forth depends on your fundamental values,

which are passed on to your kids. This intimate connection between money and values may explain why some parents are uncomfortable discussing money with their children. Lots of parents feel awkward about revealing their own finances, and that reticence makes the subject seem all the more mysterious to children.

Furthermore, help is hard to find: Any well-stocked bookstore will have two or three books on how to explain sex to a teenager. But try to find one on children and finance.

Lacking firm guidance, many parents opt for the easiest—and worst—solution: They throw money at the problem. American children receive $9 billion a year from adults, according to a study by James McNeal at Texas A&M, 53% in allowance and the rest in payment for chores or special-occasion gifts. Among 300 *Money* subscribers with children surveyed by the Gallup Organization, a third give their kids $25 a week or more by the time they reach 18. Yet, only about half of them require their children to save any of the allowance.

In an attempt to help parents, *Money* offers this common sense program based on interviews with financial experts, educators, child psychologists, and parents:

When to start. When your child is about age three, explain how things are bought and sold when you go to the grocery store or the gas station. Give the child small sums and let him or her choose what to buy. "Children need real-world experience, not just explanation, on which to base their understanding," says Sylvia C. Chard, co-author of an influential early-childhood education book, *Engaging Children's Minds: The Project Approach* (Ablex Publishing). Don't be daunted if your youngster has trouble grasping abstractions such as the notion of value. For example, a young child almost always thinks that larger coins are worth more than smaller ones. You'll have a hard time convincing a five-year-old that a dime is worth more than a nickel.

The first allowance. By age six or so, introduce the weekly dole. This is not as easy as it sounds. For one thing, there is the question of how much allowance to give: In general, *Money* parents give their children less than $10 a week until they reach their teens. Then allowances tend to escalate through high school to about $20 at age 18.

Even more critical, according to experts, is deciding the conditions under which the allowance will be given. In *Money*'s poll, more than half of the parents said they made allowance payments conditional on their children behaving well, doing chores at home, or performing well in school. Experts criticized that approach, however. "When you pay your kids for routine tasks, you open the door for your child to say, 'I'm not making my bed. I don't care if I don't get any money,' " says stockbroker Kenneth Forest Davis, who is a co-author of one of the best books on the subject (*Kids and Cash*, Oak Tree Publications, 1979), now unfortunately out of print. "The allowance then becomes a source of conflict and manipulation rather than the healthy incentive you'd planned."

Davis and others suggest instead that you give children a basic allowance with no strings just because they are family members. By the same token, as family members they should have certain chores that must be performed regardless. Then, if they do work beyond the routine, they earn extra. And as noted, don't

The Five Stages in Raising a Money-Smart Child

Here is a model program for educating your children about money based on a consensus of the financial experts *Money* consulted. The ages are approximate, depending upon each child's maturity:

3 to 5: Begin discussing money. Take your children on shopping trips to buy groceries or gifts. Talk about how you weigh choices and decide. Give them an occasional 50¢ or $1 to spend, and ask them to pick among three or four choices.

6 to 7: Introduce an allowance. Start with 50¢ or $1 a week. Don't link the money to household chores; simply assign chores as part of your child's family responsibility. Discuss what can be done with the money. Give the money every week at a set time, without fail. Don't take it away for punishment.

8 to 10: Give annual raises. Increase the child's allowance and responsibilities each year on an easy-to-remember date like July 4, and provide opportunities to earn extra money by doing additional chores. Help your child to open a savings account and talk about what to save for.

11 to 14: Start to set goals. Invite your child to join you in family budget conferences. Talk about long-range goals, such as college. As a savings incentive, match any amount that he or she contributes to a savings account.

15 to 18: Push them from the nest. Help your children attain independence by opening a checking account with an ATM card. Consider giving them a family credit card, provided they pay their own bills. Encourage them to get outside jobs. And include them in decisions about paying for college.

cut off allowance as punishment; that encourages the notion that bad behavior is negotiable and not simply unacceptable.

Raise the allowance yearly. Davis recommends that you set the amount in a regular annual conference with your children on any date that is easy to remember, such as July 4. At that time, also increase the scope of things your child must pay for. Among *Money* parents, for example, 31% insist that their kids pay for their own dates; 43% make them buy any food they want away from home (except school lunches); and 72% ask them to finance their own entertainment. Your aim should be to rear children who can manage a year's expenses on their own by the time they leave for college.

Teach them basic home economics as soon as they know enough math. Tell them they can buy their favorite cereal at the store. But show them how to find the most cost-efficient size. Also, have them figure the tip at restaurants. Or get an old newspaper to show how prices have gone up—a painless way of illustrating the essentials of inflation.

Help your child open a savings account, probably at around age 10. Check with your bank, however, before marching your little one down there. Many commercial institutions no longer accept small deposits—or they charge outrageous fees. Even if you can't find a child-friendly bank nearby, you have other options. For example, many credit unions welcome them. So do specialty banks like Young Americans Bank in Denver where the average saver is nine years old and has a deposit of only $250. Alternatively, pool holiday gifts with your child's savings and invest in a money-market fund.

Include your child in family budget talks. Start gradually with topics they might reasonably have a say in—such as whether to renovate the playroom or save the money for a topnotch swing set. Be as forthcoming about your own finances as you can, depending on your child's maturity. Obviously, you don't want your kids blabbing your salary to their friends. You do, however, want them to grasp that your money supply is not infinite. With teenagers, start discussing how to pay for their college, and get your son or daughter involved in deciding where his or her money will be invested.

Encourage them to get involved in more sophisticated money handling. By age 16 or so, your children should have a checking account, perhaps even with automated teller machine cash cards, and should reconcile the bank statement themselves. They'll soon learn that their bank balances don't always show how much money they have if there are any checks outstanding. Parents in *Money*'s poll follow this advice: Some 81% have helped their children open savings accounts, 22% have begun checking accounts, 13% have given them automatic teller machine cards, and an equal proportion have entrusted their kids with family credit cards. About one family in eight has given their children responsibility for buying their own clothes.

Finally, encourage your kids to get part-time work when they're old enough to handle it— usually between 14 and 17. Earning money is the only way kids can understand how jobs work. It will also help them appreciate how hard it is to make money.

For extra help teaching your kids about money, consult the following:

● *Children and Money: A Parents' Guide*, a book by Grace W. Weinstein (Signet, $4.50).

● *Teach Your Child the Value of Money*, a book by Harold and Sandy Moe (Harsand Press, $9.95; 800-451-0643).

● "You and Money," a free kit geared for fourth- to sixth-graders from Fidelity Investments (800-544-6666).

● *Penny Power*. A bimonthly magazine for kids, published by Consumers Union (P.O. Box 51777, Boulder, CO 80321; 800-525-0643).

Picking the Right College

Your child's freshman year can bring unpleasant surprises. To avoid disappointment, ask the tough questions before enrolling.

April is the cruelest month for tens of thousands of anxious high school seniors. Each day they go to the mailbox looking for responses from the colleges of their choice, either in a thick envelope (containing an acceptance letter and registration forms) or a thin one (with a one-page "No, thank you"). Anxiety aside, what is especially cruel about today's admissions process is that the coveted fat letters don't always guarantee happy endings: After just a few months on campus, a distressingly high percentage of incoming college students discover that they have picked the wrong school. In a 1987 nationwide poll conducted by the Higher Education Institute at UCLA, nearly one in three first-year students said they would not select their current college if they had the choice to make over again.

Why do so many kids end up disillusioned? One reason may be that they base their decisions on information from a single, biased source: the college itself. Virtually all schools tend to paint themselves as the full-color ideal while playing down the black-and-white reality—whether it is overcrowded classes, the incidence of date rape, or the lack of student housing. "With declining enrollments, admissions officers are like hotel desk clerks," warns C. Wayne Griffith, head of a computerized college-search service in Natick, Massachusetts. "Their priority is to fill up space."

So it is up to you to learn as much as you can about prospective schools. Most of the nearly 3 million young men and women who choose a college each year concentrate on factors like location, cost, school size, and academic reputation. You shouldn't stop there: Press hard for answers to the following critical questions so you and your child can avoid a costly disappointment:

Who does the teaching? Many schools boast during admissions interviews of their prominent scholars and cozy faculty/student ratios. The classroom experience can be very different, however. Ask specifically whether the superstars teach only graduate seminars or lecture in huge amphitheaters. Do the faculty rosters include professors on sabbatical? Those who only conduct research? Some courses may even be run by graduate students. At Arizona State University three years ago, freshman Kim Westley had no instructor at all for her algebra class—just a workbook and printed instructions. The department no longer offers such "self-taught" courses.

Are many students shut out of courses they want or need? Lotteries and long waiting lists for sought-after classes are common at even the priciest private schools. And because of budget constraints, not all classes are offered every semester. In some cases, a student could be forced to spend an extra year in school just to take courses required for graduation. In California State University's system, some classes are offered only every other year, which is one reason why more than 70% of freshmen take at least five years to graduate.

Is the campus overcrowded? Dorms are the center of college social life and can provide a protective environment for youngsters not quite ready to live on their own. Yet, many freshmen face a "no vacancy" sign. While literature from the University of California at Berkeley concedes there is "a high demand for on-campus or near-campus housing," it does not state that nearly one in five entering students will be forced to live elsewhere. At Stanford, the accommodations for upperclassmen include 116 three-bedroom trailers that have been parked on the campus since 1969.

Is campus crime a threat? In a recent survey by Towson State University's Center for the Study and Prevention of Campus Violence, more than one in three respondents reported being victims of thefts or assaults on campus during their college years. Yet, you will find it difficult to learn the true extent of crime at individual schools. This is the topic school officials are most reluctant to discuss. In 1988, after a Lehigh sophomore was murdered in her dorm room by a male student, the Pennsylvania legislature passed the nation's first state law requiring colleges to compile crime statistics and provide them to anyone who asks. Since then, Florida, Louisiana, and Tennessee have followed and 12 other states have legislation pending. If you are concerned about crime, ask about nighttime shuttle-bus service around campus, the size of the school's security force, and whether dorms are locked or guarded.

Will everyone feel at home? Reports of student harassment of Jews, blacks, and homosexuals have increased dramatically over the past decade, according to various advocacy groups. The Anti-Defamation League of B'nai B'rith, for example, says that reported incidents of campus anti-Semitism increased from only six in 1984 to 69 in 1989; the league believes that most incidents still go unreported. At the University of Wisconsin three years ago, a fraternity held a mock slave auction.

Will rising costs far outstrip the available financial aid? For the past decade, tuition increases have far outpaced inflation at most schools, with financial aid providing only limited relief. Increases at most schools this year will be in the 5% to 11% range; the average increase for private colleges is expected to be 9%. If you're paying the current private-college average of $8,737 this year, steady increases of 9% would mean that your annual tab would top $11,000 in four years, $12,000 in five. And that's not counting room, board, and fees, which will also rise. As your costs go up, however, financial aid may not keep pace. You might get an extra loan or help finding a job but seldom more in grants or scholarship money.

How can you get the answers? The best approach is to undertake your own thorough investigation of prospective schools. If your child already knows what subject he or she will major in, it may be worth talking to the head of that department to learn about the availability of classes. Seek out graduates of your local high school who are attending the colleges on your list and ask them about the availability of classes and housing. They can also provide important clues about the general atmosphere—whether partying is more important than studying, for example, or the school offers enough worthwhile extracurricular activities. Be sure to visit the campus while classes are in session. Take the official tour to get your bearings, then go exploring on your own. Walk through classroom buildings checking class size. Eat a few meals in the cafeteria. If at all possible, have your child spend a night in a dorm. Experiencing the school's environment can be a lot more revealing than hours spent poring over the college catalogue.

To help you ask the right questions, you might also try reading *Choosing a College* (Harper & Row, $7.95) by Thomas Sowell, a senior fellow at the Hoover Institution. An academic insider's view of the college experience, this book tells how to cut through rhetoric and identify a school's real strengths and weaknesses.

The ABCs of Investing for Education

Don't let the numbers scare you. Here's how you can cope with the increasingly high cost of learning.

If you're a parent, the $500 billion price tag of the savings and loan bailout may not seem nearly as frightening as the $22,000 a year it now costs to send a child to some of the nation's top schools. Factor in a few years of inflation, and it really looks as though you've got something to worry about: Assuming annual increases of 7%, the bill for four years at an average state university for a child born in 1990 would total $100,132 in 2008, while the tab at an average private university is expected to come to $215,000. Well, you can stop trembling. Whether your child is 16 or only six, there are moves you can make today that will enable you to meet the challenge of future education bills.

First, learn the five key rules of smart college investing:

Start saving now. Time can be your greatest ally, thanks to the power of compounding. If you start saving today for a newborn's college bills, you'd need to put about $338 a month in an investment earning an average of 8% annually to build a fund of $215,000. But if you wait just until that child is six and entering first grade, you'll need to invest $618 a month. And if you delay until the child is 14 and entering high school, you'd need to salt away a seemingly impossible $1,767 a month.

Don't be too cautious. You know you'll need a certain amount of money by a certain date, so you think first of safe, predictable investments like U.S. savings bonds and bank CDs. Think

again. Those ultraconservative choices guarantee a mediocre return.

Don't count on financial aid or loans. The financial aid system can be surprisingly generous. But while you may qualify for financial aid now, a change in your circumstances or the aid rules could make you ineligible in the future. Similarly, while there are some excellent loans available even to families who don't qualify for aid, don't assume you will simply borrow what you need, especially if you're among the growing number of parents starting families in their thirties or forties. Reason: You will be facing college bills just at the time when you should be cutting debt and boosting savings in preparation for retirement.

Save in your name, not your children's. In the past, it made sense for parents to put away money in their children's names because the earnings were taxed at the child's lower rate. But tax reform nearly closed that loophole: Under current rules, the first $500 of a child's investment income is tax-free; the second $500 is taxed at the child's tax rate (normally 15%); and everything above $1,000 is taxed at the parents' rate, usually 28% or 33%, until the child is 14. (After age 14, all earnings over $500 are taxed at the child's rate; the first $500 is still tax-free.) Such small tax breaks aren't worth the risk of losing financial aid—a risk you take when you put money in a child's name. Under the federal formulas that determine eligibility, children are expected to contribute a far higher percentage of their savings than parents are.

Be skeptical of investments pitched as "ideal for college saving." You're worried about those tuition bills, and the financial services industry knows it. Marketers hope that by linking a product to the notion of college saving, they'll boost their sales. As a result, banks, brokerages, and other financial institutions are peddling any number of familiar instruments as sure-fire college savings cures. Most are

Should You Prepay?

Frightened by the prospect of unrelenting tuition inflation, nearly 160,000 parents have latched on to plans that allow them to prepay college tuition for their kids. Should you?

While the principle is the same, details of the programs vary. Usually, you pay a lump sum or make a series of payments—the amount varies with the age of your child—and are guaranteed up to four years of tuition at a state school when the child is ready to attend. In 1989, for example, Michigan parents who put up $7,840 covered their newborn's tuition and fees for four years at any college in Michigan's public system starting in 2008. Assuming the current average four-year tuition—$10,000—grows by 7% a year, four years starting in 2008 would cost $33,800. For the parents' original $7,840 to grow to that amount, it would take an after-tax compound annual return of 8.45%.

Currently, Alabama, Florida, Ohio, and Wyoming offer similar schemes. In Ohio, you buy credits at current prices ($33 each this year) for use any time after a two-year holding period. Seven other states—Georgia, Maine, Massachusetts, Missouri, Oklahoma, Pennsylvania, and West Virginia—are contemplating plans. And a handful of individual schools offer their own versions. For example, at Indiana University, a public school with eight campuses, you can buy credits at current prices (three credit hours, enough for one class, recently cost $228). The plans offer a certain peace of mind, but before signing up, consider the following drawbacks:

Cancellation costs. What happens if your child doesn't want to go to a state college? In most cases, you will get the equivalent of the prevailing state tuition, but that may turn out to represent less than you could have got investing your original payment in stocks or bonds. And if your child chooses not to attend college at all? Michigan and Ohio will give you an amount equal to tuition at the cheapest state school. Wyoming refunds your initial investment plus 4% compounded interest. Alabama and Florida will return only your initial investment, minus a cancellation fee. Usually, however, you can transfer the plan to another family member. (Wyoming allows transfers, but not sales, to anyone you choose. Indiana University not only permits sales, it maintains a list of potential buyers.)

Tax consequences. The IRS has ruled that the difference between your initial payment and the value of the future tuition is taxable income to your child during his or her college years. Thus, an Alabama student whose parents laid out $3,857 this year to cover a projected $20,280 average tuition bill in 2008 will incur tax on $16,423, or on $4,106 a year. Moreover, you're liable for federal gift tax on whatever amount you put into the plan, a complex calculation that starts at 18% on the first $10,000 and goes up from there. You'll have to file Form 709, which will allow you to subtract the amount from the $192,800 tax credit allowed against your estate when you die.

Default risk. Only Florida puts the state's full faith and credit behind its prepayment plan. In the other states, the legislatures are not obligated to maintain the plan's fiscal soundness. Should a shortfall occur, the plan's trustees would have to rely on political pressure to force the legislatures to honor the contracts. Such concerns led Tennessee to repeal its prepayment legislation.

standard investment vehicles with new wrapping, and some are indeed new products, not all of which are good. And many scam artists have made college-cost anxiety a standard element of their sales pitches for bogus investments, too.

Now you're ready to begin setting up a college savings plan. Estimate how much money you'll need so you can figure out what you must set aside regularly starting today to cover that amount in the future. If your child is only a few years away from college and you can't set aside enough to cover the tab you face, there still are ways to make the most of what you have.

An old-fashioned investment strategy aimed at creating a diversified portfolio is the best way to accumulate money for college. Your portfolio mix should change, however, with the age of your children. If your kids are all under seven years old, you should keep half to 60% of your money in stocks, with the remainder in zero-coupon bonds, bond funds, money-market funds, or CDs. Why the emphasis on stocks? Historically, stocks have produced the highest long-term returns of any financial instrument. According to data compiled by Ibbotson Associates, an investment research firm in Chicago, over the past 64 years, when inflation averaged 3.1% annually, small-company stocks delivered a compound average annual return of 12.2% and blue-chip stocks returned 10.3%; long-term government bonds returned only 4.6% a year and Treasury bills averaged 3.6%.

When your child is ages eight through 13, stock funds should still make up about 40% of your portfolio. As your child reaches 13, however, assuming you've made substantial progress toward your target amount, you should begin shifting the bulk of your portfolio to supersafe CDs, money-market funds, or Treasuries, which you can buy from banks, brokers, or directly from the Treasury (for details, ask at the closest Federal Reserve branch). Here's a closer look at some college fund building blocks (for other investment ideas, see "Track Down Winning Investments," beginning on page 45):

Stocks. The best way for most people to invest in stocks is through no-load or low-load (3% or less sales commission) mutual funds, because you share in the ownership of a large, diversified portfolio that you could not duplicate on your own. Moreover, many funds can arrange for a set amount to be withdrawn automatically from your checking account each month or quarter to buy shares. Not only do such plans force you to save regularly, but you also benefit from an investing technique called dollar-cost averaging. Your steady, equal contributions buy fewer shares when prices are up and more when prices are down, lowering your average share cost. Dollar-cost averaging also eliminates the hazards of market timing—trying to guess the best times to buy and sell shares.

To increase the safety of your portfolio and better your chances of getting a good overall return, you should not put all your stock money into one fund. Rather, choose a mix of funds that will perform well under different circumstances. You might, for example, divide your money evenly among three types of funds: a long-term growth fund that buys shares in established, blue-chip companies; a small-company growth fund that invests in companies with market capitalizations of less than $500 million; and a global fund that buys both U.S. and foreign stocks.

Global and small-company growth funds have been long-term standouts. For the past 15 and 20 year periods, global funds were the top-performing group, delivering compound average annual returns of 21.1% and 16.4%, respectively, followed by small-company growth funds, with annual returns of 19.7% and 13.5%, respectively. The average equity fund, by comparison, managed annual returns of only 18.5% and 12.9%.

One of the points of diversifying in this manner is that you will not need to shift your assets in response to changing economic conditions. But if you are an experienced investor or are willing to do some homework, you can take advantage of market trends by tilting your contributions to the fund group that appears undervalued in relation to the others.

When choosing individual funds within a

given category, look for those with the best performance during the past 10 years or more. Of those, select funds with expense ratios—listed in the fund's prospectus—of less than 1.25%. (For more information, see the mutual fund rankings on page 193.)

Zero-coupon bonds. So named because they pay no interest until maturity, zero-coupon bonds sell at steep discounts to their face value. One appeal of zeros is that when you buy them you know exactly how much you'll have when they become due. Like all bonds, zeros increase in value when interest rates fall and lose value when rates rise, but zeros tend to be more volatile than standard corporate and government bonds, so plan to hold them until maturity. Among those best suited for college savings are "baccalaureate bonds," available in at least 12 states, and Treasury zeros.

Baccalaureates are municipal bonds which are free from federal, state, and local taxes for buyers who live in the state where they are issued. Their advantage over other munis is that they cannot be redeemed early by the issuer (or "called"), which means that you will not face the prospect of suddenly having to find another place to invest your money. To learn if your state issues baccalaureates, call a local broker who specializes in municipal bonds. Baccalaureates tend to sell out quickly, so you should ask the broker to notify you as soon as any become available.

Treasury zeros work on the same principle as baccalaureates but have one disadvantage: They are not exempt from federal tax, and you must pay tax on the interest the bond accrues each year even though you don't receive that interest until the bond matures. These bonds nonetheless can be a good choice for high-income families unlikely to qualify for financial aid. If the bonds are held in the names of children under age 14, the first $500 of interest accrued each year is tax-free.

Municipal and corporate bonds. Other good components for the fixed-income portion of your portfolio are conventional municipal or corporate bonds. As with stocks, mutual-bond funds are, for most parents, the best way to go. Investors don't have the time to do the research necessary to keep abreast of the safety of a muni or corporate issue, but fund managers are paid to monitor the safety of their portfolios day in and day out. Moreover, bond funds offer the convenience of automatic reinvestment of interest payments, so you do not have to find a place to park the twice-yearly interest payouts from individual bonds.

Unlike individual issues, however, bond funds, which are actively managed portfolios of securities, never mature. As a result, there is no guarantee you will get your principal back on a future date. And with a bond fund, you pay management and other annual fees (the average fund charges 1.8%), which can add up to far more than the one-time commission you would pay to buy an individual bond from a broker. But you can limit the cost by shopping for bond funds with expense ratios of 1% or less.

For safety, choose funds whose portfolios contain bonds rated A or higher by Moody's or Standard & Poor's rating agencies. Ask for a copy of the fund's most recent semiannual report to see the fund's portfolio, including ratings. Or you can buy Treasury funds, which invest in the safest of all securities.

To determine which type of fund, corporate or municipal, will give you a higher return, ask for the muni-fund's taxable equivalent yield for someone in your tax bracket and compare that to corporate fund yields. Under current market conditions, munis generally offer superior yields for anyone in the 28% tax bracket or higher.

In general, you will do best by sticking to the investments discussed above. But in special circumstances, there are alternatives to consider for a portion of your savings. For example, Series EE savings bonds, backed by Uncle Sam, have always been free from state and local taxes; bonds issued after December 31, 1989 are in some cases also exempt from federal taxes for parents who use the proceeds to pay for college tuition and fees. Interest on the bonds is completely tax-free for married couples filing jointly with adjusted gross incomes (modified to take into account Social Security benefits, retirement-account contributions, and passive investment losses) of $60,000 or less when they cash the bonds in; for single parents, the limit is $40,000. As income rises, the tax break is phased out, and it disappears completely at $90,000 for couples and $55,000 for singles.

Series EE bonds pay a variable rate adjusted every six months to equal 85% of the rate paid on five-year Treasuries. If you hold the bonds five years, you are guaranteed a minimum rate of 6%. Recently, the bonds were paying 7.01%—the taxable equivalent of 9.7% for parents in the 28% bracket who qualify for the full federal tax exemption and up to 10.6% for those in high-tax states. The income limits will be adjusted for inflation, but beware: Even though you meet the limits when you buy the bonds, you have no way of knowing if you will still qualify when you cash them in (you could, for example, get a promotion or land a higher-paying job). To qualify for tax breaks, the bonds must be held in the parents' names.

Annuities and life insurance offer the potential for tax-deferred growth yet come with so many conditions that it's hard to know what you're getting. Life insurance and annuities are being marketed heavily to college savers, but some financial planners are reluctant to recommend them because their many levels of fees and fine-print restrictions make them difficult for most parents to understand and compare with alternatives.

Indeed, keeping your strategy simple will make it easier to monitor and provide a sense of accomplishment as the sums mount. And once you're satisfied that you're bringing college within reach, you can start worrying about paying for the piano lessons and weddings.

Figuring Out Financial Aid

The system is maddeningly complex, but worth mastering. You may be eligible for more help than you think.

Each year, nearly half of all college undergraduates receive some form of financial assistance. The projected total for the 1990-91 school year was $29.5 billion, enough to cover about 40% of the nation's $76 billion higher-education bill. The federal government will hand out most of that aid: $13.2 billion in subsidized loans and $6.5 billion in grants. Colleges will reach into their own coffers for another $5.5 billion in grants, loans, and a variety of discounted tuition programs. States will cough up an additional $1.7 billion. (Although one of the nonprofit corporations that guarantee student loans—the Higher Education Assistance Foundation—is facing severe financial pressures, federal education officials do not expect students to be affected.)

It's anything but easy money, though. Applying for financial aid means coping with strict deadlines, cumbersome paperwork, jarring jargon, and rules that defy logic and common sense. Furthermore, while the process is meant to be uniform throughout the nation, schools often handle similar families very differently and are secretive about their policies. This story will help you understand how the game works and tell you how to arrange your family finances to get the most out of the sometimes screwball system. If nothing else, you should come away with two important understandings: People with above-average incomes can still qualify for assistance, and it's pointless to compare school prices without taking potential aid into account.

There is no simple cutoff for financial aid eligibility; when in doubt, you should apply. In general, if you have a six-figure family income and substantial assets, you probably will not qualify even at expensive colleges. But under special circumstances—if, say, you are paying college tuition for more than one child—you may qualify even with much higher income. In 1990, Princeton admitted 135 freshman from families with incomes over $105,000 who had applied for financial aid; 23 got some help.

The application process begins with forms that you fill out when your child is a senior, disclosing your income, assets, and other relevant data. Most colleges require either the Financial Aid Form (FAF) or the Family Financial Statement (FFS), available in high school guidance offices. (Some state systems have their own versions, and individual colleges may require additional paperwork.) Parents forward the FAF to the College Scholarship Service and the FFS to the American College Testing Program. These processors will not accept any forms mailed before January 1, but you should submit yours as soon as possible after that date. Some schools have early aid deadlines, and late applicants may miss out. Remember to keep copies of everything: You will have to reapply every year your child attends school.

The FAF and the FFS subject your family finances to a "needs analysis" using what is known as the congressional methodology: After minimal deductions—a family of four is given a $14,260 living expense allowance, for example—each family is expected to spend up to the following on college bills: parents, 5.6% of assets and 47% of after-tax income; students, 35% of assets and 70% of after-tax income (with a minimum of $700 for underclassmen and $900 for juniors and seniors—even if they don't work). This formula produces your expected family contribution—the magic number that every college will use as a starting point to determine your aid package. At many schools, if charges—including tuition,

room, board, books, transportation, and other miscellaneous expenses, like lab fees—exceed this amount, you will be offered help in making up the difference.

How much would the family of the median *Money* reader, with income of $48,000 and investments and home equity worth $70,000, be expected to kick in? Campus Consultants, a financial aid planning firm in New York City, gave the following estimate: Assuming the family had two children, with one about to enter his or her freshman year in college and the other in junior high, the family's expected contribution would be $8,900. So at a school costing $20,000, the *Money* family would be awarded $11,100 in aid ($20,000 minus $8,900). A school costing $10,000 would chip in only $1,100 ($10,000 minus $8,900) in financial aid.

But here's where things begin to get murky. First of all, only about a quarter of all four-year schools say they meet 100% of each student's need. The rest provide only partial assistance. Secondly, even among schools that meet all of your need, the type of aid varies greatly: Some schools are generous with their own grant money; others offer loans. What's more, many practice preferential packaging: They give their grant money to the students they want most while limiting others to government grants and loans. To complicate matters further, one school may decide you have more need than another might. The reason: While schools must follow the congressional methodology when distributing federal dollars, they tend to follow more stringent criteria in allocating their own.

When it comes to assembling your package, all financial aid officers choose from the same basic menu:

Federal grants. The largest of these is the Pell Grant—with awards ranging from $200 to about $2,300—which tends to go to families with incomes of $32,000 and less.

Federal loans. Uncle Sam delivers most of its largesse in the form of Stafford Student Loans. Loan limits for 1990-91 were $2,625 for freshmen and sophomores, $4,000 for juniors and seniors at an interest rate of 8% that jumps to 10% after four years. Staffords are made to the student (not the parents), who can take five to 10 years to repay and can defer payments until six months after he or she stops attending school. The Perkins program, which lends out money at 5%, generally gives priority to lower-income students.

Federal work/study. This subsidized program provides students with a job on or near campus. The money earned does not count as income in your needs assessment for the following year.

State loans and grants. All states offer money to residents with financial need who attend schools within their borders. Pennsylvania, Massachusetts, and others give aid to their residents no matter where they attend school; still others have reciprocity agreements with certain states.

School grants. If government money isn't enough to cover your need, private institutions with large endowments often close the gap with their own funds.

Outside grants. Some financial aid officers have discretion to distribute funds from community groups or special alumni gifts.

What kind of deal might a $20,000 school offer the median *Money* family (with income of $48,000 and assets of $70,000)? Their income would rule out the possibility of a Pell Grant. Instead, their scholar would probably get a $2,625 Stafford Loan and perhaps a work/study job good for another $1,500, for a total of $4,125. Combined with their expected family contribution of $8,900, that would still leave them about $7,000 short. Covering that amount would be up to the school itself.

Warning: Scholarships from outside sources like clubs, corporations, and religious groups usually do not have much value for families on financial aid. (For information on "How to Find Scholarships," see page 145.) "Most families don't know that scholarships may just replace financial aid awards," says Anna Leider,

co-author of *Don't Miss Out: The Ambitious Student's Guide to Financial Aid* (Octameron Press, P.O. Box 2748, Alexandria, VA 22301; $6.25).

In an ideal world, applying for financial aid would not hurt your chances of being admitted to college. But only a handful of wealthy schools ignore your financial status during the admissions process and pledge to meet 100% of each admitted student's need. The majority of the rest follow a policy under which students are admitted regardless of financial need, but not necessarily given all the aid they qualify for; as a result, some cannot attend. A small number of schools, including such prominent institutions as Smith and Brown, say they may have to reject some students—or put them on a waiting list—because those students need more money than the schools can provide.

Does this mean you should avoid applying for financial aid? Most experts say no. It is simply too difficult to anticipate whether your request for aid will hurt your chances of admission, especially because schools are not always candid about their policies. It does, however, make sense to apply to one or more "financial safety" schools—where you know you can afford the cost.

In the meantime, there are moves you can make to increase your aid eligibility:

Do not save money in your child's name. Under the financial aid formula, kids contribute a far higher percentage of their savings than parents do. So $10,000 in Mom and Dad's bank account increases the expected family contribution by up to $560; that same amount in the child's name will boost the figure by as much as $3,500.

Cash in investments. You are expected to kick in a much higher proportion of your income than of your assets. Any capital gains you incur from selling assets like stocks during the year before you apply for aid will count as income. Since you will be applying for aid each year, you should cash in any profitable investments you plan to use to pay college costs by December 31 of your child's junior year in high school.

Use a home-equity loan to pay off your debts. Another quirk of the congressional methodology is that in adding up your assets, it considers home equity but ignores consumer debt. So while borrowing against your home to pay off other loans won't alter your true net worth, it will make you poorer, and more deserving, in the eyes of an aid analyst. For example, a home-equity loan used to pay off $30,000 of auto loan or credit-card debt would cut your family contribution by $1,680 (5.6% times $30,000).

Contribute to a 401(k), IRA, or Keogh. The official formula does not count these tax-deferred retirement accounts when totting up your assets. So if you think your child will be a candidate for financial aid in a few years, it makes sense to stash as much as you can afford in these shelters (remember that you cannot withdraw funds from retirement accounts before age 59½ without paying a 10% penalty). When it comes to determining your income during the year before you apply for aid, however, contributions to retirement plans will not be deducted.

Keep a lid on your youngster's earnings. Since students on financial aid must contribute such a high percentage of their incomes, your child may be better off with a challenging non-paying internship than with a high-paying but unstimulating job. (Note that Congress may soon change the rules to let students keep more of their wages.)

Spend the student's money first. Since students are expected to contribute far more of their assets than parents are, it makes more sense for a student to dip into his own savings for big outlays like a stereo for his dorm room or a computer.

Let's say you've followed all the rules and used all the tricks and your child has been accepted at his first-choice school but you're unhappy with the financial aid package. What can you do? Sometimes there is room for negotiation. Federal regulations allow financial aid officers to exercise "professional judgment" in individual cases, though most officers are constrained by tight budgets as well. If you get a markedly better deal from another school of similar quality, mention that: Some aid officers will adjust your package to match the rival offer, although some will simply tell you to attend the other school. If your financial condition has worsened since you filed your application, be sure to tell the aid officer; usually you will get extra help.

Going for a Loan

When financial aid or savings don't cover your college costs, you may have to borrow the money you need.

What can you do when you are too well off to qualify for financial aid but not rich enough to pay the bills out of savings and income? You have one choice: borrow. Once you decide to go into debt, however, the choices may get to be dizzying—you can pick from dozens of government and private loans, many with similar rates and terms.

There is no single right way to borrow for college. In general, state education loans are the best deals, but not every state makes them. When choosing among other loans, determining what's best for you will depend not only on the interest rate but on such factors as how much money you need, how large a monthly payment you can afford, and whether you want a fixed or variable rate. Take, for example, PLUS loans, which are made by banks and other private lenders and sponsored by the Department of Education. The rate on these loans, recently 11.49%, is variable but capped at 12%, which protects you against surges in interest rates. In addition, some lenders will permit you to defer repayment until after your child leaves school. The PLUS loan is limited to $4,000 a year, however.

In contrast, the Knight Extended Repayment Plan, a commercial loan, permits you to borrow up to the full cost of education. But its variable rate was recently 12.25% and it has a higher cap (18%). Moreover, you must begin making interest and principal payments on the Knight loan immediately.

Unlike subsidized loans meant for those who qualify for financial aid, most loans discussed here are made to parents, not students. They are usually available to all comers, provided, of course, that applicants meet customary credit standards. The leading non-need-based federal, nonprofit, and commercial college-loan programs are made through banks and other lenders nationwide. Loans offered by individual states and schools are outlined below, as are some all-purpose loans that are smart ways to borrow for college:

State-sponsored loans. In 1990, 19 states offered low-cost educational loans. To ferret them out, start by checking with your high school college counselor and the financial aid officer at the college your child plans to attend. If your child is heading for an out-of-state school, be sure to ask a financial aid officer at a local college about what loans your own state may provide to residents who study elsewhere.

Pennsylvania offers one of the best deals. The state lends money to students who are Pennsylvania residents, regardless of where they attend college, and to nonresidents who attend Pennsylvania schools. Loan limits and interest rates match those of the federally subsidized Stafford Student Loan, which goes to students who qualify for financial aid. First- and second-year students can borrow $2,625 a year; juniors and seniors, $4,000 a year. The rate is 8% for the first four years of the loan, 10% thereafter. But unlike the Stafford, which lets you defer principal and interest payments, the Pennsylvania loan requires that interest payments begin immediately; principal payments can be put off until six months after the student leaves school.

Maine also offers an excellent program to parents with children attending in-state schools and to Maine residents whose children attend 2,550 participating schools out of state or in Canada. Maine lends as much as $20,000 a year per student, at a variable interest rate set anywhere from one percentage point below the prime rate to two points above prime. Principal payments on the 20-year loan can be deferred until the student leaves school. But you will be hit with up-front loan fees totaling 4.5% and a nonrefundable application fee of $35.

Massachusetts has a generous program that makes 15-year loans to cover up to the full cost of education for resident and nonresident families with students attending 51 of the Bay State's public and private colleges. A 6% origination fee boosts the fixed 9.5% rate to an effective 10.59%. Payments of principal and interest begin immediately.

School-sponsored loans. Several universities will lend parents as much as the full cost of an education. The Massachusetts Institute of Technology (which does not participate in the Massachusetts loan program) offers a typical deal: an uncapped variable-rate line of credit pegged at two percentage points above the prime. Monthly payments of principal and interest begin immediately. Stanford pegs its rate on its similar loan at 0.75 points above the seven-year Treasury note, with no cap.

Some universities offer what they call stabilization loans, which allow parents to lock in current prices by establishing a line of credit big enough to cover up to four years of costs.

Washington University in St. Louis, for example, permits parents of incoming freshmen to finance as much as $82,000 at a fixed rate of 9.6%, with 10 years to repay. Parents draw on their credit to pay each semester's bills. Interest and principal payments begin immediately. A similar loan deal offered at Case Western Reserve in Cleveland carries a 9% fixed interest rate but is limited to tuition ($12,800 for the 1990-91 school year) and does not include room and board.

Other sources. If grandparents have money in fixed-income investments, such as CDs yielding, say, 8%, ask them to lend you what they feel comfortable taking out of the bank, at perhaps 10%. That's less than what you'd pay for most loans, and you can pledge your house as collateral to make the interest payments tax deductible.

As for tapping your own assets, your cheapest option is to take out a home-equity loan. Reason: You can deduct the interest on a home-equity loan of as much as $100,000. Margin loans are another tax-advantaged way to borrow, but making use of them gets complicated. Let's say you have money invested in stocks and bonds. You can sell your securities to pay the bills (ideally, to avoid capital-gains taxes, you sell securities on which you have a loss) and then take out a margin loan to replenish your portfolio; the interest on your margin loan, usually one or two percentage points above the prime rate, will be tax deductible up to the amount of your investment income each year. Exception: You cannot deduct the interest if you borrow to buy tax-exempt securities.

If your company's 401(k) plan allows loans, you can borrow up to 50% of your vested balance, as much as $50,000, and take five years to repay. Most companies fix the interest rates at the prime plus one or two percentage points, or at what local banks are charging on commercial loans. The interest isn't tax deductible, but all the interest you pay is savings that go back into your retirement account.

Depending on your policy, you may be able to borrow up to 95% of the cash value of your life insurance, generally at the prime, give or take one or two percentage points. But your death benefit is automatically reduced by the amount outstanding, and if you've counted on the policy's earnings to cover your premiums, you may be forced to pay the premiums out of pocket or let the policy lapse.

How to Find Scholarships

Most merit-based scholarships (other than those awarded by individual schools) are better for the ego than the wallet: The overwhelming majority are less than $1,000, from such organizations as private foundations, corporations, and veterans' groups.

Among the handful of lucrative awards are the **Reserve Officer Training Corps scholarships** sponsored by the U.S. Army, Navy, and Air Force. For information, call one of the service branches or talk to a college guidance counselor.

If your child is artistically inclined, the **Arts Recognition and Talent Search** (ARTS), sponsored by the National Foundation for Advancement in the Arts, is a talent competition with cash awards of up to $3,000. For information, call or write NFAA, P.O. Box 1305, Miami, FL 33137; 305-573-0490.

For budding scientists, there is the **Westinghouse Science Talent Search**. Write to Science Service, 1719 N Street NW, Washington, D.C. 20036 or call 202-785-2255.

To find other scholarships, look close to home. Many companies help their employees' college-bound kids with grants; churches and service clubs may also hand out prizes. More obscure awards can sometimes be found in a computerized scholarship data base, such as the University of Maryland's CASHE 3000 system of 140,000 scholarships. Write to University of Maryland Financial Aid Office, 2130 Mitchell Building, College Park, MD 20742 or call 301-314-8313.

For more scholarship sources, consult the guides available in libraries and bookstores, such as *The A's and B's of Academic Scholarships* (Octameron Press) or *Financing a College Education* by Judith B. Margolin (Plenum Press).

Buy Like a Billionaire

In uncertain times, one of the surest ways to make money is to not spend it, and going into the 1990s, American consumers are taking that lesson to heart. They are cutting back on excesses and refusing to pay high prices that they might readily have accepted in the roaring 1980s.

These days smart shopping is in, and this chapter will show you how to go about it. Buying like a billionaire no longer means doing it the Trump way and piling on debt. Instead, smart shoppers, like wise investors, are making important purchases the old-fashioned way, using common sense, a little restraint, and a good bit of insider savvy to latch onto bargains. In these pages, you will find out how to:

Buy a car you can live with (or in). With sales competition hotter than ever, new-car bargains abound for the comparative shopper. But you have to ask the right questions: Should you hire an auto broker to do the haggling for you? Does leasing make sense? And how can you find out about special dealer incentives offered by manufacturers? Knowing the answers to these questions and others can save you thousands of dollars.

Then there's the equipment that goes in the car. America's love affair with the automobile will take on new dimensions in the 1990s. New technology will make the car office an extension or even a replacement for the conventional four-walled workplace with everything from phones to faxes to printers and advanced stereo and video systems.

Dress with distinction at a discount. Clothes make the person, as the saying goes, but at the prices some stores are charging, outfitting yourself for work can also break you. It doesn't have to. Beginning on page 152, find out "Where the Elite Shop—at Dizzying Discounts" on designer clothes.

Deal with high-priced eats and insults in the dark. There's an old joke about chic restaurants in which a customer complains about the low lighting and the waiter retorts: "That's atmosphere. You pay for atmosphere. If it were any darker, you couldn't afford it." In "How to Get Respect at Restaurants You Can't Afford" (page 155), former *New York Times* food critic Mimi Sheraton offers rules to follow before you make your next Saturday night reservation.

Fly smarter. Air fares are up and good ol' fashioned service—of the kind that got you and your bags where you wanted to go on time—seems to be heading for new lows. Although the airlines won't always tell you, if you're an unhappy passenger, you have more rights than you know.

Get away when you have to get away fast. Shorter and more frequent vacations are growing in popularity. The downside for impulse travelers has always been that they can't take advantage of the discounts offered those who plan trips ahead. That was then, this is now. If you know where to look, last-minute travel clubs can help you get away without paying higher prices.

Save Big Bucks on a New Car

With automobile sales down and buying incentives up, you can get a good deal with the right strategy.

In the movie "Cadillac Man," Robin Williams' character and his car salesmen co-conspirators in sleaze raise their beer bottles in a Chinese restaurant and toast the motto of the dealership: "Nobody gets out alive." So much for the movies. In reality, with heightened competition, most auto salesmen and manufacturers can't afford to treat their customers like prisoners anymore. And there are more ways than ever to save on a new car. Dealer incentives alone—factory to dealership payments that give sales managers leeway to move cars at big discounts from list prices—can save you thousands of dollars.

Despite the good deals available, buying one of life's most enjoyable products still ranks up there with a root canal as one of life's least pleasurable experiences. Manufacturers aren't making the task any easier by starting and stopping their rebate and dealer-incentive programs. And some dealers continue pressuring customers into buying quickly. The car business is based on not giving the consumer the time to compare prices.

Auto analysts agree on this key rule for making your way through the new-car market today: Keep all your transactions separate. Trading in or selling your old car, if you have one, is one deal. Financing the new car, if you won't be paying cash, is another. And negotiating the new-car price is one more. Car salesmen like to jumble the three together, making it harder for you to figure out your true costs of buying and financing.

Before setting foot in a showroom, you should decide whether you want to join the 13% of new-car customers who lease instead of buy. Leasing makes the most sense if you normally borrow when purchasing an auto and if you plan to trade in the car within five years. You won't get a tax break for taking out a car loan anymore: Starting this year, the interest is no longer deductible. And if you like to trade in cars frequently, a lease could allow you to cut your monthly payments for a mid-size model by 20% to 30% compared with a car loan. Then, too, with a lease you need not face the headache of selling or trading in your used car; you simply return it to the leasing company or dealership.

Assuming that you've decided to buy, not lease, follow these strategies:

If you plan to trade in a car, get a used-car price service to help calculate how much you can expect to receive for the auto. Once you know that number, you can determine how much money you'll need from savings or borrowing to pay for your new car. You can get a fairly reliable estimate of your old car's trade-in or resale value at your library, bank, or credit union by leafing through the latest copy of the National Automobile Dealers Association monthly *Official Used Car Guide*, a pocket-size paperback. Many bookstores and news-stands sell a competitor: *Edmund's Used Car Guide* ($4.95, published quarterly; also available by mail from Edmund's, 515 Hempstead Tpk., West Hempstead, NY 11552). For a sharper estimate, dial the recently introduced phone service known as Auto Priceline (900-999-2277), which gives prices on used cars and trucks in your state (cost: $1.75 for the first minute plus 75¢ for each minute after). You'll probably get more for your car if you sell it through the classifieds rather than trade it in at a dealership.

Pay cash if you can; if you can't, carefully analyze dealer financing or consider tapping an existing home-equity credit line. Auto-makers and dealers trumpet their cut-rate financing, but their lowest rates are usually only for loans that must be paid off in two years.

Consequently, while the rates are great, the monthly payments are exorbitant. Such short-term deals are best avoided. The other catch with below-market financing from a dealer is that if the model has a rebate attached to it, you generally won't be allowed to claim the refund, too. Yet, it almost always makes sense to choose the rebate because cutting the amount you finance reduces your total and monthly costs more than does lowering your interest rate.

If you must borrow, an existing home-equity credit line may be your best choice. (Since origination fees on home-equity loans can run as high as $2,000, it rarely makes sense to open one solely to finance a car.) The advantages of home-equity lines for car purchases are that interest on them is generally fully tax deductible up to $100,000 and that the average rate is slightly lower than the average for auto loans at banks. A taxpayer in the 28% federal bracket, for example, who wants to borrow $12,000 for a car would save roughly $800 over the life of a four-year loan by going with an 11.65% home-equity loan rather than an 11.82% loan at a bank. Remember, though: Financing a car with your home equity means putting your house on the line if you can't make the payments.

When choosing a new car to buy, don't overlook today's wallflowers. Inventory costs are a car dealer's biggest expense and, with the end of the model-year, sales managers are especially eager to unload models that aren't selling well. Select one and you could be on the road to a bargain.

Take a tough negotiating position by finding out how much dealers actually pay for the models that interest you. Here again, your library or credit union can probably help with the research. Ask to see a copy of one of the industry publications that show dealer costs for new cars and trucks. Two examples: guides from *Kelley Blue Book* and *Automobile Invoice Service*.

Look for a car's invoice price—the dealer's wholesale cost. As a rule, the dealer expects to make a profit of 5% or 6% over invoice. But if you drive a hard bargain, you can get a new car for 3% over invoice. Consider yourself a savvy negotiator if you pay no more than $300 over invoice for a new subcompact car costing $10,000 or less, $500 over invoice for a mid-price car at about $15,000, and $750 to $1,000 over invoice for a $20,000-plus car. Cars in short supply and hot sellers, including many Japanese imports, are exceptions to the rule.

Learn what special deals manufacturers now offer on the models you like. An excellent source is the "Incentive Watch" column in the weekly trade paper *Automotive News*, available at credit unions and public libraries. This table notes the size and expiration dates of all rebate and low-rate financing programs offered by domestic and foreign car makers. It also shows which models have the incentives that manufacturers award dealers for unloading specific cars; these incentives rarely appear in newspaper auto ads. Cars with such dealer incentives are perfect targets for hard bargaining, since the salesmen need your money to collect on them. Dealers will share their savings with you if you push. In late 1990, dealer incentives of $250 to $4,000 were commonly awarded on an enormous selection of cars.

Don't overlook the expiration dates of any lure. Rebates, dealer incentives, and financing terms have a shell-game quality. Some deals last for only a few weeks.

Don't let a dealer stick you with last-minute add-ons that will inflate your purchase price. If you're not careful, a salesman can tack on as much as $1,000 worth of extras. Stoutly refuse any hard sells for supposedly necessary protections such as rustproofing and fabric conditioner. The metal used in cars today is already treated to resist rust, and that $75 to $100 anti-stain fabric conditioner for resisting stains is overpriced. Refuse to pay "dealer preparation" costs—usually $100 to $200. These fees are already included in the invoice cost.

Above all, take your time. Don't be afraid to visit five or more showrooms before committing to a car. After a week of calling up 11

dealers to shop for a Plymouth Voyager SE minivan, a homemaker in Durham, North Carolina knocked nearly $3,000 off the $18,860 price she was originally quoted. "Taking my time was the biggest help," she says. "I was not anxious. The salesmen would say: 'How soon do you want the car?' and then I'd say: 'How soon do you want to sell?'"

Hiring an Auto Broker

One way to avoid haggling with car dealers is to hire someone to do it for you. Indeed, that's the main attraction of buying services—avoiding hassles—because sometimes your own hard bargaining can get you the car you want for slightly less.

Most buying services work the same way. First, you tell the service the exact model and color you want and pay a fee of $150 to $800; local American Automobile Association buying services collect their $75-per-car fees directly from dealers. (To use an AAA buying service, you must join the organization. Cost: $18 to $65 a year.) Then, the pro typically delivers the car to you at $100 to $1,100 above the invoice price. A low-cost national auto broker called Car/Puter (800-221-4001) operates a bit differently. For $22, the company refers you to the nearest of its 600 affiliated dealers. There you are likely to pay only $50 to $150 over invoice for a domestic model ($300 to $600 for imports). Lobbying muscle by car dealers has banned auto brokers in a few states such as Maryland and Texas, but AAA and Car/Puter are exempt because buyers pick up cars at dealers.

Bear in mind that auto brokers have two drawbacks: If you have a car to sell, you'll probably have to find a buyer yourself, since most services do not arrange trade-ins. And repairs may be slow if you take the car to a local dealer for warranty work. Chances are this won't be the dealer who sold the car, so you'll be asking him to fix for free an auto that didn't earn him a profit.

Fax, Phone, and Fun in the New, Improved Auto Office

How to leave those deskbound blues behind and take your state-of-the-art show on the road.

The car phone. What we have here, folks, is true romance: breakthrough technology (in the form of cellular communication) meets sexy car (already the object of a longstanding American love affair). And you don't have to stop at that voice-activated cellular speaker phone, with optional hands-free operation so you can keep both hands on the wheel while talking. Instead, you add a special cellular modem and, suddenly, your portable fax starts to spit out important papers, or your laptop computer laps up long-distance data, as you go breezing down the road.

Now throw in a printer, a dictaphone, a mobile pager or two, tape recorder, CD player, tape deck, VCR, camcorder, television, and state-of-the-art speakers, and suddenly you're no longer driving a mere car. You're in a mobile monument to some gadget-inspired, informational New Age.

In 10 years, some experts predict, cellular technology will transform the way we work as thoroughly as the steam engine did. We'll all have a home base, but that's not necessarily where the work will get done. It offers an end to the nine-to-five workday and encourages a wave of small entrepreneurial businesses geared to service and information.

Such is the promise our technological future holds, and the cellular phone is responsible. From an initial test with 5,000 users in Chicago seven years ago, these gadgets have multiplied to serve an estimated 5.2 million customers in 1990. The demand is rapidly outgrowing the existing analog networks, which are expected to handle a maximum of 18 million subscribers by 1995. On the horizon, however, is digital cellular—a faster, more accurate, and cheaper transmission system that can accommodate at least four times as many callers. In truth, we're just beginning to tap the potential of the office on wheels. Consider: If info can be faxed or retrieved on-line, it's as good as there. Sketches, blueprints, contracts—the works.

Apparently, most who know their way around an auto office are conscientious—for safety—about pulling off the road to conduct business. At least so far, there's no indication that these devices pose much of a crackup threat.

Insuring these gadgets is another matter. The standard auto policy covers only "equipment permanently installed in the car that is exclusively for reproducing sound," says a spokesperson for Insurance Services Office, which draws up forms for many insurance companies. That means no phones. Individual companies, though, sometimes take a more liberal attitude. Allstate's comprehensive policy covers anything that arrived with the car from the maker. Anything else, such as a laptop or fax, must be covered by an add-on in·the homeowners policy. Our advice? Quiz your agent.

Calling him from your car, however, won't come cheap. The phone itself starts at $500 and can run up to about $2,500 for the slip-it-in-your-pocket size. You may also want a portable fax ($600 to $1,500), in which case you'll need the special error-correcting modem ($150 to $1,000) that avoids loss of data as you drive from place to place. And then there's the phone bill—about $100 a month, for moderate calling (meaning 10 minutes or so a day) in a big city like Los Angeles.

Of course, prices for equipment and services vary depending on quality and geography, so the usual caveats apply: Shop around, fully aware that the lowest price is probably not the best deal.

Don't count on your auto dealer to do much of this customizing for you. A car company's cellular option is likely to be a "mounting space"—a rectangular hole in the console that you fill at your expense. To create a mobile office worthy of the name, you need a local converter—or "coach"—company. At Compliment Conversions in Camanche, Iowa, for instance, business-type installations were up about 40% from 1989 to 1990. The average installation—including phone, fax, and videocassette player—was $15,000, equipment included.

For the carriage trade, the Dillinger/Gaines Coach Works in New York City offered what might be called a Trumpmobile—an $85,000 stretch limo on a Cadillac chassis with two cellular phones, fax, CD player, desk and tables, safe, aircraft lighting, bar, TV and assorted accoutrements, and one more item that will be especially valuable to some clients—the paper shredder. (Donald "Art of the Deal" Trump got the prototype gratis by lending his name, but otherwise has nothing to do with the company.) So far, the company sells about 10 a year, a Dillinger spokesperson says. The limo offers a secure, air-conditioned, upholstered retreat. Furthermore, if the owner doesn't like the view out his office window, he can tell the chauffeur to drive somewhere else.

Where the Elite Shop—at Dizzying Discounts

The Kleins—Anne and Calvin—and other top labels sell for up to 80% off at designer malls.

The department store, the traditional seller of high-fashion apparel to American women, is undergoing an agonizing downsizing that may drive many shoppers elsewhere. Unwilling to pay full retail prices, dyed-in-the-wool devotees of well-designed, well-made clothes are finding a new field to graze in. And it's still a bit of a secret: the designer outlet, a small store leased by a single designer-manufacturer, usually in an out-of-the-way mall made up of a dozen or more outlet stores, including those of other designers plus assorted retailers.

The outlets offer merchandise at about the same bargain prices as conventional off-price stores—20% to 80% off. Yet, these stores have an inviting, if not luxurious, ambience. And best of all, most of their merchandise is first quality—not the irregulars sold by off-price stores.

Designer-outlet merchandise is normally manufacturers' end-of-the-season leftovers that haven't been sold to department stores and other full-price retailers. At least one designer—Harvé Benard—has been refusing to ship orders to department stores that are considered credit risks—an estimated 15% of its business. If that trend builds, designers will have convoys of clothing detouring to their outlets.

The designers don't advertise their outlets, however, and these stores operate somewhat differently from mainstream retailers. So anyone interested in designer duds at discount needs to know where to find the outlets and how to shop them.

Thanks to numbers alone, it's getting easier. The upscale outlets started appearing only about six years ago. No one has figures on their growth in particular, but the number of outlets of all kinds grew 18% in 1989, compared with 5% for full-price specialty stores and one-half of 1% for department stores.

So far, a handful of top names—Harvé Benard, Liz Claiborne, Anne Klein, Calvin Klein, Ralph Lauren, Ellen Tracy, Tahari, and Adrienne Vittadini—represent most of the action. In almost five years, Harvé Benard has built on outlet army of 76 stores scattered coast to coast—the most ambitious such expansion so far. Vittadini, a newcomer to the pack, has four. While the country's midsection is still only lightly dusted, the Northeast is already nearly saturated and California is getting there.

A look at how the rag trade works explains the quick emergence of the outlet. Major designers manufacture most of their lines in places like Hong Kong—where the cheap yet skilled labor more than offsets the superschlep to market. But factory runs must be ordered as much as a year in advance of the selling season, and the inevitable miscalculations result in piles of unsold garments. The large amount of merchandise that's left over makes it easier for off-price stores to negotiate lower and lower prices.

Anne Klein and other designers began to see advantages to opening their own outlets. Aside from not being beholden to off-price stores, they could control distribution of a valued label. Designer clothes would not hang

next to a competitor's or, worse, be sold in an off-price store next door to a major department store customer.

The greatest motive of all behind the designer outlet trend: These stores have turned out to be immensely more profitable than anyone believed possible only five years ago.

Another reason for designer boldness: the continuing turmoil among department stores. As a result of all the leveraged buy-outs and other consolidations, the number of department stores is shrinking, resulting in fewer and fewer points of distribution for manufacturers. Plus, the major stores all look the same. They cherry-pick from designers' lines. Outlets give designers a way of showcasing more of their merchandise.

If you still haven't heard about these outlets, there's a reason: Designers, to head off unfair-competition complaints by department stores carrying their labels at full price, not only haven't advertised their outlet stores but have placed them in smaller communities at least 20 miles from major retail hubs.

For the whereabouts of some of the major designer outlets, see page 154. You can also call the designers' headquarters, most of which are in New York City, and ask where outlets are. A valuable sourcebook for outlets of all types is *The Joy of Outlet Shopping*, available from the *Outlet Consumer Reporter*, Box 7867, St. Petersburg, FL 33734.

Instead of being a drag on sales, this dispersion, born out of fear of department store retaliation, has actually begun to affect American shopping habits. Often outlet centers are on major highways between two sizable cities or in tourist areas. The strategy, modeled loosely on the fabulous success of L.L. Bean and its neighbors in Freeport, Maine, is to get shoppers to plan all-day or even weekend excursions to the outlet malls and stop-offs at others while on vacation.

To serve what retail marketing executives call the destination shopper, an estimated 500 bus companies now offer a range of special tours, some just to malls, others to a mall plus a traditional tourist attraction.

So what will you find in a typical designer outlet mall? Although the phenomenon is too

The Designer Outlets' Almost-Secret Locations

Harvé Benard:

Alabama: Boaz, Foley; **Arizona:** Sedona; **California:** Citadel, Folsom, Gilroy, Pacific Grove, Palm Desert, Redding, Vacaville; **Colorado:** Silverthorne; **Connecticut:** Milford, Mystic, Norwalk; **Delaware:** Rehoboth; **Florida:** Orlando, West Palm Beach; **Georgia:** Commerce, Valdosta; **Illinois:** St. Charles; **Indiana:** Michigan City; **Kansas:** Lawrence; **Maine:** Freeport, Kittery; **Maryland:** Annapolis, Perryville, Queenstown; **Massachusetts:** Lawrence, Lenox, New Bedford; **Michigan:** Birch Run, Holland, Monroe; **Missouri:** Branson, Osage Beach; **New Hampshire:** Keene, North Conway, West Lebanon; **New Jersey:** Flemington, Manasquan, Secaucus (two); **New York:** Central Valley, Lake George, Latham, Monticello, Niagara Falls, Saratoga; **North Carolina:** Blowing Rock, Burlington, Smithfield; **Ohio:** Aurora; **Oregon:** Lincoln City; **Pennsylvania:** Lancaster, Reading, Somerset, York; **South Carolina:** Bluffton, Hilton Head; **Tennessee:** Chattanooga, Pigeon Forge; **Texas:** Hillsboro, La Marque, New Braunfels, Sulphur Springs; **Vermont:** Manchester; **Virginia:** Massaponax, Virginia Beach, Waynesboro, Williamsburg; **Washington:** Burlington, Centralia, North Bend; **West Virginia:** Martinsburg; **Wisconsin:** Kenosha, Oshkosh. Call 800-800-5012 for information on other locations.

Liz Claiborne:

Alabama: Boaz, Foley; **California:** Gilroy; **Colorado:** Silverthorne; **Georgia:** Commerce (irregulars only); **Maine:** Kittery; **Maryland:** Perryville, Queenstown; **Massachusetts:** Buzzards Bay; **Michigan:** Birch Run; **New Hampshire:** North Conway; **New Jersey:** Secaucus; **New York:** Central Valley; **North Carolina:** Brighton, Burlington (irregulars only); **Pennsylvania:** Reading; **Tennessee:** Pigeon Forge; **Texas:** Hillsboro (irregulars only); **Vermont:** Manchester; **Virginia:** Williamsburg; **Washington:** Burlington; **West Virginia:** Martinsburg; **Wisconsin:** Kenosha.

Anne Klein:

Alabama: Boaz; **California:** Barstow, Gilroy; **Florida:** Orlando; **Indiana:** Michigan City; **Maine:** Freeport, Kittery; **Maryland:** Chester; **Michigan:** Birch Run; **Missouri:** Osage Beach; **New Hampshire:** North Conway; **New Jersey:** Flemington, Shrewsbury; **New York:** Central Valley, Lake George, Niagara Falls; **North Carolina:** Blowing Rock, Hilton Head; **Tennessee:** Pigeon Forge; **Vermont:** Manchester; **Virginia:** Williamsburg; **West Virginia:** Martinsburg; **Wisconsin:** Kenosha.

Calvin Klein:

Alabama: Foley; **Florida:** Orlando; **Maine:** Freeport, Kittery; **Massachusetts:** New Bedford; **New Hampshire:** North Conway; **New Jersey:** Flemington, Secaucus (two); **New York:** Central Valley, Niagara Falls; **Vermont:** Manchester; **Virginia:** Prince William, Williamsburg; **Wisconsin:** Kenosha.

Ralph Lauren:

Alabama: Boaz, Foley; **California:** Barstow, Eureka, Mammoth; **Colorado:** Durango; **Indiana:** Michigan City; **Kentucky:** Eddyville; **Maine:** Freeport, Kittery; **Massachusetts:** Lawrence; **Missouri:** Osage Beach; **Montana:** Billings; **New Hampshire:** North Conway; **New York:** Cohoes, Niagara Falls (two), Plattsburgh, Watertown; **Pennsylvania:** Reading; **Puerto Rico:** San Juan; **South Dakota:** Rapid City; **Tennessee:** Chattanooga; **Texas:** El Paso; **Vermont:** Manchester; **Virgin Islands:** St. Thomas; **West Virginia:** Martinsburg; **Wisconsin:** Appleton; **Wyoming:** Jackson.

Adrienne Vittadini:

California: Cabazon; **Massachusetts:** New Bedford; **New York:** Central Valley, Saratoga; **Tennessee:** Chattanooga.

new and spreading too fast to have much uniformity, some generalities can be made:

There's usually a broad mix of merchandise, as designers favor their outlets over off-price stores. "If I have five beaded evening tops unsold at our first-line stores but no matching skirts, I probably won't put those pieces into our outlets even though they're top quality," says Richard Catalano, president of Adrienne Vittadini. "We'll ship them to Loehmann's."

You'll discover a new meaning of ready-to-wear. While it is impossible to predict what you will find on any given visit, stock tends to lag what you'll see in department stores and specialty stores by as much as one season. This may be a boon. For example, if you need a winter sweater in February, the place to look for it is in the outlets, not department stores which will already be pushing spring items.

You won't be put off by the look of the place. Premises are usually unglamorous but clean and easy to shop. Dressing rooms are ample and often have private booths. Return policies vary but are clearly spelled out in signs near the checkouts. Service is minimal.

Yes, shoppers, there are sales. Most outlets discount their discounts at different times during the year, especially in January and the summer. For example, in December 1989, much of the merchandise at the Calvin Klein outlet in the Woodbury Common mall in Central Valley, New York sold for 33% below the regular outlet discount. A strapless velvet dress retailing for $600 was ticketed at $300 and was on sale for $150. A suede jacket retailing for $800 and matching jodhpurs for $960 were ticketed at $400 and $480 and were on sale for $268 and $322.

In fact, if you're canny and patient, you might get what you want for next to nothing. Because department stores generally insist on a constant sense of freshness to lure traffic, most of them turn over their merchandise every six weeks or so. Outlets, like off-price stores, let goods sit on the sales floor, with numerous markdowns, until they are sold.

While the outlet may be the end of the road for merchandise, outlets themselves are dressing up and heading for town. With department stores weakened, the logical next step is to move in for the kill to those forbidden zones—the big cities and suburbs.

How to Get Respect at Restaurants You Can't Afford

Follow this famous food critic's rules when you eat out.

You might think that a powerful food critic like Mimi Sheraton would be immune to shoddy treatment in restaurants. Quite the opposite. Because she always tries to go incognito, all the things that happen to you happen to her. At Wolfgang Puck's trendy Spago in Los Angeles, for example, she says she has

been seated at a table so remote that it was practically in the parking lot.

Thus, she has learned the hard way that ordinary customers sometimes need to use strategy to get the most out of a well-known restaurant. Of course, if you are the type of person who believes that no meal can be worth the tabs that such places charge, then no meal ever will be—and it is pointless to challenge a restaurant to change your mind. But if excellent food is important to you, here are some tips that will help you get your money's worth:

Scouting the Target

The obvious first step is to select the right restaurant. When picking one in your own town, you can be guided by newspaper or magazine reviews or—better yet—the recommendations of trusted friends. When traveling in a place where you don't know anyone, however, you need to be more creative. The concierge or hotel desk clerk will be little help; they are often paid to route guests to particular spots. Instead, try calling the local newspaper restaurant critic and describing the type of restaurant you want; you can also find interesting offbeat restaurants by asking ethnic cab drivers for their favorites, but always stressing their favorites rather than spots they think tourists would like.

Be prepared to pay a premium for fancy decor. At New York City's La Grenouille, for example, where magnificent fresh bouquets adorn the dining room nightly, the annual florist's bill comes to $130,000—helping to explain why a filet mignon costs $68 as part of a prix fixe dinner as compared with only $36 for a one-pound prime sirloin plus appetizer and dessert at the rough-and-ready Palm.

If you're planning a really big occasion—a major business deal, say, or a proposal of marriage—try the restaurant first for lunch, when prices are lower and it is easier to get in. Ask to see the dinner menu, and order lunch dishes that are also available at night.

If a restaurant you plan to visit gets a rave review, cross it off your list for three to four months or get ready to face a crowd.

Making a Reservation

Call to reserve your spot well in advance. With a popular local restaurant, that may mean three to four weeks ahead if you want a table between 7:30 p.m. and 9 p.m. on a Friday or Saturday night. For a Michelin three-star restaurant in Europe, such as Taillevent in Paris, you may need three to four months. But if you're visiting Paris and suddenly decide in the morning that you would like to go to such a restaurant that night, call anyway. Or ask the hotel concierge. He can often work miracles for a not-so-small consideration.

Try to strike up a relationship over the phone with the reservations taker. If you know anyone who is a regular at that restaurant, mention that he or she referred you. Or let drop the name of the company you are with— that will mark you as a potential repeat expense-account customer. If you carry any weight at all, this is the time to swing it around.

Ask to be put on a waiting list if the restaurant is full and you must go on a particular date. Then check back periodically to reassert your interest.

State your preference in tables: banquettes, squares, or rounds, the side of the room or the center, smoking or nonsmoking, and so forth. When you expect guests, request that they be seated and served drinks if they arrive before you. Inquire about the dress code, if you have any doubts about it, and whether special dishes you have read about are served every day. And, of course, ask what forms of payment are accepted.

Reconfirm your reservation and preferences on the morning of the big day—even if the house does not require you to do so.

When You Arrive

Dress according to the custom of the crowd. Evening dress is fine for a formal restaurant such as Los Angeles' L'Ermitage, but it may not fly, so to speak, in the quirky DC3 at the Santa Monica airport, where black Spandex and a bare midriff are preferred. In general, the best tables go to guests whose appearance reinforces the image the owner wants. Frumpy people usually get tucked away out of sight in the back.

You should arrive about 10 minutes early to

see whether you like your assigned table. That will give the restaurant time to make a switch if necessary.

If you absolutely must have a certain table, tip the maître d' $10 or $15. (Mimi Sheraton says she frowns on this under nearly all other circumstances. Why should you tip for something you have coming to you?)

Spend several minutes studying appetizers, wines, and desserts if they are on display when you enter so you can see what looks appealing.

Ordering Your Meal

Once you are seated, study the menu and hear the specials. Don't just ask the waiter what he likes, ask him what the kitchen is known for. Peek at what others are eating. And get the advice of the owner or chef, if possible.

Inquire about ingredients in garnishes and sauces so you will not wind up with courses that are too similar. If you have any doubts about a sauce, for example, ask that it be served on the side.

Ask the price of any off-menu specials. Granted, this can be embarrassing if you are either host or guest. But restaurateurs realize that, and they take advantage of people's good-mannered silence to lure them into higher-priced items.

General Advice

Avoid false economies that will compromise your experience. As an impecunious student in New York years ago, Mimi Sheraton went from one fancy restaurant to another ordering chopped steak, usually the cheapest main course, and always came away wondering what made the place so special. You will get better value from a dish the kitchen prepares, rather than from one made of simple—though impeccable—ingredients.

If any food is not cooked as ordered, or if it seems spoiled, call the captain or waiter at once and quietly but firmly ask to have it replaced. Ask to speak to the owner if you get

any argument. And if the owner also protests, cancel the rest of your order and ask for the check. Then write to local restaurant critics with a copy to the owner.

As for wine, it should be returned only if it has soured or faded prematurely, but not if you simply dislike your choice. The exception: If the wine was a house recommendation, return it, explaining what displeases you—too sweet, too acidic, or whatever—so it can be replaced.

When you like a restaurant and plan to return, tell the owner and manager and leave tips for captain and waiter that total about 20% of the bill before tax. Roughly one-third of the tip should go to the captain, the rest to the waiter. And if you plan to return within two months and want to be remembered, you could slip $10 into the maître d's palm as you leave.

Unless you are an incurable food buff, bound and determined to try something new and strange every night, concentrate your business at three or four favorite restaurants. That way, you will become a regular with all of them, and gain all the accompanying privileges: last-minute reservations (restaurants almost always hold back a few tables for steady customers), better location in the dining room, and special attention when you have special guests. Don't underestimate what you might be worth. Even at a four-star eatery like Lutece, a person who shows up with no more frequency than twice a month is more important than somebody who comes in once a year.

And if all else fails, you could try the old ruse of claiming that you are the local critic, or at least related to the critic. But don't expect to get far. One man identified himself as Mimi Sheraton's cousin to a fashionable New York restaurant only to be laughed at and told, "That's what everyone says." Funny thing is, he really was her cousin.

In a perfect world, of course, no such stratagem would be necessary—especially when the restaurant is charging $50 to $100 a person. In the real world, however, it is precisely the most fashionable and expensive restaurants that are likely to give newcomers and the uninitiated short shrift.

Thirty-Seven Ways to Fly Smarter

These insider tips can help you and your bags get there safely, on time, and at the lowest fare.

If you think airline service could be better, you have company. In a recent *Money* poll, 86% of those questioned said service either hadn't improved or had gotten worse in the past three years. So what's an unhappy passenger to do? The first thing is to know your rights. Some of them are spelled out in the contract governing your ticket purchase. Others, however, are based on arcane and often unwritten airline policy. Here are some tips that can help you beat the system:

Get the Best Fare

1. Establish a continuing relationship with an honest, competent travel agent. The agent's desire to get your repeat business may overcome the many industry incentives that could bias his judgment—such as the cash and travel bonuses that airlines give to agents who bring them enough business.

2. Book in advance, and explain that you want the lowest fare. If your schedule is flexible, say so. Then emphasize the point; when quoted a price, for example, say, "Is there anything cheaper if I leave sooner, later, or on another day?"

3. Consider discount travel agencies like Travel Avenue (800-333-3335) in Chicago, which rebates four-fifths of the standard 10% ticket commission.

4. If possible, deal with an agent who has a direct-access reservation system—meaning his computer gets information on discounted seats directly from the airline. Otherwise, you may book a cheap fare today only to find tomorrow that it was sold out. If your agent lacks this service, ask him to verify your reservation by calling the airline.

5. To beat the yield-management lottery, seek out an agent who uses one of the new computer programs that automatically query and requery to find the lowest fare.

6. Don't jump to buy a special low fare the first day it is advertised. Wait a day or two to see whether competing airlines come up with a better deal.

7. Pay by credit card, so if you do get stiffed (say, your airline goes bankrupt), you can protest the charge and often get your money back.

8. After buying a nonrefundable ticket, watch your newspaper's business section for low-fare specials on the same airline. If you spot a better deal, call the airline and your travel agent. Sometimes, you can exchange your ticket.

9. Check whether so-called nested round trips would save you money. For instance, the midweek round-trip coach fare from Atlanta to Phoenix was $1,034 in early October 1990. But a discount fare purchased seven days in advance that included a Saturday night stay was only $217. So you could have bought two round trips (one starting in Atlanta, the other in Phoenix), used only half of each ticket, and saved $600.

10. If you are 62 or older, or are flying because of a family emergency, ask about discounts.

Avoid Delays

11. Don't take a flight that departs or arrives during airport rush hours, when runways and gates are most congested—generally from about 7 a.m. to 9 a.m. and then from 4 p.m. to 7 p.m.

12. When choosing between equally convenient flights, ask the travel agent for the one with the highest on-time rating. (A "9" means it arrived within 15 minutes of schedule 90% of the time last month, "8" means 80%, and so on.)

13. Get a boarding pass and seat assignment from your travel agent. If both are unavailable, the flight is probably overbooked. Take another flight or get to the gate an hour early.

14. Ask your travel agent for a list of the next three flights going your way. If you miss your plane or the flight is canceled, you'll at least know what airline to call.

15. Find out where your flight is coming from and don't book it if, for example, it is the last leg of an international flight, since those are often delayed.

16. Avoid booking the last flight out of a city, particularly as a connection. You could get stuck overnight.

17. When heading to larger cities, use less-crowded airports.

Don't Be a Chump If Bumped

18. Even if you have a boarding pass, check in at the gate—not the ticket desk—at least 10 minutes before flight time or else you forfeit rights to bumping compensation.

19. Make sure you understand the restrictions on awards offered to induce you to leave a plane.

20. If airline agents aren't finding volunteers, try negotiating a better deal—such as an extra travel voucher.

21. If you are bumped against your will, federal law requires the airline to offer you cash or a check for the cost of your one-way fare up to a maximum of $200 if it can't get you to your destination less than an hour late. For delays of two hours or more, you should receive twice the one-way fare, up to a cap of $400.

22. You won't get paid for being bumped off a plane with fewer than 60 passengers or from an international flight originating overseas; the rules don't apply to them.

Beware of Baggage Blunders

23. Avoid checking luggage if you can. Pack light and carry it on.

24. If you must check bags, do so at least 30 minutes before flight time. Otherwise, if the bags arrive late, the airline won't pay to have them delivered.

25. Notwithstanding the advice above, don't check luggage more than 90 minutes before departure either, since it may get overlooked in a corner.

26. Never check valuables like jewelry or essentials like medicine.

27. Double-check the agent filling out your baggage tags. As one gate agent put it: "PDX to Portland looks an awful lot like PHX to Phoenix."

28. If making a connection, stick with the same carrier if possible to minimize chances of a baggage mix-up.

29. If your luggage gets lost during a change of airline, the airline that carried you last is responsible for it—regardless of which airline goofed.

30. If you are missing a bag while away from home, ask the baggage supervisor for cash for necessary purchases. If the supervisor refuses, buy what you need and save receipts. Seek a refund later by complaining.

31. In case of loss or damage, keep your baggage claim tag or a photocopy; it's your only proof the bag was checked.

32. Produce original sales slips for lost items. But note: Federal law requires only that you be reimbursed for their depreciated value up to $1,250 maximum, not for what it will cost to replace them.

33. If your loss exceeds $1,250, see if you have other insurance, such as a personal-property rider on your homeowners policy, that could make up the difference.

Cope with Cancellations

34. Call right before you leave for the airport to make sure that your flight has not been delayed or canceled.

35. If the cancellation or delay is the airline's fault—because of mechanical or crew mishaps, not weather or air traffic problems—and you have a discounted or nonrefundable ticket, ask the gate agent for a FIM (flight interruption manifest). If you manage to convince the gate agent your trip is urgent, he can "FIM" you to another carrier and you won't have to pay extra.

36. If you are delayed for more than four hours, ask for a voucher to cover the cost of a meal; if it's past 10 p.m. and you're away from home, ask for a hotel voucher, too. Some airlines will give you these only if the cancellation is their fault. But many will award them for other delays, too, if you ask politely.

Complain If You Get Stuck

37. Try to get the problem resolved at the airport, of course. But if that fails, get the names and identification numbers of all airline employees you have trouble with. Then write a letter to the airline's president, its office of consumer affairs, and the Department of Transportation, Office of Consumer Affairs (400 Seventh Street SW, Washington, D.C. 20590; 202-366-2220). State briefly what happened, what loss or damage you suffered, and what compensation you expect, such as a travel voucher for $100 or a round-trip ticket. Above all, make your demand reasonable.

Easy Steps to Last-Minute Getaways

How to globe hop—or just escape for the weekend—with a maximum of fun, a minimum of hassle, and surprising discounts to boot.

For a growing number of people, it's timing, not just price, that makes a trip attractive. By jumping—or flying—at the right opportunities, they are taking shorter, more frequent vacations and, in the process, helping to change the way America travels. Between 1983 and 1988, the average length of stay dipped from 6.2 days to just 4.8 days, according to the U.S. Travel Data Center, while the number of trips rose 17%.

There are perhaps a dozen specialized firms that now cater to the thousands of vacationers who—by choice or by chance—travel without a lot of advance planning. By combining attractive destinations with a hint of adventure, these clubs and discount travel brokers have captured the imagination of a wide group of people. In particular, they appeal to two-career couples, trying to juggle conflicting and often unpredictable schedules and still sneak away for an occasional weekend—with or without the kids.

And you don't have to spend more to keep your itinerary flexible. In fact, you may spend less. That's because of outfits like Last Minute Travel that buy unsold space on airlines, cruises, and tours and pass it on at savings of 25% to 40%—without the long advance purchase that would otherwise be required.

The easiest way to make a quick getaway is

to call one of the clubs listed in the table below. Some specialize in international flights, cruises, and tours, others in domestic flights. In either case, for an annual fee of $40 and up, you typically get a monthly newsletter, a hotline with recorded information on late-breaking discounts, and, of course, services of the club as your agent. The clubs can also respond quickly to events: The awakening of Eastern Europe in 1989, for example, spurred clubs to look for bargain flights because of interest by travelers.

On the other hand, it's easy to arrange last-minute trips yourself—if you don't mind swimming against the tide. Reason: Neither airlines, tour operators, nor many travel agents can be counted on to help because it's in their interest to sell you full-price fares. Here, travel experts offer suggestions:

Start by searching for an airfare. The rule here is to be a contrarian. Look for values on lesser-known carriers and lesser-flown routes; avoid flights to the most heavily toured spots in high season (Rome and the French Riviera are just as pleasant in spring or fall as in July).

Last-Minute Travel Clubs

The groups listed below offer unsold space on flights, tours, or cruises at discounts ranging from 20% to 65%. Last-minute travel clubs deal mainly in cruises and international tours, weekend clubs are mainly for domestic trips, and consolidators sell airline tickets only.

Name	Phone	Annual fee	Region	Comments
LAST-MINUTE CLUBS				
Discount Travel International (DTI)	800-334-9294	$45/family	National	One of the largest; administers AFL-CIO's travel club.
Last Minute Travel	617-267-9800	None	Boston area	Has 20 travel consultants and a reputation for personal service.
Moment's Notice	212-486-0503	$45/family	New York	"One of the best last-minute clubs," says Arthur Frommer.
Worldwide Discount Travel	305-534-2082	$40/ individual $50/family	National	Recent offerings included Bali, China, and Southeast Asia.
WEEKEND CLUBS				
Amex's Express Weekends	800-421-8758	$75/ individual $135/couple	Chicago New York Boston	Many domestic mini-vacations; will add more cities in 1991.
TWA's Travel Club	800-872-8364	$50/ individual $95/couple	Regional clubs in 9 major cities	Frequent fliers get 3,000 bonus miles after first travel club trip.
AIRLINE CONSOLIDATORS				
C. L. Thomson	Deals only through your travel agent	None	National	Well respected; known for Hawaiian tours and trans-Pacific flights.
Travac	800-872-8800	None	National	Offers mainly flights to Europe.
UniTravel	800-325-2222	None	National	In business 22 years; international and coast-to-coast flights.

Seek out smaller carriers for domestic flights. America West and Southwest Air are two possibilities according to Ed Perkins, editor of *Consumer Reports Travel Letter* (P.O. Box 53629, Boulder, CO 80322; $37 a year). Their walk-up fares—the ones you get at the airport—are often lower than those of larger competitors. The same is true for international travel; several airlines, especially those based in the Third World, often have last-minute deals.

Shop for a high-quality charter. Like any flight operator, a charter company occasionally winds up with unsold seats. George Albert Brown, author of the *Airline Passenger's Guerrilla Handbook* (Blakes Publishing Group), calls this one of the best last-minute deals. But he warns that charter tickets are typically nonrefundable, late departures are common, and, most important to lanky travelers, legroom can be scarce since the planes are designed to pack in as many people as possible. Two of the most respected charter operations, experts say, are run by Balair (212-581-3411) and Tower (718-917-8500).

Purchase from a ticket consolidator (a broker who deals only in discounted airline seats). You can book directly, but you may get better service if you work through your travel agent. If the agent balks, find another. If price is an object and you travel light, you can even get discounts of 50% or more if you escort freight for an air courier service like Halbart Express (718-656-8279). But bring only carry-on luggage, since the package of freight counts as your checked bag.

In searching for a last-minute cruise, do not rely on the reverse logic you applied to airfares. For while it's true that the steepest savings occur off-season, berths on little-known carriers can be undesirable considering that you will spend days—maybe weeks—on board. Instead, scan the travel section of your local newspaper for cruise ads or find a travel agent who specializes in last-minute promotions.

As for lodging, the best bargains are often at smaller hotels off the tourist trail (you can find

them with any reputable guidebook, such as *Fodor's*). Start with a reservation at such a hotel, then parlay it into better lodging by telling the second hotel that you already have a room but would like to be closer to town (cancel your reservation at the first hotel if the ploy works, of course). Or try calling hotels on the day you plan to arrive, when they may be stuck with space left vacant by no-shows.

For domestic trips, some of the best last-minute bargains can be had by extending a business trip to fill the weekend. One way to do this is by consulting the North American edition of *Pocket Flight Guide* (800-323-3537, $65 a year), which lists all flights through major cities.

Even airlines are starting to market their unsold seats as bargains. Eastern and TWA, for instance, offer "Weekenders" and "Breakaway" club memberships, respectively, that give 20% to 50% off coach fare to places like Seattle and New York. And American Express is promoting its $75-a-year "Express Weekends" club. Though tours emanate only from New York, Boston, and Chicago thus far, the savings are substantial.

Finally, some last-minute thoughts:

If you're traveling because of a family tragedy, such as a death or illness, many airlines will give you a price discount or credit for future travel.

Check visa requirements for international travel. Though many popular destinations don't require them—including Canada, Mexico, England, much of the Caribbean and Europe, Japan, Thailand, and Hong Kong—the majority of countries still do. The booklet *Foreign Entry Requirements* tells all (available from the Consumer Information Center, Box 455W, Pueblo, CO 81009).

If you feel the slightest bit uneasy about any of the companies you are buying from, check whether the American Society of Travel Agents (703-739-2782) or the U.S. Department of Transportation's Office of Consumer Affairs (202-366-2220) has received any complaints about them.

Pay by credit card. That way, if somebody does stiff you, you can protest the charge and possibly avoid paying.

Walt Disney World Doesn't Mean Mickey Mouse Prices

It costs a family of four about $500 a day to visit the country's premier amusement park.

On a typical morning at Florida's Walt Disney World, crowds vie for an early spot on the indoor roller coaster known as Space Mountain. By midmorning, visitors might wait in line an hour for this wild, two-minute-and-36-second ride located in the Magic Kingdom, the most famous of the three Disney World parks. But cognoscenti know that you can get into Main Street, U.S.A.—the nostalgic, turn-of-the-century boulevard that serves as the Kingdom's gateway—half an hour before official starting time. Thus, you can position yourself for the mad dash to Space Mountain or any other ride.

Is beating the wait all that important? You bet. Say you go on a busy day and experience an average delay of 30 minutes at popular attractions. If you hope to ride eight of them, you will waste four hours. Not all of the lines are in the park, either. After waiting in traffic to reach Disney-MGM Studios, the hot new amusement area with a Hollywood spin, it is not unheard of to be turned away because the parking lot is full. The solution? If you still want to join the crowds at MGM, park at EPCOT Center—the permanent world's fair that is the third major Disney World site—and take the free 10-minute shuttle bus to MGM.

Delays and lockouts are all the more galling because the cost of Disney's brand of enchantment has never been higher. The basic one-day admission more than doubled between 1980 and 1989 to $32.75 for "adults" ages 10

and up, and $26.40 for kids ages three to nine. (All prices are from a May 1990 visit.) Even with four-day passes ($105.60 each), standard air fare ($250 a person), a mid-size rental car ($150 a week), and a modest hotel (one room with two double beds at $85 a night), a family of four can expect to spend $2,900—including food, souvenirs, and incidentals—for a typical five-night stay at peak season. That leaves aside what the family might spend on visits to Disney's local competitors, such as Sea World (admission: $25.40 a day) and Universal Studios Florida ($30.74).

Not that the escalating costs have dampened enthusiasm for Disney World itself or for U.S. amusement parks in general, which marked a record 254 million visits in 1989 alone (for a rundown on the top 10, see the table on page 166). But 18-year-old Disney World and 35-year-old Disneyland—the Anaheim, California original after which it was modeled—always scoop up the most people: 43.3 million in 1989. And those numbers are growing globally: Tokyo Disneyland, which opened in 1983, had 13.4 million visits in 1989; Euro Disneyland, outside Paris, is slated to begin operating in 1992. Already, two out of three Americans visit a Disney park at some time in their lives.

Most guests say the World is worth the price, and the Disney folks are banking on that good will—literally. Walt Disney Company revenues in 1989 reached $2.6 billion. That is a 27% increase from the year before, in part due to price hikes. Mickey's marketeers argue that you pay more because you get more: Besides the MGM park, Disney is always adding new attractions—such as EPCOT's Body Wars, a jolting flight-simulator.

But hold on to your wallet, because the marketing blitz never lets up. When you take MGM's hot new ride, Star Tours, for example, you exit directly into—where else?—the Star Tours gift shop. Suddenly, your kids are clamoring for an $85 silver satin jacket or a $26.95 cotton sweatshirt, both emblazoned with the Star Tours logo. Even more amazing, many of the parents around you are buying.

Here's how you can get the most for your Disney dollars:

Study the guidebooks thoroughly. The frankest one, the *Unofficial Guide to Walt Disney World & EPCOT* by Bob Sehlinger (Prentice-Hall, $7.95), claims to save you more than three hours in line a day with field-tested touring plans. The official guide, Steve Birnbaum's *Guide to Walt Disney World 1990* (Avon, $9.95), is encyclopedic but less critical.

Go off-season. The least busy time is the first two weeks of December, followed by the months of September and October. You'll generally save about 10% to 20% off the high-season hotel rates. And the mid-afternoon wait for popular rides like Jungle Cruise could be only about six minutes instead of 60.

If you're staying several days, buy the four-day pass. Some veterans are still furious that Disney canceled its three-day $82.68 discounted pass in 1989; now you can get only a four-day ($105.60) or five-day ($123.55) ticket. Still, they get you into any of the three parks. (The single-day pass is good for only one park.) And a pass remains valid for a lifetime, so if you don't use up your days, file it away for your next visit. In fact, ticket hawkers and crafty tourists are making a black market in unexpired passes, though the Disney folks warn of fakes.

Stay over a weekend. Contrary to what you might think, the mobs are thickest Monday through Thursday because families—especially those who drive—often arrive Sunday and leave by week's end. So Fridays and Sundays are usually 20% less crowded.

Visit in the morning or evening. Go an hour before official opening time since the parks sometimes open 30 to 60 minutes early. Head back to the hotel for a snooze or a swim during the noon-to-3 p.m. craziness, then return that evening. This works best, of course, if you are staying nearby. Those at Disney World hotels sometimes get an "8 a.m. curtain call"—a slip of paper that admits you to Disney-MGM an hour before the hordes.

Look for package deals. These sometimes offer the best value, since the so-called wholesalers who create them buy flights and hotel space in bulk. But savings vary, and you have to book through an agent, so find one who knows the tour business and Orlando. Also ask him to call the airlines and hotels directly to see if he can get a better deal. Get written confirmation for everything. And ask whether your employer offers Disney admission discounts (some do). If yours doesn't, buy full-price tickets three weeks in advance from Disney (407-934-7639). There's a $2 postal fee, but it means one less line to contend with.

Choose carefully where you stay. The big debate here is between on-property hotels—meaning those within Disney's 28,000-acre confines—or off-property. Basically, the trade is between dollars and convenience: The on-property hotels can be $50 a night more expensive than comparable lodging outside the perimeter. And while Disney hotels have excellent free shuttle service to the parks, so do some of their off-property competitors—a few of which are only blocks farther away.

Here's a rundown on some of the more than 350 hotels in the area:

Disney hotels. At $69 to $99 a night, the Caribbean Beach—a sprawling two-story hotel with man-made lagoons—is the best value. As a result, it's often booked months in advance.

Call Disney's central reservation number (407-934-7639) to hold a spot. If that's not available, consider Fort Wilderness ($155 to $165), an upscale trailer park in a beautiful woodsy setting. The Grand Floridian Beach ($195 to $285) is the most elegant of the three hotels on the monorail (the others are the Polynesian Village at $170 to $225 a night and the Contemporary at $160 to $230). Although travel experts rave about Disney cleanliness, *Money* staffers' hotel stays turned up two minor lapses: shaving cream on a towel at the Disney Village Resort Villas and food on the wall at the Grand Floridian.

On-property hotels not owned by Disney. These offer free shuttle service but tend to be expensive. They include the Hilton ($160 to $195; 800-782-4414) and Howard Johnson ($95 to $145; 800-654-2000) in the Lake Buena Vista area. Closer to EPCOT is the newest and most extravagant—the Swan ($185 to $285; 800-248-7926).

Off-property hotels. The fanciest is the Hyatt Regency Grand Cypress ($140 to $185; 800-228-9000), the only AAA five-diamond hotel in the area. But the recently renovated Hyatt Orlando ($89 to $129; 800-228-9000) is also a safe bet, and the Comfort Inn at Lake Buena Vista ($29 to $65; 800-999-7300), although it eschews frills, is cheap, clean, and convenient to Disney World.

Ignore—discreetly, of course—the rule about not bringing food into the park. Lines at Disney food stands are often long, service is slow, and the prices are steep—$22 for a burger, Coke, and fries for four, compared with $10 at an Orlando McDonald's.

Make your show reservations before leaving home. Recommended are the Hoop-Dee-Doo Revue ($31.80 for adults, $25.44 or $16.96 for kids), a wacky western musical that includes an all-you-can-eat country dinner. Problem is, you may be shut out unless you reserve a month beforehand at 407-934-7639.

Although it's tempting to let Disney eat up your entire vacation, you'll miss some of the fun if you do. Here's a rundown on five other parks, all of which are within easy driving distance of Disney World:

Universal Studios Florida. (adults $30.74, children $24.38) Attractions include Jaws, King Kong, E.T., and Earthquake—all said to be different from the ones at Universal Studios in California. There's also a Hard Rock Cafe shaped like an electric guitar.

Sea World of Florida. (adults $25.40, children $21.15) Dipping attendance—down about 10% in 1989, owing in part to Disney-MGM's opening—has a bright side: You rarely have to wait for seats at Legend of Shamu, which stars killer whales, or New Friends, the whale-and-dolphin show. Most people find this park a refreshing reality check after Disney.

Wet 'n Wild. (adults $17.95, children $15.95) This park's allure is based on stupendous water slides—like Der Stuka, which feels like a 76-foot free-fall, and the new Black Hole, where you slide through a winding black, 500-foot-long, four-foot diameter tube. There are also kiddie slides for the youngsters.

Kennedy Space Center. This educational diversion is located on the coast an hour and a half east of Disney World. The attraction part, called Spaceport USA, includes the Imax film *The Dream Is Alive* (adults $2.75, children $1.75), and there are bus tours (adults $4, children $1.75) of the space center and Cape Canaveral Air Force Station, 10 miles away.

Busch Gardens The Dark Continent. ($23.95 over age two) An hour and a half up Interstate 4 and Interstate 75 in Tampa, this park offers the illusion of a zoo without bars: Many of the animals live in open areas similar to their natural, mostly African, origins. "It's a nice way to ease out of the vacation," says Jeffrey O'Donnell of Cape Cod, Massachusetts, who came with his wife, Sherry, and three children. Was it anticlimactic after hurtling through Space Mountain and Star Tours? Says O'Donnell: "We made sure the kids went on all the Disney rides three or four times—so now they're Disneyed out."

A Tour Guide to the Top 10 Amusement Parks

The old Army adage "Hurry up and wait" applies to America's amusement parks, as this overview of the 10 most popular ones shows. *Money* reporters visited each park—once on a sunny weekday and once on a sunny weekend—and recorded the longest time they waited in line for the best rides. (The Ohio parks were closed, so 1989 data was used.) The worst wait-

Park (1989 attendance)	Admission Price	Best Times To Visit	Medical/ Total Staff Per Million Visitors	Double Room At a Good Nearby Hotel
WALT DISNEY WORLD **Lake Buena Vista, Florida** **407-824-4321** **(30 million)**	Adult: $32.75 Child: $26.40	September to mid-February (except holidays)	1.8/1,067	Caribbean Beach 407-934-7639 $69 to $99
DISNEYLAND **Anaheim, California** **714-999-4565** **(13.3 million est.)**	Adult: $25.50 Child: $20.50	September to mid-February (except holidays)	N.A./752	Disneyland Hotel 714-635-8600 $125 to $215
UNIVERSAL STUDIOS HOLLYWOOD **Universal City, California** **818-508-9600** **(5.1 million)**	Adult: $21 Child: $15.50	November to January, March to May (except holidays)	1.2/588	Beverly Garland Hotel 800-238-3759 $98
KNOTT'S BERRY FARM **Buena Park, California** **714-220-5200** **(4 million)**	Adult: $21 Child: $16	May to early June, November to February, September (except holidays)	4.5/375	Embassy Suites 800-362-2779 $89 to $149
SEA WORLD OF FLORIDA **Orlando, Florida** **407-351-3600** **(4 million)**	Adult: $25.40 Child: $21.15	October, November, February, March (except holidays)	3.5/500	Sheraton World Resort 800-327-0363 $108 to $128
SEA WORLD OF CALIFORNIA **San Diego, California** **619-226-3901** **(3.6 million)**	Adult: $21 Child: $15.50	Last two weeks in June, September, April, and May (except holidays)	3.3/1,111	Dana Inn & Marina 800-345-9995 $69.50 to $129.50
KINGS ISLAND **Kings Island, Ohio** **513-398-5600** **(3.2 million)**	Adult: $20.95 Child: $10.45	Late May to early June, late August to early September	9.4/1,563	Kings Island Inn 800-727-3050 $85 to $105
CEDAR POINT **Sandusky, Ohio** **419-626-0830** **(3.2 million est.)**	Adult: $19.95 Child: $10.95	May, June, and weekends in September	15.6/1,000	Radisson Harbour Inn 800-333-3333 $65 to $135
SIX FLAGS MAGIC MOUNTAIN **Valencia, California** **805-255-4100** **(3.2 million)**	Adult: $22 Child: $11	First two weekends in December, September to early May	N.A./938	Hampton Inn 800-426-7866 $72 to $78
BUSCH GARDENS THE DARK CONTINENT **Tampa, Florida** **813-971-8282** **(3.1 million)**	Adult: $23.95 Child: $23.95	Last three weeks in September, early January, late May to early June	7.4/807	Embassy Suites/ Busch Gardens 800-362-2779 $89 to $129

to-ride ratio was at Cedar Point's Demon Drop, where *Money*'s reporter stood in line 30 minutes for a terrifying 15-second ride. The only parks with few delays were the two Sea Worlds.

No wait times were available for Sea World of California's Forbidden Reef. All prices were current in May 1990 and, except hotels, include tax.

Recommended Rides (wait time in minutes and seconds; ride time; wait-to-ride ratio; rides per hour)	Cost of a Hamburger, Cola, and Fries	Comments
Space Mountain (45:14; 2:36; 17 to 1; 2,000) Body Wars (64:48; 5:40; 11 to 1; 1,400) Captain EO (14:29; 16:47; 1 to 1; 1,685) For kids: Peter Pan (20:37; 3:09; 7 to 1; 1,000)	$5.46	At Michael Jackson's popular Captain EO show at EPCOT, don't get in the line in front of the Journey into Imagination building. EO has its own side entrance.
Pirates of Caribbean (4:52; 16:00; 1 to 3; 2,500) Splash Mountain (42:36; 9:16; 5 to 1; 2,000) Star Tours (31:00; 4:46; 7 to 1; 1,600) For kids: Small World (2:28; 12:35; 1 to 5; 2,800)	$4.71	A good time to beat the crowds is when school is in session.
Earthquake, King Kong (both part of a 90-minute tram ride; wait 40 minutes) Star Trek (30:00; 20:00; 2 to 1; 5,400) For kids: American Tail (to open late May)	$5.74	At the Star Trek show, 29 audience members get cameo roles. If you volunteer, there's a catch: They'll try to sell you a $35 video of your performance.
XK-1 (2:30; 1:30; 2 to 1; 800) Timber Mountain Log (9:22; 4:25; 2 to 1; 1,620) Montezooma's Revenge (1:30; 0:37; 2 to 1; 1,344) For kids: Red Baron (0:55; 2:00; 1 to 2; 240)	$4.72	Knott's has the best food we found, such as a complete chicken dinner with appetizer, salad, vegetables, and pie for $9.51 at Mrs. Knott's Chicken Dinner Restaurant.
Penguin Encounter (0:00; N.A.; N.A.; N.A.) Legend of Shamu (0:00; 26:53; N.A.; 5,200) Sharks! (27:58; 19:42; 1 to 1; 1,000) For kids: New Friends (0:00; 29:50; N.A.; 3,000)	$6.54	You can see the Sharks and Penguin Encounter anytime, so plan your day around the times for the big shows like Shamu and New Friends.
Baby Shamu Celebration (0:00; 27:05; N.A.; 6,500) Forbidden Reef (N.A.; N.A.; N.A.; N.A.) Shark Exhibit (0:00; 10:00; N.A.; 3,000) For kids: Cap'n Kid's World (0:00; N.A.; N.A.; 1,200)	$7.00	The sea otter exhibit includes animals rescued from the Exxon Valdez disaster. Sea World saves about 200 stranded or wounded sea mammals each year.
The Beast (45:00; 4:30; 10 to 1; 1,200) Vortex (30:00; 2:30; 12 to 1; 1,500) The Racer (15:00; 2:15; 7 to 1; 2,640) For kids: Beastie (10:00; 1:30; 7 to 1; 1,300)	$4.28	Stash valuables, food (concealed, since it's against park rules), jackets, or whatever else you don't want to carry at the lockers near the main gate for 75¢.
Demon Drop (30:00; 0:15; 120 to 1; 1,500) Cedar Downs (5:00; 2:30; 2 to 1; 1,000) Magnum XL-200 (60:00; 2:30; 24 to 1; 2,000) For kids: Sir Rub-a-Dub's Tubs (15:00; 3:00; 5 to 1; 500)	$4.17	The Hotel Breakers (419-627-2106) is less modern than the Radisson but offers early- and late-season packages (two nights, four people, $133 to $186).
Ninja (25:00; 2:30; 10 to 1; 1,600) Free Fall (20:00; 1:12; 17 to 1; 1,750) Revolution (35:00; 2:30; 14 to 1; 2,000) For kids: Bugs Bunny World (0:00; N.A.; N.A.; 3,900)	$6.51	Better ride the new Viper—the world's tallest, fastest looping roller coaster—before lunch: It will hurl you upside down seven times at speeds of up to 70 mph.
Congo River Rapids (7:56; 7:34; 1 to 1; 1,200) Tanganyika Tidal Wave (5:22; 5:39; 1 to 1; 1,795) The Scorpion (24:04; 1:38; 15 to 1; 1,100) For kids: Serengeti Plain (7:47; 25:35; 1 to 3; 1,600)	$4.34	To minimize crowds, start at Bird Gardens and head clockwise against the flow toward Nairobi. And bring a change of clothes for water rides—you'll get drenched.

Realize Your Retirement Dreams

Whether your retirement is 30 years away or at hand, the aim of this chapter is to help you leave your career with no regrets. By following the fairly simple strategies explained here, you can have the active, comfortable life in retirement that so many of us want but few will achieve without careful planning.

There are some immutable facts of retirement in the 1990s and beyond which will have a great impact on your future: First, you'll live much longer after you stop working than people did just two generations ago, when the concept of retirement at 65 began to catch on. Today, you can expect to live for 35 more years if you're a 40-year-old man; 40 years if you're a woman of the same age.

Second, you can no longer take for granted the generous company pensions and reliable Social Security benefits that are largely responsible for the affluence of many current retirees. Old folks today may turn out to have been living in a golden era. Although anticipated cuts probably won't be as bad as most people think, Social Security will be squeezed by the glut of retiring baby boomers, while companies by the thousands will be emphasizing do-it-yourself 401(k)-type plans over traditional pensions. That leaves you as the chief architect of your future.

And you may not be able to save heavily in the years just before you retire. Current retirees typically polished off their last major pre-retirement financial commitment—their children's educations—in their early fifties. That left them a decade or more to devote to accumulating money for the future. Many baby boomers, on the other hand, have postponed parenthood until well into their thirties. As a result, more than a few will find themselves on the verge of retirement still swamped with tuition bills.

Then, too, there's the likelihood that you will have to spend the final years of your career caring for dependent parents. Already, an estimated 20% to 25% of workers spend six to 35 hours a week tending to elderly relatives. By the time the oldest baby boomers start retiring around 2010, those over 85—the group most likely to need assistance from their adult children—will have doubled to 6.6 million.

All of these trends point toward one conclusion: More than ever, your financial security in retirement will depend on the money you put aside now. Fortunately, no generation has ever had so many powerful retirement planning tools at its disposal.

When should you begin? Right away. Start early and the magic of compounding alone will make you rich in retirement. For example, a 30-year-old who puts $3,000 a year—with 5% annual increases to cover inflation—in a tax-deferred account earning 10% will have $1,422,000 by age 65.

Even if you are in your forties or fifties, you may yet have time to build a sizable reserve by following the sensible investment strategies explained in "Building a Retirement Fund" on page 178. And if you are already retired, that same story will tell you how to boost income from your investments and stay ahead of inflation. Still worried about preserving your standard of living in your later years? Learn the ins and outs of working in retirement in "Should You Take a Post-Job Job?" on page 173.

As you accumulate assets for retirement, you'll naturally want to preserve them. Counting your home, life insurance, and investments, your estate can easily surpass $600,000, the point at which federal estate taxes start kicking in. To reduce those taxes to the minimum—if not zero—read the estate-planning stories beginning with "Making Your Legacy Trouble-Free" on page 186.

The Truth about Retirement

Don't believe everything you hear about the finances of old age. Here are some time-honored retirement rules that ought to be retired.

Most conventional wisdom is harmless enough when it's wrong. So what if the early bird doesn't catch the worm? At least he'll catch the sunrise. But running your financial life on clichés can be hazardous, particularly when it comes to retirement. By the time you realize your plans were based on faulty assumptions, you may not be able to recover.

The retirement years, unfortunately, come in for more than their share of falsehoods—eight of the most dangerous of which are presented below. Some of these myths were never true. Others once were, but demographic, economic, or social changes have since made them obsolete. Either way, whether you are near or far from retiring, here are some misconceptions to avoid:

MYTH NO. 1: Most people need to save for no more than about 10 or 15 years of life in retirement.

This myth rests on the fact that the average life span is 75 years and that most people retire by age 62. The average life span, however, takes into account the entire population, including the 21% who die before age 65. By the time you reach retirement age, your projected life expectancy will already be well past that average.

Reality: You need to plan for age 90, at least.

MYTH NO. 2: If you stay with one employer your entire career, you'll have a richer retirement than if you job hop to chase higher salaries.

It is true that if you change jobs a lot, vesting requirements may prevent you from building up much money in fixed pension plans. But you may still come out ahead. The reason is that even with the maximum number of years of service, fixed pensions usually offer a retirement benefit of no more than about 50% of the highest salary you reach before retiring. Thus, if you stay in a job for decades just to build your pension, but work for lower pay as a result, your benefit will be less. If you can raise your salary by changing employers more often, though, you will boost your benefit from any fixed plan that you happen to get vested in. Also, you will be able to contribute more to the increasingly popular self-funded retirement plans such as 401(k)s. They sometimes vest sooner than fixed plans and, in any case, let you take your money with you even if you leave before the company's payments are vested. You must, of course, plow some of your extra income into a 401(k), Individual Retirement Account, or other savings.

Reality: You shouldn't stay in the wrong job for the right pension.

MYTH NO. 3: Preserving capital should be a retiree's main objective.

Preserving spending power should be your objective. If you retire at 55 and live until 90, your retirement may last almost as long as your working years. That's enough time for inflation to erode even the fattest nest egg. A $500,000 retirement account earning 8% would yield a comfortable $40,000 a year. But assuming a modest inflation rate of 4.5%, the income would buy only $27,000 worth of goods in 10 years, $17,000 in 20 years, and

only $11,000 after 30 years. To stay ahead, your best strategy is to increase wealth in the early years by working part time (provided, of course, your added earnings don't cause an offsetting reduction in Social Security benefits) and by including growth investments in your portfolio. If you bank an extra $20,000 a year in your $500,000 retirement fund for the first 10 years, you will probably outrun inflation forever and never use up your money.

Reality: You shouldn't stop earning and saving just because you are retired.

MYTH NO. 4: You will pay a smaller fraction of your income in taxes.

Sure, you may drop into a lower tax bracket the year after you retire, provided your income goes down far enough. But forget about brackets for a moment and concentrate instead on the effective tax rate—that is, the actual fraction of your income the government claims. The effective tax rate has risen fairly consistently ever since individual income taxes were first levied in 1913. Even under tax reform, which cut the top bracket to just 33% in 1989, down from a recent peak of 70% in 1981, the effective rate held steady. If the effective rate continues to rise in the future, as seems very likely, then you may pay as much or more of your income for federal, state, and local taxes after retiring as you did while working. Furthermore, if your retirement includes part-time work, the taxes you pay for Social Security will almost certainly have risen to keep the system solvent. For the same reason, you can probably expect more of your benefits to be taxed.

Reality: Even if your retirement income puts you in a lower bracket someday, you can't assume that a smaller percentage will go for taxes.

MYTH NO. 5: Your housing costs will go down.

Even if you pay off a 30-year mortgage by the time you retire, inflation will have made it only an incidental expense. Your real costs will be property taxes and maintenance, which continue to rise. Since most retirees' incomes drop, people ages 65 and older actually spend a larger portion of their income on housing than those ages 45 to 64, according to the Bureau of Labor Statistics (31% for the older people versus 27% for younger ones). Of course, you can always reduce costs by buying a smaller house or renting, but it won't just happen by itself.

Reality: If your house needs lots of maintenance and is in an area with high taxes, you should count on a rising housing budget—or figure on moving.

MYTH NO. 6: Your retirement nest will be empty.

If your adult offspring flock back, or if you or your spouse's elderly parents need care, you could find yourself retired in a house full of permanent guests instead. Since 1975, the number of young adults ages 25 to 29 living with their parents has nearly doubled. When kids need to save for a house or their marriages fail or they're simply scared to go out on their own, they rush back to Mom and Dad. Meanwhile, as people live longer, retirees increasingly become responsible for very old parents, many of whom need day-to-day care; an estimated 60% of dependent elderly live with their adult children. And even if your children or parents don't actually move in with you, they may still need your financial help— which could have just as big an impact on your retirement plans.

Reality: Unless you are a childless orphan, you may well face dilemmas about what support to give to the generations that preceded and succeeded you.

MYTH NO. 7: Your employer will provide good basic health insurance, and Medicare will cover the rest of your medical bills.

Two developments are making it increasingly unlikely that your employer will offer future retirees anywhere near the kind of coverage that current retirees get. One is the annual double-digit rise in insurance premium costs; even well-heeled employers are having trouble swallowing that. The other is a change in federal accounting guidelines that discourages companies from making generous promises of future support to retirees. Under the

change, such obligations reduce the profit a company can show on its balance sheet today— thus cutting the all-important bottom line. Given these two influences, it's no wonder that a survey by Wyatt Company, a Washington, D.C. benefits consulting firm, showed 38% of corporations planning to reduce health benefits for those retiring in the near future. The far future looks even worse. A worker currently at mid-career may get no health insurance at all when he or she retires. As for Medicare, remember that you usually can't collect until age 65, even if you retire sooner. And on average, it will pay less than half of your health-care bills.

Reality: You'd better take good care of yourself, put aside money for insurance, and check into cost cutters such as health maintenance organizations.

MYTH NO. 8: Chances are good you will spend your last years in a nursing home, but long-term-care insurance can protect your wealth.

First, your odds of winding up in a nursing home for more than short periods of time are fairly small—only about an 8% chance for women, 5% for men. True, that may become more likely as people live longer in the future, but it will probably still be a long shot. Unfortunately, if you do fall into the unlucky minority that requires long-term care (at an average annual cost of $25,000 to $30,000), nursing-home insurance may not preserve your nest egg. Virtually all such policies pay only a fixed daily benefit, and the cost of care has been rising 5.5% per annum. Even if you are willing to pay more over the years to raise the benefit, because medical costs have been increasing so much faster than inflation, in the end your insurance will probably only defray, not absorb, them. You may do just as well taking the money you would otherwise spend on premiums and investing it conservatively. That way, if you don't need long-term care, or if a government program comes along to bail you out, the money will still be yours.

Reality: You shouldn't rush into nursing-home insurance unless frailty or Alzheimer's disease runs in your family.

Should You Take a Post-Job Job?

Going back to work may not be worth it financially, yet for many retirees it is essential emotionally. Only you can tell which course is for you.

Why people choose to work or not to work after retirement is rarely simple. Nearly a quarter of retirees hold jobs. Half of the working retirees recently surveyed by Travelers Corporation reported financial need as their main reason for returning to the job market. For the other half, the reasons were a skein of emotional hungers from companionship to self-esteem. And what of those retirees who have happily turned their backs on work for good? Many retirees discover that they have been waiting all their lives to do nothing.

The problem is that few people really come to grips with the questions of continuing to work until they have retired. Then, they are in a far less flexible position to start a new career or find the perfect part-time position. People often have only hazy notions of what retirement will be like, and they don't realistically think about how they are going to spend all those thousands of hours. You should begin exploring the options at least five years before you retire. The basic ones: full- or part-time work for your former employer or a new one, experimenting with a job in a new field, taking temporary positions with a variety of employers, doing volunteer work, or launching a new business of your own.

Your first step should be estimating a job's effect on your finances; perversely, working in retirement doesn't always put much more money in your pocket. Many people—like a growing number of early retirees who took reduced pension packages and face a longer post-work life—wind up as inflation's orphans. They simply have to work.

But you need to figure out how much going back to work might cost you. When you take into account increased tax payments and reduced Social Security benefits, for instance, you could pocket less than $11,000 from a $30,000 post-job-job paycheck if you are between ages 65 and 70. (See "How a Retiree Can Pay 64% Tax on $30,000" on page 174.)

From age 70 on, you may earn as much as you like without losing any benefits. If you're going to be so highly compensated that your earnings would wipe out your Social Security benefits anyway, it can make sense to defer filing for benefits as long as possible, because the longer you defer, the higher the payment you'll receive when you do apply.

Next come taxes. Even though you may be receiving Social Security benefits, you still must pay FICA taxes out of your earnings, which was at a rate of 7.65% in 1990. Your job earnings may also push you into a higher combined federal, state, and local tax bracket and could make up to half of your Social Security benefits subject to federal income tax. Run through the calculations with the help of a planner or tax professional to determine what your net gain would be from a job at various earning levels.

Now you are ready to weigh the emotional side of the work issue. If you don't need the extra income, stop and consider what may be the most fulfilling kind of work for the retired person: volunteering. Unpaid work can handle many of those ego needs that are satisfied by a job, like a sense of contributing and expertise.

Challenging volunteer opportunities abound. The National Executive Service Corps (257 Park Avenue South, New York, NY 10010) offers management consultant positions for nonprofit groups ranging from the National Football Foundation & Hall of Fame to the New York Philharmonic. NESC is also developing a special program that trains retired engineers and scientists to fill the need for high school science and math teachers. And the Service Corps of Retired Executives (800-368-5855), sponsored by the Small Business Administration, matches members with the owners of small and start-up businesses who need counseling.

Whatever you decide to do, don't try to remake yourself into someone you're not. While many people view retirement as some kind of Camelot, the truth is that you're the same person you were before, driven by the same likes and dislikes. So a salesman probably shouldn't think about becoming a librarian. And if you've been setting your own pace, you are not going to be happy working under close supervision now.

If you're looking for executive or professional work, you'll need patience. Easy starting points like newspapers, personnel departments, and employment agencies will probably lead nowhere. More than 80% of jobs are never advertised but are filled instead by people who become experts at networking, job consultants say. Getting the word out to friends, relatives, and former co-workers that you are in the market for a particular type of job can turn up fruitful contacts.

And don't let the specter of age discrimination stop you for a moment. Representatives of Forty Plus of the Greater Washington, D.C. area, one of the network of self-help groups for job-seeking executives and professionals over 40, found it takes about seven months on average to get the kinds of jobs its members are seeking, during which you'll have to make about 450 contacts, fill out 90 job applications, and go through six interviews. So the group tells members to forget about age discrimination and get to work.

Another reason to ignore age discrimination: It's being done in by the baby bust, which is adding too few new workers to the market. Happily, this in turn has nurtured a growing appreciation of older workers. In 1981, Travelers started a job bank at its Hartford headquarters to recruit retirees to meet 60% of its temporary employment needs; by 1985, demand for retirees had grown so much that the company began recruiting them from other insurance companies.

Opportunities for flexible, part-time work are on the rise. Reason: All the restructuring and downsizing of corporations has eliminated full-time jobs while creating part-time ones. When Kelly Services began actively recruiting retirees in 1987, 7% of the 580,000 employees it places annually were aged 55 or older; now

How a Retiree Can Pay 64% Tax on $30,000

The table below shows how little a 65-year-old retiree actually pockets from a job that pays $30,000. The biggest outrage: He must give back Social Security benefits at the rate of $1 for every $3 earned above $9,360.

Next, there is a 7.65% FICA tax on the $30,000. Then income taxes. The calculations assume he gets $20,000 in pension and investment income, including the maximum Social Security benefit ($11,700 in 1990), files as a single taxpayer, and pays state and local tax totaling 20% of the federal tax.

Gross salary	$30,000
Minus lost Social Security benefits	$6,880
Minus FICA tax	$2,295
Minus federal, state, and local tax	$9,947
Net salary	$10,878

the proportion is nearly 10%.

While most such jobs are clerical and secretarial, temporary employment in professional and management positions is also on the rise. Interim Management Corporation in New York City, for example, places retired and between-jobs senior executives in temporary posts ranging from chief executive officer to operations manager. Assignments average six months, and interim managers are amply rewarded. For instance, a woman who retired as controller of one corporation recently took a five-month stint at another for $44,000—

more than half of the $80,000 she earned annually in her previous position.

If, on the more ambitious end of the work spectrum, you have long harbored the dream of becoming an entrepreneur after retirement, be warned: A mountain of preliminary research is required to see whether there is a healthy market for your service or product to get an accurate idea of all costs involved. And once launched, you'll have to work harder than you ever have to make a go of it. Too often people discover too late that self-employment is not for them.

Don't Give Up on Social Security Yet

Despite the system's much publicized woes, you are likely to receive higher benefits than you think.

If you're like many middle-class working Americans, you're not overly optimistic about what you will eventually get from Social Security. In a recent poll of *Money* subscribers, 53% said that they believe benefit levels are likely to be cut for people who retire in the future, and 54% said they think that payouts could be eliminated for upper-income retirees.

Is the widespread cynicism about Social Security justified? The answer may surprise you: Despite all the belt-tightening talk, your benefits will probably be higher than you expect. In fact, you are likely to get more, in today's dollars, than someone retiring now does.

To be sure, Social Security's looming fiscal problems will cause benefits to be cut—though not from this year's levels or even from current levels adjusted for inflation. Few people realize that under the present law, annual benefits for people retiring in the future at age 65 will almost certainly be much higher than those received by today's retirees; it's from

those bountiful levels that the cuts will come. The reductions will take the form of increases in the normal retirement age (probably to as high as 69) and in taxes.

Such cuts will not be painless. If you are 30 years old today and plan to retire at age 65 in 2025, you are likely to receive only 80% of your full retirement benefits and to have 85% of what you get subject to income tax (compared with a maximum of 50% today). Nonetheless, payment levels at that time will be so generous that you could still collect a check as much as 18% larger than a comparable 65-year-old today, even after inflation and taxes are taken into account. Your standard of living, however, is likely to be so much higher 35 years from now that Social Security will probably provide a smaller part of your retirement income. So you'll have to rely more on other sources to maintain your pre-retirement living standard.

The table, "What Social Security Will Pay

You at Age 65," on the opposite page shows how much you can expect to get if the Social Security system is amended in ways that appear most likely.

Most people know that once they retire, their Social Security benefits will rise with inflation. But Social Security's promise to current wage earners is more extravagant: The system pledges to pay a starting benefit equal to a certain percentage of salary, up to a maximum that rises each year with the average wage rate. Because the formula is tied to wages, which tend to outpace inflation, each new crop of retirees will start out at a higher level of real benefits than their predecessors did. The maximum age-65 payout in 2025, for example, is projected to be $17,829 a year in 1990 dollars, compared with $11,700 today.

A problem will arise, however, when the baby-boom generation begins to file for retirement benefits around the year 2010. Over the 20 years that follow, the ratio of Social Security taxpayers to beneficiaries will drop from around 3 to 1 to less than 2 to 1, sending the program's costs, relative to wages subject to Social Security taxes, soaring by 47%. If there are no further changes, costs will begin to exceed revenues around 2017.

What happens then? Many politicians believe that the system can plug the gap by drawing down the vast sums that will have accumulated in Social Security's trust fund—essentially, the program's bank account at the Treasury. The trust fund buildup will occur because tax hikes and benefit cuts enacted in 1977 and 1983 will raise much more money over the next few decades than the system needs.

Projections for 1990, for example, indicated workers would pay $46 billion more in Social Security taxes than retirees would collect. Each year's surplus fattens the trust fund, which could swell to around $7 trillion by 2017, when the system starts to go into the red. In theory, the fund can then be tapped to cover annual deficits that will reach more than $387 billion in 2025.

So the problem's solved, right? Wrong. The Social Security trust fund, it turns out, is a bookkeeping illusion. By law, the trust fund

must invest entirely in Treasury bonds. This is just another way of saying that the Treasury borrows the money—to spend on bombers, paper clips, congressmen's junk mail, and other routine government expenses—and issues the fund an IOU in return. If Social Security eventually cashes in the IOUs, taxpayers would have to pay them off. Thus, drawing on the trust fund merely supplements Social Security tax revenue with money from income and other taxes.

Obviously, the burden that the system will impose in the future depends in large part on trends in population—specifically the ratio of taxpayers to retirees. For the sake of consistency, this story relies on the Social Security Administration's own demographic assumptions, such as a stable birth rate and increasing life expectancy for the elderly.

The story also relies on Social Security's own economic assumptions. The key one is that worker productivity will rebound from its depressed levels of the past two decades and increase by 1% to 2% a year; it's rising productivity that leads to higher wages. In the unlikely event that this expectation proves far too optimistic, the taxes required to support the system could double or triple. Even if Social Security's economic assumptions are on the mark, at some point workers of the future will balk at the rising cost of maintaining the benefits now being promised.

Once it becomes evident that the system is going to drain hundreds of billions of dollars needed to fund other federal government programs, it is hard to imagine that taxpayers will not demand reform. The likely date: a few years before 2017, when Social Security's finances swing into deficit.

To keep the system on a pay-as-you-go basis, Congress will probably eliminate the deficit partly by cutting benefits and partly by hiking payroll taxes. A set of likely changes, developed for *Money* by Bruce D. Schobel, a former senior policy adviser with Social Security:

● The age at which new retirees become entitled to full benefits would be moved back by two months each year starting in 2000, until it reaches 69 in 2023.

● The fraction of benefits subject to income tax would rise from a maximum of 50% today to 85%, effective in 2025.

● The Social Security payroll tax would go up from 6.2% to 7% in 2025.

The following describes the effects of these changes on three broad age groups:

If you are retired now or are planning to retire before 2000. You have little to fear from changes in the Social Security law. Despite the current proposals to include benefit cuts in a budget accord that reduces the federal deficit, congressional inertia will probably postpone any serious action for 20 years. Because of the 1983 reforms, though, you may see more of your benefits taxed away. Under current law,

up to half your benefits are subject to income tax if the sum of your non-Social Security income plus half your benefits exceeds $32,000 ($25,000 if you are single). Unlike most other thresholds in the tax code, these aren't indexed to inflation. Thus, if your income goes up along with the cost of living, an increasing portion of your benefits will be taxed.

If you are now between the ages of 37 and 52. Sometime during your retirement, which will most likely start between 2000 and 2018, Congress and taxpayers will have to confront the shortfall in Social Security's revenues. Chances are very good that your benefits will be stingier than the system is promising.

One such curtailment is already in the law: The normal retirement age will creep up by two months a year between 2000 and 2005,

What Social Security Will Pay You at Age 65

This table, prepared with the help of Ira Siegler, a partner at the benefits consulting firm Kwasha Lipton, compares the Social Security benefits that you are promised under current law with those that you would receive if the system is changed in ways that *Money* considers likely. Because *Money* is forecasting that taxes on Social Security will be increased, we show benefits on both a pretax and an after-tax basis. To

eliminate the effects of inflation, all amounts have been converted into today's dollars. Workers destined to receive average benefits currently earn about $20,500 a year; maximum payouts will go to those now making $51,300 or more. After-tax figures assume that average earners will have other retirement income equal to their benefits and that maximum earners will have $25,000 of outside income.

If you're now age...	ANNUAL BENEFITS FOR AVERAGE WAGE EARNERS				MAXIMUM ANNUAL BENEFITS			
	Before taxes		After taxes		Before taxes		After taxes	
	Under current law	Under *Money* forecast	Under current law	Under *Money* forecast	Under current law	Under *Money* forecast	Under current law	Under *Money* forecast
65	$8,648	$8,648	$8,648	$8,648	$11,700	$11,700	$10,062	$10,062
60	9,002	9,002	9,002	9,002	12,515	12,515	10,763	10,763
55	9,529	9,529	9,529	9,529	13,767	13,767	11,840	11,840
50	9,799	9,799	9,647	9,647	14,694	14,694	12,637	12,637
45	10,068	9,828	9,490	9,304	15,542	15,172	13,366	13,048
40	10,715	9,822	9,911	9,085	16,867	15,461	14,506	13,297
35	11,265	9,772	10,420	9,039	17,815	15,454	15,321	13,290
30	11,265	9,857	10,420	8,600	17,829	15,600	15,333	11,887
25	11,988	10,374	11,089	9,052	18,974	16,420	16,318	12,512
20	12,756	11,039	11,799	9,631	20,189	17,471	17,363	13,313

and again between 2017 and 2022. Very likely, the increases would continue between 2005 and 2017 and extend through 2023. With that scenario, those workers who are now under 30 could not claim full benefits before age 69.

In either case, you will still be able to retire as early as 62, but you would pay a bigger penalty than early retirees do now. For example, if you retire at 62 today, when the normal retirement age is still 65, you get 80% of your full benefits. If you are now 41 and you retire at 62 in 2011, under current law you would get 75%. With the further tightening predicted, you'd be entitled to just 70%. Similarly, if you are now 44 and you retire at 65 in 2011, the current law would grant you 95% of your full benefits; in *Money*'s scenario, you'd get 90%. Nonetheless, because of wage growth, you would still receive more, even after inflation, than someone retiring at 65 today.

If you are now 36 or younger. Today's 36-year-olds, slated to start retiring in 2016, are likely to file for benefits in the midst of a fierce national debate on Social Security reform. Whatever changes in the program are adopted, they will probably be phased in, granting those now in their mid-thirties or younger a few years to prepare. But the bulk of the new rules will almost certainly be in place by 2025, the year today's 30-year-olds reach 65.

Beginning in that year, if you retire at age 65, your check will be only 80% of the full age-69 benefit, according to *Money*'s forecast. In addition, as much as 85% of what you receive will be taxable. But even so, annual wage growth of 5% to 6% between now and 2025 would push real, after-tax benefits nearly a fifth higher than those of workers retiring this year.

One note of caution: Although benefit levels will increase, they may not seem quite as munificent in 2025 as they would today. Thanks to rising wages, average 65-year-olds preparing to retire in 2025 will have incomes 57% greater than the average pre-retiree does now. So even though their pretax checks will be 30% higher, their benefits will amount to only about 36% of their lofty pre-retirement wages, compared with about 42% currently. Thus, you may have to supplement Social Security with private pensions and savings to a greater degree than retirees do now, and you should factor that into your retirement planning.

Building a Retirement Fund

Whether you are decades from leaving work or already out on your own, your portfolio must strike a balance between risk and return.

Even a generous company pension, coupled with the maximum Social Security benefit, probably won't provide you with enough income for a carefree retirement. To keep your standard of living from dropping after you leave work, you must shore up your finances with investments. Future generations of elderly will be divided into the dids and the did-nots; those who did save will retire comfortably. Those who didn't will not.

To be sure of ranking among the "dids," it isn't enough simply to sock your money away;

you also have to invest it wisely. Consider this: If you had the discipline to save $500 a month for 30 years but stashed it all in a risk-free, bank money-market deposit account paying 6.5% annually, you would accumulate about $553,000. But if you put your money into a growth-oriented mix of stocks and bonds or mutual funds earning 10%—a reasonable long-term return for such a portfolio—you'd wind up with a cool $1.1 million. The price for nearly doubling your return over 30 years, however, is much greater uncertainty in the short run. With even a moderately risky growth portfolio, you should be prepared to ride out market drops that could be as grim as 30% in a year.

The crucial issue in retirement investing, then, is how much risk you can afford to take in pursuit of higher gains. The answer depends on the coolness of your nerve, the security of your current economic circumstances, and, most important, your age. In general, you can afford to emphasize relatively chancy growth investments when you are young, but you should gradually switch to a less aggressive combination of investments as you near retirement and rely more heavily on stable, income-producing assets after you stop working. At every stage, though, you should invest part of your portfolio for growth. Only that way can you build up the money you need and be sure of keeping ahead of rising prices in your retirement years.

In the footrace with inflation, you get an important head start from Uncle Sam. Basically, the government agrees not to tax the earnings on certain retirement savings plans until you withdraw the money. Some of these plans, such as employer-sponsored 401(k)s, postpone taxes on both the investment

Why 401(k)s Are Good Investments

If your employer offers a 401(k) savings plan, put every dollar you can into it, for three reasons: First, you can defer taxes on contributions—up to $7,979 for 1990—until you withdraw the money. Second, your earnings will also grow tax deferred. Third, most companies match part of an employee's savings, typically 50¢ on the dollar on contributions up to 6% of your pay. Together, these advantages can give you an unbeatable return. Until you reach age 59½, however, you can generally withdraw money from your 401(k) only in cases of hardship, and the federal government will slap you with a 10% early-withdrawal penalty.

Companies typically provide three investment options in a 401(k), though some offer as many as seven. The common choices include:

Stock funds. If you have few growth investments outside of your 401(k), you might put the bulk of your account into your plan's stock funds. Some companies let you choose among portfolios, ranging from conservative balanced funds to more aggressive growth funds.

Guaranteed investment contracts. These are fixed-income investments, sponsored by insurance companies, that guarantee payment of interest and return of principal. Because GICs are safe and their yields are predictable—comparable to those on one-year bank CDs—they are the most popular 401(k) investment, attracting some 60% of employees' money. Unlike CDs, however, GICs are not federally insured.

Bond funds. These can be excellent choices if you have growth investments outside of your 401(k). Most 401(k) bond funds hold a mix of high-grade corporates and Treasuries and, thus, carry little credit risk, though the value of your holdings will rise and fall as interest rates fluctuate.

Your employer's stock. As a rule, you should keep less than 10% of your retirement portfolio in your company's stock. That way, you'll be protected in the event that the firm hits hard times and its share price drops.

earnings and your contributions to the account. In many 401(k)s, the company also kicks in 50¢ or so for every dollar you save.

Because of advantages like these, tax-deferred accounts should be central to your strategy all through your retirement planning. Let's say that you are in the 28% tax bracket and contribute $250 a month to a 401(k) earning 8%. With no matching contributions from your employer, you will have more than $117,000 in 20 years, even after paying taxes upon withdrawal. If your plan includes a 50% match, you would amass more than $170,000 after taxes. By contrast, if you set aside the same amount of money at the same return outside a tax-deferred plan, the tax man's nips and tucks would leave you with only about $81,000.

There are trade-offs, however, for that tax deferral. Tax law limits the amount you can contribute to these accounts—for instance, the maximum for a 401(k) was $7,979 for 1990. And with the exception of Individual Retirement Accounts and Keogh plans, tax-sheltered plans usually also restrict you to a handful of investment choices. Worst of all, the tax code curtails your ability to withdraw money from an account before you turn 59½. And if you do take out savings before then, you generally have to pay a 10% penalty to the IRS in addition to regular income taxes on the withdrawal. The best advice: Contribute as much money as you can to your tax-deferred accounts before you start investing for retirement elsewhere, but be reasonably sure you won't need the money until after 59½.

Below and on the following pages, you will find portfolio strategies recommended by John Markese, research director for the American Association of Individual Investors (AAII).

20 + Years to Retirement: Go for Growth
Stocks or stock funds: 70%
Cash equivalents: 30%

With memories still fresh of the 1987 stock-market crash and the more recent mini-crash in summer 1990, you may think that putting 70% of your nascent retirement fund into stocks is as rash as torching Old Glory at an American Legion rally. But when retirement is still decades distant, you should emphasize making your investments grow as fast as is prudently possible, and that means investing in stocks. The AAII's Markese expects the equity-oriented portfolio recommended above to earn a compound annual return of 10% to 12% for the next decade. The risks, though, are considerable: He concedes that the investments could plunge as much as 30% in any one year.

For most novice investors, it makes sense to delegate the job of selecting individual stocks to professionals. You can do this easily and inexpensively by putting your money into managed stock funds, which include both those offered in employer-sponsored savings plans and publicly sold mutual funds and variable annuities. (See "The Pros and Cons of Annuities" on the opposite page.)

Experts recommend that mid-career investors devote most of the stock portion of their portfolios to growth funds. Managers of these funds seek out firms with sharply rising earnings. In a healthy economy, such stocks often outperform the market averages by a wide margin; if a recession occurs and corporate profits shrivel, however, prices can drop sharply.

Within a company-sponsored retirement plan, the fund that most closely fits this approach might be identified as the aggressive equity fund or the growth fund. If you are investing outside an employer's plan, you can choose among literally hundreds of mutual funds that fit the bill. (See "Mutual Fund Rankings," beginning on page 193.)

If you have faith in your stock-picking abilities and decide not to use funds, you will need at least $12,000 to assemble a minimally diversified portfolio of four or five stocks. You should also be prepared to pay a broker stiff commissions, which on stock orders of $3,000 or less can run as high as 3% a transaction.

For stock pickers who can handle the ante and are willing to accept above-average risk, experts recommend light blue chips—medium-size companies with leading positions in niche markets and steady earnings gains over a decade or longer.

As for the 30% of your portfolio in cash equivalents, put your emphasis on yield and safety. Suitable investments in employer-sponsored plans typically include money-market funds and guaranteed investment contracts, which are fixed-income vehicles similar to bank certificates of deposit but issued by insurance companies. Outside such plans, you can choose among publicly offered money-market funds, Treasury bills, and short-term bank certificates of deposit.

Once you've settled on a mix of investments, stick with your allocation until you enter the next phase of your retirement planning. In the meantime, don't shuffle money between stocks and cash whenever you think a bull or bear market is due: Not even professionals can consistently outguess the market. But you should realign your portfolio occasionally, perhaps once a year. For example, if a bull market pushes your equity holdings from 70% to 80% of your retirement fund, you should bring your portfolio back into line by selling some of your holdings and adding the proceeds to your cash investments. Likewise, when market declines shrink the equity allotment in your portfolio, you should rebalance by shifting some cash into stocks. These periodic adjustments will ensure that you tend to buy undervalued assets and sell overvalued ones.

The Pros and Cons of Annuities

Insurance companies like to tout their deferred annuities as perfect investments for retirement. Depending on the type, deferred annuities—so-called because your money is paid to you at a future date—resemble either mutual funds or CDs. And they do indeed have one major advantage: Taxes on your investment earnings are postponed until you withdraw them. But annuities also have sales commissions as high as 8%, annual expenses of up to 3%, and early-withdrawal penalties that in some cases can hit 15%. In addition, you must pay a 10% federal tax penalty on any earnings you withdraw before age 59½. As a result, you should not consider a deferred annuity unless you have no other tax-deferred investment and won't need your money for at least a decade. By then, early-withdrawal penalties have usually expired and the buildup of earnings will compensate for other costs. When you retire, you can annuitize, which is effectively the same as rolling over your money into a so-called immediate annuity. But you'll have more flexibility if you leave your money in the annuity and withdraw cash as you need it. There are two types of deferred annuities:

Variable annuities, which require initial investments of $500 to as much as $5,000, function as tax-deferred umbrella accounts that shelter stock, bond, money-market, and other kinds of investment funds. Your eventual payout will depend on how well the funds do; if they do poorly, the insurer will not make up your losses.

Fixed-rate annuities typically have minimum initial investments of $5,000 and offer yields that are close to those on one-year CDs. To attract new investors, many insurance companies guarantee an enticing initial rate on their fixed annuities for one to five years. After that, however, the insurer is free to lower the rate. Your broker or insurance agent should be able to help you avoid insurers with a history of slashing returns after the initial guarantee period ends.

Insurance companies also offer immediate annuities to retired people who need income starting right away. In return for a lump-sum payment of $5,000 or more, an immediate annuity pays you a fixed monthly income guaranteed to last either for your life, the joint lives of you and your spouse, or some specific period, such as 20 years. That may sound attractive, but remember: Those fixed payments could leave you at the mercy of rising prices.

10 Years to Retirement: Don't Get Timid
Stocks or stock funds: 60%
Bonds or bond funds: 20%
Cash equivalents: 20%

As your investments grow and you get closer to retirement, you have more to lose—and less time to recover from losses. So you should begin gradually pruning your stockholdings and moving into high-quality bonds or bond mutual funds. To ensure that you don't buy all of your bonds when prices are peaking, make this transition over at least two years. For example, if you want to move $20,000 into bond funds, plan on eight quarterly transfers of $2,500 each.

Despite your growing sensitivity to investment risk, you must continue to keep most of your retirement fund in stocks to keep it ahead of inflation. People suddenly become very conservative when they approach retirement. But unless you plan to die on the day you quit work, you must continue to invest for growth. The AAII's Markese estimates the portfolio recommended above might drop about 25% in a single year. But over a decade or longer, he expects it to deliver a compound annual return of around 10%—about five percentage points above the current inflation rate.

If maintaining this level of risk so close to retirement will cost you sleep, invest your stockholdings more conservatively. For example, over a two-year transition period, you might swap half the money you have in growth funds for shares of total-return funds, which usually hold bonds and cash to cushion their equity investments during market slumps. In company-sponsored plans, such funds are often identified as equity income, or balanced, funds.

If you are investing in individual stocks, you might shift your focus to traditional blue chips—stocks issued by leading firms in major industries. Choose those with divided yields above the market average to provide a safety net against stock market slips and a reliable source of appreciation. A stock with a rising dividend and a high yield offers the potential for consistent long-term growth even if the stock market doesn't deliver big capital gains,

financial experts say. Even without changing the nature of your stockholdings, you will take some of the risk out of your portfolio simply by gradually switching 10% of your money from stocks to bonds, which are historically far more stable in price. As with stocks, small investors may find investing in bond mutual funds more affordable than buying corporate or municipal bonds directly. Another option is buying Treasuries which you can get in denominations as small as $1,000 without commission directly from a Federal Reserve bank or branch.

Funds that invest in high-quality bonds—either Treasuries or corporates and munis graded BBB or better by rating services such as Standard & Poor's—with maturities between four and 10 years usually offer the best trade-off between risk and reward. Unfortunately, only about a third of company-sponsored 401(k) plans offer a bond fund; to find out the average maturity of the bonds in the portfolio of your plan's fund, check with your employee-benefits counselor.

The Newly Retired: Look Beyond Yield
Stocks or stock funds: 50%
Bonds or bond funds: 30%
Cash equivalents: 20%

Traditionally, retirees have viewed their last day of work as a signal to cash in their stocks for safe, high-yielding income investments. While understandable, the tradition has a serious flaw: It leaves you at the mercy of inflation.

Over a typical retiree's life span, inflation can drastically shrink the value of a fixed income from bonds or CDs. For example, $500,000 invested in government bonds yielding 8% will produce $40,000 in annual income. But after just 10 years of 5% inflation, that income will buy less than $25,000 does today.

Once again, the solution is to maintain a sizable commitment to blue-chip stocks or total-return funds. You should also reduce your risks, however, by shifting 10% of your portfolio from stocks into high-grade bonds or bond funds over a two-year period. According to Markese, the recommended portfolio above would yield only about 4.2% compared with the 8% available from long-term government bonds. But stock dividends usually rise over the years, while bond payments stay the same. And, thanks to stocks' higher growth rates, the portfolio should provide a compound annual total return—the sum of stock dividends and bond interest plus capital gains from the stocks—of about 9.5%.

Thus, if inflation were running at 5%, you could withdraw 4.5% of your portfolio for living expenses and have enough left to reinvest and keep your retirement fund growing. As long as the fund continues expanding, the dollar amount of your 4.5% withdrawal will automatically increase as well, keeping pace with your rising cost of living. In years when the market slumps, you may need to pull out more than your portfolio earns, eating into your capital. But growth in good years should make up for such setbacks. Also, when a market surge sharply boosts the value of your assets, you can reduce your withdrawal rate to build up a cushion against bad years. Retirees who fixate on yield lose the battle against inflation.

How Good Is Your GIC's Guarantee?

Don't be lulled by having a guaranteed investment contract—that wonderful-sounding name for a place to put money for retirement. Indeed, GICs, as they are called, now attract 62% of new contributions to the company-sponsored 401(k) savings plans that offer them. If you work for any of the two-thirds of companies that offer GICs as part of their 401(k) plans, it's key that you understand the product's ins and outs.

On the face of it, a GIC looks a lot like a bank CD—investors get a fixed yield for one to five years and the promise that their principal will not lose value. But while federal deposit insurance backs most CDs, the guarantee behind a GIC is only as solid as the life insurance company issuing the contract. GICs are nothing more than the unsecured credit of insurance companies.

None of the 61 insurers that offer the contracts have defaulted on their GIC obligations in the 17 years that the contracts have been available to employees, and it's unlikely that any will in the next year or two. But the risk of calamity among the $150 billion in outstanding GICs is growing, because more and more insurers have packed their own investment portfolios with risky mortgages and as much as 45% in junk bonds.

Generally, company plans buy several GICs from one or more insurers. What would happen to your contributions and earnings if an insurance company defaulted on its contracts? That may depend on where the insurance company is based. If it operates out of one of the 44 states that maintain so-called guarantee funds, you might get back as much of your money as the fund could afford—perhaps all of your principal but less interest than the insurer had promised. But it's possible that some state funds would not cover GICs. In that case, or if the insurance company that issued your GIC operates out of Alabama; California; Colorado; Louisiana; New Jersey; Washington, D.C.; or Wyoming—none of which maintain guaranteed funds—you could end up losing your whole account. You can better assess your GIC risk by asking your employee-benefits counselor these two questions:

How is the GIC issuer rated for claims-paying ability? The safest GIC issuers get ratings of AA or better from Standard & Poor's or Moody's. S&P rates one company, Union Labor Life, BBB—comparable to the lowest credit rating on an investment-grade bond—and six are unrated by either service.

What is the average maturity of the GIC portfolio? Ideally, it will be two or three years at most. If your 401(k) plan buys mostly GICs maturing in five years or longer, there is a greater risk that the issuer will stumble while in possession of your money.

With a balanced portfolio, you can spend part of your capital gains and still have enough growth to keep up with rising prices.

Elderly Retirees: Put Safety First
Stocks or stock funds: 40%
Bonds or bond funds: 40%
Cash equivalents: 20%

Once you reach age 75, inflation can become less of a concern; accordingly, over a two-year period, it makes sense to further trim your equity holdings to reduce investment risks. But in case you outlast your expected life span—and, thus, are exposed to more years of inflation than you planned for—you should keep 40% of your portfolio in stocks. For safety, consider shifting some holdings into high-dividend stocks, such as banks or utilities. But such issues should not account for more than 25% of your stockholdings; otherwise, you sacrifice diversification. Among bonds, stick with intermediate-term Treasuries.

If you have prudently managed your retirement fund up to this point, you may now pleasantly discover that you have more than you need to live on and can leave a big inheritance to your children. But even if you must gradually begin to draw down capital—which most financial planners say is no cause for worry at this stage in your life—your heirs will have every reason to be grateful. After all, one of the greatest gifts you can give your children is your own financial independence.

Where to Put Your IRA Money

Even a small improvement in your annual return can make a big difference in your retirement fund.

Once, your Individual Retirement Accounts might have been the focus of your investment life. But since the Tax Reform Act of 1986 drastically curtailed the deductibility of IRA contributions, many Americans have lost more than their incentive to contribute; they have lost interest in tending to their old ones as well.

Yet, neglecting your IRA can be a costly mistake. Many IRAs now hold substantial sums. Nearly a third of the respondents in a *Money* poll reported having $15,000 or more in their accounts, and that did not include any funds rolled over from company savings plans. With that kind of money involved, even a small improvement in your annual return can add up to a big difference in your retirement fund. In 20 years at 7%, $15,000 grows to $58,045; at 8%, it reaches $69,914; and at 9%, you're talking about a sizable $84,066.

Although under the old rules all workers could make tax-deductible contributions to an IRA of as much as $2,000 a year, currently your contribution is not fully deductible if you are covered by a pension plan and your adjusted gross income is $40,000 or above for married couples filing jointly ($25,000 for individuals). Couples who have AGIs between $40,000 and $50,000 can deduct part of their contributions (singles can if their AGI is $25,000 to $35,000).

Whether or not you can still make deductible IRA contributions, it is still important to tend to the money stashed in your old IRAs. Your first chore may be simply to make a list of your accounts and total how much is in each. Did the double-digit yields available in the mid-1980s lead you to put everything into

CDs? Today those CDs are probably returning no more than 7% to 8%. Indeed, 49% of the people responding to *Money*'s poll admitted making less than 10% a year on their IRAs. Or perhaps you sampled a different investment each year and are now left with a ragtag assortment of accounts. Some planners report that they have had clients with as many as 15 separate accounts.

Once you determine how much you have and where it is, you can begin to organize your portfolio. Your strategy will depend on several factors, including how much risk you want to take, the number of years before you retire, and how much income you will need. An often-quoted rule of thumb: It will take 70% to 80% of your current income to maintain your life-style in retirement.

Most financial experts share one basic belief: Over the long term, meaning at least 10 years, equities offer investors the best total return and the best chance to stay ahead of inflation year to year. So, even if you are squeamish about the stock market, keeping at least 25% of your retirement portfolio in equities is prudent. In addition, you should be more aggressive when you are younger, shifting to more conservative fixed-income investments as you get closer to retirement.

When setting up your asset mix, remember to include all your retirement accounts, such as 401(k)s and Keoghs, along with your IRAs. Say you are a moderately conservative, growth-oriented 40-year-old with $45,000 in your 401(k) and $15,000 in your IRA, and want to divide your money evenly between equities and fixed-income investments. To achieve this mix, begin with your 401(k). If your company plan offers an attractive guaranteed investment certificate (GIC) and a quality equity fund, you might consider putting $30,000 in the GIC and $15,000 in the equity portfolio. You would then want to stash your $15,000 IRA money in two or three no-load or low-load mutual funds invested in stocks; the average general equity fund returned a solid 16% annually over the past five years.

Among the stock funds recommended by Paul Westbrook, a retirement planner in Watchung, New Jersey: Neuberger & Berman's Partners Fund (no load; 800-877-9700; 17.65% five-year average annual return; $250 IRA minimum) and the Janus Fund (no load; 800-525-3713; 19.7% five-year average annual return; $500 IRA minimum). Another frequently mentioned favorite is Vanguard's Index Trust-500 Portfolio (no load; 800-662-7447; 19.9% five-year average annual return; $500 IRA minimum), which is designed to mirror the performance of Standard & Poor's 500-stock index and has outperformed 72% of all general equity mutual funds over the past decade. (For more detailed information on the performance of 960 funds, including *Money*'s risk-adjusted grades, see "Mutual Fund Rankings," beginning on page 193.) Some mutual funds cater to IRA contributors.

If you want to take a more defensive approach, you might consider equity-income funds or growth and income funds, categories that have averaged 14.7% and 16.8% annual returns respectively over the past five years. The income portion of such funds, which consists mainly of dividend-paying stocks, may prove more stable in an uncertain investing climate. Steven Enright, president of Enright Financial Advisors in River Vale, New Jersey, likes Mutual Beacon (no load; 800-448-3863; 19.8% five-year average annual return; $2,000 IRA minimum) and Evergreen Total Return (no load; 800-235-0064; 14.2% five-year average annual return; no IRA minimum).

For the nonequity part of your portfolio, some planners recommend that you buy Treasury securities, and in particular, they like zero-coupon bonds. The pricing and commissions on bonds can vary widely, so shop around and check with a discount broker. Or you can invest in bond funds. Andrew Chipok, a planner with L.J. Altfest & Company in New York City, recommends Vanguard's Fixed Income GNMA Fund (no load; 800-662-7447; 11.4% five-year average annual return; $500 IRA minimum) and Dreyfus' A Bonds Plus Fund (no load; 800-645-6561; 11.8% five-year average annual return; $750 IRA minimum). Once you do get your portfolio in order, make sure you maintain an asset mix that suits your goals and age.

Making Your Legacy Trouble-Free

You won't be around forever to take care of your loved ones. But with a well-drawn will and a few simple trusts, you can create an estate plan that could earn your heirs' lifelong gratitude.

Whatever your age, you can always find reasons to put off estate planning. There's the hassle of finding a lawyer, the expense, and all that off-putting jargon. Worst of all, perhaps, is the uncomfortable feeling you get from thinking about the ultimate retirement: your own death.

None of these excuses, however, justifies the price—in both money and frustration—that your survivors will pay if you don't put your affairs in order. If you die without a will, you effectively leave your family's financial security to the ungentle mercy of inflexible state laws, frequently plodding courts, and sometimes greedy lawyers. You could also wind up bequeathing far more than necessary to your Uncle Sam. Federal tax brackets start at 37% on estates above $600,000 and top out at a back-bending 55% on multimillion-dollar ones. And the rules may well change—for the worse.

A carefully drawn estate plan can spare your family both expense and anguish. By using a few relatively straightforward techniques, most families can pass their estates on with a minimum of red tape and without a penny of federal estate tax. At the same time, you can also protect the special needs of youthful, disabled, or spendthrift heirs.

There are three fundamental issues that every estate plan must address: providing for heirs, minimizing estate taxes, and lightening the administrative burden on survivors.

How property passes to your heirs depends on whether you hold it in your name or through some other form of ownership. Assets that you own jointly with rights of survivorship, for example, will automatically go to the surviving joint owner after your death. Assets for which you designate a beneficiary, such as Individual Retirement Accounts, pensions, and life insurance policies, will pass to whomever you name.

But there is only one way to make sure that property you own outright reaches your heirs: by leaving it to them in your will (see "With a Will, You Get Your Way" on page 191). An effective will need not be complicated or expensive. According to the National Resource Center for Consumers of Legal Services, the average cost nationwide for a simple will is only $83. A more elaborate will might cost $150 to $500, depending on the complexity of your finances. Yet, an estimated seven of 10 adults have never written a will.

Should you die without a will, the assets in your estate will be disbursed according to your state's laws of intestacy. These laws are essentially rigid formulas for dividing property, and they make little or no allowance for a family's special needs. In most states, for example, one-half to two-thirds of what you own would go to your children, regardless of how young or irresponsible they may be or how much your spouse may need.

No doubt many people without wills have simply put off thinking about them. But others may assume that their estates are in order without wills because they own everything jointly with their heirs. That could be a costly mistake. Suppose, for example, a widow makes her son the joint owner of her house with the understanding that he will sell the property after her death and divide the proceeds with his sister. In reality, the daughter may get nothing; the son's obligation is merely moral, not legal.

If your heirs are minors or financially inept adults, you also need to ensure that your property is managed for their benefit. Financially inexperienced widows, for example, are frequent victims of bad advice, well intentioned or otherwise. And though minors' inheritances will be managed by the guardian of their property—whom you name in your will—that person will have to seek a probate judge's approval for all but the most routine investment and spending decisions. While the law's intent is to protect your children from a thieving or incompetent guardian, it creates a burden that can work to their detriment.

You can solve this problem by bequeathing the kids' inheritances to a trust. Contrary to popular belief, trusts are not just for the charity-ball set; in fact, uncomplicated trusts can cost as little as $300 to $600 to set up, and an experienced estate lawyer can customize them to fit just about any family's needs.

Simply put, a trust is a legal device that holds property you place in it for the sake of one or more beneficiaries. The trust is managed by a trustee in accordance with instructions you set forth in the written agreement that creates the trust. Unlike a guardian, a trustee can usually manage your children's money without interference from a court.

While income taxes may be one of life's certainties, estate taxes need not be. In fact, you can escape the federal estate tax entirely by making sure that the value of your taxable estate is below $600,000. Federal taxes on estates under that amount are entirely offset by a $192,800 credit, which is available to everyone. That doesn't mean, however, that you can avoid the tax by just giving away everything but $600,000 on your deathbed. The federal estate and gift taxes are unified—meaning that

the value of taxable gifts as of the time you made them will be added to the property you hold at death in calculating your estate-tax liability.

Fortunately, the tax law leaves you plenty of loopholes. You can give as much as $10,000 a year each to as many people as you wish without triggering the gift tax; married couples can jointly give up to $20,000. You can also make tax-free gifts of any amount to charities and unlimited payments to health-care and educational institutions to cover a relative or friend's medical or tuition bills.

An even bigger bonanza is the so-called marital deduction, which lets you give during your lifetime or bequeath at your death as much as you want to your spouse tax-free as long as he or she is a U.S. citizen. (If your spouse is not a citizen, consult a tax adviser.) The write-off has its limitations, though: If your spouse ends up with more than $600,000, you may only postpone the estate tax until his or her death.

One way to solve that problem is through the judicious use of trusts. For example, a bypass trust (sometimes called a family or credit-shelter trust) lets both partners in a marriage take advantage of their separate $600,000 estate-tax exemptions to pass as much as $1.2 million to their heirs tax-free. In this arrangement, you bequeath assets worth up to $600,000 tax-free to the trust. The rest goes directly to your spouse and, because of the marital deduction, that bequest also escapes taxes.

For the rest of your spouse's life, he or she can collect the trust's income and usually up to $5,000 or 5% a year of the principal, whichever is greater. After your spouse's death, your children or other heirs become the trust's beneficiaries. But because the trust was not under your spouse's control, the assets do not count toward his or her taxable estate. And as long as your spouse's own assets are less than $600,000, your estate makes the entire trip from you to your spouse to your children free of federal taxes.

Property that you pass to your heirs by means of a trust, life insurance, or joint ownership goes directly to the beneficiary or co-owner. Property passed by your will, however, must go through probate, the legal process by which your will is proved valid in court, your assets are inventoried, your creditors paid off, and the balance of your estate distributed to your heirs. Depending on the complexity of your estate and the efficiency of your local probate system, your survivors might have to wait anywhere from a few months to several years for their inheritances. Meantime, legal and administrative costs could consume 5% to 10% of your estate.

You can sidestep the whole mess by transferring your assets to a revocable living trust (for more information, see "Beyond the Hype of Living Trusts" below). In contrast to testamentary trusts, living trusts start operating while you are still alive. With a revocable living trust, you retain the right to change the trust's provisions, terminate it, and usually serve as both trustee and beneficiary during your lifetime. (You will, of course, pay taxes on the trust's income.) Then, at your death, the trust effectively does the work of your will, either distributing your property among your heirs or remaining in force for their benefit. Nothing passes through probate.

If you have a revocable living trust, you will need what's known as a pour-over will, which directs that any property you failed to put into your living trust go into the trust at your death. Those assets will be subject to probate, but most states have streamlined proceedings for estates of $500 to $60,000.

Once you've grasped the basics of estate planning, your next question may well be: Can I buy a book of forms or computer software and cobble together my own living trusts? The short answer is yes—at your heirs' peril. Drafting your own estate plan is like do-it-yourself brain surgery. At least an attorney is accountable for his mistakes. But if you mess up, your spouse can't sue you after you're gone.

Unfortunately, because such trusts are just catching on, you may have trouble tracking down an attorney experienced in setting them up. To find one, ask your relatives, friends, accountant, or the trust officer at your bank for recommendations, or get in touch with lawyers who belong to your local estate-planning council. (You can get the association's phone number from your city's bar association.) Interview at least three of the attorneys. While you probably can't judge their legal expertise, their responses can give you an idea of the care they take and their grasp of the problems you face. It's also important to consider how well you get along with them. Remember that you will be sharing with your estate planner the intimate details of your finances.

Beyond the Hype of Living Trusts

Fewer people need these heavily promoted devices to duck probate costs than promoters want you to think.

Maybe you've seen one of the dozens of newspaper ads placed by lawyers and financial planners urging you to attend special no-charge seminars where you'll hear about the wonders of living trusts, which allow you to pass assets to your heirs outside your will. Or perhaps you've seen commercials on television in which lawyers hawk living-trust booklets, cassettes, or services. You might even have been visited by a door-to-door salesman for one of the smooth outfits known among attorneys as living-trust factories—actually, firms that mass market trusts composed mostly of boilerplate language for $1,000 or so.

Why the intense salesmanship? Simple: Living trusts are easy to peddle and command big fees. "You can learn how to sell living trusts in less than one day," promises an insurance magazine ad for the sales training program of American Family Living Trusts of Rancho Cordova, California. "Producers are now averaging over $2,000 a week."

Unhappily, that boast may well be true. A custom-designed trust can cost $600 to $3,500 or more, depending on the size and complexity of your estate. Yet, a growing number of middle- and upper-middle-income Americans are persuaded to spend such sums by the new marketeers.

The trusts were once used almost exclusively by the rich. Not anymore. To hear some trust-meisters talk, everyone should have a revocable living trust—so named because you transfer ownership of assets to the trust while you are alive and can alter the document's terms at any time. You can serve as trustee and manage the assets yourself; after your death, a successor trustee, typically a family member or friend, will distribute the assets to your beneficiaries according to your instructions in the trust document.

Do living trusts ever live up to their star billing? The answer: yes, but less frequently than their advocates claim. Proponents are quick to point out that the trusts avoid the "evil" and the "ordeal" of probate, the legal process in which a court approves your will and supervises the distribution of your assets. While that language may be hyperinflated, the point is correct: Probating an estate can take a year or longer, and legal fees and court costs often amount to 5% of the assets. Boston attorney Alexander Bove, author of the *Complete Book of Wills & Estates* (Henry Holt, $19.95), estimates that a lawyer settling a $1 million estate in Massachusetts might charge $25,000 to $40,000 in probate fees, compared with $6,000 to $8,000 for settling the same estate in a living trust.

Proponents also argue correctly that unlike a will, a living trust will protect your family's privacy. Once your will is admitted to probate, anyone can read it at the courthouse. But a trust document will remain secret even after the assets are distributed, except when a trustee needs a court to interpret the trust's instructions or a beneficiary—usually one who feels shortchanged—persuades the court to make the documents public. (This doesn't mean, however, that you can use a revocable trust to keep assets out of your creditors' hands. After a will is admitted to probate, creditors have four to six months to present claims to the executor for payment. With a trust, your assets can be transferred to the heirs immediately, so your creditors have to go to greater lengths to collect—they must sue the trustee in court or the beneficiaries if the trust has been dissolved. But since there is no time limit, such suits can be brought years after you die.)

Contrary to what many trust salesmen say, living trusts don't confer any tax benefits that a married couple can't get with a will. In either case, you can leave your heirs as much as $1.2 million free of federal estate taxes. You do it with a will through testamentary trusts that let you and your spouse each make full use of your $600,000 federal estate-tax exemption. Similarly, a couple can set up a living trust that splits into two trusts after the death of the first spouse. With both types, each trust contains up to the maximum of $600,000 in assets that can pass tax-free to the heirs. When the first spouse dies, his or her trust pays income to the survivor. Upon the second death, the assets of both trusts are distributed free of estate tax to the couple's ultimate beneficiaries—their children, for example.

Are living trusts better estate-planning tools than wills? The answer depends on your circumstances. For most people, living trusts aren't worth the cost and trouble. For couples whose houses are jointly owned and who have few other assets, a living trust would be overkill. And a trust will be worthless if you don't bother to transfer to it title to your real estate, stocks, mutual funds, bank accounts, and other property. Some seminar showmen barely mention those tasks—and an estimated 50% of people with living trusts neglect to do them. Retitling bank accounts, securities, and mutual funds can require hours of work and reams of forms that must be filled out. Moreover, you'll probably need your lawyer to retitle your house and any other real estate (cost: about $150 a property).

The best way to decide whether a living trust is appropriate is to consult an experienced estate lawyer. In general, however, you are a candidate for a trust if one of the following applies to you:

The cost of going through probate in your state is high. Figuring this out is tricky. Fees for executors and attorneys vary enormously from state to state. So do court costs. In addition, states calculate the size of estates in different ways. Some include the market value of a decedent's home; others don't. Thus, estates of the same size might be valued for probate purposes at $600,000 in Texas but $1 million in California. For help in estimating your estate's probate costs, consult the 50-state appendix in *Probate: How to Settle an Estate* (Random House, $8.95) by Kay Ostberg and HALT, a nonprofit consumer advocacy group in Washington, D.C. In general, say estate lawyers, the probate process is particularly costly in California, New York, and Pennsylvania, where total fees could top $35,000 on a $600,000 estate. For an estate of the same size in comparatively bargain states like North Carolina, Texas, and Virginia, probate would run less than $16,000.

Your estate is likely to prove contentious. For example, you may plan to leave a large inheritance to a second spouse, which could anger children from your first marriage. Only rarely have embittered heirs been able to invalidate living trusts, so if your objectives could put your estate in jeopardy, you should definitely consider a living trust.

You want to keep your estate private. As your estate grows more substantial, so do the benefits of nondisclosure. You might not want the world to know that your spouse inherited $250,000 in securities. His or her name would end up on a lot of investment marketing lists.

You fear becoming physically or mentally incompetent. A living trust can let you avoid a conservatorship—that is, being placed under a court-appointed guardian if you become unable to manage your own affairs. When setting up the trust, you can provide for a successor trustee to manage your assets if you are incapacitated. If your successor trustee is a professional at a bank or investment firm, you will usually pay an annual fee of 1% to 2% of the assets under management.

If you do set up a living trust and transfer your property to it, you should also have a simple will, which will cost $250 or so. Only in a will can you name a guardian for your minor children. Also, you may leave assets out of your trust on purpose or by accident. Without a will, those assets will be distributed according to your state's laws rather than your wishes. But if you have a will with a pour-over provision, the assets will shift to your trust and pass the way you intend.

Do You Need a Living Trust?

Benefits include:

- Gives you full control of your assets while you are alive and competent and avoids probate costs.

- Permits assets to be distributed quickly upon your death and keeps the details of your estate private.

- Arranges for a successor trustee to manage your assets should you become incapacitated and is difficult to contest.

Drawbacks include:

- Costs more in legal fees than drafting a will and requires retitling all assets that the trust will hold, which can be tedious and expensive.

- May require you or your heirs to pay annual fees of 1% to 2% of assets to a professional trustee and leaves your trust assets vulnerable to creditors' claims longer than a will does.

With a Will, You Get Your Way

Ensure that your last wishes are carried out and your legacy remains in the family.

When it comes to a will, all too many people act as if they'll get around to drafting it sometime soon—just before they die. Like stock market timers, however, they forget one important thing: Death, as well as market turns, has a way of happening when least expected. Consider the consequences of dying without a will:

The state will select your heirs. Should you die intestate—meaning with no will—the courts will gladly step in and put your personal affairs in order. But the law's notion of who gets what after you're gone probably doesn't match your own. In most states, your property will be split among your spouse and children, often with one-half to two-thirds going to your offspring. Without a single stroke of your pen, you could be assuring your mate's impoverished old age.

A probate court judge will name a guardian for your minor children. The court will have to look out for your children's welfare because you neglected to do so.

You may leave an unnecessarily large bequest to the tax collector. When a will is part of a carefully drawn estate plan that includes trusts, a married couple can pass up to $1.2 million to their heirs free of federal estate tax.

The state will charge you for its services, such as they are. Only in a will can you name an executor to inventory your estate, pay your debts, file income and estate-tax returns, and distribute assets to your heirs. If you perish without making such provisions, a judge may tap a public administrator for the job.

Executors, like public administrators, are entitled to fees, which may be set by state law or the probate court. In Mississippi, an executor's commission may not exceed 7% of a gross estate. If you name a family member or friend to do the job, he or she may waive the fee.

Clearly, a will should be the foundation on which you build your estate plan, unless you use a revocable living trust as a substitute. Unlike wills, such trusts aren't subject to probate. A living trust is not for everyone, though, because the lawyer's fee for drawing one up typically runs to $1,000, versus a high of around $250 for a simple will. In addition, you must transfer title of your assets to your trust. Young people who are unlikely to die for many years should write wills, then after they've accumulated more property and are closer to death, revise their estate plans to include revocable living trusts. Even if you establish a revocable living trust, you will still need a pour-over will, which stipulates that any assets you neglected to place in your living trust will go there after your death. To learn more about living trusts, see "Beyond the Hype of Living Trusts" on page 188.

Before you begin to set down your wishes in a will, however, you should know that the law doesn't give you free rein to disinherit your spouse. In the 41 common-law states, for instance, your spouse is entitled to a portion, usually a third, of your estate. As a result, the most effective way to disinherit your spouse is by getting him or her to sign a prenuptial or nuptial agreement to that effect. If you live in one of the nine community property states (Arizona, California, Idaho, Louisiana, Nevada, New Mexico, Texas, Washington, and Wisconsin), you can leave your half of the community property and all of your separate property to whomever you please. In Louisiana, you cannot disinherit your children.

Indeed, cutting your offspring out of your will is tricky in most states because the law considers your children to be the "natural objects of your bounty." So if you fail to mention a wayward son in your will, he could contest its validity by claiming that you were incompetent when you wrote it. To avoid litigation, it's wise to state in your will: "I make no provision for my son so-and-so." That statement shows that you considered your son while writing your will and consciously decided to leave him out.

People who plan to use their wills to hurl a final round of insults at family members and former friends who have wronged them should find another outlet for their frustrations. If you refer to your kid sister in your will as a lazy lummox who is unworthy of an inheritance, for example, she could sue your estate for libel.

When making bequests, it's generally best to leave percentages of your estate rather than fixed dollar amounts to your heirs because your assets may shrink or swell over the years. You may, however, wish to earmark specific sums for distant relatives, charities, or your household help. Remember that you cannot use your will to bequeath property that is jointly held—your share goes to your co-owner—or that has a named beneficiary, as does an Individual Retirement Account or life insurance policy.

You should list contingent beneficiaries in your will in case your first choices die before you do, cannot be located, or refuse to accept your bequests. By naming your church, college, or the Salvation Army as your contingent beneficiary, you're assured of making a complete disposition of your estate even if everyone you ever cared about goes before you do.

Don't catalogue everything you own in your will, because your holdings will change. Instead, inventory your assets and list their whereabouts in a separate letter of instruction that you give to your executor and loved ones. In that letter, which generally isn't legally binding, you can also convey your wishes regarding organ donation and funeral services.

Many people are tempted to save the lawyer's fees by drafting their own wills. The temptation rises further at the sight of how-to books, software, or even blank statutory wills, which are available from state legislatures, bar associations, and office-supply stores in California, Maine, Michigan, and Wisconsin. (Other states have not passed laws yet authorizing the use of statutory wills.) It's best to resist any such impulse because you run the risk of having a sloppy, do-it-yourself will that may be contested by heirs who are confused by its provisions. Besides, statutory wills cannot be customized to fit your particular needs. Michigan's version, for example, doesn't allow you to create a trust. A statutory will is a good stopgap for someone who's planning to see a lawyer next month about writing a will but is getting on a plane to Europe tomorrow.

Once you have written a will, store it somewhere that's safe from fire and other calamities. Your bank safe-deposit box is a suitable choice only if state law permits your survivors to retrieve your will from your box immediately after your death. In some states, banks must seal safe-deposit boxes at death and can't open them without a court order or without the presence of a state tax collector. If that's the case in your state, leave your will in a depository provided by some probate courts or with your lawyer, who should store it with other wills in a bank vault.

Don't forget about your will after you have put it away. Some provisions in the document may become invalid if you marry or divorce. You may also have to amend it if you move to another state or grow considerably richer or poorer. But you needn't throw out your will to make minor changes. You can add or remove a beneficiary, change the amount of a bequest, or replace an executor or guardian by asking your attorney to add an amendment to your will called a codicil.

Mutual Fund Rankings

What a decade it's been for mutual funds. New funds—and whole categories—were spawned in the 1980s, and investors couldn't read enough about them. Up-front sales loads lightened, but other expenses didn't. Hot hands went cold; service became a selling point. And Fidelity's Magellan Fund grew larger than most small nation's economies, from assets of $35.1 million in January 1980 to $12.4 billion a decade later.

Sure, the 1980s brought crashes and program trading. But for the typical stock-fund investor, the decade was one long tailgate party. The average stock fund cruised along at an annualized rate of 15.2%—more than half again as much as the stock market's historic average yearly gain of 10%. The only blemish on the decade was that stock funds fell a full 2.4 percentage points short of the S&P 500's 17.6% average annualized return.

Of course, if you'd selected any of the 10 best-performing funds of the 1980s you'd have aced the S&P easily, especially if you got aboard early in the decade. The records of most of the top 10, including overall champ Fidelity Magellan, which had a 10-year compound annual return of 28.4%, were launched during the 149% boom in small-company shares before mid-1983.

The decade's deadbeats were largely among funds saddled with gold stocks and technology shares. The latter bore the brunt of 1983's small-stock massacre, and gold funds sank when cooling inflation caused the commodity to belly-flop after 1980.

The 1980s were an equally congenial period for bond funds. The average taxable portfolio produced a compound annual gain of 10.9%

for the 10 years to December 1, 1990; the typical tax-exempt fund, 8.8%. The reason was that inflation, which stormed into the decade at a 13% rate, tiptoed out at 4.7%. Interest rates fell commensurately, lifting nearly all bond funds.

Of course, the top fund did more than simply reflect the healthy environment. Under manager Kenneth Urbaszewski, Kemper High Yield navigated adroitly among high-yielding junk bonds and safer Ginnie Maes, high-grade corporates and cash to produce an average annual return of 13.4%. By contrast, funds that chased high yields earned mediocre returns. One such fund, National Bond, finished dead last among taxables tracked by *Money*. It posted a paltry 7.1% average annual gain.

As all experienced investors know, the true test of mutual-fund performance is long term. That's why in this—*Money*'s most complete mutual fund listings ever—funds are ranked by their five-year returns. Some hits and misses of the past half-decade:

Best-performing category. Aided by a weak buck and strong foreign stock markets, international funds scored the biggest average gains, up 237.2% for the period.

Top-gaining fund. Not surprisingly, the highest-flying fund was the one that led the hottest category: Fidelity Overseas, up 324.9%.

Most disappointing. High-yield corporates, up just 54.8% overall (or 9% compounded annually), gained this dubious distinction as the funds devoured investors' principal while paying seductive double-digit yields. The fund category's worst: National Bond, up 19.3%—or a paltry 3.6% on average annually.

Worst individual performance. The slump in technology stocks clobbered Fidelity's Select-Technology fund, which lost 1.4% over the five years to the December 22, 1989 cutoff date.

Total returns alone don't tell you all you need to know about a fund you're considering or one you already own. That's why *Money* also graded the risk-adjusted performances of all 960 large, widely available funds we follow. Also assigned are three additional grades—for performance in different market phases—to five-year top performers. You'll find the funds listed category by category starting below. Complete alphabetical listings begin on page 202.

The *Money* risk-adjusted grade—a telling measure based on a formula developed by Stanford University professor William

Sharpe—compares funds within broad categories (equity, tax-exempt bond, taxable bond, international and global, and gold and sectors). Specifically, it rewards them for superior total return and docks them for outsize risk. To win an A, a fund must rank among the top 10% in its category; a B goes to the upper-middle 20%; C, the middle 40%; D, the next 20%; and F, the bottom 10%. *Money*'s grade thus allows you to distinguish between funds with similar total returns: The one with the higher grade has achieved its return more smoothly. For example, Hartwell Emerging Growth ranks first among small-company growth funds in total return over the past five years but still merits a risk-adjusted grade of only C. To see why, look under the column headed five-year analysis, which records the fund's gain or loss during its best and worst quarters in the five-year period that ended September 20, 1989. There you see that even though Hartwell rose as much as 46% in a three-month period, it has also taken a beating

THE Money RANKINGS: TOP TAX-EXEMPT BOND FUNDS

Ranked by five-year performance	MONEY risk-adjusted grade	% gain (or loss) to Dec. 1, 1989				% compound annual return		Five-year analysis		Lipper market phase rating			Net assets (million)
		One year	Three years	Five years	10 years	Five years	10 years	Best quarter	Worst quarter	Current	Prior up	Prior down	
HIGH-GRADE TAX-EXEMPTS		**10.8**	**20.5**	**76.5**	**134.2**	**12.0**	**8.8**						
1. United Municipal	A	12.8	24.7	93.0	129.6	14.1	8.7	11.3	(6.5)	C	A	A	$618
2. Putnam Tax-Exempt Income	A	12.7	23.0	88.7	202.6	13.5	11.7	11.1	(6.0)	E	C	A	1,305
3. Financial Tax-Free Income	B	14.7	22.9	88.6	—	13.5	—	12.1	(7.5)	D	A	B	163
4. Delaware Grp.–Tax-Free USA	A	11.7	24.3	88.1	—	13.5	—	10.4	(6.2)	A	A	A	553
5. Mutual of Omaha Tax-Free	B	11.7	23.5	88.0	129.5	13.5	8.7	10.4	(6.0)	C	A	C	357
6. SteinRoe Managed Municipals	B	11.5	21.5	87.2	165.5	13.4	10.3	12.2	(4.6)	B	A	C	550
7. Seligman Tax-Exempt–National	B	10.8	22.2	84.9	—	13.1	—	10.8	(5.7)	E	A	B	142
HIGH-YIELD TAX-EXEMPTS		**10.3**	**21.3**	**71.4**	**159.3**	**11.3**	**10.0**						
1. Vanguard Muni–High Yield	B	12.8	23.3	83.9	140.3	13.0	9.2	9.8	(5.9)	D	A	A	928
2. SteinRoe High Yield Municipals	A	11.8	25.3	83.7	—	12.9	—	9.1	(4.3)	B	B	A	282
3. IDS High Yield Tax-Exempt	B	11.7	22.1	81.6	154.5	12.7	9.8	10.6	(4.9)	C	B	C	4,516
4. Fidelity High Yield Muni	C	12.6	20.4	78.1	141.0	12.2	9.2	9.4	(5.9)	D	A	D	1,731
5. Merrill Lynch Muni–High Yield	C	9.8	20.3	76.0	172.3	12.0	10.5	9.6	(4.4)	D	C	D	1,574
6. Colonial Tax Exempt High Yield	C	8.3	18.6	69.3	188.4	11.1	11.2	7.9	(3.0)	D	D	D	1,500
7. GIT Tax-Free–High Yield	D	7.0	16.0	65.2	—	10.6	—	10.6	(4.1)	E	C	E	42
SHORT/INTERMEDIATE-TERM TAX-EX.		**7.6**	**17.3**	**48.5**	**102.4**	**8.2**	**7.3**						
1. Vanguard Muni–Intermediate	C	10.2	21.2	68.6	111.7	11.0	7.8	7.4	(3.6)	D	A	A	1,076
2. USAA Tax Exempt–Intermediate	D	9.3	19.9	61.4	—	10.1	—	6.5	(2.8)	E	C	B	448
3. Fidelity Limited Term Muni	D	8.1	16.5	60.3	118.6	9.9	8.1	7.4	(3.6)	E	B	C	444
4. Dreyfus Intermediate Tax-Exempt	D	8.8	18.1	60.1	—	9.9	—	6.7	(2.8)	B	B	B	1,093
5. Limited Term Municipal	D	7.6	20.4	51.6	—	8.7	—	4.7	(0.7)	A	—	E	201
6. Scudder Tax-Free Target–1993	D	6.9	14.6	51.2	—	8.6	—	6.2	(2.0)	D	A	C	78
7. Scudder Tax-Free Target–1990	D	5.9	14.1	41.7	—	7.2	—	4.6	(1.0)	D	B	C	57
SHEARSON LEHMAN HUTTON MUNI INDEX		13.1	26.0	91.8	164.6	13.9	10.3	11.1	(0.5)				

of as much as 31%.

You can get a further indication of a top performer's consistency by consulting the other important grade, the Lipper Market Phase Rating. Here, *Money*'s supplier of fund data, Lipper Analytical Services, rates funds during three distinct investment periods: the current market phase (since the analysis is based on data from late 1989, "current" may have changed by publication date; however, the information is still valuable in measuring a fund's stability); the previous up phase; and the prior down phase. (For equity funds, the phases begin and end at major turning points in the Lipper Growth Fund Index, an average of major stock funds; for bond funds, they are determined by changes in the trend of the prime rate.) In each period, funds that rank in the top 20% of their category earn an A, those in the next 20% a B, and so on, with an E for funds in the bottom quintile.

None of *Money*'s top-performing funds scored straight A's. But a few came close. IAI Regional, the No. 2 growth fund, up 177.6%, registered three A's and a B, as did New York Venture, the fifth-ranked growth fund. Several funds, including Putnam Voyager, United Income, and Massachusetts Financial Total Return Trust, scored three aces and a C.

For an idea of a fund's management style, see the portfolio analysis section. Also be sure to check the expense analysis column. Of particular interest: the five-year projection. It sums up how much you would pay in sales charges and operating expenses, assuming you invest $1,000 at an annual return of 5%, reinvest all dividends and capital gains, and sell your shares after five years. One cost not included in that projection is the impact of a fund's % turnover, which measures how much of the portfolio is bought and sold each year. The more a fund trades, the higher its brokerage costs—and the higher your capital-gains tax is likely to be in up years. Leave it to the IRS to toss cold water on some pretty hot performances.

Portfolio analysis				Expense analysis				Telephone	
% yield	Average maturity (years)	% cash	Senior fund manager, age (years managing fund)	% turnover	% maximum initial sales charge	Five-year projection	Minimum initial investment	Toll-free (800)	In state
6.8									◄ CATEGORY AVERAGE
6.7	24.0	5.2	John M. Holliday, 54 (9)	225	4.25	$74	$500	—	816-283-4122
6.8	25.6	1.4	David Eurkus, N.A.	113	4.75	75	500	225-1581	—
6.7	25.7	5.3	William Veronda, 43 (5)	27	None	41	250	525-8085	—
7.2	24.1	0.0	J. Michael Pokorny, 50 (6)	8	4.75	87	1,000	523-4640	215-988-1333 (Pa.)
6.9	22.0	2.0	Mark L. Winter, 37 (3)	73	8.0	113	1,000	228-9596	800-642-8112 (Neb.)
6.5	17.6	1.8	David Snowbeck, 47 (12)	102	None	36	1,000	338-2550	—
6.2	24.5	2.2	Thomas Moles, N.A. (5)	41	4.75	91	1,000	221-2450	212-912-8200 (N.Y.)
7.5									◄ CATEGORY AVERAGE
7.3	22.9	8.5	Ian A. MacKinnon, 41 (8)	40	None	15	3,000	662-7447	—
7.2	19.5	6.7	Tom Conlin, 35 (2)	208	None	41	1,000	338-2550	—
7.4	21.4	3.4	Kurt A. Larson, 49 (10)	13	5.0	82	2,000	328-8300	—
7.0	22.3	7.9	Guy E. Wickwire, 41 (8)	47	None	33	2,500	544-6666	—
7.4	N.A.	6.0	Vincent Giordano, 45 (10)	77	4.0	70	1,000	637-3863	—
7.6	9.8	3.6	Michael Hardie, 42 (5)	22	4.75	105	250	426-3750	—
6.7	18.0	10.5	Rick Gunn, 42 (5)	58	None	64	1,000	336-3063	703-528-6500 (Va.)
6.3									◄ CATEGORY AVERAGE
7.0	10.5	4.3	Ian A. MacKinnon, 41 (8)	89	None	15	3,000	662-7447	—
7.0	9.2	2.4	Kenneth E. Willmann, 44 (8)	113	None	27	3,000	531-8000	—
6.7	10.5	10.2	John F. Haley Jr., N.A. (5)	30	None	37	2,500	544-6666	—
7.1	8.5	0.1	Monica Wieboldt, 39 (5)	34	None	40	2,500	645-6561	—
6.7	N.A.	2.0	Brian McMahon, 34 (5)	45	2.0	89	2,500	847-0200	505-984-0200 (N.M.)
6.1	3.2	5.0	Donald C. Carleton, 55 (6)	54	None	44	1,000	225-2470	—
5.6	0.7	4.0	Donald C. Carleton, 55 (6)	31	None	44	1,000	225-2470	—

Key to MONEY grades: A = Top 10%   B = Next 20%   C = Middle 40%   D = Next 20%   F = Bottom 10%

THE Money RANKINGS: TOP STOCK FUNDS

Ranked by five-year performance	MONEY risk-adjusted grade	% gain (or loss) to Dec. 22, 1989				% compound annual return		Five-year analysis		Lipper market phase rating			Net assets (millions)
		1989	Three years	Five years	10 years	Five years	10 years	Best quarter	Worst quarter	Current	Prior up	Prior down	
GROWTH		**24.7**	**43.6**	**113.1**	**331.8**	**16.1**	**15.2**						
1. Fidelity Magellan	A	32.4	62.2	188.8	1,116.2	23.6	28.4	22.9	(24.7)	A	A	D	$12,412.6
2. IAI Regional	A	29.3	57.9	177.6	—	22.6	—	17.0	(16.0)	B	A	A	121.2
3. AIM Weingarten	A	34.0	58.7	173.3	535.8	22.3	20.3	23.9	(21.8)	A	A	D	427.8
4. Scudder Capital Growth	A	31.8	66.5	165.4	423.1	21.5	18.0	18.5	(24.2)	A	B	D	972.4
5. New York Venture	A	31.8	55.7	163.8	518.2	21.4	20.0	19.1	(18.4)	A	A	B	320.4
6. IDS New Dimensions	A	29.0	58.5	160.2	516.0	21.1	19.9	26.6	(14.6)	B	A	B	752.0
7. Thomson McKinnon—Growth	A	35.5	56.9	155.1	—	20.6	—	23.0	(21.3)	B	A	C	357.0
8. SteinRoe Special	B	36.0	66.9	152.8	502.8	20.4	19.7	19.3	(19.5)	A	B	C	319.6
MAXIMUM CAPITAL GAINS		**25.5**	**46.4**	**114.3**	**366.6**	**16.3**	**16.4**						
1. Putnam Voyager	A	33.5	61.1	168.9	415.9	21.9	17.8	24.2	(20.2)	A	A	C	717.3
2. AIM Constellation	B	34.1	56.2	165.6	365.1	21.6	16.6	36.1	(26.9)	A	A	E	82.2
3. SLH Aggressive Growth	B	41.1	63.7	164.9	—	21.5	—	34.9	(23.7)	A	B	E	97.7
4. Twentieth Century Growth	B	42.5	60.6	159.8	432.5	21.0	18.2	32.0	(27.3)	B	A	D	1,600.0
5. Oppenheimer Time	B	25.4	51.5	146.3	401.6	19.7	17.5	24.1	(19.6)	C	B	C	332.9
6. Twentieth Century Vista	C	46.4	57.0	142.9	—	19.4	—	40.5	(26.2)	A	B	E	279.0
7. Pacific Horizon Aggressive Growth	C	33.3	46.7	141.0	—	19.2	—	39.3	(20.1)	D	A	B	96.2
8. Keystone America Omega	C	29.1	56.1	139.9	229.4	19.1	12.7	26.9	(19.4)	A	A	D	39.6
SMALL-COMPANY GROWTH		**21.6**	**37.2**	**90.6**	**252.1**	**13.4**	**13.2**						
1. Hartwell Emerging Growth	C	35.7	67.0	156.9	305.5	20.8	15.0	46.4	(31.3)	A	A	E	24.5
2. Putnam OTC Emerging Growth	B	26.0	50.9	156.8	—	20.8	—	26.4	(23.1)	B	A	D	178.8
3. Evergreen Limited Market*	B	20.4	44.0	156.5	—	20.7	—	23.8	(24.6)	C	A	B	38.9
4. Alliance Quasar	C	26.9	52.7	152.6	—	20.4	—	29.6	(26.7)	A	A	D	266.5
5. Acorn Fund	B	24.1	58.8	145.5	352.6	19.7	16.3	17.1	(20.8)	B	A	A	836.6
6. New Beginning Growth	C	32.7	49.4	141.3	—	19.3	—	29.6	(22.0)	B	A	B	57.9
7. Babson Enterprise	C	22.4	45.8	121.5	—	17.2	—	21.9	(28.2)	B	B	B	87.3
8. Nicholas II	C	16.4	44.5	115.0	—	16.5	—	22.6	(16.8)	D	B	A	399.8
GROWTH AND INCOME		**21.9**	**42.0**	**114.3**	**329.3**	**16.4**	**15.5**						
1. Nationwide Fund	B	30.1	53.9	148.8	349.7	20.0	16.2	19.4	(21.9)	A	A	E	480.6
2. Investment Co. of America	A	27.1	49.4	144.6	412.2	19.6	17.7	17.5	(18.8)	B	A	B	5,384.2
3. Washington Mutual Investors	A	25.8	47.8	143.2	500.5	19.4	19.6	16.9	(19.0)	B	A	C	4,272.9
4. Vanguard Index Trust—500 Port.	B	28.5	53.3	143.2	368.9	19.4	16.7	21.2	(22.7)	A	A	E	1,718.6
5. Fundamental Investors	B	27.0	50.1	143.0	419.0	19.4	17.9	20.9	(22.2)	B	A	D	767.6
6. Oppenheimer Total Return	A	18.3	47.8	140.8	253.0	19.2	13.4	17.0	(14.9)	D	A	B	381.3
7. Safeco Equity	C	35.0	55.3	139.6	297.0	19.1	14.8	22.8	(26.8)	A	B	E	56.0
8. Dean Witter Dividend Growth	A	29.0	49.6	139.5	—	19.1	—	14.6	(17.6)	A	C	B	2,679.8
EQUITY INCOME		**20.0**	**36.7**	**104.3**	**364.7**	**15.3**	**16.4**						
1. United Income	A	25.1	58.7	161.8	469.9	21.2	19.0	22.6	(11.2)	A	A	C	1,554.2
2. Financial Industrial Income	A	30.0	55.3	134.5	371.6	18.6	16.8	17.6	(17.0)	A	A	D	446.0
3. Delaware Group—Decatur I	B	19.9	45.7	129.9	407.9	18.1	17.6	16.5	(18.9)	B	A	E	1,836.0
4. Oppenheimer Equity Income	A	17.7	44.9	122.1	408.9	17.3	17.7	15.9	(12.6)	C	B	B	1,163.0
5. Safeco Income	C	17.9	30.2	107.9	367.9	15.8	16.7	14.4	(19.2)	B	A	D	223.4
6. Income Fund of America	A	21.8	39.3	107.8	367.9	15.7	16.7	11.0	(7.7)	C	D	A	1,534.9
7. Fidelity Equity-Income	C	16.9	39.7	105.9	474.1	15.5	19.1	14.9	(18.0)	B	B	D	4,961.3
8. National Total Return	C	25.8	37.6	104.5	356.5	15.4	16.4	12.8	(15.5)	B	C	C	275.2
BALANCED		**18.0**	**33.2**	**103.0**	**322.3**	**15.1**	**15.4**						
1. Loomis-Sayles Mutual	B	19.7	39.1	137.5	345.6	18.9	16.1	19.6	(14.4)	C	A	E	320.2
2. USAA Inv. Trust—Cornerstone	B	21.1	43.0	131.2	—	18.2	—	21.3	(17.7)	B	B	E	538.0
3. Mass. Financial Total Return Trust	A	21.3	45.8	129.9	365.6	18.1	16.6	14.4	(12.4)	A	A	C	647.0
4. Vanguard Wellington	B	20.1	41.1	118.4	364.1	16.9	16.6	14.0	(12.4)	A	B	D	2,034.1
5. Putnam (George) Fund of Boston	B	21.3	39.5	118.2	314.3	16.9	15.3	14.1	(13.6)	B	B	D	396.3
6. Phoenix Balanced Series	A	23.4	38.3	116.6	407.2	16.7	17.6	15.4	(8.8)	D	A	B	455.0
7. IDS Mutual	A	17.3	40.6	115.6	325.3	16.6	15.6	13.3	(9.2)	C	C	B	1,696.0
8. Fidelity Puritan	A	18.9	38.4	115.6	412.5	16.6	17.8	12.8	(14.7)	C	B	C	4,824.1
S&P 500-STOCK INDEX**		**31.6**	**61.5**	**152.5**	**403.9**	**20.4**	**17.6**	**21.4**	**(22.5)**				

*Currently closed to new investors   **To 1/1/90   †Fund may impose back-end load or exit fee.

Portfolio analysis			Senior fund manager, age (years managing fund)	Expense analysis			Minimum initial investment	Telephone	
% yield	P/E ratio	% cash		% turnover	% maximum initial sales charge	Five-year projection		Toll-free (800)	In state
1.8									◀ CATEGORY AVERAGE
1.5	15.0	9.7	Morris Smith, 33 (8 months)	87	3.0	$88	$2,500	544-6666	—
1.6	17.9	30.0	Bing Carlin, 52 (9)	94	None	55	5,000	—	612-371-2884
0.9	18.7	3.9	Heinz Hutzler, 65 (20)	93	5.5	118	1,000	374-1919	—
0.3	N.A.	8.0	Steven Aronoff, 46 (3 months)	49	None	53	1,000	225-2470	—
1.0	17.9	10.9	Shelby M.C. Davis, 52 (21)	58	4.75	99	1,000	545-2098	—
0.4	24.4	25.1	Arch Spencer, 50 (2)	119	5.0	93	2,000	328-8300	—
0.5	19.8	10.0	Irwin Smith, N.A. (3)	104	None†	117	1,000	628-1237	212-482-5894 (N.Y.)
1.0	21.6	0.5	Richard Weiss, 38 (8)	42	None	55	1,000	338-2550	—
1.7									◀ CATEGORY AVERAGE
0.4	N.A.	9.9	Matthew A. Weatherbie, N.A.	71	5.75	122	500	225-1581	—
0.0	19.2	0.0	Heinz Hutzler, 65 (13)	131	5.5	141	1,000	374-1919	—
0.0	37.5	4.1	Richard Freeman, 55 (7)	10	5.0	115	500	—	212-528-2744
1.8	19.8	1.0	James E. Stowers, 65 (31)	143	None	55	None	345-2021	—
2.3	23.2	18.6	Donna Calder, 38 (3)	67	8.5	136	1,000	525-7048	—
0.1	29.0	1.0	James E. Stowers, 65 (6)	145	None	55	None	345-2021	—
0.0	28.5	1.5	William H. Duncan, 46 (6)	276	4.5	112	1,000	332-3863	—
0.8	17.3	6.4	Maureen Cullinane, N.A. (6 months)	84	2.0	97	1,000	343-2898	—
0.7									◀ CATEGORY AVERAGE
0.0	37.2	4.2	John Hartwell, 73 (21)	110	3.0	154	2,000	624-3863	—
0.0	N.A.	4.4	Richard Jodka, N.A.	74	5.75	141	500	225-1581	—
0.2	18.2	34.9	Robin D. Kelly, 36 (6)	47	None	74	25,000	235-0064	
0.0	20.9	9.8	F. Burr, 52 (17); P. Jenkel, 50 (17)	58	5.5	123	250	227-4618	
1.9	27.8	4.0	Ralph Wanger, 55 (19)	36	None†	44	4,000	922-6769	
1.1	N.A.	2.0	Douglas C. Jones, 45 (8)	88	None	65	2,000	332-5580	—
0.9	21.8	8.5	Peter Schliemann, 44 (5)	41	None	75	1,000	422-2766	—
1.6	19.3	9.9	Albert O. Nicholas, 59 (6)	18	None	41	1,000	—	414-272-6133
3.2									◀ CATEGORY AVERAGE
2.9	14.9	6.3	Charles S. Bath, 35 (5)	13	7.5	107	250	848-0920	800-282-1440 (Ohio)
3.5	14.7	17.0	Committee management	16	5.75	87	250	421-0180	714-671-7000 (Calif.)
3.0	13.5	5.0	Committee management	21	5.75	94	250	421-0180	714-671-7000 (Calif.)
2.7	15.6	1.3	George Sauter, 35 (2)	10	None	12	3,000	662-7447	—
3.4	16.1	9.3	Committee management	8	5.75	96	250	421-0180	714-671-7000 (Calif.)
3.7	13.7	24.9	Diane Jarmusz, 37 (6)	127	4.75	97	1,000	525-7048	—
3.6	19.1	4.9	Douglas Johnson, 35 (5)	88	None	53	1,000	426-6730	800-562-6810 (Wash.)
2.6	17.1	3.3	Paul Vance, 52 (8)	8	None†	104	1,000	869-3863	—
5.0									◀ CATEGORY AVERAGE
3.0	14.9	4.6	Russell Thompson, 49 (20)	49	8.5	119	500	—	816-283-4122
4.0	16.5	9.4	John Kaweske, 48 (4)	124	None	43	250	525-8085	—
4.2	12.5	7.7	Paul Ehrsam, 33 (7)	39	8.5	122	25	523-4640	215-988-1333 (Pa.)
5.1	15.0	21.2	Diane Jarmusz, 37 (9)	91	8.5	128	1,000	525-7048	—
5.0	13.5	1.4	Arley N. Hudson, 55 (11)	34	None	51	1,000	426-6730	800-562-6810 (Wash.)
6.7	13.7	20.8	Committee management	34	5.75	94	1,000	421-0180	714-671-7000 (Calif.)
5.3	12.7	6.1	C. Bruce Johnstone, 48 (17)	68	2.0	54	2,500	544-6666	—
4.3	15.8	9.0	John Doney, 59 (2)	35	7.25	125	250	223-7757	203-863-5600 (Conn.)
5.1									◀ CATEGORY AVERAGE
4.6	14.6	0.8	G. Kenneth Heebner, 48 (13)	218	None	56	1,000	345-4048	—
3.5	25.4	6.4	David Peebles, 50 (2)	28	None	67	1,000	531-8000	—
5.4	14.6	10.0	Richard Dahlberg, 49 (5)	52	4.75	109	250	225-2606	—
5.3	11.8	2.2	Vincent Bajakian, 59 (18)	28	None	26	3,000	662-7447	—
5.8	12.4	1.4	Thomas V. Reilly, N.A.	139	5.75	126	500	225-1581	—
5.0	21.4	12.0	Patricia Bannan, 29 (4)	226	6.9	110	500	243-4361	—
5.6	10.1	9.1	Tom Medcalf, 42 (7)	60	5.0	86	2,000	328-8300	—
6.3	17.2	8.7	Richard Fentin, 33 (3)	77	2.0	55	2,500	544-6666	—
3.2	**14.7**		**Key to MONEY grades:** A = Top 10% B = Next 20% C = Middle 40% D = Next 20% F = Bottom 10%						

N.A. Not available

THE Money RANKINGS: TOP STOCK FUNDS

Ranked by five-year performance	MONEY risk-adjusted grade	% gain (or loss) to Dec. 22, 1989				% compound annual return		Five-year analysis		Lipper market phase rating			Net assets (millions)
		One year	Three years	Five years	10 years	Five years	10 years	Best quarter	Worst quarter	Current	Prior up	Prior down	
FLEXIBLE INCOME		**11.4**	**27.5**	**84.8**	**247.3**	**13.0**	**13.1**						
1. National Total Income	A	20.8	43.4	124.0	380.2	17.5	17.0	13.5	(8.3)	A	A	C	$198.4
2. Vanguard Wellesley Income	A	20.1	33.0	103.6	318.6	15.3	15.4	12.0	(2.5)	B	B	B	766.1
3. Mutual of Omaha Income	B	15.3	37.8	86.1	213.7	13.2	12.1	9.0	(4.5)	C	C	B	169.0
4. Seligman Income	C	14.7	21.0	81.6	256.0	12.7	13.5	12.2	(2.7)	D	B	B	160.0
5. USAA Mutual—Income	B	16.7	32.9	79.2	233.2	12.4	12.8	9.0	(3.6)	A	C	D	349.3
6. Northeast Investors Trust	B	0.7	15.0	75.2	214.8	11.9	12.2	9.2	(2.1)	E	A	E	355.0
CONVERTIBLES		**14.9**	**24.0**	**93.6**	**307.1**	**14.1**	**15.1**						
1. Dreyfus Convertible Securities	C	14.0	36.3	110.4	281.3	16.0	14.3	12.6	(20.0)	B	A	C	265.8
2. Phoenix Convertible	B	18.7	35.6	95.2	—	14.3	—	12.8	(8.3)	C	C	A	158.7
3. American Capital Harbor	C	20.1	32.6	89.3	317.1	13.6	15.4	13.5	(20.4)	A	D	E	385.4
4. Putnam Convert. Income & Growth	D	15.8	21.6	79.5	322.8	12.4	15.5	12.1	(19.3)	C	B	E	823.0
5. Alliance Convertible	—	11.5	22.0	—	—	—	—	12.8	(17.3)	C	—	B	71.8
6. Dean Witter Convertible Securities	—	12.8	8.1	—	—	—	—	16.2	(23.3)	D	—	E	745.5
OPTION INCOME		**14.4**	**32.6**	**80.9**	**223.0**	**12.6**	**12.4**						
1. Oppenheimer Premium Income	C	5.6	56.8	90.6	245.6	13.8	13.2	19.3	(5.0)	E	D	A	272.3
2. Franklin Option	D	13.1	35.1	83.0	256.1	12.8	13.5	10.6	(15.1)	C	B	C	45.0
3. Analytic Optioned Equity	C	16.8	39.2	82.3	226.6	12.8	12.6	9.2	(10.7)	C	C	B	109.2
4. Gateway Option Index	D	17.8	32.2	75.1	177.1	11.9	10.7	7.0	(16.4)	B	E	B	31.1
5. Putnam Option Income	D	13.6	26.6	73.5	209.6	11.6	12.0	13.3	(25.4)	B	A	E	935.6
6. SLH Income—Option Income	—	15.4	31.2	—	—	—	—	12.5	(18.1)	A	—	C	575.5
SECTORS		**27.9**	**46.0**	**112.5**	**267.0**	**15.8**	**13.8**						
1. Fidelity Select—Leisure	A	29.6	66.6	208.6	—	25.3	—	24.1	(25.0)	A	A	D	61.0
2. Vanguard Spec. Port.—Health Care	A	31.0	64.6	192.8	—	24.0	—	23.7	(25.6)	B	B	B	72.2
3. Fidelity Select—Health Care	A	37.7	49.0	191.8	—	23.9	—	31.2	(28.5)	D	A	D	223.5
4. Pru-Bache Utility	A	35.3	49.2	169.5	—	21.9	—	18.4	(10.7)	A	A	E	2,213.7
5. Putnam Health Sciences Trust	B	37.8	59.6	163.2	—	21.3	—	25.9	(22.9)	D	D	A	291.8
6. Seligman Comm. & Information	B	27.6	56.2	148.5	—	20.0	—	29.7	(19.3)	B	A	B	43.2
INTERNATIONAL		**23.0**	**64.8**	**237.2**	**463.3**	**27.2**	**18.2**						
1. Fidelity Overseas	A	15.4	47.3	324.9	—	33.5	—	38.5	(17.4)	D	—	C	925.6
2. Merrill Lynch Pacific A	B	14.7	69.5	318.0	928.4	33.1	26.2	30.9	(25.9)	B	A	E	357.4
3. Japan Fund	A	8.1	68.2	289.4	663.9	31.2	22.5	27.8	(8.7)	D	B	A	417.5
4. Vanguard Trustees' Comm.—Intl.	A	23.9	82.9	282.8	—	30.8	—	19.4	(12.0)	B	C	B	587.1
5. Vanguard World—Int. Growth	A	23.0	54.7	271.7	—	30.0	—	25.9	(13.0)	B	A	B	600.3
6. Kleinworth Benson—Intl. Equity	B	21.3	60.6	270.8	363.8	30.0	16.6	24.9	(18.4)	B	C	C	70.1
GLOBAL		**22.3**	**46.5**	**169.5**	**417.0**	**21.6**	**17.8**						
1. Paine Webber Classic Atlas	B	19.5	49.3	239.1	—	27.6	—	20.1	(24.8)	C	A	D	202.4
2. Oppenheimer Global	C	32.5	58.8	237.1	450.4	27.5	18.6	25.7	(32.0)	A	B	E	509.0
3. Putnam International Equities	C	21.8	42.6	225.7	480.2	26.6	19.2	23.4	(18.0)	C	A	C	489.0
4. First Investors Global	C	34.2	100.2	214.7	—	25.8	—	24.9	(18.9)	A	C	B	120.8
5. Pru-Bache Global	D	10.5	29.7	168.3	—	21.8	—	24.4	(21.5)	E	B	B	391.0
6. New Perspective	C	23.9	54.0	161.4	414.3	21.2	17.8	18.3	(18.0)	C	B	B	1,232.3
GOLD & METALS		**29.0**	**49.7**	**93.0**	**175.7**	**13.4**	**10.2**						
1. Oppenheimer Gold & Spec. Min.	B	39.7	160.5	229.7	—	26.9	—	44.7	(9.2)	A	B	A	160.9
2. Lexington Goldfund	C	25.4	59.7	135.9	161.7	18.7	10.1	42.7	(17.1)	B	A	B	140.0
3. Franklin Gold	C	43.8	97.8	130.0	316.1	18.1	15.3	58.1	(22.7)	A	C	C	347.0
4. Vanguard Spec. Port.—Gold & PM	C	31.4	54.7	125.6	—	17.7	—	52.9	(22.6)	B	A	B	187.2
5. International Investors	D	53.2	62.6	113.7	297.5	16.4	14.8	52.9	(21.8)	A	C	B	917.6
6. Keystone Precious Metals	D	28.1	53.8	95.4	150.5	14.3	9.6	52.4	(24.8)	B	B	C	220.0
S&P 500-STOCK INDEX**		**31.6**	**61.5**	**152.5**	**403.9**	**20.4**	**17.6**	**21.4**	**(22.5)**				

*Figure reflects borrowing to boost investment　　**To 1/1/90　　†Fund may impose back-end load or exit fee.

Portfolio analysis			Senior fund manager, age (years managing fund)	Expense analysis			Minimum initial investment	Telephone	
% yield	P/E ratio	% cash		% turnover	% maximum initial sales charge	Five-year projection		Toll-free (800)	In state
9.0									◄ CATEGORY AVERAGE
5.8	17.2	19.0	John Doney, 59 (2)	23	7.25	$121	$250	223-7757	203-863-5600 (Conn.)
6.0	12.7	4.3	Earl E. McEvoy, 41 (8)	19	None	29	3,000	662-7447	—
8.0	N.A.	1.0	Eugenia M. Simpson, 33 (3)	87	8.0	121	250	228-9596	800-642-8112 (Neb.)
8.1	N.A.	7.4	J. Paul Rodriguez, 60 (6)	74	4.75	90	1,000	221-2450	212-912-8200 (N.Y.)
8.9	N.A.	1.5	John W. Saunders Jr., 54 (4)	11	None	34	1,000	531-8000	—
14.2	N.A.	(4.0)*	Ernest E. Monrad, 59 (29)	17	None	42	1,000	225-6704	—
5.6									◄ CATEGORY AVERAGE
3.9	N.A.	8.8	Jeffrey F. Friedman, 43 (8)	46	None	60	2,500	645-6561	—
5.4	N.A	22.0	John G. Martin, 50 (9)	213	6.9	112	500	243-4361	—
5.9	N.A.	6.0	Jim Behrmann, 46 (7)	95	5.75	103	500	421-5666	—
6.1	N.A.	4.5	Tony Kreisel, N.A.	116	5.75	134	500	225-1581	—
5.3	N.A.	3.2	A. Berry, N.A. (4); R. Cresci, N.A. (4)	54	5.5	134	250	227-4618	—
6.3	N.A.	2.2	Donald Johansen, N.A. (1)	472	None†	117	1,000	869-3863	—
6.6									◄ CATEGORY AVERAGE
9.1	20.0	29.9	Diane Jarmusz, 37 (2)	335	8.5	139	1,000	525-7048	—
2.8	17.6	9.0	Martin Wiskemann, 62 (17)	80	4.0	84	100	342-5236	—
8.1	15.8	6.4	Chuck Dobson, 48 (11)	66	None	62	5,000	—	714-833-0244
1.9	14.9	0.0	Peter W. Thayer, 41 (12)	10	None	82	500	354-6339	—
3.5	16.2	5.1	Robert S. Stephenson, N.A.	38	6.75	129	500	225-1581	—
8.7	13.2	9.2	Don Fullerton, N.A. (4)	41	None†	105	500	—	212-528-2744
2.3									◄ CATEGORY AVERAGE
0.0	23.1	4.1	Karen Firestone, N.A. (1)	249	2.0†	144	1,000	544-6666	—
1.6	24.3	12.9	Edward P. Owens, 43 (5)	19	None†	35	3,000	662-7447	—
0.7	23.8	9.2	Steve Kaye, N.A. (2)	114	2.0†	133	1,000	544-6666	—
3.5	16.5	8.5	Warren Spitz, 34 (4)	66	None†	94	1,000	225-1852	—
1.3	20.8	6.6	Cheryl D. Alexander, N.A.	25	5.75	139	500	225-1581	—
0.0	N.A.	3.5	Paul Wick, N.A. (1 month)	117	4.75	131	1,000	221-2450	212-912-8200 (N.Y.)
0.8									◄ CATEGORY AVERAGE
2.1	N.A.	3.6	George Noble, N.A. (5)	115	3.0	103	2,500	544-6666	—
1.3	N.A.	6.0	Stephen I. Silverman, 39 (6)	39	6.5	118	250	637-3863	
0.2	N.A.	12.0	Laura Luckyn-Malone, 37 (4)	39	None	56	1,000	535-2726	
1.8	N.A.	11.7	John Callahan, 65 (5)	14	None	29	10,000	662-7447	—
1.3	N.A.	8.2	Richard R. Foulkes, 42 (9)	0	None	36	3,000	662-7447	—
0.0	27.2	7.5	Henry de Vismes, 42 (18)	55	None	141	1,000	233-9164	212-687-2515 (N.Y.)
1.5									◄ CATEGORY AVERAGE
0.9	N.A.	15.0	Nimrod Fachler, N.A. (3)	95	4.5	127	1,000	544-9300	—
0.3	N.A.	6.9	Kenneth Oberman, 59 (8)	27	8.5	178	1,000	525-7048	—
1.8	17.8	3.3	Anthony Regan, N.A.	103	5.75	165	500	225-1581	—
0.0	N.A.	1.0	Daniel J. Duane, 43 (3)	115	8.5	171	200	423-4026	—
2.9	N.A.	4.2	Peter Lehman, 30 (5)	82	None†	111	1,000	225-1852	—
2.7	16.6	13.1	Committee management	21	5.75	100	250	421-0180	714-671-7000 (Calif.)
1.6									◄ CATEGORY AVERAGE
1.2	27.0	3.8	Kenneth Oberman, 59 (2)	112	8.5	146	1,000	525-7048	—
0.3	40.9	5.5	Caesar M.P. Bryan, 35 (3)	20	None	87	1,000	526-0057	—
2.9	28.0	14.0	Martin Wiskemann, 62 (17)	3	4.0	82	100	342-5236	—
2.4	24.9	15.6	David J. Hutchins, 28 (4)	18	None†	27	3,000	662-7447	—
1.9	28.0	0.7	John C. Van Eck, 73 (35)	5	8.5	127	1,000	221-2220	212-687-5200 (N.Y.)
0.0	22.5	N.A.	Frederick G.P. Thorne, 53 (15)	82	None†	91	250	343-2898	—
3.2	**14.7**		Key to MONEY grades: A = Top 10% B = Next 20% C = Middle 40% D = Next 20% F = Bottom 10%						

N.A. Not available

THE Money RANKINGS: TOP TAXABLE BOND FUNDS

Ranked by five-year performance	MONEY risk-adjusted grade	% gain (or loss) to Dec. 22, 1989				% compound annual return		Five-year analysis		Lipper market phase rating			Net assets (million)
		One year	Three years	Five years	10 years	Five years	10 years	Best quarter	Worst quarter	Current	Prior up	Prior down	
U.S. GOVERNMENT BONDS		**13.7**		**62.0**	**187.8**	**10.1**	**11.1**						
1. Lord Abbett U.S. Gov. Securities	B	13.8	25.6	76.1	227.1	12.0	12.6	10.6	(3.8)	D	A	B	$1,241
2. AMEV U.S. Government Securities	B	12.7	25.4	70.8	208.5	11.3	11.9	8.3	(2.0)	C	B	A	120
3. Colonial Gov. Securities Plus	C	13.9	23.3	70.4	—	11.2	—	9.0	(5.3)	D	B	B	2,700
4. Value Line U.S. Gov. Securities	C	12.2	25.2	68.2	—	11.0	—	9.4	(2.9)	C	B	A	258
5. United Government Securities	C	12.0	16.0	67.6	—	10.9	—	10.0	(7.4)	C	—	C	107
6. Carnegie Gov. Sec.–High Yield	C	12.2	21.4	65.2	—	10.6	—	9.2	(2.2)	D	C	C	45
7. Fidelity Government Securities	C	13.0	20.8	64.1	188.8	10.4	11.2	7.5	(2.1)	C	C	C	542
MORTGAGE-BACKED SECURITIES		**12.7**	**23.2**	**62.9**	**158.7**	**10.2**	**9.9**						
1. Kemper U.S. Government Securities	A	14.5	24.2	78.2	179.6	12.2	10.8	8.6	(3.0)	B	A	C	4,593
2. Van Kampen Merritt U.S. Gov.	C	14.8	23.6	73.5	—	11.6	—	8.2	(4.5)	A	—	C	3,579
3. Smith Barney U.S. Gov. Securities	B	15.2	29.3	72.4	—	11.5	—	8.5	(3.6)	B	—	A	333
4. Vanguard Fixed Income—GNMA	B	14.6	27.6	71.8	—	11.4	—	8.0	(3.8)	A	A	B	2,122
5. Franklin U.S. Gov. Sec. Series	A	12.8	26.6	69.5	156.6	11.1	9.9	7.2	(1.5)	C	B	B	11,340
6. Merrill Lynch Federal Securities	B	14.0	24.9	68.4	—	11.0	—	8.4	(3.1)	B	—	B	2,677
7. Alliance Mortgage Securities	C	11.1	24.9	66.6	—	10.7	—	7.9	(2.6)	D	C	B	564
HIGH-GRADE CORPORATES		**11.9**	**23.5**	**71.7**	**197.1**	**11.4**	**11.5**						
1. United Bond	A	11.0	26.4	82.7	221.3	12.8	12.4	9.8	(4.1)	C	A	A	396
2. Bond Fund of America	A	10.1	24.3	81.6	227.6	12.7	12.6	9.1	(3.8)	D	B	B	1,443
3. IDS Selective	B	12.6	25.2	81.0	229.1	12.6	12.7	9.2	(4.5)	A	C	C	1,166
4. Axe-Houghton Income	B	10.8	22.7	80.1	234.1	12.5	12.8	11.8	(4.1)	C	A	E	64
5. SLH Investment—Inv. Grade	C	15.7	18.8	79.3	—	12.4	—	13.5	(7.6)	A	A	E	490
6. Alliance Bond—Monthly Inc. Port.	B	14.2	27.2	77.8	205.9	12.2	11.8	9.7	(2.7)	A	A	D	69
7. American Capital Corporate Bond	A	4.8	26.0	76.8	182.4	12.1	10.9	9.3	(2.2)	E	C	A	233
HIGH-YIELD CORPORATES		**0.1**	**14.2**	**54.8**	**184.2**	**9.0**	**10.9**						
1. Cigna Income	A	14.2	24.8	83.7	220.3	12.9	12.3	10.3	(4.4)	A	B	C	230
2. Kemper High Yield	A	(0.6)	24.8	80.4	251.6	12.5	13.4	8.4	(1.5)	D	A	A	1,461
3. IDS Bond	B	11.7	22.8	80.2	228.2	12.5	12.6	10.9	(4.3)	B	A	C	1,843
4. Eaton Vance Income of Boston	A	4.1	23.3	78.8	234.4	12.3	12.8	8.8	(2.5)	B	A	A	82
5. Financial Bond Shares—High Yield	A	4.2	22.1	76.9	—	12.1	—	9.5	(1.8)	A	A	B	51
6. Cigna High Yield	B	1.4	21.8	74.5	218.8	11.8	12.3	7.8	(2.1)	C	B	A	268
7. Delaware Group—Delchester I	B	1.5	21.9	74.0	199.6	11.7	11.6	7.5	(2.5)	B	A	B	626
SHORT/INTERMEDIATE-TERM TAXABLES		**11.0**	**21.0**	**61.3**	**193.0**	**10.0**	**11.3**						
1. Boston Co. Managed Income	A	6.6	23.8	72.7	188.5	11.5	11.2	8.8	(1.5)	E	A	A	85
2. Scudder Short-Term Bond	B	12.9	21.3	69.2	—	11.1	—	9.9	(4.6)	A	B	E	59
3. Merrill Lynch Corp.—Intermediate	B	12.5	21.6	68.3	—	11.0	—	7.8	(2.9)	A	A	D	87
4. Fidelity Intermediate Bond	C	12.2	21.7	68.0	222.3	10.9	12.4	9.2	(2.0)	D	B	C	617
5. Pru-Bache Gov.—Intermediate	C	12.6	20.8	61.6	—	10.1	—	7.3	(1.5)	C	D	B	396
6. John Hancock—U.S. Gov. Securities	C	11.9	17.2	61.4	168.2	10.0	10.4	7.8	(2.9)	B	C	D	176
7. Benham Government Treasury Note	C	12.4	16.0	60.1	—	9.9	—	9.5	(3.9)	C	D	E	98
WORLD INCOME		**6.4**	**21.0**	**132.7**	**—**	**18.4**							
1. Mass. Fin. International Trust—Bond	A	7.5	41.3	132.7	—	18.4	—	17.7	(3.4)	C	—	A	123
2. Merrill Lynch Ret. Global Bond B	—	7.0	36.9	—	—	—	—	16.9	(3.8)	C	—	B	270
3. T. Rowe Price International Bond	—	(3.4)	24.7	—	—	—	—	16.7	(7.4)	E	—	A	286
4. Van Eck World Income	—	10.9	—	—	—	—	—	6.2	(2.1)	A	—	E	37
5. Fidelity Global Bond	—	7.8	—	—	—	—	—	14.7	(1.9)	B	—	C	63
6. Merrill Lynch Global Convertible B	—	6.7	—	—	—	—	—	5.9	(2.0)	C	—	—	30
7. Capital World Bond	—	4.4	—	—	—	—	—	14.3	(3.6)	D	—	C	30
SALOMON BROS. INVESTMENT-GRADE INDEX		**14.4**	**26.8**	**79.0**	**221.2**	**12.3**	**12.4**	**8.0**	**(2.8)**				

†Fund may impose back-end load or exit fee.   ‡Figure reflects borrowing to boost investments.

Portfolio analysis				Expense analysis				Telephone	
% yield	Average maturity (years)	% cash	Senior fund manager, age (years managing fund)	% turnover	% maximum initial sales charge	Five-year projection	Minimum initial investment	Toll-free (800)	In state
8.0								◄ CATEGORY AVERAGE	
10.6	N.A.	0.7	Carroll Coward, 32 (2)	332	4.75	$94	$500	426-1130	—
9.3	15.2	1.7	Dennis M. Ott, 44 (4)	109	4.5	91	500	872-2638	—
8.2	21.1	0.3	Robert Busby, 41 (1)	66	6.75	126	250	426-3750	—
9.3	22.7	6.2	Charles Heebner, 53 (1)	34	None	37	1,000	223-0818	—
8.5	21.8	(2.3)‡	Robert G. Alley, 41 (2)	189	4.25	84	500	—	816-283-4122
7.5	14.0	8.5	John Shriver, 33 (4)	39	4.5	109	1,000	321-2322	—
8.1	6.4	5.5	James Wolfson, N.A. (3)	283	None	44	2,500	544-6666	—
9.0								◄ CATEGORY AVERAGE	
9.9	8.8	1.0	Patrick Beimford, N.A. (8)	203	4.5	72	1,000	621-1048	—
8.9	11.0	0.6	Jack Doyle, 55 (5)	167	4.9	87	1,500	225-2222	—
8.9	27.5	6.4	Committee management	2	4.0	63	3,000	544-7835	—
9.1	N.A.	7.0	Paul G. Sullivan, 47 (9)	8	None	20	3,000	662-7447	—
10.0	28.0	4.0	Jack Lemein, 45 (5)	34	4.0	68	100	342-5236	—
9.4	7.2	6.0	Gregory M. Maunz, 35 (1)	364	4.0	77	1,000	637-3863	—
11.1	4.0	0.0	Paul Zoschke, N.A. (1)	239	5.5	113	250	227-4618	—
8.9								◄ CATEGORY AVERAGE	
9.1	21.2	(8.4)‡	Robert G. Alley, 41 (5)	179	8.5	118	500	—	816-283-4122
9.5	14.9	8.8	Committee management	93	4.75	87	1,000	421-0180	714-671-7000 (Calif.)
8.6	15.1	12.9	Ray S. Goodner, N.A. (4)	86	5.0	91	2,000	328-8300	—
9.1	10.0	3.0	Robert E. Manning, 53 (3)	258	None	79	1,000	366-0444	—
8.0	25.9	0.0	George Mueller, 47 (4)	72	None†	99	500	—	212-528-2744 (N.Y.)
9.1	N.A.	10.4	Wayne D. Lyski, N.A. (2)	104	5.5	148	250	227-4618	—
10.8	11.0	5.4	David R. Troth, 55 (10)	56	4.75	96	500	421-5666	—
13.5								◄ CATEGORY AVERAGE	
8.9	16.3	2.5	Gary Brown, 36 (1 month)	361	5.0	101	500	628-0372	—
14.0	7.8	8.0	Kenneth T. Urbaszewski, 41 (10)	76	4.5	83	1,000	621-1048	—
9.1	18.4	5.2	Fred Quirsfeld, N.A. (4)	76	5.0	90	2,000	328-8300	—
14.9	9.1	6.9	Hooker Talcott Jr., 58 (4)	61	4.75	116	1,000	225-6265	—
13.1	8.5	8.1	William Veronda, 43 (5)	42	None	46	250	525-8085	—
13.2	9.3	7.1	Alan Peterson, 39 (6)	76	5.0	100	500	628-0372	—
13.5	10.1	2.2	J. Michael Pokorny, 50 (10)	66	6.75	111	25	523-4640	215-988-1333 (Pa.)
8.3								◄ CATEGORY AVERAGE	
8.4	10.1	4.0	David Gray, 48 (1 month)	139	None	63	1,000	225-5267	—
6.8	2.6	7.0	Thomas M. Poor, 47 (N.A.)	24	None	28	1,000	225-2470	—
8.8	5.1	9.0	Martha S. Reed, 52 (7)	152	2.0	54	1,000	637-3863	—
8.8	8.2	6.5	Michael Gray, N.A. (2)	59	None	35	2,500	544-6666	—
10.0	3.7	2.5	Donna Blair, 36 (1)	28	None	46	1,000	225-1852	—
8.7	3.8	1.0	David Turner, 43 (8)	12	4.5	137	500	225-5291	—
7.6	3.7	0.2	Jeffrey Tyler, N.A. (1)	386	None	42	1,000	472-3389	—
8.6								◄ CATEGORY AVERAGE	
9.9	4.9	10.0	Leslie Nanberg, 43 (5)	232	4.75	130	250	225-2606	—
11.7	12.8	7.0	David Walter, 44 (3)	199	None†	94	1,000	637-3863	—
8.2	7.0	10.0	Edward A. Taber III, 46 (3)	368	None	66	2,500	638-5660	301-547-2308 (Md.)
9.7	7.0	4.1	Klaus Buescher, 59 (2)	386	5.75	138	1,000	221-2220	212-687-5200 (N.Y.)
7.9	4.2	20.5	Judy Pagliuca, N.A. (2)	227	None	82	1,000	544-6666	—
5.3	10.5	16.0	Harry Dewdney, 55 (2)	20	None†	132	1,000	637-3863	—
7.4	8.6	7.7	Committee management	94	4.75	121	1,000	421-0180	714-671-7000 (Calif.)
8.7	**9.5**		Key to MONEY grades: A = Top 10% B = Next 20% C = Middle 40% D = Next 20% F = Bottom 10%						

N.A. Not available

THE Money RANKINGS

THE ALPHABETICAL GUIDE TO
960 Mutual Funds

ABBREVIATIONS

Bal Balanced; **Conv** Convertibles; **Eql** Equity income; **Flex** Flexible income; **G&I** Growth and income; **Glo** Global; **Gold** Gold/metals; **Gro** Growth; **HGC** High-grade corporates; **HGT** High-grade tax-exempts; **HYC** High-yield corporates; **HYT** High-yield tax-exempts; **Intl** International; **ITT** Intermediate-term tax-exempts; **Max** Maximum capital gains; **MBS** Mortgage-backed securities; **OpInc** Option income; **SCG** Small-company growth; **Sec** Sectors; **STT** Short-term taxables; **USG** U.S. Government bonds; **WI** World income

BENCHMARKS FOR INVESTORS

	% gain (or loss) to Jan. 1, 1990				
	One year	Three years	Five years	10 years	% yield
S&P 500-stock index	31.6	61.5	152.5	403.9	3.2
Dow Jones industrial average	32.2	62.2	175.8	427.3	3.9
Lipper growth fund index*	26.6	45.5	122.3	297.7	—
Lipper growth and income fund index*	20.6	46.6	119.0	322.6	—
Salomon Bros. investment-grade bond index	14.4	26.8	79.0	221.2	8.7
Shearson Lehman Hutton long-term Treasury index	18.9	26.4	106.4	233.7	8.2
Shearson Lehman Hutton municipal bond index†	13.1	26.0	91.8	164.6**	7.3

*To Dec. 22, 1989   †To Dec.1, 1989   **From Jan. 1, 1980

STOCK FUNDS

FUND NAME	Type	MONEY risk-adjusted grade	% gain (or loss) to Dec. 22, 1989				Portfolio analysis			Net assets (millions)	Expense analysis	
			One year	Three years	Five years	10 years	% yield	P/E ratio	% cash		% maximum initial sales charge	Five-year projection
ABT Growth & Income Trust	G&I	C	14.3	38.4	121.4	274.9	3.1	11.2	26.3	$100.1	4.75	$123
ABT Utility Income	Sec	B	32.6	44.0	115.0	198.5	5.9	14.0	4.9	138.8	4.75	114
Acorn Fund	SCG	B	24.1	58.8	145.5	352.6	1.9	27.8	4.0	836.6	None†	44
Advest Advantage Growth	Gro	—	22.9	41.2	—	—	1.2	19.4	10.5	29.5	None†	143
Advest Advantage Income	Flex	—	16.5	24.1	—	—	6.0	17.0	3.5	58.2	None†	122
AIM Charter	G&I	C	36.1	53.2	127.2	314.9	2.6	19.0	20.6	75.7	5.5	125
AIM Constellation	Max	B	34.1	56.2	165.6	365.1	0.0	19.2	0.0	82.2	5.5	141
AIM Summit*	Gro	D	28.4	41.5	112.7	—	1.6	N.A.	2.6	255.1	8.5	142
AIM Weingarten	Gro	A	34.0	58.7	173.3	535.8	0.9	18.7	3.9	427.8	5.5	118
Alliance Balanced	Bal	C	13.9	30.1	110.5	306.9	3.4	16.6	1.5	157.0	5.5	128
Alliance Canadian	Intl	F	22.0	77.2	108.0	230.6	0.6	13.0	0.0	32.7	5.5	150
Alliance Convertible	Conv	—	11.5	22.0	—	—	5.3	N.A.	3.2	71.8	5.5	134
Alliance Counterpoint	G&I	—	32.0	53.0	—	—	1.2	21.5	1.0	59.8	5.5	145
Alliance Fund	Gro	C	22.2	44.8	116.9	242.6	1.2	18.1	1.9	831.3	5.5	98
Alliance Growth & Income	G&I	B	23.2	42.9	132.7	361.8	2.6	15.3	3.1	365.9	5.5	112
Alliance International	Intl	B	27.9	59.1	270.0	—	0.5	N.A.	1.2	195.7	5.5	128
Alliance Quasar	SCG	C	26.9	52.7	152.6	—	0.0	20.9	9.8	266.5	5.5	123
Alliance Surveyor	Gro	C	23.1	49.1	121.1	245.0	0.0	23.1	0.0	97.4	5.5	134
Alliance Technology	Sec	C	5.3	21.9	75.1	—	0.0	19.6	10.6	142.3	5.5	125
AMA Classic Growth	Gro	D	19.2	25.9	76.3	155.2	3.4	11.9	18.0	33.7	None	89
AMA Global Growth	Glo	—	19.9	—	—	—	3.3	14.4	16.0	108.3	None	88
AMCAP Fund	Gro	C	25.8	49.1	112.7	342.4	1.8	22.0	19.2	2,051.2	5.75	97
American Balanced	Bal	B	20.1	39.6	112.3	317.5	5.1	13.0	10.5	271.1	5.75	100
American Capital Comstock	Gro	D	28.1	43.5	100.0	383.8	2.1	14.9	9.1	934.7	8.5	121
American Capital Enterprise	Gro	D	29.3	43.4	104.5	317.2	1.6	17.9	9.4	598.3	5.75	103
American Capital Harbor	Conv	C	20.1	32.6	89.3	317.1	5.9	N.A.	6.0	385.4	5.75	103
American Capital OTC Securities	SCG	F	31.4	2.0	15.8	—	0.0	24.6	4.8	45.1	5.75	151
American Capital Pace	Max	D	26.4	40.4	95.5	479.0	0.9	15.5	6.4	2,470.3	5.75	103

Key to MONEY grades: A = Top 10%   B = Next 20%   C = Middle 40%   D = Next 20%   F = Bottom 10%

†Fund may impose back-end load or exit fee.   *Investment by contractual plan only   N.A. Not available

THE Money RANKINGS: STOCK FUNDS

FUND NAME	Type	MONEY risk-adjusted grade	% gain (or loss) to Dec. 22, 1989				Portfolio analysis			Net assets (millions)	Expense analysis	
			One year	Three years	Five years	10 years	% yield	P/E ratio	% cash		% maximum initial sales charge	Five-year projection
American Capital Venture	Max	F	26.4	33.7	58.6	266.6	2.1	20.7	4.5	$198.2	5.75	$113
American Growth	Gro	F	22.7	36.0	71.1	212.8	4.3	25.6	7.9	64.3	8.5	158
American Investors Growth	Gro	F	30.2	47.5	68.4	55.3	0.7	30.6	0.1	68.6	8.5	162
American Leaders	G&I	C	10.3	27.3	89.8	343.6	4.6	10.3	28.0	151.0	4.5	98
American Mutual	G&I	A	23.2	43.8	125.2	422.8	4.7	14.3	23.0	3,245.0	5.75	91
American National Growth	Gro	C	21.4	43.3	110.0	280.9	2.5	15.9	5.6	106.3	8.5	148
American National Income	EqI	D	26.3	42.7	100.4	334.2	3.6	12.8	10.4	68.4	8.5	144
AMEV Capital	G&I	B	35.7	44.1	133.0	504.5	1.4	28.8	15.6	142.5	8.5	141
AMEV Fiduciary	Gro	B	36.7	44.8	146.4	—	0.5	28.3	7.5	32.4	4.5	126
AMEV Growth	Max	C	38.8	45.9	139.5	494.2	0.4	28.7	9.7	235.2	8.5	138
Analytic Optioned Equity	OpInc	C	16.8	39.2	82.3	226.6	8.1	15.8	6.4	109.2	None	62
Axe-Houghton Fund B	Bal	C	20.7	26.2	106.7	272.6	5.8	16.0	4.0	166.4	None	74
Axe-Houghton Stock	Gro	F	27.1	16.9	73.8	194.7	0.7	23.3	6.0	68.9	None	96
Babson Enterprise	SCG	C	22.4	45.8	121.5	—	0.9	21.8	8.5	87.3	None	75
Babson Growth	Gro	C	20.0	40.2	121.3	252.1	2.7	15.5	6.3	273.8	None	45
Babson Shadow Stock	SCG	—	11.3				1.6	18.0	3.5	27.8	None	73
Bailard Biehl & Kaiser Diversa	Bal	—	12.3				6.7	23.3	2.4	104.6	None	73
Baron Asset	SCG	—	24.3				0.3	28.0	25.0	50.1	None†	116
Bartlett Basic Value	G&I	C	9.9	32.8	89.7	—	5.2	15.2	2.0	110.7	None	68
Blanchard Precious Metals	Gold	—	9.5	—	—	—	0.0	N.A.	23.0	32.6	$125	130*
Blanchard Strategic Growth	Max	—	15.5	44.5	—	—	1.2	N.A.	15.0	252.5	$125	164
Boston Co. Capital Appreciation	Gro	B	23.5	45.4	142.1	349.7	1.9	14.0	19.6	604.8	None	72
Boston Co. International	Intl	—	13.9	—			0.2	N.A.	11.1	26.7	None	95
Boston Co. Special Growth	Gro	D	16.6	34.3	96.5	—	2.0	19.0	10.0	41.0	None	88
Brandywine Fund	Gro	—	30.8	55.9	—	—	0.2	19.3	1.6	166.4	None	63
Bull & Bear Capital Growth	Gro	D	26.6	35.6	81.6	197.6	0.0	25.1	0.0	65.1	None	123
Bull & Bear Gold Investors	Gold	D	19.9	37.4	90.0	96.4	0.2	17.8	0.0	47.0	None	131
Burnham Fund	G&I	A	20.7	43.6	133.2	348.9	5.5	N.A.	17.6	156.4	5.0	106
Calvert Ariel Growth	SCG	—	22.0	89.8	—	—	0.5	15.2	23.0	163.5	4.5	126
Calvert Social Inv. Managed Growth	Bal	B	17.6	34.9	103.1	—	3.4	N.A.	2.0	219.4	4.5	115
Capital Income Builder	EqI	—	19.2	—	—	—	5.2	13.6	18.5	198.8	5.75	123
Cardinal Fund	G&I	B	20.9	40.4	128.7	364.2	3.5	11.8	13.1	176.8	8.5	121
Carnegie Cappiello Growth	Gro	C	24.0	49.8	117.0	—	1.2	N.A.	11.9	69.7	4.5	130
Carnegie Cappiello Total Return	G&I	—	32.9	45.2	—	—	4.6	N.A.	3.5	81.3	4.5	130
Century Shares Trust	Sec	B	37.3	43.4	130.1	359.6	2.6	11.5	7.3	155.0	None	48
Cigna Growth	Gro	C	26.8	40.3	105.2	272.1	1.5	16.2	4.5	187.2	5.0	102
Cigna Utilities	Sec	—	32.9	—	—	—	5.2	19.8	0.8	52.3	5.0	115
Cigna Value	G&I	C	31.9	60.9	118.0	—	1.5	19.0	9.4	74.2	5.0	102
Clipper Fund	G&I	B	20.2	45.1	119.3	—	2.1	16.1	7.0	121.6	None	70
Colonial Advanced Strategies Gold	Gold	—	16.1	51.9	—	—	1.2	39.4	5.8	89.0	6.75	164
Colonial Diversified Income	Flex	F	10.2	30.8	68.4	185.7	8.2	N.A.	5.3	510.0	6.75	124
Colonial Fund	G&I	B	23.5	40.8	120.9	325.9	4.4	12.6	9.4	325.0	6.75	115
Colonial Growth Shares	Gro	B	27.5	60.7	138.5	345.5	1.7	15.1	7.3	123.0	6.75	140
Colonial Small Stock Index	SCG	—	13.5	25.4	—	—	0.4	17.9	5.8	45.0	4.75	138
Colonial U.S. Equity Index	G&I	—	26.6	47.4	—	—	1.9	15.7	1.4	34.0	4.75	142
Columbia Growth	Gro	C	26.6	58.4	124.3	408.6	1.9	23.0	11.8	262.3	None	57
Columbia Special	Max	—	30.6	84.6	—	—	0.0	22.1	4.2	94.0	None	76
Common Sense Growth	Gro	—	25.9	—	—	—	0.8	17.2	5.0	797.4	8.5	180
Common Sense Growth & Income	G&I	—	24.8	—	—	—	2.3	17.0	10.2	297.3	8.5	163
Composite Bond & Stock	Bal	C	11.1	25.8	78.4	240.2	4.8	14.3	4.9	71.8	4.0	103
Composite Growth	G&I	C	10.4	28.4	98.2	298.9	2.9	14.2	12.4	72.1	4.0	102
Copley Fund	G&I	D	16.3	24.8	88.9	275.7	0.0	14.5	8.0	26.8	None	93
Counsellors Capital Appreciation	Gro	—	25.1	—	—	—	1.7	17.2	17.0	59.0	None	59
Counsellors Emerging Growth	SCG	—	20.4	—	—	—	0.9	14.8	16.0	27.0	None	40

Key to MONEY grades: A = Top 10%   B = Next 20%   C = Middle 40%   D = Next 20%   F = Bottom 10%

†Fund may impose back-end load or exit fee.   *Three-year expense projection   N.A. Not available

THE Money RANKINGS: STOCK FUNDS

FUND NAME	Type	MONEY risk-adjusted grade	One year	Three years	Five years	10 years	% yield	P/E ratio	% cash	Net assets (millions)	% maximum initial sales charge	Five-year projection
			% gain (or loss) to Dec. 22, 1989				**Portfolio analysis**				**Expense analysis**	
Cowen Income & Growth	EqI	—	23.4	34.6	—	—	3.9	N.A.	3.2	$46.2	4.85†	$155
Dean Witter American Value	Gro	C	23.7	37.7	110.1	—	2.2	22.7	6.2	99.0	None†	116
Dean Witter Convertible Securities	Conv	—	12.8	8.1	—	—	6.3	N.A.	2.2	745.5	None†	117
Dean Witter Developing Growth	SCG	F	13.9	18.4	42.6	—	0.0	20.3	2.3	84.0	None†	122
Dean Witter Dividend Growth	G&I	A	29.0	49.6	139.5	—	2.6	17.1	3.3	2,679.8	None†	104
Dean Witter Natural Resources Dev.	Sec	C	30.3	63.4	109.9	—	1.4	15.5	2.4	141.9	None†	124
Dean Witter Option Income	OpInc	—	19.9	24.2	—	—	7.5	15.7	0.4	215.5	None†	126
Dean Witter World Wide Investment	Glo	D	15.6	38.1	149.9	—	1.0	N.A.	6.7	310.6	None†	137
Delaware Fund	Bal	D	23.9	39.6	104.3	374.7	5.3	18.4	9.1	380.0	6.75	107
Delaware Group–Decatur I	EqI	B	19.9	45.7	129.9	407.9	4.2	12.5	7.7	1,836.0	8.5	122
Delaware Group–Decatur II	EqI	—	24.6	47.9	—	—	3.6	14.1	8.3	317.0	4.75	114
Delaware Group–Delcap I	Max	—	32.0	81.1	—	—	0.6	23.9	24.9	136.0	4.75	122
Delaware Group–Trend	Max	C	50.0	69.5	128.7	416.8	0.2	27.4	26.8	78.9	8.5	149
Dreyfus Capital Value	Max	—	27.2	85.3	—	—	5.0	N.A.	7.7	715.2	4.5	117
Dreyfus Convertible Securities	Conv	C	14.0	36.3	110.4	281.3	3.9	N.A.	8.8	265.8	None	60
Dreyfus Fund	G&I	A	22.3	41.8	111.0	307.9	3.6	15.9	20.1	2,726.9	None	43
Dreyfus General Aggressive Growth	Max	C	25.2	48.2	135.6	—	1.3	N.A.	8.0	42.3	None	94
Dreyfus Growth Opportunity	Gro	C	13.5	42.1	115.3	233.9	3.3	17.5	14.3	534.3	None	57
Dreyfus Leverage	Max	C	19.4	34.3	110.2	306.5	3.9	20.4	1.4	482.6	4.5	114
Dreyfus New Leaders	SCG	—	29.1	48.0	—	—	0.7	21.4	19.5	194.8	None	77
Dreyfus Strategic Aggressive Investing	Max	—	10.0	—	—	—	0.0	22.4	(3.3)††	110.5	3.0	134
Dreyfus Strategic Investing	Max	—	28.9	64.4	—	—	6.8	25.0.	7.5	108.7	4.5	152
Dreyfus Third Century	Gro	D	15.7	43.6	97.9	217.2	4.6	16.8	30.0	166.7	None	57
Eaton Vance Growth	Gro	C	27.5	51.1	117.3	328.1	0.9	17.5	11.2	91.1	4.75	97
Eaton Vance Investors	Bal	C	19.3	38.1	91.9	278.8	5.4	12.5	12.8	212.8	4.75	97
Eaton Vance Special Equities	Gro	F	21.3	37.1	59.8	247.4	0.0	20.8	7.1	54.0	4.75	109
Eaton Vance Stock	G&I	B	26.6	45.5	126.6	313.6	3.3	14.1	11.1	88.9	4.75	98
Eaton Vance Total Return Trust	G&I	C	31.6	21.3	129.1	—	5.5	14.1	(2.9)††	506.1	4.75	110
Eclipse Equity	SCG	—	15.5	—	—	—	3.6	N.A.	18.0	188.6	None	62
Enterprise Growth & Income	G&I	—	15.4	—	—	—	1.9	14.3	18.0	29.9	4.75	125
Enterprise Growth Portfolio	Gro	C	20.2	47.1	110.7	358.7	0.6	18.8	2.0	52.7	4.75	130
Equitec Siebel Aggressive Growth	Max	—	14.6	20.1	—	—	0.6	16.4	15.0	37.0	None†	133
Equitec Siebel Total Return	G&I	—	17.7	27.2	—	—	3.3	15.5	12.0	130.8	None†	114
EuroPacific Growth	Intl	C	23.4	61.0	199.7	—	1.5	N.A.	20.8	354.0	5.75	126
Evergreen Fund	Gro	C	13.0	32.4	104.7	363.1	1.6	16.4	14.9	813.3	None	57
Evergreen Limited Market*	SCG	B	20.4	44.0	156.5	—	0.2	18.2	34.9	38.9	None	74
Evergreen Total Return	EqI	C	15.5	22.1	95.7	408.3	5.7	14.5	9.1	1,365.6	None	56
Evergreen Value Timing	Max	—	24.6	45.8	—	—	1.5	16.3	13.6	30.9	None	85
Fairmont Fund	Max	F	4.3	(1.9)	48.8	—	1.5	N.A.	5.1	43.6	None	69
FBL Series–Growth Common Stock	G&I	F	13.6	11.6	56.4	150.1	5.4	11.1	68.0	37.0	None†	105
Fenimore International–Equity Series	Intl	—	28.0	33.0	—	—	0.8	N.A.	4.6	49.3	5.0	171
Fidelity Balanced	Bal	—	19.8	40.4	—	—	5.7	17.2	4.7	157.1	2.0	81
Fidelity Blue Chip Growth	Gro	—	33.0	—	—	—	0.7	19.6	5.9	63.7	2.0†	114
Fidelity Canada	Intl	—	26.3	—	—	—	0.8	N.A.	3.3	24.1	2.0†	140
Fidelity Capital Appreciation	Max	—	25.2	103.4	—	—	0.7	17.3	5.0	2,179.1	2.0†	105
Fidelity Contrafund	Gro	C	41.7	67.2	142.7	325.4	1.8	1.45	18.5	277.9	None	54
Fidelity Convertible Securities	Conv	—	26.4	—	—	—	6.1	N.A.	11.7	58.6	None	87
Fidelity Destiny I‡	Gro	B	23.6	53.4	137.7	509.1	2.0	N.A.	7.2	1,764.9	9.0	33
Fidelity Destiny II‡	Gro	—	24.0	60.9	—	—	1.3	N.A.	0.5	173.1	9.0	54
Fidelity Equity–Income	EqI	C	16.9	39.7	105.9	474.1	5.3	12.7	6.1	4,961.3	2.0	54
Fidelity Europe	Intl	—	31.5	60.2	—	—	1.8	N.A.	20.3	135.7	2.0†	140
Fidelity Freedom**	Max	C	28.4	57.8	136.9	—	1.3	15.3	5.7	1,421.0	None	60
Fidelity Fund	G&I	C	26.5	51.4	126.8	387.2	2.9	16.4	9.0	1,059.9	None	37
Fidelity Growth & Income	G&I	—	27.5	63.9	—	—	3.4	16.2	10.1	1,454.6	2.0	51

Key to MONEY grades: A = Top 10%   B = Next 20%   C = Middle 40%   D = Next 20%   F = Bottom 10%

*Currently closed to new investors **Open to retirement plans only †Fund may impose back-end load or exit fee. ‡Investment by contractual plan only ††Figure reflects borrowing to boost investments

FUND NAME	Type	MONEY risk-adjusted grade	% gain (or loss) to Dec. 22, 1989				Portfolio analysis			Net assets (millions)	Expense analysis	
			One year	Three years	Five years	10 years	% yield	P/E ratio	% cash		% maximum initial sales charge	Five-year projection
Fidelity Growth Company	Gro	C	38.3	55.4	150.4	—	0.5	20.8	20.8	$280.7	3.0	$85
Fidelity International Growth & Income	Intl	—	17.5	—	—	—	1.5	N.A.	12.2	27.1	1.0†	129
Fidelity Magellan	Gro	A	32.4	62.2	188.8	1,116.2	1.5	15.0	9.7	12,412.6	3.0	88
Fidelity OTC	SCG	—	28.1	57.5	—	—	1.7	20.3	11.4	736.2	3.0	100
Fidelity Overseas	Intl	A	15.4	47.3	324.9	—	2.1	N.A.	3.6	925.6	3.0	103
Fidelity Pacific Basin	Intl	—	10.6	53.2	—	—	0.6	N.A.	4.5	112.3	2.0†	127
Fidelity Puritan	Bal	A	18.9	38.4	115.6	412.5	6.3	17.2	8.7	4,824.1	2.0	55
Fidelity Real Estate	Sec	—	13.1	14.9	—	—	5.8	25.3	13.1	54.4	2.0	90
Fidelity Select–American Gold	Gold	—	26.6	56.8	—	—	0.0	32.9	0.0	286.1	2.0†	138
Fidelity Select–Biotechnology	Sec	—	42.7	43.0	—	—	0.0	34.5	7.7	82.8	2.0†	149
Fidelity Select–Broadcast	Sec	—	31.2	92.0	—	—	0.0	27.7	1.3	14.4	2.0†	53
Fidelity Select–Chemicals	Sec	—	16.2	58.4	—	—	0.0	14.1	1.8	27.2	2.0†	136
Fidelity Select–Energy	Sec	C	40.5	59.1	100.8	—	1.9	19.5	11.6	77.0	2.0†	144
Fidelity Select–Energy Services	Sec	—	57.1	35.1	—	—	0.0	35.7	5.7	35.1	2.0†	163
Fidelity Select–Financial Services	Sec	C	16.5	7.2	75.7	—	3.2	10.2	2.6	27.2	2.0†	157
Fidelity Select–Health Care	Sec	A	37.7	49.0	191.8	—	0.7	23.8	9.2	223.5	2.0†	133
Fidelity Select–Leisure	Sec	A	29.6	66.6	208.6	—	0.0	23.1	4.1	61.0	2.0†	144
Fidelity Select–Medical	Sec	—	50.8	47.9	—	—	0.2	N.A.	16.7	44.6	2.0†	161
Fidelity Select–Precious Metals	Gold	D	35.1	42.1	70.8	—	3.2	34.1	4.4	260.1	2.0†	135
Fidelity Select–Technology	Sec	F	15.7	(1.9)	(1.4)	—	0.0	21.4	6.3	71.3	2.0†	144
Fidelity Select–Telecommunications	Sec	—	46.2	112.5	—	—	0.5	22.7	0.0	102.8	2.0†	144
Fidelity Select–Utilities	Sec	B	36.5	41.8	137.1	—	2.0	15.6	8.1	123.2	2.0†	132
Fidelity Special Situations–Plymouth	Max	—	29.8	49.5	—	—	2.8	N.A.	0.4	199.1	4.0	134
Fidelity Trend	Gro	C	30.0	49.7	122.6	272.8	1.2	18.4	3.2	861.8	None	26
Fidelity Utilities Income	Sec	—	24.6	—	—	—	5.1	12.0	7.0	153.4	2.0	99
Fidelity Value	Max	D	22.0	39.6	99.8	344.1	1.5	N.A.	2.6	141.0	None	61
Fiduciary Capital Growth	SCG	F	17.2	23.1	61.6	—	0.9	17.9	12.2	33.8	None	69
Financial Dynamics	Max	D	20.1	34.7	86.1	201.4	1.5	22.8	15.1	89.3	None	54
Financial Industrial	G&I	D	28.9	33.2	88.3	218.6	2.2	16.3	13.9	367.9	None	45
Financial Industrial Income	EqI	A	30.0	55.3	134.5	371.6	4.0	16.5	9.4	446.0	None	43
Financial Strategic–Gold	Gold	D	24.9	17.3	56.9	—	0.9	N.A.	15.4	55.5	None	87
Financial Strategic–Pacific Basin	Intl	C	20.3	60.4	244.9	—	0.1	N.A.	4.3	24.2	None	89
Financial Strategic–Utilities	Sec	—	28.9	38.4	—	—	3.6	N.A.	5.9	26.3	None	77
First Eagle Fund of America	Max	—	25.0	—	—	—	0.0	N.A.	14.4	84.8	None†	171
First Investors Fund for Growth	Gro	F	23.6	23.7	23.6	89.2	1.7	N.A.	2.0	32.5	8.5	139
First Investors Global	Glo	C	34.2	100.2	214.7	—	0.0	N.A.	1.0	120.8	8.5	171
Flexfunds–Growth Portfolio	Gro	—	10.1	10.4	—	—	5.7	16.1	48.0	31.0	None	74
Flexfunds–Muirfield	Gro	—	13.0	—	—	—	1.4	N.A.	41.0	27.0	None	75
Founders Blue Chip	G&I	B	31.7	45.8	129.6	326.9	2.1	18.8	7.6	230.5	None	55
Founders Frontier	SCG	—	40.0	—	—	—	0.0	26.9	14.3	52.3	None	102
Founders Growth	Gro	B	38.9	55.4	144.0	385.0	1.4	23.4	18.7	117.5	None	75
Founders Special	Max	C	35.7	58.5	119.3	311.5	0.5	34.3	14.0	95.2	None	62
FPA Capital	Gro	C	25.5	59.9	134.0	281.0	1.5	20.8	0.4	78.3	6.5	126
FPA Paramount*	G&I	B	21.5	74.1	122.4	418.5	3.1	26.1	50.0	214.2	6.5	117
FPA Perennial	G&I	C	24.2	45.8	94.9	—	3.2	14.9	20.8	55.8	6.5	125
Franklin DynaTech Series	Sec	D	29.5	50.7	67.1	246.2	0.5	22.3	26.0	38.0	4.0	86
Franklin Equity	Gro	C	15.7	39.7	126.4	331.2	2.6	11.1	5.0	409.0	4.0	77
Franklin Gold	Gold	C	43.8	97.8	130.0	316.1	2.9	28.0	14.0	347.0	4.0	82
Franklin Growth Series	Gro	A	22.0	57.7	131.6	331.7	1.9	16.7	13.0	146.0	4.0	81
Franklin Income Series	EqI	C	12.1	27.9	81.3	303.1	10.7	N.A.	29.0	1,289.0	4.0	73
Franklin Managed–Rising Dividend	G&I	—	17.1	—	—	—	3.1	N.A.	22.0	41.0	4.0	130
Franklin Option	OpInc	D	13.1	35.1	83.0	256.1	2.8	17.6	9.0	45.0	4.0	84
Franklin Utilities Series	Sec	B	25.2	30.0	101.4	372.2	6.9	12.3	11.0	712.0	4.0	74
Freedom Gold & Government	Gold	C	18.1	26.9	66.7	—	6.5	N.A.	0.4	67.5	None†	89

Key to MONEY grades: A = Top 10%   B = Next 20%   C = Middle 40%   D = Next 20%   F = Bottom 10%

*Currently closed to new investors   †Fund may impose back-end load or exit fee.   N.A. Not available

THE Money RANKINGS: STOCK FUNDS

FUND NAME	Type	MONEY risk-adjusted grade	One year	Three years	Five years	10 years	% yield	P/E ratio	% cash	Net assets (millions)	% maximum initial sales charge	Five-year projection
Freedom II—Global	Glo	—	32.1	55.5	—	—	0.0	17.6	0.8	$36.3	None†	$127
Freedom Regional Bank	Sec	—	16.6	50.2	—	—	1.2	13.5	5.0	78.5	None†	111
Fund of America	G&I	D	16.3	42.1	78.7	347.8	1.9	17.5	5.3	175.6	5.75	108
Fundamental Investors	G&I	B	27.0	50.1	143.0	419.0	3.4	16.1	9.3	767.6	5.75	96
FundTrust—Growth	Gro	D	16.6	29.9	85.6	—	1.3	N.A.	2.0	23.6	1.5	111
FundTrust—Growth & Income	G&I	C	17.4	32.2	88.9	—	2.1	N.A.	1.5	36.9	1.5	104
Gabelli Asset	Gro	—	26.3	91.4	—	—	1.3	35.3	39.7	351.6	None†	72
Gabelli Growth	Gro	—	37.7	—	—	—	0.3	19.6	18.8	98.5	None	123
Gateway Option Index	OpInc	D	17.8	32.2	75.1	177.1	1.9	14.9	0.0	31.1	None	82
Gradison Established Growth	Gro	B	15.1	45.7	135.3	—	2.7	10.2	30.0	125.2	None	79
Growth Fund of America	Gro	B	29.4	61.5	142.2	403.8	1.4	20.2	25.6	1,776.5	5.75	98
Growth Fund of Washington	Gro	—	13.2	37.1	—	—	1.6	N.A.	14.0	58.5	5.0	139
Growth Industry Shares	Gro	D	28.1	46.0	99.3	307.6	0.8	20.1	13.0	68.0	None	51
G.T. Europe Growth	Intl	—	37.4	63.6	—	—	0.0	N.A.	9.6	176.6	4.75	146
G.T. International Growth	Intl	—	35.0	71.6	—	—	0.0	N.A.	7.2	110.9	4.75	144
G.T. Japan Growth	Intl	—	50.8	188.0	—	—	0.0	N.A.	9.6	38.8	4.75	160
G.T. Pacific Growth	Intl	C	47.8	91.5	248.8	527.9	0.0	N.A.	5.9	150.4	4.75	149
G.T. Worldwide Growth	Glo	—	33.7	—	—	—	0.0	N.A.	4.2	32.0	4.75	151
Guardian Park Avenue	Gro	B	22.2	50.2	137.5	460.4	2.6	12.9	8.0	224.0	4.5	82
Harbor Growth	Gro	—	21.2	39.7	—	—	0.9	N.A.	1.4	142.8	None	60
Harbor International	Intl	—	35.0	—	—	—	0.6	N.A.	8.7	31.0	None	78
Harbor U.S. Equities	G&I	—	23.3	—	—	—	1.3	N.A.	1.0	61.2	None	56
Hartwell Emerging Growth	SCG	C	35.7	67.0	156.9	305.5	0.0	37.2	4.2	24.5	3.0	154
Heartland Value	Max	—	7.5	23.1	—	—	0.8	N.A.	14.3	31.6	None†	133
Heritage Capital Appreciation	Max	—	20.4	42.5	—	—	0.4	N.A.	30.4	63.4	4.0	149
IAI Apollo	Max	D	21.2	67.8	98.5	—	0.7	17.5	30.0	27.6	None	55
IAI Regional	Gro	A	29.3	57.9	177.6	—	1.6	17.9	30.0	121.2	None	55
IAI Stock	Max	B	28.4	57.3	122.5	371.9	1.6	20.8	30.0	72.8	None	55
IDEX Fund*	Gro	—	39.5	75.4	—	—	1.3	N.A.	17.4	85.8	8.5	159
IDEX II*	Gro	—	40.4	80.6	—	—	1.4	N.A.	18.9	84.2	8.5	158
IDEX 3	Gro	—	38.7	—	—	—	1.1	23.4	18.0	104.2	8.5	160
IDEX Total Income	Flex	—	5.2	—	—	—	10.1	N.A.	7.0	27.3	7.0	121
IDS Discovery	SCG	F	28.5	28.3	79.3	—	0.6	24.6	23.0	157.4	5.0	85
IDS Equity Plus	G&I	C	26.5	46.3	129.1	298.5	3.0	17.5	12.3	392.0	5.0	87
IDS Growth	Gro	C	33.6	39.0	126.8	438.0	0.4	27.6	15.8	700.8	5.0	84
IDS International	Intl	D	15.0	30.5	183.7	—	0.2	N.A.	11.2	203.6	5.0	123
IDS Managed Retirement	G&I	—	33.0	50.3	—	—	2.5	17.9	19.6	700.7	5.0	101
IDS Mutual	Bal	A	17.3	40.6	115.6	325.3	5.6	10.1	9.1	1,696.0	5.0	86
IDS New Dimensions	Gro	A	29.0	58.5	160.2	516.0	0.4	24.4	25.1	752.0	5.0	93
IDS Pan Pacific Growth	Glo	—	10.2	—	—	—	0.6	N.A.	4.2	48.2	None†	116
IDS Precious Metals	Gold	—	19.8	58.9	—	—	1.6	N.A.	14.5	105.6	5.0	123
IDS Progressive	Max	D	9.8	32.4	93.4	336.5	1.0	18.3	22.0	168.5	5.0	90
IDS Stock	G&I	C	26.9	50.8	123.7	295.7	3.3	15.4	16.9	1,373.0	5.0	82
IDS Strategy—Aggressive Equity	Max	C	29.4	28.8	136.5	—	0.0	21.3	15.7	273.4	None†	91
IDS Strategy—Equity Portfolio	G&I	B	19.4	51.1	124.3	—	3.3	N.A.	22.0	293.8	None†	90
IDS Utilities Income	Sec	—	28.0	—	—	—	6.2	N.A.	15.6	123.7	5.0	96
Income Fund of America	EqI	A	21.8	39.3	107.8	367.9	6.7	13.7	20.8	1,534.9	5.75	94
Integrated Capital Appreciation	Gro	—	12.0	30.3	—	—	0.9	N.A.	19.5	210.8	None†	139
Integrated Equity—Aggressive Growth	SCG	—	19.3	—	—	—	0.0	N.A.	2.2	50.0	4.75	159
Integrated Equity—Growth	Gro	—	28.9	—	—	—	4.9	N.A.	5.6	48.2	4.75	144
Integrated Multi-Asset—Total Return	G&I	—	16.0	—	—	—	3.3	N.A.	6.6	39.6	4.75	150
International Investors	Gold	D	53.2	62.6	113.7	297.5	1.9	28.0	0.7	917.6	8.5	127
Investment Co. of America	G&I	A	27.1	49.4	144.6	412.2	3.5	14.7	17.0	5,384.2	5.75	87
Investment Portfolio—Equity	Gro	D	28.2	46.9	91.7	—	1.2	20.5	10.0	300.0	None†	128

Key to MONEY grades: A = Top 10% B = Next 20% C = Middle 40% D = Next 20% F = Bottom 10%

*Currently closed to new investors   †Fund may impose back-end load or exit fee.   N.A. Not available

FUND NAME	Type	MONEY risk-adjusted grade	% gain (or loss) to Dec. 22, 1989 One year	Three years	Five years	10 years	% yield	P/E ratio	% cash	Net assets (millions)	% maximum initial sales charge	Five-year projection
Investment Portfolio—Total Return	Bal	—	18.3	32.8	—	—	4.4	18.9	9.0	$543.0	None†	$123
Investment Trust of Boston—Growth Opp.	G&I	C	24.8	35.3	102.6	221.9	2.9	14.8	0.6	62.9	4.25	132
Investors Research	Max	D	20.0	29.3	98.0	420.3	2.9	18.9	30.0	73.3	8.5	127
ISI Trust	G&I	D	24.5	44.5	72.2	171.9	5.1	15.8	22.1	109.8	6.0	112
Ivy Growth	Gro	C	25.3	36.0	108.3	456.8	2.3	16.1	5.5	199.9	None	74
Ivy Institutional	Gro	B	16.0.	40.8	132.6	—	4.6	12.2	6.3	24.7	None	69
Ivy International	Intl	—	28.4	98.9	—	—	0.6	N.A.	8.6	53.3	None	103
Janus Fund	Max	A	42.0	71.9	138.5	537.3	3.4	20.3	14.0	695.7	None	54
Janus Twenty	Max	—	45.3	50.8	—	—	5.3	27.0	10.0	69.8	None	102
Janus Venture	SCG	—	36.3	70.7	—	—	4.0	23.6	26.0	99.4	None	70
Japan Fund	Intl	A	8.1	68.2	289.4	663.9**	0.2	35.0	12.0	417.5	None	56
J.P. Growth	Gro	C	29.6	36.8	98.3	315.3	2.6	16.3	13.7	27.1	6.75	113
John Hancock Global Trust	Glo	—	16.3	34.4	—	—	1.0	22.3	10.0	100.0	4.5	168
John Hancock Growth	Gro	C	28.4	47.8	118.4	296.5	1.3	24.1	12.0	105.8	4.5	139
Kaufmann Fund	SCG	—	39.1	38.6	—	—	0.0	N.A.	11.1	34.3	None	184
Kemper Growth	Gro	C	27.5	47.2	115.5	307.7	1.9	22.6	15.0	338.0	8.5	127
Kemper International	Intl	C	18.2	45.9	224.4	—	1.0	N.A.	25.0	176.0	8.5	139
Kemper Summit	SCG	D	23.3	30.8	92.0	303.0	2.5	21.3	12.0	259.0	8.5	129
Kemper Technology	Sec	C	22.5	32.4	94.7	241.0	3.0	17.6	11.0	536.0	8.5	120
Kemper Total Return	Bal	D	18.9	23.8	90.7	289.5	3.9	19.1	10.0	939.0	8.5	125
Keystone America Omega	Max	C	29.1	56.1	139.9	229.4	0.7	17.3	6.4	39.6	2.0	97
Keystone International	Intl	D	4.0	33.2	170.4	280.9	0.0	N.A.	0.3	112.7	None†	110
Keystone K-1	EqI	C	18.3	35.7	100.9	284.0	5.8	N.A.	5.0	755.2	None†	103
Keystone K-2	Gro	C	22.1	30.7	112.2	264.3	2.4	N.A.	4.7	333.4	None†	92
Keystone Precious Metals	Gold	D	28.1	53.8	95.4	150.5	0.0	22.5	0.0	220.0	None†	91
Keystone S-1	G&I	C	26.7	40.5	108.9	223.2	2.4	14.9	1.5	182.4	None†	96
Keystone S-3	Gro	D	23.1	37.5	99.1	258.6	2.3	17.8	7.1	254.0	None†	79
Keystone S-4	Gro	F	20.0	23.8	70.5	147.3	0.0	22.6	2.1	521.0	None†	64
Kidder Peabody Equity Income	EqI	—	27.7	32.9	—	—	3.0	N.A.	1.2	60.3	None†	129
Kleinworth Benson—Intl. Equity	Intl	B	21.3	60.6	270.8	363.8	0.0	27.2	7.5	70.1	None	141
Legg Mason Special Investment	SCG	—	33.6	40.4	—	—	0.6	16.7	18.0	65.6	None	133
Legg Mason Total Return	Gro	—	14.9	27.6	—	—	1.9	13.5	9.9	30.1	None	128
Legg Mason Value	Gro	C	18.9	36.5	99.2	—	2.1	13.9	16.3	833.3	None	106
Lehman Capital	Max	D	39.5	29.6	86.2	416.8	0.0	29.9	13.0	74.1	5.0	116
Lehman Investors	G&I	C	19.8	37.9	103.0	320.6	2.9	13.9	3.2	401.0	5.0	85
Lehman Opportunity	Max	B	19.9	49.5	116.3	438.6	2.0	15.2	12.0	117.0	None	66
Lexington Global	Glo	—	24.0	—	—	—	0.3	17.7	0.0	49.6	5.0	143
Lexington Goldfund	Gold	C	25.4	59.7	135.9	161.7	0.3	40.9	5.5	140.0	None	87
Lexington Growth	Gro	C	27.0	38.0	115.4	172.3	1.1	17.4	5.1	29.6	None	73
Lexington Research	G&I	C	26.6	34.6	109.6	275.8	2.8	17.9	8.7	131.1	None	61
Lindner Dividend	EqI	B	11.9	32.7	88.1	550.7	9.2	N.A.	5.5	138.3	None†	54
Lindner Fund	Gro	B	20.5	56.6	114.7	589.9	4.2	10.6	17.0	602.4	None†	51
LMH Fund	G&I	D	10.4	20.5	70.5	—	3.7	12.8	25.0	36.0	None	79
Loomis-Sayles Capital Development*	Gro	C	13.6	29.0	144.0	590.9	3.4	18.4	0.1	197.8	None	51
Loomis-Sayles Mutual	Bal	B	19.7	39.1	137.5	345.6	4.6	14.6	0.8	320.2	None	56
Lord Abbett Affiliated	G&I	B	22.1	39.5	123.0	363.2	4.4	N.A.	3.6	3,595.2	7.25	96
Lord Abbett Developing Growth	SCG	F	12.0	15.7	33.7	142.1	0.4	N.A.	12.0	133.1	7.25	128
Lord Abbett Value Appreciation	Gro	C	17.3	27.9	103.7	—	3.0	16.3	10.0	189.4	7.25	129
MacKenzie American	Gro	—	16.1	66.0	—	—	2.3	25.1	37.0	52.1	8.5	173
MacKenzie N. American Total Return	Bal	—	14.3	18.7	—	—	9.6	10.9	1.0	123.3	5.0	108
MainStay Capital Appreciation	Max	—	23.3	22.9	—	—	0.0	N.A.	18.0	34.3	None†	170
MainStay Value	G&I	—	20.2	32.0	—	—	1.2	N.A.	23.0	27.1	None	170
Mass. Capital Development	Gro	D	26.5	40.0	90.3	360.4	2.0	14.3	18.0	821.0	7.25	117
Mass. Financial Development	G&I	C	24.2	42.2	113.7	308.4	3.1	13.9	23.0	242.0	7.25	117

Key to MONEY grades: A = Top 10%   B = Next 20%   C = Middle 40%   D = Next 20%   F = Bottom 10%

* Currently closed to new investors   †Fund may impose back-end load or exit fee.   ** To 1/1/90   N.A. Not available

THE Money RANKINGS: STOCK FUNDS

FUND NAME	Type	MONEY risk-adjusted grade	% gain (or loss) to Dec. 22, 1989				Portfolio analysis			Net assets (millions)	Expense analysis	
			One year	Three years	Five years	10 years	% yield	P/E ratio	% cash		% maximum initial sales charge	Five-year projection
Mass. Financial Emerging Growth	SCG	F	23.0	24.3	79.5	—	0.0	34.6	5.0	$215.0	7.25	$148
Mass. Fin. Lifetime–Capital Growth	Max	—	27.1	—	—	—	1.1	N.A.	15.0	202.0	None†	136
Mass. Fin. Lifetime–Dividends Plus	G&I	—	15.5	—	—	—	5.8	N.A.	14.0	186.0	None†	133
Mass. Fin. Lifetime–Emerging Growth	SCG	—	23.6	—	—	—	0.0	N.A.	4.0	81.0	None†	143
Mass. Fin. Lifetime–Global Equity	Glo	—	25.2	—	—	—	2.9	N.A.	19.0	50.0	None†	152
Mass. Fin. Lifetime–Managed Sectors	Sec	—	35.5	—	—	—	0.7	N.A.	10.0	180.0	None†	134
Mass. Financial Managed Sectors Trust	Sec	—	37.5	47.2	—	—	1.3	N.A.	10.0	130.0	4.75	124
Mass. Financial Special	Max	C	20.7	53.5	127.5	—	1.9	10.5	22.0	131.0	4.75	140
Mass. Financial Total Return Trust	Bal	A	21.3	45.8	129.9	365.6	5.4	14.6	10.0	647.0	4.75	109
Mass. Investors Growth Stock	Gro	C	33.0	42.7	104.6	282.7	0.8	27.8	8.0	901.0	7.25	103
Mass. Investors Trust	G&I	B	33.6	55.4	132.0	326.5	2.7	15.8	11.0	1,412.0	7.25	101
Mathers Fund	Gro	B	13.0	58.9	132.2	292.8	1.9	17.8	75.5	214.2	None	56
Merrill Lynch Basic Value A	G&I	B	16.3	46.5	131.7	419.2	3.9	10.8	25.0	2,369.0	6.5	95
Merrill Lynch Capital A	G&I	A	21.5	47.5	132.7	411.3	5.4	13.9	6.0	1,076.0	6.5	96
Merrill Lynch Eurofund B	Intl	—	23.4	—	—	—	0.2	N.A.	10.0	238.0	None†	112
Merrill Lynch Fund for Tomorrow B	Gro	C	25.2	42.5	110.5	—	1.3	20.0	15.0	659.2	None†	101
Merrill Lynch International A	Glo	D	20.8	41.1	147.8	—	3.8	20.7	15.0	200.3	6.5	132
Merrill Lynch Natural Resources B	Sec	—	25.4	38.9	—	—	1.8	24.9	19.0	464.5	None†	100
Merrill Lynch Pacific A	Intl	B	14.7	69.5	318.0	928.4	1.3	N.A.	6.0	357.4	6.5	118
Merrill Lynch Phoenix A	G&I	B	12.9	49.8	131.3	—	4.7	20.4	19.0	275.6	6.5	125
Merrill Lynch Retirement Benefit B	Bal	—	15.7	25.8	—	—	6.7	N.A.	2.0	1,692.8	None†	99
Merrill Lynch Retirement Equity B	G&I	—	29.2	—	—	—	1.1	20.9	1.0	498.5	None†	104
Merrill Lynch Science-Tech. Holdings A	Sec	C	9.1	28.2	83.0	—	1.2	20.5	12.0	150.6	6.5	137
Merrill Lynch Special Value A	Gro	F	(0.2)	(7.2)	26.0	104.5	1.9	21.1	6.0	68.5	6.5	125
Metlife–State Street Cap. Appreciation	Max	—	28.5	62.9	—	—	0.2	21.9	6.0	43.5	4.5	123
MetLife–State Street Equity Income	EqI	—	24.3	36.6	—	—	4.3	15.8	22.0	42.9	4.5	123
MidAmerica Mutual	Gro	D	15.6	33.0	88.7	251.0	3.8	N.A.	28.4	36.7	5.75	110
Mutual of Omaha Growth	Gro	C	33.5	54.1	129.7	274.6	0.7	21.0	14.0	46.8	8.0	143
Mutual of Omaha Income	Flex	B	15.3	37.8	86.1	213.7	8.0	N.A.	1.0	169.0	8.0	121
Mutual Qualified*	G&I	A	13.9	59.7	135.0	—	1.2	21.5	23.8	1,482.0	None	43
Mutual Shares*	G&I	A	14.4	58.8	135.3	451.6	1.4	21.2	25.2	3,477.2	None	46
National Aggressive Growth	SCG	F	8.5	15.6	74.4	194.0	0.5	47.4	11.0	32.2	8.5	155
National Aviation & Technology	Sec	C	35.4	43.4	106.7	228.9	1.0	22.6	17.8	89.5	4.75	118
National Industries	G&I	D	23.7	40.3	72.3	132.6	0.9	N.A.	23.0	31.5	None	92
National Stock	G&I	C	24.3	42.0	113.5	289.2	3.2	N.A.	9.0	240.2	7.25	111
National Strategic Allocation	Max	—	16.5	—	—	—	2.3	15.5	2.0	100.9	7.75	163
National Telecom. & Technology	Sec	D	14.9	27.8	56.2	—	0.8	23.8	4.7	40.6	4.75	138
National Total Income	Flex	A	20.8	43.4	124.0	380.2	5.8	17.2	19.0	198.4	7.25	121
National Total Return	EqI	C	25.8	37.6	104.5	356.5	4.3	15.8	9.0	275.7	7.25	125
Nationwide Fund	G&I	B	30.1	53.9	148.8	349.7	2.9	14.9	6.3	480.6	7.5	107
Nationwide Growth	Gro	C	13.0	40.8	125.0	382.0	2.2	14.9	8.5	254.1	7.5	110
Neuberger & Berman Guardian	G&I	C	19.2	47.9	110.4	350.8	2.5	12.9	5.8	574.0	None	48
Neuberger & Berman Manhattan	Max	B	26.6	46.7	139.4	429.9	1.4	15.8	5.4	401.3	None	66
Neuberger & Berman Partners	Gro	B	20.8	43.1	122.0	409.3	3.5	16.1	13.0	767.9	None	54
Neuberger & Berman Selected Sec. Plus	Sec	C	27.1	46.8	101.5	225.4	2.3	16.4	8.8	432.0	None	58
Neuwirth Fund	SCG	D	16.1	33.3	103.0	243.3	0.5	16.9	6.9	25.6	None	104
New Beginning Growth	SCG	C	32.7	49.4	141.3	—	1.1	N.A.	2.0	57.9	None	65
New Economy	Gro	A	29.9	54.4	148.3	—	1.8	21.1	21.5	887.8	5.75	105
New England Equity Income	G&I	D	8.1	18.9	79.5	255.3	3.7	15.5	0.0	58.6	6.5	143
New England Growth	Gro	C	18.5	40.5	127.2	548.6	2.6	17.5	0.0	574.3	6.5	130
New England Retirement Equity	G&I	C	21.0	29.8	120.0	347.7	2.7	17.7	0.0	151.8	6.5	131
New Perspective	Glo	C	23.9	54.0	161.4	414.3	2.7	16.6	13.1	1,232.3	5.75	100
Newton Growth	Gro	D	16.2	24.7	80.1	292.0	1.8	16.0	19.0	33.9	None	69
New York Venture	Gro	A	31.8	55.7	163.8	518.2	1.0	17.9	10.9	320.4	4.75	99

Key to MONEY grades: A = Top 10% B = Next 20% C = Middle 40% D = Next 20% F = Bottom 10%

*Currently closed to new investors   †Fund may impose back-end load or exit fee.   N.A. Not available

FUND NAME	Type	MONEY risk-adjusted grade	% gain (or loss) to Dec. 22, 1989				Portfolio analysis			Net assets (millions)	Expense analysis	
			One year	Three years	Five years	10 years	% yield	P/E ratio	% cash		% maximum initial sales charge	Five-year projection
Nicholas Fund	Gro	B	22.0	40.2	105.2	460.4	2.6	15.6	12.8	$1,374.1	None	$48
Nicholas Income	Flex	D	4.2	18.3	60.7	176.0	10.8	N.A.	7.9	76.6	None	46
Nicholas Limited Edition	SCG	—	16.3	—	—	—	0.7	16.7	18.3	56.1	None	72
Nicholas II	SCG	C	16.4	44.5	115.0	—	1.6	19.3	9.9	399.8	None	41
Nomura Pacific Basin	Intl	—	20.3	86.9	—	—	0.2	N.A.	9.0	69.7	None	71
Northeast Investors Trust	Flex	B	0.7	15.0	75.2	214.8	14.2	N.A.	(4.0)††	355.0	None	42
Olympus Premium Income	OpInc	—	10.1	18.1	—	—	13.2	17.5	14.0	42.8	4.25	152
Oppenheimer Asset Allocation	Bal	—	17.5	—	—	—	4.3	17.2	19.7	80.0	4.75	125
Oppenheimer Directors	Max	F	20.5	35.3	77.1	228.5	1.6	18.7	22.1	137.4	8.5	142
Oppenheimer Equity Income	EqI	A	17.7	44.9	122.1	408.9	5.1	15.0	21.2	1,163.0	8.5	128
Oppenheimer Fund	Gro	F	22.8	27.7	75.3	146.2	1.8	20.1	19.1	205.6	8.5	139
Oppenheimer Global	Glo	C	32.5	58.8	237.1	450.4	0.3	N.A.	6.9	509.0	8.5	178
Oppenheimer Gold & Special Minerals	Gold	B	39.7	160.5	229.7	—	1.2	27.0	3.8	160.9	8.5	146
Oppenheimer OTC	SCG	—	30.8	75.0	—	—	0.6	29.3	20.5	52.5	4.75	126
Oppenheimer Premium Income	OpInc	C	5.6	56.8	90.6	245.6	9.1	20.0	29.9	272.3	8.5	139
Oppenheimer Regency**	Max	D	19.5	33.0	90.2	—	1.6	23.3	17.5	126.7	8.5	143
Oppenheimer Special	Gro	D	19.8	26.6	72.5	232.0	2.9	14.7	15.1	549.0	8.5	134
Oppenheimer Target	Max	F	16.9	25.2	76.9	—	1.6	14.3	19.2	67.0	4.75	115
Oppenheimer Time	Max	B	25.4	51.5	146.3	401.6	2.3	23.2	18.6	332.9	8.5	136
Oppenheimer Total Return	G&I	A	18.3	47.8	140.8	253.0	3.7	13.7	24.9	381.3	4.75	97
Over-the-Counter Securities	SCG	D	18.3	28.8	86.3	266.1	0.8	19.4	6.0	309.9	4.5	126
Pacific Horizon Aggressive Growth	Max	C	33.3	46.7	141.0	—	0.0	28.5	1.5	96.2	4.5	112
Paine Webber Asset Allocation	G&I	—	10.0	22.1	—	—	5.9	13.7	57.2	608.5	None†	125
Paine Webber Classic Atlas	Glo	B	19.5	49.3	239.1	—	0.9	N.A.	1.4	202.4	4.5	127
Paine Webber Classic Growth	Gro	—	33.5	61.0	—	—	0.2	27.4	7.3	76.4	4.5	140
Paine Webber Classic Growth & Income	G&I	C	23.9	39.0	93.5	—	2.9	18.4	8.8	63.6	4.5	134
Paine Webber Master Growth	Gro	—	28.7	44.6	—	—	0.0	21.5	12.6	96.0	None†	138
Pasadena Growth	Gro	—	34.7	60.0	—	—	0.0	21.0	2.4	23.3	3.0	135
Pax World	Bal	C	23.3	38.8	92.7	257.4	4.5	17.1	2.9	91.2	None	61
Penn Square Mutual	G&I	C	22.5	44.9	112.5	329.8	3.5	15.5	18.4	213.5	4.75	96
Pennsylvania Mutual	SCG	C	15.9	44.8	105.1	400.3	1.6	19.3	25.0	554.0	None†	56
Permanent Portfolio	Bal	F	6.6	23.2	56.0	—	0.0	19.7	25.0	97.8	None	184
Philadelphia Fund	G&I	C	31.1	51.9	102.5	237.0	1.5	19.2	40.0	110.2	None	77
Phoenix Balanced Series	Bal	A	23.4	38.3	116.6	407.2	5.0	21.4	12.0	455	6.9	110
Phoenix Convertible	Conv	B	18.7	35.6	95.2	—	5.4	N.A.	22.0	158.7	6.9	112
Phoenix Growth Series	Gro	B	24.8	46.3	133.9	597.5	3.1	17.5	11.0	700.2	6.9	113
Phoenix Stock Series	Max	C	18.2	35.1	103.8	535.0	3.3	24.0	14.0	130.0	6.9	112
Phoenix Total Return	G&I	D	16.8	32.9	79.6	—	4.0	20.8	10.0	32.9	4.75	126
Pilgrim MagnaCap	Gro	C	21.0	37.6	119.1	361.6	1.4	14.6	5.0	218.5	4.75	128
Pine Street	G&I	C	23.4	32.9	100.3	275.6	3.5	13.4	3.2	54.0	None	65
Pioneer Fund	G&I	C	21.8	49.7	113.2	280.4	2.6	16.2	1.0	1,650.0	8.5	124
Pioneer II	G&I	C	20.5	43.5	114.8	368.0	3.0	15.2	9.7	4,344.0	8.5	126
Pioneer Three	G&I	D	19.6	40.3	94.4	—	2.1	16.7	2.4	724.0	8.5	124
Piper Jaffray Value	Gro	—	35.4	—	—	—	1.4	N.A.	1.3	38.1	4.0	108
Plymouth—Growth Opportunities	Gro	—	21.9	—	—	—	0.2	17.5	3.8	37.6	4.0	169
Plymouth—Income & Growth	G&I	—	24.7	—	—	—	4.5	14.8	17.8	48.8	4.0	146
Primary Trend	G&I	—	8.1	31.3	—	—	1.7	N.A.	12.0	49.3	None	61
Princor Capital Accumulation	Max	C	13.4	33.9	111.8	383.0	3.1	16.2	0.5	124.6	5.0	102
Princor Growth	Gro	D	18.6	30.6	102.6	246.4	1.8	19.7	0.3	31.8	5.0	107
Provident Fund for Income	EqI	D	20.8	36.3	83.5	316.5	6.7	12.2	4.5	102.4	7.25	113
Pru-Bache Equity	Gro	C	28.8	47.2	127.2	—	1.6	16.9	10.0	606.1	None†	88
Pru-Bache Equity Income	EqI	—	18.3	—	—	—	2.5	16.2	10.6	149.4	None†	133
Pru-Bache Flexifund—Aggressive	G&I	—	18.4	—	—	—	3.4	N.A.	6.7	109.3	None†	138
Pru-Bache Flexifund—Conservative	G&I	—	14.6	—	—	—	4.5	N.A.	31.6	139.1	None†	122

Key to MONEY grades: A = Top 10%   B = Next 20%   C = Middle 40%   D = Next 20%   F = Bottom 10%

†Fund may impose back-end load or exit fee.   **Open to retirement plans only   †† Figure reflects borrowing to boost investments.   N.A. Not available

THE Money RANKINGS: STOCK FUNDS

FUND NAME	Type	MONEY risk-adjusted grade	% gain (or loss) to Dec. 22, 1989				Portfolio analysis			Net assets (millions)	Expense analysis	
			One year	Three years	Five years	10 years	% yield	P/E ratio	% cash		% maximum initial sales charge	Five-year projection
Pru-Bache Global	Glo	D	10.5	29.7	168.3	—	2.9	N.A.	4.2	$391.0	None†	$111
Pru-Bache Global Natural Resources	Sec	—	24.0	—	—	—	0.6	N.A.	17.0	49.2	None†	140
Pru-Bache Growth Opportunity	SCG	D	18.0	32.2	87.6	—	0.4	19.5	9.9	142.5	None†	106
Pru-Bache IncomeVertible Plus	Sec	—	20.6	37.6	—	—	5.8	N.A.	19.0	563.7	None†	120
Pru-Bache Option Growth	Max	B	21.4	41.6	117.8	—	3.1	17.7	16.3	65.3	None†	105
Pru-Bache Research	Gro	C	21.1	38.2	122.9	—	2.6	16.4	2.0	362.4	None†	89
Pru-Bache Utility	Sec	A	35.3	49.2	169.5	—	3.5	16.5	8.5	2,213.7	None†	94
Putnam Convertible Income & Growth	Conv	D	15.8	21.6	79.5	322.8	6.1	N.A.	4.5	823.0	5.75	134
Putnam Energy Resources	Sec	C	32.8	71.8	103.1	—	3.1	15.2	0.4	112.0	5.75	158
Putnam Fund for Growth & Income	G&I	B	19.6	46.4	132.7	387.6	4.7	12.9	20.4	1,938.4	5.75	126
Putnam (George) Fund of Boston	Bal	B	21.3	39.5	118.2	314.3	5.8	12.4	1.4	396.3	5.75	126
Putnam Health Sciences Trust	Sec	B	37.8	59.6	163.2	—	1.3	20.8	6.6	291.8	5.75	139
Putnam Information Sciences	Sec	C	35.1	56.0	107.8	—	0.5	30.3	3.1	89.9	5.75	166
Putnam International Equities	Glo	C	21.8	42.6	225.7	480.2	1.8	17.8	3.3	489.0	5.75	165
Putnam Investors	Gro	C	31.2	44.5	118.9	326.2	1.7	N.A.	5.5	697.3	5.75	125
Putnam Option Income	OpInc	D	13.6	26.6	73.5	209.6	3.5	16.2	5.1	935.6	6.75	129
Putnam Option Income II	OpInc	—	17.6	30.0	—	—	4.7	15.4	6.0	1,120.2	6.75	126
Putnam OTC Emerging Growth	SCG	B	26.0	50.9	156.8	—	0.0	N.A.	4.4	178.8	5.75	141
Putnam Vista Basic Value	Max	B	23.0	45.6	129.5	404.9	3.3	N.A.	10.5	271.0	5.75	116
Putnam Voyager	Max	A	33.5	61.1	168.9	415.9	0.4	N.A.	10.0	717.3	5.75	122
Quest for Value	Max	C	17.6	34.0	97.1	—	1.0	15.4	19.2	78.5	5.5	140
Rea-Graham Balanced	Bal	D	7.3	19.1	69.4	—	4.7	N.A.	70.0	49.0	4.75	140
Reich & Tang Equity	Gro	—	16.0	48.0	—	—	2.9	19.8	16.0	109.0	None	61
Rightime Blue Chip	G&I	—	18.4	—	—	—	5.8	15.6	2.0	98.0	4.75	177
Rightime Fund	G&I	—	10.2	26.5	—	—	0.4	N.A.	1.0	167.3	None	137
Rightime Growth	Gro	—	18.5	—	—	—	1.1	17.8	1.0	42.5	4.75	178
Rodney Square Growth	Gro	—	25.5	—	—	—	1.0	N.A.	14.0	37.7	5.75	147
Rodney Square International Equity	Intl	—	17.1	—	—	—	0.4	N.A.	6.2	67.3	5.75	147
Royce Value	SCG	C	15.1	41.4	93.9	—	1.3	19.0	26.0	192.8	None†	113
Rushmore Stock Market Index	G&I	—	20.5	41.3	—	—	1.9	N.A.	0.0	30.4	None	51
Safeco Equity	G&I	C	35.0	55.3	139.6	297.0	3.6	19.1	4.9	56.0	None	53
Safeco Growth	Gro	D	17.4	51.0	86.9	249.5	3.0	18.0	4.9	76.8	None	52
Safeco Income	EqI	C	17.9	30.2	107.9	367.9	5.0	13.5	1.4	223.4	None	51
SBSF Growth	Gro	C	31.5	47.4	107.6	—	2.4	N.A.	33.0	99.0	None	64
Schroder Capital–International Equity	Intl	—	19.7	49.1	—	—	0.2	N.A.	11.0	54.5	None	71
Schroder Capital–U.S. Equity	Gro	D	20.7	33.1	85.1	166.1	1.8	18.4	3.1	24.0	None	88
Scudder Capital Growth	Gro	A	31.8	66.5	165.4	423.1	0.3	N.A.	8.0	972.4	None	53
Scudder Development	SCG	F	22.6	30.8	71.3	230.2	0.0	24.8	5.0	290.7	None	72
Scudder Global	Glo	—	36.0	66.3	—	—	0.4	14.6	1.0	125.1	None	107
Scudder Growth & Income	G&I	B	24.7	42.7	130.4	283.5	4.0	15.0	7.0	477.8	None	51
Scudder International	Intl	C	24.9	50.6	229.3	441.0	0.0	N.A.	2.0	701.6	None	67
Security Action*	Gro	D	17.4	24.9	84.4	—	1.2	18.1	1.0	211.3	8.5	47
Security Equity	Gro	C	29.0	57.7	130.7	331.0	1.9	20.8	9.4	270.5	8.5	139
Security Investment	G&I	D	19.0	31.9	78.7	191.9	5.9	16.2	3.8	83.5	8.5	147
Security Ultra	Max	F	13.6	9.0	49.1	191.5	0.3	19.8	(15.3) **	58.4	8.5	258
Selected American Shares	G&I	B	18.6	42.6	124.1	368.3	1.6	14.1	23.0	363.3	None	61
Selected Special Shares	Gro	D	27.7	49.9	101.7	227.4	0.9	15.9	25.0	47.1	None	68
Seligman Capital	Max	D	29.0	26.2	96.9	334.8	0.0	20.6	7.1	123.6	4.75	100
Seligman Comm. & Information	Sec	B	27.6	56.2	148.5	—	0.0	22.4	3.5	43.2	4.75	131
Seligman Common Stock	G&I	C	24.7	36.0	122.3	353.9	3.2	17.8	6.1	512.1	4.75	84
Seligman Growth	Gro	C	31.0	44.7	122.7	246.5	2.1	22.2	6.8	575.4	4.75	85
Seligman Income	Flex	C	14.7	21.0	81.6	256.0	8.1	N.A.	7.4	160.0	4.75	90
Sentinel Balanced	Bal	C	17.8	29.3	98.5	308.4	5.8	13.0	15.0	74.0	8.5	136
Sentinel Common Stock	G&I	C	24.2	38.5	125.8	411.4	3.7	13.6	3.0	597.0	8.5	128

Key to MONEY grades: A = Top 10%   B = Next 20%   C = Middle 40%   D = Next 20%   F = Bottom 10%

*Investment by contractual plan only   †Fund may impose back-end load or exit fee.   **Figure reflects borrowing to boost investments.   N.A. Not available

FUND NAME	Type	MONEY risk-adjusted grade	% gain (or loss) to Dec. 22, 1989 — One year	Three years	Five years	10 years	Portfolio analysis — % yield	P/E ratio	% cash	Net assets (millions)	Expense analysis — % maximum initial sales charge	Five-year projection
Sentinel Growth	Gro	C	24.2	33.8	107.6	354.5	1.2	18.0	2.0	$52.0	8.5	$152
Sentry Fund	Gro	C	21.6	32.4	104.6	249.6	1.9	17.9	1.0	46.4	8.0	115
Sequoia Fund*	Gro	A	26.9	48.1	115.9	489.3	2.6	16.2	38.4	929.0	None	56
Sigma Capital Shares	Max	D	10.5	18.2	86.5	337.3	3.3	20.8	11.1	85.8	6.0	125
Sigma Investment Shares	G&I	B	27.5	43.4	132.9	374.0	3.1	15.8	24.2	112.9	6.0	109
Sigma Trust Shares	Bal	B	22.1	33.1	103.2	273.2	4.8	13.4	27.9	56.3	6.0	115
Sigma Venture Shares	SCG	F	20.8	6.9	51.5	193.2	0.2	23.2	11.7	45.3	6.0	129
SLH Aggressive Growth	Max	B	41.1	63.7	164.9	—	0.0	37.5	4.1	97.7	5.0	115
SHL Appreciation	Gro	A	27.5	52.7	148.1	437.7	2.1	17.4	17.3	965.9	5.0	96
SLH Equity–Growth & Opportunity	Gro	—	16.9	34.4	—	—	0.3	14.6	29.1	210.3	None†	129
SLH Equity–International	Intl	—	16.6	22.1	—	—	0.8	N.A.	7.2	69.1	None†	155
SLH Equity–Strategic Investors	G&I	—	19.6	—	—	—	3.1	N.A.	19.0	208.8	None†	133
SLH Equity–Sector Analysis	Max	—	21.0	—	—	—	4.4	N.A.	(3.4)††	290.8	None†	119
SLH Fundamental Value	Gro	D	17.2	42.2	80.1	—	1.5	19.8	26.6	83.7	5.0	108
SLH Global Opportunities	Glo	F	17.1	15.8	121.8	—	1.1	15.0	5.1	88.5	5.0	139
SLH Income–Convertible Securities	Conv	—	9.2	24.1	—	—	6.5	N.A.	12.3	136.5	None†	104
SLH Income–Option Income	OpInc	—	15.4	31.2	—	—	8.7	13.2	9.2	575.5	None†	105
SLH Investment–Basic Value	Gro	—	20.9	30.9	—	—	2.1	11.8	12.2	333.1	None†	110
SLH Investment–Growth	Gro	D	24.5	33.1	92.2	—	3.8	18.9	34.3	923.5	None†	109
SLH Investment–Precious Metals	Gold	—	21.3	51.7	—	—	2.1	N.A.	14.0	95.1	None†	135
SLH Investment–Special Equities	SCG	F	17.1	16.5	67.9	—	0.0	23.8	12.5	138.2	None†	128
SLH Precious Metals & Minerals	Gold	—	17.9	26.2	—	—	0.0	29.4	7.8	36.6	5.0	135
SLH Small Capitalization	SCG	—	13.1	—	—	—	0.0	27.2	1.4	26.9	5.0	139
SLH Utilities	Sec	—	20.2	—	—	—	6.3	N.A.	11.6	581.5	None†	96
Smith Barney Equity	Gro	C	28.9	43.4	122.8	308.5	2.2	14.6	8.9	83.8	5.75	102
Smith Barney Income & Growth	G&I	B	23.2	39.6	118.9	430.0	4.9	12.0	3.5	577.2	5.75	83
SoGen International	Gro	A	16.5	51.9	151.5	512.6	4.2	17.6	20.2	158.0	3.75	111
Southeastern Growth	Gro	—	15.6	19.4	—	—	0.1	15.4	11.0	105.0	None†	128
Sovereign Investors	G&I	B	22.3	34.5	115.6	353.5	4.6	14.1	18.0	66.0	5.0	114
State Bond Common Stock	Gro	C	37.9	58.5	138.3	239.9	1.4	20.4	7.5	35.8	8.5	142
SteinRoe Capital Opportunities	Max	D	34.5	39.6	106.0	255.6	0.4	22.1	1.7	251.2	None	56
SteinRoe Prime Equities	G&I	—	28.4	—	—	—	1.9	18.6	0.8	31.4	None	80
SteinRoe Special	Gro	B	36.0	66.9	152.8	502.8	1.0	21.6	0.5	319.6	None	55
SteinRoe Stock	Gro	C	32.3	38.7	106.4	268.2	1.8	20.9	1.7	201.8	None	42
SteinRoe Total Return	EqI	C	18.9	27.2	90.1	207.6	5.4	15.3	1.2	144.3	None	48
Strategic Investments	Gold	F	63.0	15.4	7.1	60.4	4.3	N.A.	5.0	57.7	8.5	162
Stratton Monthly Dividend Shares	Sec	C	19.6	13.5	79.9	—	8.0	11.9	2.6	34.3	None	66
Strong Discovery	Max	—	21.7	—	—	—	6.9	21.6	36.2	56.3	2.0	126
Strong Income	Flex	—	1.3	19.1	—	—	12.8	N.A.	44.8	208.8	None	67
Strong Investment	Bal	D	10.9	19.5	69.1	—	8.8	21.5	40.9	239.2	1.0	74
Strong Opportunity	Max	—	17.8	51.7	—	—	8.1	23.4	31.0	204.7	2.0	103
Strong Total Return	G&I	D	1.8	24.1	87.5	—	12.3	23.0	16.9	1,095.9	1.0	75
Templeton Foreign	Intl	B	28.3	95.3	215.7	—	2.7	N.A.	12.0	493.0	8.5	126
Templeton Global	Glo	F	16.1	31.6	104.2	—	2.4	19.4	12.8	893.0	8.5	112
Templeton Growth	Glo	D	20.8	51.7	136.2	347.5	3.6	12.7	5.9	2,350.9	8.5	120
Templeton World	Glo	D	20.0	46.2	127.8	392.8	3.1	13.9	1.9	4,612.8	8.5	120
Thomson McKinnon–Convertible	Conv	—	10.7	—	—	—	4.4	N.A.	12.0	42.6	None†	93**
Thomson McKinnon–Global	Glo	—	27.3	47.6	—	—	0.0	20.9	7.7	53.4	None†	148
Thomson McKinnon–Growth	Gro	A	35.5	56.9	155.1	—	0.5	19.8	10.0	357.0	None†	117
Thomson McKinnon–Opportunity	Max	C	27.8	54.4	110.6	—	0.0	20.1	7.3	46.4	None†	128
Transamerica Growth & Income	EqI	C	19.6	35.5	88.2	268.1	5.5	N.A.	3.4	67.6	4.75	115
Transamerica Sunbelt Growth	Gro	F	24.1	33.1	78.0	—	3.3	25.9	6.1	32.5	4.75	134
Transamerica Technology	Sec	—	17.9	70.0	—	—	0.5	32.9	11.8	59.6	4.75	174
T. Rowe Price Capital Appreciation	Max	—	20.8	51.5	—	—	2.1	N.A.	29.7	132.4	None	82

Key to MONEY grades: A = Top 10%   B = Next 20%   C = Middle 40%   D = Next 20%   F = Bottom 10%

*Currently closed to new investors **Three-year expense projection †Fund may impose back-end load or exit fee. ††Figure reflects borrowing to boost investments.   N.A. Not available

THE Money RANKINGS: STOCK FUNDS

FUND NAME	Type	MONEY risk-adjusted grade	% gain (or loss) to Dec. 22, 1989				Portfolio analysis			Net assets (millions)	Expense analysis	
			One year	Three years	Five years	10 years	% yield	P/E ratio	% cash		% maximum initial sales charge	Five-year projection
T. Rowe Price Equity Income	EqI	—	12.3	46.6	—	—	5.1	13.4	22.4	$951.4	None	$69
T. Rowe Price Growth & Income	G&I	D	17.5	38.2	83.4	—	4.4	13.6	10.4	551.4	None	57
T. Rowe Price Growth Stock	Gro	C	23.3	33.2	121.3	223.6	1.8	17.0	11.9	1,515.7	None	43
T. Rowe Price International Stock	Intl	B	22.1	56.3	260.7	—	2.2	N.A.	12.4	871.6	None	64
T. Rowe Price New America Growth	Gro	—	35.3	42.3	—	—	0.0	23.9	4.9	136.2	None	82
T. Rowe Price New Era	Sec	B	24.1	58.4	131.5	295.8	2.3	21.8	10.6	796.1	None	49
T. Rowe Price New Horizons	SCG	F	24.3	29.1	61.1	208.8	0.5	21.4	3.9	955.4	None	47
T. Rowe Price Small-Cap Value	SCG	—	16.7	—	—	—	0.8	N.A.	13.6	31.6	None	65
Tudor Fund	Max	D	23.0	40.6	107.4	466.0	0.6	23.2	1.3	184.9	None	63
Twentieth Century Balanced	Bal	—	23.8	—	—	—	3.1	N.A.	4.0	32.5	None	55
Twentieth Century Growth	Max	B	42.5	60.6	159.8	432.5	1.8	19.8	1.0	1,600.0	None	55
Twentieth Century Heritage	Gro	—	33.1	—	—	—	0.8	19.4	2.0	127.0	None	55
Twentieth Century Select	Gro	B	35.9	48.1	144.0	534.8	1.9	19.0	1.0	2,800.0	None	55
Twentieth Century Ultra	Max	D	34.3	57.4	121.1	—	0.0	28.0	1.0	349.0	None	55
Twentieth Century Vista	Max	C	46.4	57.0	142.9	—	0.1	29.0	1.0	279.0	None	55
United Accumulative	Gro	B	25.1	51.2	125.9	425.4	3.8	16.3	10.5	869.2	8.5	117
United Continental Income	Bal	C	22.0	24.1	99.6	347.7	5.7	17.3	2.7	319.7	8.5	129
United Gold & Government	Gold	—	19.2	49.6	—	—	1.8	22.4	11.5	84.3	8.5	156
United Income	EqI	A	25.1	58.7	161.8	469.9	3.0	14.9	4.6	1,554.2	8.5	119
United International Growth	Intl	C	11.7	44.1	155.8	470.3	1.9	N.A.	4.2	275.2	8.5	143
United New Concepts	SCG	F	8.0	7.2	55.9	—	2.1	22.3	27.0	72.0	8.5	147
United Retirement Shares	G&I	C	21.4	37.8	93.7	285.4	4.4	20.5	11.7	136.7	8.5	130
United Science & Energy	Sec	B	25.5	52.3	123.5	302.0	1.6	22.2	11.0	247.7	8.5	130
United Services Gold Shares	Gold	F	64.6	41.4	45.3	147.0	4.2	N.A.	5.0	345.2	None	89
United Services New Prospector	Gold	—	19.8	29.5	—	—	0.0	33.3	6.0	104.2	None†	112
United Services Prospector	Gold	D	25.0	39.5	87.9	—	0.0	22.0	6.0	41.4	None†	117
U.S. Trend	Gro	C	28.1	52.4	110.6	276.5	2.7	15.5	0.5	87.1	4.75	101
United Vanguard	Gro	C	17.9	42.5	108.2	504.8	2.7	18.5	17.6	755.2	8.5	136
USAA Investors Trust—Cornerstone	Bal	B	21.1	43.0	131.2	—	3.5	25.4	6.4	538.0	None	67
USAA Investors Trust—Gold	Gold	F	22.2	17.6	46.8	—	1.6	34.7	7.4	190.4	None	78
USAA Mutual—Aggressive Growth	SCG	F	15.4	27.9	68.7	—	0.7	24.7	3.9	149.6	None	55
USAA Mutual—Growth	Gro	D	25.6	38.1	86.7	215.3	2.6	14.6	1.8	230.0	None	67
USAA Mutual—Income	Flex	B	16.7	32.9	79.2	233.2	8.9	N.A.	1.5	349.3	None	34
USAA Mutual—Income Stock	EqI	—	24.4	—	—	—	4.3	N.A.	5.1	61.1	None	55
Value Line Convertible	Conv	—	10.3	18.9	—	—	5.4	16.2	16.9	55.2	None	57
Value Line Fund	G&I	C	28.7	45.5	132.2	277.3	1.9	20.3	6.7	203.6	None	40
Value Line Income	EqI	C	20.9	32.0	91.5	306.5	5.3	13.6	7.3	147.4	None	44
Value Line Leveraged Growth	Max	C	29.1	38.0	120.6	318.3	1.4	19.2	7.4	253.2	None	58
Value Line Special Situations	Gro	F	19.5	9.6	42.5	138.6	0.5	29.5	6.1	114.9	None	64
Vance Sanders Special	Gro	F	18.2	20.1	30.0	115.7	0.7	19.4	6.3	57.3	4.75	107
Van Eck Gold Resources	Gold	—	21.9	41.3	—	—	0.2	36.5	4.3	261.0	6.75	138
Van Eck World Trends	Glo	—	12.3	28.0	—	—	1.2	N.A.	2.2	61.1	5.75	141
Van Kampen Merritt Growth & Income	G&I	—	16.6	33.1	—	—	2.7	N.A.	4.6	37.1	4.9	127
Vanguard Asset Allocation	G&I	—	22.3	—	—	—	2.0	15.5	12.1	121.6	None	27
Vanguard Convertible Securities	Conv	—	14.4	16.9	—	—	5.9	N.A.	8.0	58.5	None	49
Vanguard Equity Income	EqI	—	24.8	—	—	—	3.7	N.A.	6.3	308.5	None	35
Vanguard Explorer*	Sec	D	8.1	24.8	40.9	200.7	1.1	19.9	10.7	261.0	None	36
Vanguard Explorer II	SCG	—	17.3	35.0	—	—	0.4	23.3	10.4	83.7	None	41
Vanguard High Yield Stock*	EqI	C	1.5	21.6	95.8	502.5	5.5	10.8	24.5	153.9	None	30
Vanguard Index Trust—Extended Market	SCG	—	22.4	—	—	—	1.3	20.2	0.6	138.6	1.0	23
Vanguard Index Trust—500 Portfolio	G&I	B	28.5	53.3	143.2	368.9	2.7	15.6	1.3	1,718.6	None	12
Vanguard Preferred Stock	EqI	C	18.7	18.2	91.3	223.6	6.0	N.A.	6.5	64.5	None	37
Vanguard PrimeCap	Gro	C	19.5	29.8	121.5	—	0.7	N.A.	10.5	277.4	None	46
Vanguard Quantitative Portfolio	G&I	—	29.3	52.8	—	—	1.7	13.2	5.0	171.8	None	36

Key to MONEY grades: A = Top 10%   B = Next 20%   C = Middle 40%   D = Next 20%   F = Bottom 10%

*Currently closed to new investors   †Fund may impose back-end load or exit fee.   N.A. Not available

FUND NAME	Type	MONEY risk-adjusted grade	% gain (or loss) to Dec. 22, 1989				Portfolio analysis			Net assets (millions)	Expense analysis	
			One year	Three years	Five years	10 years	% yield	P/E ratio	% cash		% maximum initial sales charge	Five-year projection
Vanguard Small Capitalization Stock	SCG	F	9.5	24.9	58.7	186.1	1.1	N.A.	0.9	$29.6	1.0	$77
Vanguard Specialized Portfolio—Energy	Sec	C	41.1	80.1	136.6	—	2.4	23.6	11.3	58.2	None†	22
Vanguard Specialized Port.—Gold & PM	Gold	C	31.4	54.7	125.6	—	2.4	24.9	15.6	187.2	None†	27
Vanguard Specialized Port.—Health Care	Sec	A	31.0	64.6	192.8	—	1.6	24.3	12.9	72.2	None†	35
Vanguard Spl.—Service Economy	Sec	C	27.8	30.0	112.8	—	1.3	17.7	2.4	24.9	None†	48
Vanguard STAR	Bal	—	17.5	41.0	—	—	3.9	N.A.	12.7	935.8	None	26
Vanguard Trustees' Commingled—Intl.	Intl	A	23.9	82.9	282.8	—	1.8	N.A.	11.7	587.1	None	29
Vanguard Trustees' Commingled—U.S.	G&I	D	15.3	43.0	102.9	—	2.2	12.5	3.1	123.0	None	32
Vanguard Wellesley Income	Flex	A	20.1	33.0	103.6	318.6	6.0	12.7	4.3	766.1	None	29
Vanguard Wellington	Bal	B	20.1	41.1	118.4	364.1	5.3	11.8	2.2	2,034.7	None	26
Vanguard Windsor*	G&I	B	13.2	46.1	129.6	511.6	4.2	8.5	18.8	8,179.2	None	26
Vanguard Windsor II	G&I	—	25.6	50.8	—	—	3.6	11.2	7.6	2,232.2	None	33
Vanguard W. L. Morgan Growth	Gro	C	20.9	53.0	118.5	326.4	1.9	16.2	9.7	737.6	None	31
Vanguard World—International Growth	Intl	A	23.0	54.7	271.7	—	1.3	N.A.	8.2	600.3	None	36
Vanguard World—U.S. Growth	Gro	C	34.2	36.0	102.4	302.1	0.6	19.4	11.2	192.7	None	53
Washington Mutual Investors	G&I	A	25.8	47.8	143.2	500.5	3.0	13.5	5.0	4,272.9	5.75	94
Westwood Fund	Max	—	26.7	—	—	—	2.7	N.A.	15.0	61.0	4.0	107
Winthrop Focus Growth	Gro	—	22.7	33.8	—	—	3.7	N.A.	0.8	53.7	None†	75
WPG Fund	Max	C	25.4	42.9	111.4	294.8	0.9	19.7	0.5	38.7	None	83

Key to MONEY grades: A = Top 10%   B = Next 20%   C = Middle 40%   D = Next 20%   F = Bottom 10%

*Currently closed to new investors   †Fund may impose back-end load or exit fee.
Notes: To be ranked, a fund must be one year old, accept a minimum initial investment of $25,000 or less and have had assets of at least $25 million as of Sept. 30, 1989. Gain or (loss) figures include reinvestment of dividends and capital-gains distributions through Nov. 30, 1989. The MONEY risk-adjusted rating appears for funds with at least five-year records and covers the 60-month period through Nov. 30. The prospectuses of bond funds in the high-grade categories require them to invest primarily in issues rated BBB or better by Moody's or Standard & Poor's. Short-intermediate-term taxables and tax-exempts have average weighted maturities of up to 10 years. Stock and bond fund yields are the latest 12 months' dividends divided by the most recent share prices adjusted for capital-gains distributions.   **Source: Lipper Analytical Services**

Why Gurus Don't Always Make Good Fund Managers

By now it's become almost routine: You see the ace stock picker lionized on "Wall Street Week." Next thing you know, he or she is running a mutual fund. Should you invest? It's chancy: All too often celebrated seers get knocked off their pedestals when they try to duplicate their success running a mutual fund.

Among the reasons:

That sizzling nonfund performance record may be phony. Outside of mutual funds, it is easy—and quite common—for pros to quietly omit their less-successful investments when assembling results for public consumption. Fund performance, on the other hand, is tabulated daily and printed in the next morning's newspapers.

Unlike hypothetical portfolios, funds incur real-world trading costs. Portfolio strategists and newsletter editors never pay a penny in brokerage commissions on their oft-touted model portfolios. By contrast, funds have to overcome not only trading costs but also administrative and management expenses. The latter can run particularly high on funds led by big-name managers.

Fund regulations cramp some strategists' style. Funds can make only limited use of techniques like short selling and options trading, though some stars rely on those tactics to boost their nonfund returns.

The pressure of running a mutual fund can tempt a manager to abandon his or her basic strategy. The constant temptation to get swept up by the emotions of the market is exacerbated in a fund, because shareholders inevitably pour new money in when stocks are rising and cash out when the market falls. Unlike private managers, fund managers often have to sell stocks into a declining market to meet redemptions.

THE Money RANKINGS: TAXABLE BOND FUNDS

FUND NAME	Type	MONEY risk-adjusted grade	% gain (or loss) to Dec. 22, 1989				Portfolio analysis			Net assets (millions)	Expense analysis	
			One year	Three years	Five years	10 years	% yield	Average maturity (years)	% cash		% maximum initial sales charge	Five-year projection
Advest Advantage Gov. Securities	USG	—	11.6	8.5	—	—	8.5	N.A.	3.0	$123.8	None†	$80
AIM High-Yield Securities	HYC	F	(4.2)	5.4	35.6	148.5	15.2	8.8	8.3	57.5	4.75	122
AIM Limited Maturity Treasury	STT	—	9.9	—	—	—	8.5	1.4	2.1	69.3	1.75	42
Alliance Bond—High Yield Portfolio	HYC	—	(13.3)	(5.9)	—	—	16.6	8.9	14.9	183.4	5.5	121
Alliance Bond—Monthly Income Portfolio	HGC	B	14.2	27.2	77.8	205.9	9.1	7.5	10.4	69.3	5.5	148
Alliance Bond—U.S. Gov. Portfolio	USG	—	13.0	24.6	—	—	10.0	N.A.	0.0	529.5	5.5	114
Alliance Mortgage Securities	MBS	C	11.1	24.9	66.6	—	11.1	4.0	0.0	564.1	5.5	113
AMA Income—U.S. Gov. Plus Port.	USG	D	9.1	15.6	54.2	150.2	8.5	N.A.	2.0	40.9	None	95
American Capital Corporate Bond	HGC	A	4.8	26.0	76.8	182.4	10.8	11.0	5.4	233.5	4.75	96
American Capital Federal Mortgage	MBS	—	13.5	18.6	—	—	8.8	11.0	0.0	38.6	4.75	111
American Capital Government Securities	USG	D	15.6	21.2	59.7	—	9.8	10.0	4.0	4,743.2	4.75	92
American Capital High Yield	HYC	F	(11.3)	3.8	39.1	144.1	17.0	10.0	12.5	443.5	4.75	95
American High Income Trust	HYC	—	5.7	—	—	—	11.9	9.5	12.1	123.9	4.75	99
AMEV U.S. Government Securities	USG	B	12.7	25.4	70.8	208.5	9.3	15.2	1.7	120.4	4.5	91
Axe-Houghton Income	HGC	B	10.8	22.7	80.1	234.1	9.1	N.A.	3.0	64.4	None	79
Babson Bond Trust—Long-Term Portfolio	HGC	B	13.1	22.7	70.7	191.3	8.9	12.3	4.0	77.1	None	54
Bartlett Fixed Income	HYC	—	12.7	25.8	—	—	8.7	N.A.	4.0	160.1	None	55
Benham GNMA Income	MBS	—	14.2	27.4	—	—	9.0	N.A.	10.0	279.1	None	42
Benham Government Treasury Note	STT	C	12.4	16.0	60.1	—	7.6	3.7	0.2	98.4	None	42
Benham Target—1995	STT	—	16.2	19.3	—	—	0.0	5.8	0.1	42.0	None	39
Benham Target—2000	USG	—	20.5	25.7	—	—	0.0	11.0	0.5	44.3	None	39
Benham Target—2005	USG	—	25.6	27.7	—	—	0.0	15.6	0.6	31.0	None	39
Benham Target—2010	USG	—	31.9	27.8	—	—	0.0	20.4	0.5	45.0	None	39
Benham Target—2015	USG	—	35.9	20.2	—	—	0.0	25.4	0.3	310.3	None	39
Bond Fund of America	HGC	A	10.1	24.3	81.6	227.6	9.5	14.9	8.8	1,443.3	4.75	87
Boston Co. Managed Income	STT	A	6.6	23.8	72.7	188.5	8.4	10.1	4.0	85.9	None	63
Bull & Bear High Yield	HYC	F	(3.3)	(4.6)	22.5	—	13.4	N.A.	1.0	65.3	None	91
Bull & Bear U.S. Gov. Guaranteed Sec.	MBS	—	11.2	22.3	—	—	8.4	N.A.	1.0	37.4	None	94
Capital World Bond	WI	—	4.4	—	—	—	7.4	8.6	7.7	36.0	4.75	121
Cardinal Government Guaranteed	MBS	—	12.5	26.1	—	—	9.6	N.A.	1.2	118.5	4.75	86
Carnegie Gov. Securities—High Yield	USG	C	12.2	21.4	65.2	—	7.5	14.0	8.5	45.4	4.5	109
Cigna Government Securities	USG	—	11.5	—	—	—	8.5	N.A.	4.0	56.4	5.0	102
Cigna High Yield	HYC	B	1.4	21.8	74.5	218.8	13.2	9.3	7.1	268.4	5.0	100
Cigna Income	HYC	A	14.2	24.8	83.7	220.3	8.9	16.3	2.5	230.0	5.0	101
Colonial Government Securities Plus	USG	C	13.9	23.3	70.4	—	8.2	21.1	0.3	2,700.0	6.75	126
Colonial High Yield Securities	HYC	C	0.4	18.4	64.0	191.0	13.7	9.4	4.6	381.0	4.75	111
Colonial Income Plus	HYC	D	13.6	22.6	50.5	—	6.1	10.8	3.7	97.0	6.75	124
Colonial Income	HGC	B	8.4	22.0	65.5	186.3	10.3	17.7	5.3	163.0	4.75	109
Colonial U.S. Government Trust	MBS	—	10.7	—	—	—	9.9	N.A.	0.0	63.0	4.75	113
Colonial VIP—High Income	HYC	—	3.4	—	—	—	11.1	9.5	5.5	66.0	None†	142
Columbia Fixed Income Securities	HGC	C	14.6	25.2	70.2	—	8.1	10.1	3.1	109.0	None	43
Common Sense Government	USG	—	14.8	—	—	—	9.0	10.0	1.0	104.3	8.5	141
Composite Income	HYC	C	6.9	21.1	55.1	166.8	10.6	N.A.	7.2	110.8	4.0	94
Composite U.S. Government Securities	USG	C	13.5	25.1	63.6	—	8.8	N.A.	3.7	82.0	4.0	95
Counsellors Fixed Income	STT	—	8.9	—	—	—	9.6	7.0	2.0	11.3	None	41
Dean Witter Government Sec. Plus	USG	—	15.2	—	—	—	7.6	19.6	1.4	1,780.1	None†	100
Dean Witter High Yield Securities	HYC	F	(13.1)	(4.7)	37.1	143.0	20.0	10.0	10.3	1,191.9	5.5	81
Dean Witter U.S. Government Securities	MBS	D	11.2	23.6	52.7	—	9.6	14.3	1.6	10,200.1	None†	86
Delaware Group—Delchester I	HYC	B	1.5	21.9	74.0	199.6	13.5	10.1	2.2	626.3	6.75	111
Delaware Group—Delchester II	HYC	—	1.2	—	—	—	13.2	10.1	2.2	85.6	4.75	107
Delaware Group—Gov. Income	MBS	—	11.5	23.7	—	—	8.9	8.2	2.5	144.6	4.75	111
Delaware Treasury Rsvs.—Investors Ser.	STT	—	9.5	23.0	—	—	8.7	2.4	3.0	114.1	None	50
Dreyfus A Bond Plus	HGC	C	15.1	24.8	75.3	209.9	8.4	22.5	2.9	311.1	None	56
Dreyfus GNMA	MBS	—	11.5	21.8	—	—	8.8	25.6	2.2	1,586.5	None	56

Key to MONEY grades:　A = Top 10%　B = Next 20%　C = Middle 40%　D = Next 20%　F = Bottom 10%

†Fund may impose back-end load or exit fee.　N.A. Not available

FUND NAME	Type	MONEY risk-adjusted grade	% gain (or loss) to Dec. 22, 1989				Portfolio analysis			Net assets (millions)	Expense analysis	
			One year	Three years	Five years	10 years	% yield	Average maturity (years)	% cash		% maximum initial sales charge	Five-year projection
Dreyfus Short-Intermediate Government	STT	—	11.4	—	—	—	9.1	2.1	3.4	$32.0	None	$0††
Dreyfus Strategic Income	HYC	—	14.6	33.3	—	—	9.1	19.4	23.6	42.3	4.5	80
Dreyfus U.S. Government Intermediate	STT	—	13.4	—	—	—	9.0	5.2	2.2	61.1	None	26
Eaton Vance Government Obligations	USG	C	13.4	28.0	62.4	—	9.7	5.2	(8.5)**	298.2	4.75	143
Eaton Vance High Income Trust	HYC	—	1.5	20.4	—	—	13.5	N.A.	6.6	257.6	None†	137
Eaton Vance Income of Boston	HYC	A	4.1	23.3	78.8	234.4	14.9	9.1	6.9	82.3	4.75	116
Enterprise High Yield Bond	HYC	—	(0.9)	—	—	—	12.0	8.4	21.0	28.9	4.75	115
Equitec Siebel High Yield	HYC	—	4.8	16.4	—	—	11.5	7.6	8.0	25.9	None†	126
Equitec Siebel U.S. Government	USG	—	8.4	20.9	—	—	9.9	12.0	1.0	368.8	None†	115
Fidelity Flexible Bond	HGC	C	13.6	22.2	69.0	178.5	8.7	11.0	1.9	412.6	None	37
Fidelity Global Bond	WI	—	7.8	—	—	—	7.9	4.2	20.5	63.5	None	82
Fidelity Government Securities	USG	C	13.0	20.8	64.1	188.8	8.1	6.4	5.5	542.9	None	44
Fidelity High Income	HYC	C	(2.6)	13.1	64.1	226.3	14.3	9.1	12.0	1,386.7	None	43
Fidelity Income—GNMA Portfolio	MBS	—	13.8	23.2	—	—	8.2	26.1	3.9	662.4	None	47
Fidelity Income—Mortgage Securities	MBS	—	13.3	24.5	—	—	8.2	22.3	8.2	405.1	None	49
Fidelity Income—Short-Term Government	STT	—	10.5	—	—	—	8.1	2.2	17.3	135.7	None	56
Fidelity Intermediate Bond	STT	C	12.2	21.7	68.0	222.3	8.8	8.2	6.5	617.9	None	35
Fidelity Short-Term Bond Portfolio	STT	—	10.8	21.5	—	—	8.6	2.6	2.5	205.7	None	49
Financial Bond Shares—High Yield	HYC	A	4.2	22.1	76.9	—	13.1	8.5	8.1	51.3	None	46
Financial Independence—U.S. Gov. Sec.	MBS	C	10.6	21.6	60.7	—	8.3	28.6	4.9	29.6	4.0	112
Financial Independence—U.S. Treasury	USG	—	15.4	—	—	—	6.8	24.2	1.4	78.5	4.0	105
Financial Select Income	HGC	C	8.5	17.3	71.3	168.8	10.0	9.3	10.5	32.8	None	55
First Investors Fund for Income	HYC	F	(7.0)	4.3	38.9	116.9	15.4	9.0	8.0	1,356.0	8.5	135
First Investors Government	MBS	D	12.0	20.6	60.6	—	8.9	N.A.	0.0	235.5	7.25	123
First Investors High Yield	HYC	—	(7.8)	2.4	—	—	14.4	9.0	10.0	762.9	7.25	139
Franklin AGE High Income	HYC	D	(3.0)	12.0	51.1	170.5	15.4	10.1	5.0	1,968.0	4.0	70
Franklin IS Trust—Adjustable Rate Mort.	MBS	—	10.2	—	—	—	9.2	30.0	1.0	60.0	4.0	91
Franklin IS Trust—Short-Intermediate U.S.	STT	—	9.9	—	—	—	8.0	N.A.	2.0	30.0	1.5	58
Franklin Partners—Tax-Adv. High Yield	HYC	—	4.9	—	—	—	13.8	10.8	0.0	35.0	4.0	50
Franklin Partners—Tax-Adv. U.S. Gov.	USG	—	13.2	—	—	—	9.5	28.5	4.0	66.0	4.0	54
Franklin U.S. Government Sec. Series	MBS	A	12.8	26.6	69.5	156.6	10.0	28.0	4.0	11,340.0	4.0	68
Freedom Government Plus	USG	—	15.3	24.5	—	—	8.0	N.A.	1.4	145.1	None†	76
Freedom Global Income Plus	WI	—	8.2	50.0	—	—	7.9	7.5	18.7	261.4	None†	98
Fund for U.S. Government Securities	MBS	C	13.4	28.9	64.0	177.9	9.0	N.A.	3.9	1,059.0	4.5	96
FundTrust—Income	HYC	D	8.2	17.8	48.5	—	8.1	N.A.	1.1	53.7	1.5	112
Government Income Securities	USG	—	14.5	27.8	—	—	9.2	N.A.	2.9	1,351.0	1.0†	58
Gradison Government Income	USG	—	12.7	—	—	—	8.2	N.A.	18.0	37.5	2.0	87
GT Global Bond	WI	—	10.1	—	—	—	7.1	N.A.	32.0	38.6	4.75	143
GT Global Government Income	WI	—	10.4	—	—	—	11.2	N.A.	12.2	131.3	4.75	136
IAI Bond	HGC	C	16.6	26.3	70.3	202.8	7.0	16.4	20.0	66.7	None	50
IAI Reserve	STT	—	8.7	22.9	—	—	7.6	0.4	50.0	101.5	None	47
IDS Bond	HYC	B	11.7	22.8	80.2	228.2	9.1	18.4	5.2	1,843.0	5.0	90
IDS Extra Income	HYC	D	(3.5)	10.1	54.7	—	13.3	11.5	2.9	1,182.0	5.0	93
IDS Federal Income	USG	—	11.0	22.7	—	—	8.4	6.5	2.9	200.8	5.0	92
IDS Selective	HGC	B	12.6	25.2	81.0	229.1	8.6	15.1	12.9	1,166.0	5.0	91
IDS Strategy—Income Portfolio	HGC	B	10.2	22.1	75.5	—	7.4	16.7	5.9	225.6	None†	118
IDS Strategy—Short-Term Income‡	STT	F	9.5	22.5	36.5	—	8.0	4.2	33.7	117.6	None†	118
Integrated Home Investors Gov. Guar.	MBS	C	12.4	22.0	57.1	—	8.3	N.A.	7.1	154.8	None†	110
Integrated Income—High Yield	HYC	—	(4.0)	12.8	—	—	14.8	N.A.	37.8	31.7	4.75	140
Integrated Income—Government Plus	USG	—	8.0	—	—	—	11.3	N.A.	2.7	55.4	4.75	123
Integrated Income Plus	HYC	—	(6.4)	8.9	—	—	14.4	N.A.	30.5	29.7	None†	155
Intermediate Bond Fund of America	STT	—	10.6	—	—	—	8.9	10.1	10.8	109.4	4.75	95
International Cash—Global Portfolio	WI	—	4.2	31.6	—	—	8.0	N.A.	100.0	75.6	2.25	125
Investment Portfolio—Diversified Income	HYC	F	7.5	10.3	25.9	—	14.2	6.4	18.0	335.0	None†	123

Key to MONEY grades: A = Top 10%   B = Next 20%   C = Middle 40%   D = Next 20%   F = Bottom 10%

‡To 1/1/90   †Fund may impose back-end load or exit fee.   **Figure reflects borrowing to boost investments.   ††Manager absorbing expenses   N.A. Not available

THE Money RANKINGS: TAXABLE BOND FUNDS

FUND NAME	Type	MONEY risk-adjusted grade	% gain (or loss) to Dec. 22, 1989				Portfolio analysis			Net assets (millions)	Expense analysis	
			One year	Three years	Five years	10 years	% yield	Average maturity (years)	% cash		% maximum initial sales charge	Five-year projection
Investment Portfolio—Government Plus	USG	D	12.1	18.4	47.1	—	9.6	N.A.	8.0	$5,918.0	None†	$117
Investment Portfolio—High Yield	HYC	C	(2.9)	16.4	64.7	—	13.2	7.5	15.0	743.2	None†	120
John Hancock Bond	HGC	B	12.3	25.4	74.2	196.5	9.4	14.9	3.0	1,065.0	4.5	127
John Hancock High Income—Federal Sec.	USG	—	10.4	—	—	—	9.7	N.A.	5.0	77.0	4.5	111
John Hancock High Income—Fixed Income	HYC	—	(0.9)	18.2	—	—	13.6	9.2	4.0	89.6	4.5	112
John Hancock—U.S. Gov. Guar. Mortgages	MBS	—	13.4	24.2	—	—	8.9	N.A.	2.0	334.6	4.5	130
John Hancock—U.S. Government Securities	STT	C	11.9	17.2	61.4	168.2	8.7	3.8	1.0	176.0	4.5	137
Kemper Diversified Income	HYC	D	8.8	15.4	39.2	153.0	15.4	7.3	7.0	285.0	8.5	134
Kemper Enhanced Government Income	USG	—	13.5	—	—	—	8.8	N.A.	0.0	81.0	4.5	119
Kemper High Yield	HYC	A	(0.6)	24.8	80.4	251.6	14.0	7.8	14.0	1,461.0	4.5	83
Kemper Income & Capital Preservation	HGC	A	8.4	23.1	72.7	193.1	10.7	8.4	14.0	409.0	4.5	82
Kemper U.S. Government Securities	MBS	A	14.5	24.2	78.2	179.6	9.9	8.8	0.0	4,593.0	4.5	72
Keystone America Government	USG	—	12.5	—	—	—	7.4	11.9	1.0	67.6	2.0†	121
Keystone America High Yield	HYC	—	0.9	—	—	—	13.9	10.5	3.7	112.0	2.0†	116
Keystone America Investment Grade	HGC	—	6.3	—	—	—	8.3	11.3	0.0	28.0	2.0†	99
Keystone B-1	HGC	C	12.1	16.1	60.6	185.4	8.3	12.9	8.2	487.5	None†	89
Keystone B-2	HYC	C	5.5	17.7	63.7	198.5	10.7	16.2	5.7	986.0	None†	91
Keystone B-4	HYC	F	(4.8)	2.0	35.2	158.1	15.8	10.7	5.0	947.8	None†	106
Kidder Peabody Government Income	USG	—	13.2	24.7	—	—	7.8	26.5	2.4	110.4	None†	118
Legg Mason U.S. Gov. Intermediate	STT	—	13.0	—	—	—	7.7	4.9	6.7	40.8	None	55
Lexington GNMA Income	MBS	C	15.1	25.7	65.7	155.2	8.6	12.0	1.1	96.1	None	59
Liberty High Income Securities	HYC	C	0.1	15.7	58.8	183.4	14.2	11.1	4.4	333.0	4.5	98
Lord Abbett Bond Debenture	HYC	C	5.0	21.2	62.8	191.6	11.6	9.9	1.2	647.7	7.25	106
Lord Abbett U.S. Government Securities	USG	B	13.8	25.6	76.1	227.1	10.6	10.9	0.7	1,241.2	4.75	94
MacKenzie Fixed Income	HGC	—	16.0	42.8	—	—	7.7	10.0	47.0	37.5	4.75	115
MainStay Government Plus	USG	—	12.7	23.2	—	—	9.6	11.3	0.0	542.5	None†	129
MainStay High Yield Bond	HYC	—	(4.2)	11.8	—	—	17.0	N.A.	19.0	178.0	None†	134
Mass. Financial Bond	HGC	B	13.5	22.2	76.1	209.8	8.7	10.1	6.0	320.0	7.25	112
Mass. Fin. Government Guaranteed	MBS	C	12.3	20.7	55.8	—	8.8	9.6	2.0	349.0	4.75	109
Mass. Fin. Gov. Income Plus	USG	—	13.8	18.2	—	—	7.1	N.A.	6.0	1,376.0	4.75	119
Mass. Fin. High Income Trust—Series I*	HYC	D	(1.6)	10.8	51.3	213.9	14.6	9.7	7.0	665.0	7.25	117
Mass. Fin. High Income Trust—Series II	HYC	—	(2.6)	—	—	—	13.0	9.9	9.0	39.0	4.75	124
Mass. Fin. International Trust—Bond	WI	A	7.5	41.3	132.7	—	9.9	4.9	10.0	123.0	4.75	130
Mass. Fin. Lifetime—Gov. Income Plus	USG	—	12.2	—	—	—	6.6	N.A.	4.0	3,664.0	None†	128
Mass. Fin. Lifetime—High Income	HYC	—	(4.2)	—	—	—	12.6	9.7	9.0	127.0	None†	136
Mass. Fin. Lifetime—Intermed. Income	STT	—	8.1	—	—	—	8.9	5.1	16.0	75.4	None†	138
Merrill Lynch Corporate—High Income A	HYC	C	4.4	23.3	69.3	192.9	13.3	10.4	6.0	717.0	4.0	74
Merrill Lynch Corporate—High Quality A	HGC	B	14.2	24.3	73.8	—	8.8	12.6	10.0	423.0	4.0	72
Merrill Lynch Corporate—Intermed. Bond	STT	B	12.5	21.6	68.3	—	8.8	5.1	9.0	87.4	2.0	54
Merrill Lynch Federal Securities	MBS	B	14.0	24.9	68.4	—	9.4	7.2	6.0	2,677.8	4.0	77
Merrill Lynch Global Convertible B	WI	—	6.7	—	—	—	5.3	10.5	16.0	30.0	None†	132
Merrill Lynch Retirement Global Bond B	WI	—	7.0	36.9	—	—	11.7	12.8	7.0	270.1	None†	94
Merrill Lynch Retirement Income	MBS	—	13.3	22.0	—	—	8.8	7.7	7.0	1,743.3	None†	75
MetLife—State Street Gov. Income	USG	—	13.2	—	—	—	9.0	16.8	2.6	1,120.7	None	57
MetLife—State Street Gov. Securities	USG	—	12.9	18.3	—	—	8.3	12.4	3.0	30.5	4.5	111
MetLife—State Street High Income	HYC	—	1.4	23.7	—	—	13.0	9.1	3.0	142.8	4.5	111
Midwest Income—Intermediate-Term Gov.	STT	D	11.2	19.1	52.2	—	7.6	3.4	3.4	40.9	1.0	66
Mutual of Omaha America	USG	C	14.6	24.7	61.6	164.4	8.2	12.0	7.0	50.8	None	57
National Bond	HYC	F	(11.6)	(8.5)	19.3	97.7	14.7	9.2	7.0	462.7	7.25	123
National Federal Securities Trust	USG	F	14.1	11.8	42.3	—	9.1	27.8	4.0	532.8	6.75	111
Nationwide Bond	HGC	C	11.3	20.2	61.6	—	8.9	17.5	5.1	37.0	7.5	109
Neuberger & Berman Limited Mat. Bond	STT	—	11.2	22.8	—	—	8.2	2.6	23.9	110.6	None	36
Neuberger & Berman Money Market Plus	STT	—	8.8	—	—	—	9.3	0.7	79.2	112.5	None	36
New England Bond Income	HGC	C	12.1	22.7	67.2	167.8	7.7	N.A.	2.0	76.1	4.5	127

Key to MONEY grades: A = Top 10%   B = Next 20%   C = Middle 40%   D = Next 20%   F = Bottom 10%

*Currently closed to new investors   †Fund may impose back-end load or exit fee.   N.A. Not available

FUND NAME	Type	MONEY risk-adjusted grade	% gain (or loss) to Dec. 22, 1989				Portfolio analysis			Net assets (millions)	Expense analysis	
			One year	Three years	Five years	10 years	% yield	Average maturity (years)	% cash		% maximum initial sales charge	Five-year projection
New England Global Government	WI	—	4.2	—	—	—	4.4	5.0	0.0	$26.1	6.5	$130*
New England Government Securities	USG	—	13.3	20.7	—	—	7.3	8.0	5.0	184.8	6.5	129
Olympus U.S. Government Plus	USG	—	10.5	18.9	—	—	8.6	N.A.	3.0	115.2	4.25	131
Oppenheimer GNMA	MBS	—	12.0	24.6	—	—	9.0	N.A.	4.3	57.0	4.75	105
Oppenheimer High Yield	HYC	C	4.8	24.6	64.5	168.8	13.2	6.0	4.6	753.2	6.75	113
Oppenheimer U.S. Government Trust	USG	—	12.1	22.5	—	—	9.4	N.A.	12.9	257.8	4.75	110
Paine Webber Fixed Income—GNMA	MBS	C	13.4	21.9	61.8	—	8.4	11.9	23.2	991.4	4.25	78
Paine Webber High Yield	HYC	D	(0.1)	5.0	45.6	—	14.5	8.9	8.2	323.5	4.25	80
Paine Webber Investment Grade Bond	HGC	C	13.2	19.7	69.1	—	8.5	12.0	15.3	269.4	4.25	80
Paine Webber Master Global	WI	—	5.0	—	—	—	12.2	N.A.	25.6	1,084.8	None†	130
Paine Webber Master Income	HGC	—	9.6	14.4	—	—	7.6	20.4	1.4	207.4	None†	121
Phoenix High Yield Series	HYC	C	(0.8)	15.0	60.1	—	13.0	9.5	14.0	135.4	4.75	88
Pilgrim GNMA	MBS	D	13.3	22.5	51.9	—	9.4	25.8	2.0	132.0	4.75	103
Pilgrim High Yield	HYC	D	1.7	16.7	49.0	170.9	13.9	10.4	0.0	30.6	4.75	140
Pioneer Bond	HGC	C	11.6	23.5	64.7	180.3	8.9	N.A.	1.2	72.0	4.5	92
Piper Jaffray Government Income	USG	—	10.2	—	—	—	8.8	7.0	9.0	86.0	4.0	105
Principal Preservation Government Port.	USG	—	11.8	21.7	—	—	8.2	N.A.	2.0	30.6	4.5	108
Princor Government Securities Income	MBS	—	15.9	26.3	—	—	7.9	25.1	0.0	56.8	5.0	100
Pru-Bache GNMA	MBS	D	12.8	18.8	55.8	—	7.7	N.A.	1.1	221.9	None†	93
Pru-Bache Government—Intermed. Term	STT	C	12.6	20.8	61.6	—	10.0	3.7	2.5	396.5	None	46
Pru-Bache Government Plus	USG	—	12.7	20.0	—	—	7.5	8.5	20.9	3,912.3	None†	84
Pru-Bache High Yield	HYC	D	0.6	14.0	57.2	179.5	12.4	N.A.	2.6	2,478.2	None†	83
Pru-Bache U.S. Government	USG	—	16.9	21.6	—	—	6.7	16.2	0.5	179.0	None†	114
Putnam Capital Preservation—Income	USG	—	10.4	—	—	—	8.7	N.A.	0.0	53.3	4.75	79
Putnam Global Government Income	WI	—	6.0	—	—	—	12.4	4.0	0.0	167.4	4.75	133
Putnam GNMA Plus	MBS	—	14.2	19.7	—	—	8.2	N.A.	2.3	990.9	4.75	98
Putnam High Income Government	USG	—	14.1	18.1	—	—	8.3	N.A.	10.6	7,867.6	6.75	111
Putnam High Yield	HYC	C	(2.7)	16.4	58.2	210.2	15.1	7.9	14.4	2,075.3	6.75	104
Putnam High Yield Trust II	HYC	—	(4.0)	17.6	—	—	14.7	8.0	5.7	346.9	6.75	128
Putnam Income	HGC	B	12.0	26.3	72.0	222.8	9.7	15.9	6.5	428.4	4.75	107
Putnam U.S. Gov. Guaranteed Securities	MBS	B	12.8	27.1	65.0	—	9.9	N.A.	6.7	1,441.1	4.75	81
Quest for Value—U.S. Gov. High Income	USG	—	11.4	—	—	—	8.3	24.0	12.7	69.6	5.5	115
Rightime Government Securities	USG	—	15.8	—	—	—	5.9	N.A.	4.0	37.7	4.75	130
Rodney Square Benchmark—U.S. Treasury	USG	—	4.8	4.0	—	—	7.7	N.A.	0.0	35.5	4.5	103
Safeco U.S. Government	USG	—	13.0	22.9	—	—	8.5	4.5	3.8	28.5	None	56
Scudder GNMA	MBS	—	12.9	22.6	—	—	8.7	N.A.	4.0	260.2	None	57
Scudder Income	HGC	B	13.1	23.8	73.5	198.1	8.2	7.5	2.0	273.7	None	52
Scudder Short-Term Bond	STT	B	12.9	21.3	69.2	—	6.8	2.9	7.0	59.3	None	28
Security Income—Corporate Bond	HGC	C	9.9	20.7	64.1	177.0	10.0	21.3	3.9	56.0	4.75	105
Seligman High Yield Bond	HYC	—	4.1	18.0	—	—	14.4	8.8	5.4	46.0	4.75	107
Seligman Secured Mort. Income	MBS	—	10.3	20.8	—	—	9.8	15.6	2.2	37.0	4.75	105
Seligman U.S. Gov. Guaranteed	USG	—	10.0	13.3	—	—	9.3	10.3	2.0	86.0	4.75	105
Sentinel Bond	HGC	C	12.9	23.7	68.7	190.2	8.9	8.4	7.0	29.0	8.5	131
Sentinel Government Securities	USG	—	12.8	23.2	—	—	8.5	10.8	1.9	33.0	8.5	129
Sigma Income Shares	HGC	C	10.1	16.2	70.3	180.3	8.3	26.0	18.3	37.6	4.5	94
SLH High Yield	HYC	D	(3.6)	12.1	50.3	—	14.9	9.6	16.7	378.9	5.0	93
SLH Income—Global Bond	WI	—	5.8	30.5	—	—	5.8	7.4	5.7	85.3	None†	116
SLH Income—High Income Bond	HYC	—	(3.7)	15.6	—	—	12.9	N.A.	15.0	441.5	None†	99
SLH Income—Intermed.-Term Government	STT	—	9.4	16.8	—	—	7.5	N.A.	16.4	37.7	None†	88
SLH Income—Mortgage Securities	MBS	—	10.8	16.8	—	—	8.3	N.A.	4.3	764.6	None†	107
SLH Investment—Gov. Securities	USG	D	14.5	15.2	56.7	—	8.1	N.A.	0.6	2,064.5	None†	90
SLH Investment—Inv. Grade	HGC	C	15.7	18.8	79.3	—	8.0	25.9	0.0	490.5	None†	99
SLH Managed Governments	MBS	C	10.0	19.3	55.6	—	9.1	23.6	9.6	585.4	5.0	93
Smith Barney U.S. Gov. Securities	MBS	B	15.2	29.3	72.4	—	8.9	27.5	6.4	333.7	4.0	63

Key to MONEY grades: A = Top 10% B = Next 20% C = Middle 40% D = Next 20% F = Bottom 10%

*Three-year expense projection †Fund may impose back-end load or exit fee. N.A. Not available

THE Money RANKINGS: TAXABLE BOND FUNDS

FUND NAME	Type	MONEY risk-adjusted grade	One year	Three years	Five years	10 years	% yield	Average maturity (years)	% cash	Net assets (millions)	% maximum initial sales charge	Five-year projection
			% gain (or loss) to Dec. 22, 1989				Portfolio analysis				Expense analysis	
SteinRoe Government Plus	USG	—	13.6	21.2	—	—	6.7	17.0	4.0	$122.2	5.5	$103
SteinRoe Income	HGC	—	6.8	24.4	—	—	10.3	14.6	0.2	98.5	None	50
SteinRoe Managed Bond	HGC	C	12.7	21.4	72.6	191.0	8.4	14.6	0.5	168.2	None	41
Strong Advantage	STT	—	9.4	—	—	—	10.4	2.0	87.1	134.7	None	61
Strong Government Securities	USG	—	11.5	24.0	—	—	8.0	4.4	26.8	34.6	None	24
Strong Short-Term Bond	STT	—	9.5	—	—	—	10.0	1.2	47.8	134.1	None	56
T. Rowe Price GNMA	MBS	—	14.0	22.1	—	—	9.1	N.A.	0.0	380.5	None	54
T. Rowe Price High Yield Bond	HYC	—	(0.9)	20.3	—	—	14.1	10.1	8.4	853.5	None	57
T. Rowe Price International Bond	WI	—	(3.4)	24.7	—	—	8.2	7.0	10.0	286.1	None	66
T. Rowe Price New Income	HGC	C	12.8	23.4	66.5	177.2	8.9	7.4	5.1	1,039.3	None	48
T. Rowe Price Short-Term Bond	STT	D	10.0	22.0	50.5	—	8.5	2.6	42.8	214.0	None	53
Templeton Income	WI	—	8.5	26.1	—	—	8.7	6.6	29.0	115.9	4.5	103
Thomson McKinnon—Income	HGC	C	6.9	22.1	59.9	—	10.4	12.2	6.8	554.6	None†	107
Thomson McKinnon—U.S. Government	USG	—	13.6	19.1	—	—	8.6	N.A.	1.0	583.0	None†	112
Transamerica Gov. Securities Trust	USG	—	11.0	21.0	—	—	10.6	4.2	18.3	990.4	4.75	105
Transamerica Invest. Quality Bond	HGC	C	12.4	21.1	67.3	—	9.9	10.0	3.2	102.3	4.75	108
Transamerica Spec.—Gov. Income	USG	—	11.2	—	—	—	10.0	5.5	14.9	29.5	None†	127
Transamerica Spec.—High Yield	HYC	—	(4.9)	—	—	—	14.6	8.8	10.9	34.9	None†	128
Twentieth Century Long-Term Bond	HGC	—	15.2	—	—	—	8.5	13.8	1.0	65.0	None	55
Twentieth Century U.S. Governments	STT	D	10.4	20.7	50.4	—	8.9	2.5	4.0	451.0	None	55
United Bond	HGC	A	11.0	26.4	82.7	221.3	9.1	21.2	(8.4)**	396.7	8.5	118
United Government Securities	USG	C	12.0	16.0	67.6	—	8.5	21.8	(2.3)**	107.2	4.25	84
United High Income*	HYC	D	(7.5)	4.4	47.5	177.8	15.2	9.5	13.0	1,064.2	8.5	123
United High Income II	HYC	—	(2.7)	12.6	—	—	13.3	9.4	36.4	302.1	8.5	130
U.S. Gov. Guaranteed Securities	USG	—	12.0	20.6	—	—	9.7	17.6	7.1	539.8	4.75	99
UST Master Managed Income	HGC	—	16.4	35.1	—	—	7.5	N.A.	4.2	37.3	4.5	101
Value Line Aggressive Income	HYC	—	2.3	6.9	—	—	12.0	10.0	10.8	33.0	None	63
Value Line U.S. Government Securities	USG	C	12.2	25.2	68.2	—	9.3	22.7	6.2	258.7	None	37
Van Eck World Income	WI	—	10.9	—	—	—	9.7	7.0	4.1	37.6	5.75	138
Vanguard Bond Market	STT	—	14.3	22.8	—	—	8.8	13.1	8.1	133.1	None	17
Vanguard Fixed Income—GNMA	MBS	B	14.6	27.6	71.8	—	9.1	N.A	7.0	2,122.2	None	20
Vanguard Fixed Income—High Yield	HYC	C	1.9	19.2	68.6	200.8	13.2	7.4	8.9	952.7	None	23
Vanguard Fixed Income—Invest. Grade	HGC	B	15.5	27.3	76.3	216.1	8.9	18.9	2.8	968.3	None	21
Vanguard Fixed Income—Short-Term Bond	STT	B	11.6	24.8	60.1	—	8.5	N.A.	5.8	577.9	None	19
Vanguard Fixed Income—Short-Term Gov.	STT	—	11.6	—	—	—	8.5	N.A.	8.1	198.7	None	18
Vanguard Fixed Income—U.S. Treasury	USG	—	18.9	25.1	—	—	7.8	N.A.	1.7	474.2	None	20
Van Kampen Merritt High Yield	HYC	—	(6.1)	12.1	—	—	14.5	8.0	7.5	275.0	4.9	115
Van Kampen Merritt U.S. Government	MBS	C	14.8	23.6	73.5	—	8.9	11.0	0.6	3,579.4	4.9	87
Venture Income Plus	HYC	F	(5.3)	3.0	35.0	—	17.1	7.7	8.4	36.0	4.75	121
Venture Ret. Plan of America—Bond	MBS	D	9.1	16.8	50.3	124.1	9.6	N.A.	28.2	64.7	None†	132
WPG Government Securities	USG	—	14.1	26.0	—	—	8.5	N.A.	3.9	89.7	None	46
Zweig Series—Government Securities	USG	—	13.2	15.5	—	—	6.7	N.A.	4.0	122.2	None†	103

THE Money RANKINGS: TAX-EXEMPT BOND FUNDS

FUND NAME	Type	MONEY risk-adjusted grade	One year	Three years	Five years	10 years	% yield	Average maturity (years)	% cash	Net assets (millions)	% maximum initial sales charge	Five-year projection
			% gain (or loss) to Dec. 1, 1989				Portfolio analysis				Expense analysis	
Alliance Muni Income—Insured National	HGT	—	11.1	—	—	—	6.5	N.A.	1.5	$109.1	4.0	$109
Alliance Muni Income—National Port.	HGT	—	11.1	—	—	—	7.3	26.9	1.7	130.7	4.0	62
American Capital Muni Bond	HGT	D	12.3	17.6	71.3	122.1	7.1	25.0	2.8	242.6	4.75	92
American Capital Tax-Exempt—High Yield	HYT	—	10.4	16.5	—	—	8.2	22.0	2.8	232.6	4.75	92
American Capital Tax-Exempt—Insured	HGT	—	10.0	8.9	—	—	7.0	25.0	1.8	38.4	4.75	92

Key to MONEY grades: **A** = Top 10%　**B** = Next 20%　**C** = Middle 40%　**D** = Next 20%　**F** = Bottom 10%

*Currently closed to new investors　**Figure reflects borrowing to boost investments.　†Fund may impose back-end load or exit fee.　N.A. Not available

THE Money RANKINGS: TAX-EXEMPT BOND FUNDS

FUND NAME	Type	MONEY risk-adjusted grade	% gain (or loss) to Dec. 1, 1989				Portfolio analysis			Net assets (millions)	Expense analysis	
			One year	Three years	Five years	10 years	% yield	Average maturity (years)	% cash		% maximum initial sales charge	Five-year projection
AMEV Tax Free—National	HGT	—	9.2	19.8	—	—	7.2	24.8	1.7	$37.1	4.5	$102
Benham National Tax-Free—Long-Term	HGT	D	10.6	12.3	63.4	—	6.8	22.4	9.0	40.7	None	28
Calvert Tax-Free Reserves—Limited	ITT	F	7.0	18.7	39.7	—	6.3	1.0	5.0	133.7	2.0	64
Calvert Tax-Free Reserves—Long	HGT	D	11.2	16.8	66.4	—	6.3	24.0	1.0	47.3	4.5	90
Cigna Municipal Bond	HGT	C	11.2	19.9	81.8	128.8	7.0	26.3	3.4	262.5	5.0	97
Colonial Tax-Exempt High Yield	HYT	C	8.3	18.6	69.3	188.4	7.6	9.8	3.5	1,500.0	4.75	105
Colonial Tax-Exempt Insured	HGT	—	10.1	17.1	—	—	6.6	8.0	2.9	124.0	4.75	108
Colonial VIP—High Muni	HYT	—	6.3	—	—	—	6.9	18.8	4.7	36.0	None†	142
Composite Tax-Exempt Bond	HGT	C	8.5	17.7	71.4	100.6	6.9	8.9	3.9	103.9	4.0	83
Dean Witter Tax-Exempt Securities	HGT	C	12.0	22.2	81.9	—	7.3	20.3	0.1	1,033.6	4.0	69
Delaware Group Tax-Free—USA	HGT	A	11.7	24.3	88.1	—	7.2	24.1	0.0	553.6	4.75	87
Delaware Group Tax-Free—USA Insured	HGT	—	10.2	20.4	—	—	6.8	23.0	0.0	56.0	4.75	91
Dreyfus Insured Tax Exempt Bond	HGT	—	9.6	17.0	—	—	6.7	26.0	2.6	191.6	None	55
Dreyfus Intermed. Tax Exempt Bond	ITT	D	8.8	18.1	60.1	—	7.1	8.5	0.1	1,093.8	None	40
Dreyfus Short-Intermediate Tax Exempt	ITT	—	6.9	—	—	—	6.2	1.9	10.3	61.6	None	24
Dreyfus Tax Exempt Bond	HGT	C	10.0	19.0	70.0	118.2	7.3	N.A.	10.2	3,708.1	None	40
Eaton Vance High Yield Muni Trust	HYT	—	8.9	16.1	—	—	7.6	23.7	1.3	1,011.2	None†	124
Eaton Vance Muni Bond	HGT	B	12.1	24.1	81.5	139.6	7.1	25.6	4.8	76.5	4.75	101
Fidelity Aggressive Tax-Free	HYT	—	10.4	25.1	—	—	7.7	21.6	9.4	540.6	None†	41
Fidelity High Yield Municipals	HYT	C	12.6	20.4	78.1	141.0	7.0	22.3	7.9	1,731.0	None	33
Fidelity Insured Tax-Free	HGT	—	10.9	18.4	—	—	6.5	23.0	7.9	172.3	None	42
Fidelity Limited Term Muni	ITT	D	8.1	16.5	60.3	118.6	6.7	10.5	10.2	444.6	None	37
Fidelity Municipal Bond	HGT	C	10.8	20.7	77.2	110.7	6.9	24.3	11.1	1,059.9	None	29
Fidelity Short-Term Tax-Free	ITT	—	6.2	—	—	—	5.7	2.8	2.1	59.4	None	36
Fidelity Tax Exempt—Limited Term	ITT	—	7.6	16.7	—	—	6.4	9.2	7.0	121.5	None	35
Financial Tax-Free Income Shares	HGT	B	14.7	22.9	88.6	—	6.7	25.7	5.3	163.9	None	41
First Investors Insured Tax Exempt	HGT	C	9.5	23.2	69.1	134.0	6.6	N.A.	0.0	1,063.0	7.25	126
Fortress High Yield Municipal	HYT	—	10.9	—	—	—	7.4	N.A.	4.9	64.3	1.0†	59
Franklin Federal Tax-Free Income	HGT	C	9.9	20.4	75.9	—	7.6	25.0	1.0	3,871.0	4.0	67
Franklin High Yield Tax-Free Income	HYT	—	10.4	29.8	—	—	8.5	25.0	2.0	1,510.0	4.0	75
Franklin Insured Tax-Free Income	HGT	—	8.7	19.3	—	—	7.2	23.0	2.0	692.0	4.0	71
Freedom Managed Tax-Exempt	HGT	—	11.4	—	—	—	6.7	22.0	1.4	111.3	None†	53
GIT Tax-Free—High Yield	HYT	D	7.0	16.0	65.2	—	6.7	18.0	10.5	42.0	None	64
IDS High Yield Tax-Exempt	HYT	B	11.7	22.1	81.6	154.5	7.4	21.4	3.4	4,516.0	5.0	82
IDS Insured Tax-Exempt	HGT	—	10.9	19.8	—	—	6.4	22.8	10.5	105.2	5.0	88
IDS Tax-Exempt Bond	HGT	C	12.1	19.8	78.0	128.6	6.8	23.0	17.0	1,027.0	5.0	83
Integrated Insured Tax-Free—STRIPES	HGT	—	8.9	20.6	—	—	6.5	N.A.	4.2	103.5	4.75	117
John Hancock Tax-Exempt Income	HGT	B	10.0	21.2	81.2	107.7	6.9	25.4	4.0	333.8	4.50	92
Kemper Municipal Bond	HGT	A	12.0	23.3	82.7	148.7	7.1	17.0	0.0	1,947.0	4.5	72
Keystone America Tax-Free Income	HGT	—	9.9	—	—	—	6.1	26.8	2.0	162.9	2.0†	114
Keystone Tax-Exempt Trust	HGT	—	10.0	18.3	—	—	6.7	23.5	3.4	603.4	None†	93
Keystone Tax-Free*	HGT	C	10.1	19.9	74.3	137.8	7.3	23.6	3.3	912.5	None†	92
Liberty Tax-Free Income	HGT	C	11.3	22.0	78.5	119.0	6.7	27.4	3.2	482.0	4.5	95
Limited Term Muni	ITT	D	7.6	20.4	51.6	—	6.7	4.9	2.0	201.1	2.75	89
Lord Abbett Tax-Free Income—National	HGT	B	10.4	22.9	81.5	—	7.0	23.4	1.7	313.2	4.75	83
MainStay Tax-Free Bond	HGT	—	7.6	17.1	—	—	6.5	23.5	0.0	121.4	None†	108
Mass. Fin. Lifetime—Managed Muni	HGT	—	10.2	—	—	—	6.0	25.2	6.0	343.0	None†	132
Mass. Fin. Man. High Yield Muni Bond*	HYT	C	10.8	20.8	60.4	—	8.4	21.8	3.0	484.0	4.75	82
Mass. Fin. Managed Muni Bond	HGT	B	10.6	23.3	79.9	201.6	6.7	21.1	6.0	1,286.0	4.75	82
Merrill Lynch Muni—High Yield A	HYT	C	9.8	20.3	76.0	172.3	7.4	N.A.	6.0	1,574.3	4.0	70
Merrill Lynch Muni—Insured A	HGT	C	10.7	21.5	73.3	125.9	7.2	N.A.	8.0	2,342.8	4.0	68
Merrill Lynch Muni—Limited Maturity	ITT	F	6.7	16.5	34.0	88.8	6.1	N.A.	17.0	360.0	0.75	30
Mutual of Omaha Tax-Free Income	HGT	B	11.7	23.5	88.0	129.5	6.9	22.0	2.0	357.4	8.0	113
National Securities Tax-Exempt	HGT	C	10.9	21.1	79.9	120.9	7.2	24.5	7.0	97.0	4.5	88
Nationwide Tax-Free Income	HGT	—	10.7	15.3	—	—	6.5	22.0	2.1	74.0	None†	48

Key to MONEY grades: A = Top 10%   B = Next 20%   C = Middle 40%   D = Next 20%   F = Bottom 10%

*Currently closed to new investors   †Fund may impose back-end load or exit fee.

THE Money RANKINGS: TAX-EXEMPT BOND FUNDS

FUND NAME	Type	Money risk-adjusted grade	% gain (or loss) to Dec. 1, 1989				Portfolio analysis			Net assets (millions)	Expense analysis	
			One year	Three years	Five years	10 years	% yield	Average maturity (years)	% cash		% maximum initial sales charge	Five-year projection
New England Tax-Exempt Income	HGT	C	10.9	17.7	78.1	144.6	6.6	N.A.	0.0	$142.1	4.5	$97
Nuveen Insured Tax-Free—National Port.	HGT	—	12.3	—	—	—	6.5	24.0	2.6	102.0	4.75	93
Nuveen Municipal Bond	HGT	A	11.1	23.5	81.2	131.8	6.7	22.0	2.1	1,170.6	4.75	81
Oppenheimer Tax-Free Bond	HGT	C	9.8	19.7	77.8	147.3	7.0	27.2	0.3	223.7	4.75	86
Paine Webber Classic High Yield Muni	HYT	—	10.9	—	—	—	7.4	22.0	0.0	61.3	4.0	85
Paine Webber Tax-Ex. Income—National	HGT	—	9.8	21.2	—	—	7.2	N.A.	4.4	332.6	4.0	82
Piper Jaffray National Tax-Exempt	HGT	—	8.5	—	—	—	6.8	21.0	1.9	37.3	4.0	83
Principal Preservation—Tax-Exempt	HGT	F	9.1	13.5	29.1	—	6.7	16.9	2.0	73.6	4.5	100
Princor Tax-Exempt Bond	HGT	—	12.9	23.1	—	—	6.4	22.9	1.3	37.8	5.0	106
Pru-Bache Muni Bond—High-Yield Series	HYT	—	11.4	—	—	—	7.6	26.5	2.0	576.0	None†	43
Pru-Bache Muni—Insured Series	HGT	—	11.0	—	—	—	6.7	24.7	2.0	471.2	None†	44
Pru-Bache Muni—Modified-Term Series	ITT	—	8.8	—	—	—	6.4	15.1	1.0	47.9	None†	42
Pru-Bache National Municipal Bond	HGT	D	8.3	14.4	67.7	—	6.4	22.9	3.6	1,038.8	None†	65
Putnam Tax Exempt Income	HGT	A	12.7	23.0	88.7	202.6	6.8	25.6	1.4	1,305.7	4.75	75
Putnam Tax-Free High Yield	HYT	—	9.3	21.0	—	—	6.9	N.A.	2.6	634.9	None†	126
Putnam Tax-Free Insured	HGT	—	10.9	20.8	—	—	5.6	27.0	1.4	296.2	None†	116
Safeco Municipal Bond	HGT	B	11.6	25.3	83.1	—	6.8	16.2	1.6	281.6	None	33
Scudder High-Yield Tax Free	HYT	—	11.4	—	—	—	6.6	19.4	4.0	113.9	None	55
Scudder Managed Muni Bond	HGT	C	12.1	23.5	74.6	132.7	6.7	20.5	1.0	687.1	None	34
Scudder Tax-Free Target—1990	ITT	D	5.9	14.1	41.7	—	5.6	0.7	4.0	57.3	None	44
Scudder Tax-Free Target—1993	ITT	D	6.9	14.6	51.2	—	6.1	3.2	5.0	78.6	None	44
Scudder Tax-Free Target—1996	ITT	—	7.8	15.4	—	—	6.1	5.2	3.0	34.4	None	54
Seligman Tax-Exempt—National	HGT	B	10.8	22.2	84.9	—	6.2	24.5	2.2	142.0	4.75	91
Sigma Tax-Free Bond	HGT	C	10.8	21.4	76.2	107.3	6.4	23.0	14.7	24.9	4.5	105
SLH Income—Tax-Exempt	HGT	—	9.9	21.8	—	—	6.6	22.4	2.4	561.1	None†	89
SLH Managed Muni	HGT	B	10.4	22.2	77.7	—	7.3	23.8	1.0	1,522.4	5.0	86
Smith Barney Muni Bond—National Port.	HGT	—	12.0	22.3	—	—	8.0	24.4	0.0	141.6	4.0	59
State Bond Tax-Exempt	HGT	C	11.3	22.5	72.3	—	6.9	24.5	6.7	51.1	4.5	86
SteinRoe High Yield Municipals	HYT	A	11.8	25.3	83.7	—	7.2	19.5	6.7	282.2	None	41
SteinRoe Intermediate Municipal	ITT	—	7.9	15.7	—	—	5.9	6.1	0.6	96.2	None	44
SteinRoe Managed Municipals	HGT	B	11.5	21.5	87.2	165.5	6.5	17.6	1.8	550.6	None	36
Tax-Exempt Bond of America	HGT	C	10.4	18.7	72.5	147.7	6.6	23.2	10.2	485.6	4.75	86
Thomson McKinnon Tax Exempt	HGT	—	11.0	17.6	—	—	5.8	21.5	1.8	59.9	None†	117
Transamerica Spl.—High Yield Tax-Free	HYT	—	9.0	16.7	—	—	6.5	21.0	7.1	31.1	None†	131
T. Rowe Price Tax-Free High Yield	HYT	—	10.6	21.6	—	—	7.3	22.4	7.6	416.8	None	55
T. Rowe Price Tax-Free Income	HGT	D	9.9	12.4	58.9	123.0	6.8	22.3	3.8	1,133.4	None	38
T. Rowe Price Tax-Free Short-Intermed.	ITT	F	6.7	13.7	37.0	—	5.8	N.A.	34.4	216.9	None	43
United Municipal Bond	HGT	A	12.8	24.7	93.0	129.6	6.7	24.0	5.2	618.6	4.25	74
United Municipal High Income	HYT	—	11.8	21.2	—	—	8.3	23.2	2.3	174.9	4.25	85
USAA Tax Exempt—High Yield	HGT	C	11.7	22.6	76.5	—	7.2	22.9	2.4	1,135.2	None	25
USAA Tax Exempt—Intermediate	ITT	D	9.3	19.9	61.4	—	7.0	9.2	2.4	448.9	None	27
USAA Tax Exempt—Short	ITT	F	7.5	18.0	41.3	—	6.4	1.9	6.5	256.6	None	29
UST Master Intermed.-Term Tax-Exempt	ITT	—	8.6	20.9	—	—	6.5	9.4	1.2	77.8	4.5	81
UST Master Tax-Ex.—Long Term	HGT	—	13.6	37.4	—	—	5.9	22.2	4.6	32.8	4.5	85
Value Line Tax Exempt—High Yield	HGT	C	8.8	19.7	66.9	—	7.7	N.A.	8.7	273.3	None	35
Vanguard Muni—High-Yield	HYT	B	12.8	23.3	83.9	140.3	7.3	22.9	8.5	928.7	None	15
Vanguard Muni—Insured Long-Term	HGT	C	12.5	24.1	79.1	—	7.0	21.7	6.2	1,003.3	None	15
Vanguard Muni—Intermediate-Term	ITT	C	10.2	21.2	68.6	111.7	7.0	10.5	6.6	1,076.2	None	15
Vanguard Muni—Limited-Term	ITT	—	7.8	—	—	—	6.3	3.2	12.0	188.2	None	15
Vanguard Muni—Long-Term	HGT	B	12.9	23.0	81.5	118.4	7.1	20.8	7.3	674.5	None	15
Vanguard Muni—Short-Term	ITT	F	6.8	17.3	35.1	90.5	5.8	1.3	52.0	715.5	None	15
Van Kampen Merritt Ins. Tax Free Inc.	HGT	—	10.4	21.2	—	—	6.6	23.9	2.1	625.7	4.9	94
Van Kampen Merritt Tax Free High Inc.	HYT	—	10.8	26.5	—	—	8.0	24.4	4.8	623.6	4.9	93
Venture Muni Plus	HYT	D	10.7	22.0	44.7	—	8.1	20.0	6.2	75.0	None†	131
Zweig Tax-Free—Limited Term	ITT	—	6.0	15.5	—	—	6.7	4.5	2.2	42.3	1.5	55

Key to MONEY grades: A = Top 10% B = Next 20% C = Middle 40% D = Next 20% F = Bottom 10%

†Fund may impose back-end load or exit fee. N.A. Not available

Index

R

Real estate investments. *See* Resolution Funding Corporation
Reassessment, property, 107-109
Recession, 10, 45
Resolution Funding Corporation (Refcorp), 39, 69-70
Resolution Trust Corporation (RTC), 79
Restaurants, 155-157
    choosing, 156
    ordering, 157
    reservations, 156
Retirement. *See also* Guaranteed investment contracts, Health insurance, Individual retirement accounts, Keoghs, Pension and benefits plans, Social Security
    and discrimination, 174
    housing costs, 171-172
    and inflation, 182-184, 185
    investing for, 178-185
    myths, 170-172
    post-retirement employment, 173-175
    and taxes, 171, 173
Risk
    tolerance for, 48

S

Savings, 36-39. *See also* College investments, Money-market funds, Pension and benefits plans
    figuring your savings rate, (worksheet) 38
    strategies, 36-37, 39
Savings and loan bailout, 55, 69-70
Savings accounts
    and children, 132, 133
    money-market, 36
Series EE savings bonds, 111, 130, 136, 139, 140

Social Security
    benefits, (table) 177
    changes, 175-178
    eligibility, 177-178
    and taxes, 107, 111, (table) 174, 175, 176, 177, 178
    and working after retirement, 171, 173
Standard & Poor's Register, 60
Stocks
    blue chip, 39, 180
    buy and sell orders, 67-69
    in Europe, 50-54
    high-yield, 56
    money-flow trend investing, 71
    P/E analysis, 65-67
    reinvestment plans, 68

T

Tax deductions and credits
    charitable donations, 112
    child care, 111
    child's unearned income, 115
    home offices, 117-118
    passive versus active losses, 110
    rental property, 116
    stock shifts, 112
    unusual write-offs, 125
Tax-deferred savings plans. *See* Pension and benefits plans
Tax-free investments. *See* Municipal-bond funds, Municipal bonds
Tax preparers, 114-117
Tax records, 111
Tax Reform Act of 1986, 59, 116, 184
Taxes. *See also* Flexible spending accounts, 401(k), Individual retirement accounts, Internal Revenue Service, Keoghs
    assessments, challenging, 107-109
    capital gains, 112, 116-117, 142, 145
    college prepayment, 137
    and credit-card balance, 110, 116

    estimated payments, 116
    gifts, 137, 187
    gray areas, 114
    and marriage, 111, 114-115, 187
    property, 104, 105, 107-109
    in retirement, 171, 173
    second homes, 116
    and Social Security, 107, 111, (table) 174, 175, 176, 177, 178
    state and local, 104-107
Telecommunications investments, 47-48
Travel, last-minute, 160-162. *See also* Air travel
    clubs, (table) 161
    lodging, 162
Treasury notes, 39
Trusts, 188-190, 191, 192
    bypass, 187
    charitable remainder, 112
    and pour-over wills, 188, 191
    tax benefits, 189
    trustee, 189, 190
12b-1 fee. *See* Mutual funds

U

Unit trust. *See* Municipal-bond unit trust
U.S. savings bonds. *See* Series EE savings bonds
U.S. Tax Court, 117-118

W

Wills, 186-188, 189-190, 191-192. *See also* Estate planning
    disinheritance, 191-192
    executor, 191, 192
    statutory, 192

Z

Zero-coupon bonds. *See* Bonds
Zero-coupon Treasuries, 36, 139